KU-005-880

Local Authorities and Human Rights

Richard Drabble QC, James Maurici

and

Tim Buley

144 1632
LIBRARY
ACC. No.
01122090
DEPT.
CLASS No.
342·41085 DRA
UNIVERSITY
COLLEGE CHESTER

Series Editor: John Wadham

OXFORD
UNIVERSITY PRESS

OXFORD
UNIVERSITY PRESS

Great Clarendon Street, Oxford ox2 6dp

Oxford University Press is a department of the University of Oxford.
It furthers the University's objective of excellence in research, scholarship,
and education by publishing worldwide in

Oxford New York

Auckland Bangkok Buenos Aires Cape Town Chennai
Dar es Salaam Delhi Hong Kong Istanbul Karachi Kolkata
Kuala Lumpur Madrid Melbourne Mexico City Mumbai Nairobi
São Paulo Shanghai Taipei Tokyo Toronto

Oxford is a registered trade mark of Oxford University Press
in the UK and in certain other countries

Published in the United States
by Oxford University Press Inc., New York

© Drabble, Maurici and Buley 2004

The moral rights of the authors have been asserted

Crown copyright material is reproduced under Class Licence Number CO1P0000148
with the permission of HMSO and the Queen's Printer for Scotland

Database right Oxford University Press (maker)

First published 2004

All rights reserved. No part of this publication may be reproduced,
stored in a retrieval system, or transmitted, in any form or by any means,
without the prior permission in writing of Oxford University Press,
or as expressly permitted by law, or under terms agreed with the appropriate
reprographics rights organization. Enquiries concerning reproduction
outside the scope of the above should be sent to the Rights Department,
Oxford University Press, at the address above

You must not circulate this book in any other binding or cover
and you must impose this same condition on any acquirer

British Library Cataloguing in Publication Data
Data applied for

Library of Congress Cataloging in Publication Data
Data available

ISBN 1–84174–135–3

1 3 5 7 9 10 8 6 4 2

Typeset by RefineCatch Limited, Bungay, Suffolk
Printed in Great Britain by Ashford Colour Press Ltd, Gosport, Hampshire

Accession no.
01122090

CANCELLED
14 JAN 2008

Local Authorities and Human Rights

Contents

Preface

As was widely predicted, the courts have been kept extremely busy since the Human Rights Act 1998 came into force on 2 October 2000. Whether it has met the hopes, or realized the fears, of those involved in the debates that preceded it will be a matter for individual decision. We take the view however that, whatever answer one gives to that question, it is now possible to step back from the detail of debate about individual issues and see a coherent picture emerging. While more fine-tuning may be required, it is now possible to give relatively clear answers to many of the burning questions that attended the inauguration of the Act, and to identify and delineate a number of important principles which any lawyer will need to have in mind when dealing with the Act. We hope that this book provides a clear and useful account of those principles and their operation in the local authority context.

This book has been a long time in the making and it would be impossible to do justice to all of those who have had some part in its making. We must however mention in particular all those at OUP who have provided support in the production process, and thank them for their (at times much strained) patience.

Three people merit particular mention. Firstly, David Blundell provided crucial assistance in bringing Chapter 10 up-to-date. Secondly, Chris Campbell-Holt has been an outstanding research assistant for all aspects of the book and also had the less glamorous, but vital, task of proof-reading. Finally, Zoë Leventhal, a pupil at Landmark Chambers, provided invaluable last minute assistance in readying the book for publication. It goes without saying that final responsibility for any errors remains our own.

John Howell QC was extensively involved in the preparation of the first drafts of Chapter 2 but it should be made clear that he has not been involved in subsequent amendments made in the light of more recent changes.

The law is as stated on 1 December 2003, although efforts have been made in individual chapters to incorporate subsequent changes.

Richard Drabble QC
James Maurici
Tim Buley

Landmark Chambers

Abbreviations

CPR	Civil Procedure Rules 1998
DETR	Department of Energy, Transport and the Regions
ECHR	European Convention on Human Rights
EPA	Environmental Protection Act 1990
HRA	Human Rights Act 1998
LGA	Local Government Act 1972 and 2000
MHA	Mental Health Act 1983
RSL	Registered social landlord
SENs	Special educational needs
SSSI	Site of special scientific interest
TCPA	Town and Country Planning Act 1990

Table of Cases

Table of Primary Legislation

Table of Secondary Legislation

Table of International Instruments

Chapter One

Introduction to the Human Rights Act 1998

Richard Drabble QC

1.1 INTRODUCTION

The purpose of this introductory chapter is to outline the basic structure of the
Human Rights Act (HRA) 1998, which represents a sophisticated constitutional
settlement, enabling domestic courts to give direct effect to the European Convention on Human Rights (ECHR) whilst maintaining the sovereignty of Parliament.
The principal provisions can be shortly described. They will in any event be
familiar to many readers and have been described in many other publications.
However, in the time since the commencement of the 1998 Act, there have been
significant case law developments addressing some of the issues that arise out of
the Act itself, as well as the application of the Convention to particular subject
areas. The principal case law developments affecting the Act itself are discussed
in the course of this chapter. The provisions of the HRA 1998 relating to remedies
are discussed in Chapter Three.

One thing that has become clear is the extent to which it has become impossible to describe English law in terms of a dichotomy between domestic common
law on the one hand and the Convention on the other. Any practitioner in the areas
of local authority work described in this book needs to be aware not only of
domestic cases concerning the 1998 Act and the Convention, but also of decisions
of the European Court of Human Rights (the European Court) in the area. Now
that the Act has 'brought rights home', decisions of the European Court are
immediately part of the domestic legal order. As we shall see, the Act requires
domestic courts to have regard to the European jurisprudence: in the case of
immediately contemporary decisions of the European Court it is highly likely that
they will be followed. Decisions such as *Z and others* v *UK* (App. No. 29392/95)
(discussed in Chapter Three) have a profound, immediate and irreversible impact
on local authority affairs.

The decision of the Court of Appeal in *JD and others* v *East Berkshire Community Health Trust and others* [2003] 2 WLR 58 provides a graphic example of

the impact of *Z and others*. In that case the Court of Appeal felt obliged to depart from the approach of the House of Lords in *X* v *Bedfordshire County Council* [1995] 2 AC 633 because of the impact of *Z*. Both cases are discussed further in Chapter Three.

It has also become clear that the process is not one way. As the UK case law develops, so it will influence Strasbourg itself.

1.2   BASIC STRUCTURE OF THE HUMAN RIGHTS ACT

1.2.1   'Convention rights'

'Convention rights' are defined in s. 1(1) of the HRA 1998. These are 'the rights and fundamental freedoms' set out in Articles 2–12 and 14 ECHR, Articles 1–3 of the First Protocol, and Articles 1 and 2 of the Sixth Protocol, as read with Articles 16 and 18 of the Convention.

The Articles of most relevance to local authorities are discussed in Chapter Two and in the individual chapters. In general terms, the most relevant Articles are likely to be Article 6 (right to a fair trial), Article 8 (right to respect for a home, private and family life, etc.), and Articles 1 and 2 of Protocol 1 (the rights to property and education). However, it is clear that the activities of local authorities may be affected by the higher-order rights such as Article 2 (right to life, in (say) a child care or an environmental regulatory context), Article 3 (prohibition of inhuman or degrading treatment, in similar contexts), and Article 5 (right to liberty, where, for example, local authority social services' obligations interface with mental health functions). Article 14 (prohibition of discrimination), is also of very considerable importance. As discussed in Chapter Two, Article 14 is very much wider in scope than traditional concepts of discrimination on the grounds of sex or race, and it may be possible to formulate a challenge to many questionable administrative practices by relying on Article 14 read together with a relevant substantive right such as Article 8. Thus, while there may be, for example, no right under Article 8 to public sector housing, discrimination (in the wide Article 14 sense) is prohibited.

1.2.2   Interpretation of Convention rights

Section 2 of the HRA 1998 imposes an obligation on domestic courts and tribunals to 'take into account' the Strasbourg jurisprudence. This is defined as including not only the judgments of the European Court of Human Rights, but also decisions of the Commission and other matters (for full details, see the text of s. 2(1)(a)–(d) of the Act in Appendix 1). The obligation is to take these matters 'into account'. They are not binding, but the weight to be given to them will vary. Recent decisions of the Court will inevitably be given very considerable weight indeed; at the other end of the spectrum, a domestic court may feel able to place little weight on an old admissibility decision of the Commission, particularly in an area where the case law of the European Court is sparse or has moved on.

The approach above has been followed in decided cases since the commencement of the 1998 Act. In *R v Secretary of State for the Environment, Transport and the Regions, ex parte Alconbury Developments Ltd and others* [2001] 2 WLR 1389, Lord Slynn said (at para. 26):

> Your Lordships have been referred to many decisions of the European Court of Human Rights on article 6 of the Convention. Although the Human Rights Act 1998 does not provide that a national court is bound by these decisions it is obliged to take account of them so far as they are relevant. In the absence of some special circumstance it seems to me that the court should follow any clear and constant jurisprudence of the European Court of Human Rights. If it does not do so there is at least a possibility that the case will go to that court, which is likely in the ordinary case to follow its own constant jurisprudence.

In the same case Lord Hoffmann hinted at one circumstance where this course might not be taken, i.e. if that jurisprudence 'compelled a conclusion fundamentally at odds with the distribution of powers under the British constitution' (para. 76). However, the chances of such an occurrence happening might be thought to be rare. In *Alconbury* itself, Lord Hoffmann's own analysis demonstrated the compatibility of the emerging Strasbourg case law with the demands of the British constitution. Both the House of Lords and the European Court of Human Rights are anxious to ensure (so far as possible) that the case law of each is consistent with that of the other.

In *R v Secretary of State for Work and Pensions, ex parte Carson* [2002] 3 All ER 994, Stanley Burnton J had to consider the status of decisions of the Commission. He said (at para. 38) that they 'are not of the same level as those of the Court. Where, however, there is a clear and constant line of decisions of the Commission that are not inconsistent with those of the Court, good reason is required if this Court is not to follow them'.

In *Runa Begum v Tower Hamlets* [2002] 1 WLR 2491, Laws LJ had to consider whether Runa Begum's rights under the statutory scheme in play in that case were 'civil rights' for the purposes of Article 6 of the Convention. He considered the case law of the European Court of Human Rights and decided that they were, although he observed:

> I acknowledge, however, that the exercise of categorisation cannot be ignored. The terms of Article 6 require it to be undertaken, and I shall proceed to deal with it. But I should say that I think it important to have in mind that the Court's task under the HRA, in this context as in many others, is not simply to add on to the Strasbourg learning to the corpus of English law, as if it were a compulsory adjunct taken from an alien source,

but to develop a municipal law of human rights by the incremental method of the common law, taking account of the Strasbourg jurisprudence as HRA s. 2 enjoins us to do.

In the same case in the House of Lords ([2003] 2 WLR 388) the Secretary of State argued that the conclusion on the extent of the concept of 'civil rights' went beyond the Strasbourg case law. All members of the House found it unnecessary to decide whether Runa Begum's rights were indeed within Article 6; but instead proceeded on the basis that there was no breach of the Article in any event. Relevantly for present purposes, a major reason for doing so was a recognition of the fact that (in judicial policy terms) the extent of the rights conferred by Article 6 was closely related to the nature of the protection required to comply with Article 6. The wider the ambit of Article 6, the greater the difficulty that might be created if very strong protection were required in order to comply with Article 6. Thus Lord Hoffmann said (paras 69–70) that to apply Runa Begum's argument:

> . . . to the provision of benefits in kind, involving the amount of discretion which is inevitably needed in such cases, is to go further than the Strasbourg court has so far gone. This would not matter — domestic courts are perfectly entitled to accord greater rights than those guaranteed by the Convention — provided that it was acceptable that the scope of judicial review should be limited in the way that it is by s. 204. If, however, it should be decided in Srasbourg that the administration of social welfare benefits falling within the *Salesi* principle requires a more intrusive form of judicial review, I would not wish to place any obstacle in the way of the UK government arguing that, in a case such as this, the principle does not apply at all.
>
> For that reason only, I would prefer not to decide whether rights under s. 193 should be classified as civil rights. It is sufficient to say that, assuming that they are, the right of appeal under s. 204 is sufficient to satisfy article 6.

Thus the decision in *Runa Begum* in the Lords is a clear example of the sensitivity of that Court to the need to ensure that domestic case law develops as one piece with Strasbourg case law.

In *R* v *Spear* [2002] 3 WLR 437 the House of Lords felt able not to follow the decision of the European Court of Human Rights (*Morris* v *UK* (2002) 34 EHRR 1253) on one aspect of the Courts Martial system. Lord Bingham observed (at para. 12) that:

> It goes without saying that any judgment of the European Court commands great respect, and section 2(1) of the Human Rights Act 1998 requires the House to take any such judgment into account, as it routinely does. There were, however, a large number of points in issue in *Morris*, and it seems clear that on this particular aspect the European Court did not receive all the help which was needed to form a conclusion.

Following the decision in *Spear*, the European Court has adopted a practice of adjourning its own hearing to await the decision of in any related domestic proceedings.

Finally, and as another example of the relationship between domestic and Strasbourg courts, the cases of *Wynne* v *UK* (1994) 19 EHRR 333 (ECtHR); *R* v *Secretary of State for the Home Department, ex parte Anderson* [2002] 2 WLR 1143 (CA); *Stafford* v *UK* (2002) 35 EHRR 32 (Grand Chamber of ECtHR); and *R* v *Secretary of State for the Home Department, ex parte Anderson* [2002] 3 WLR 1800 fall to be mentioned. In *Wynne* the European Court of Human Rights had held that the role of the Secretary of State in fixing a tariff in mandatory life sentence cases was contrary to the Convention. In *Anderson* the Court of Appeal followed *Wynne*, although unpersuaded that it was correct. The position was then reviewed by the Grand Chamber of the European Court in *Stafford*. The European Court cited extensively from the judgments of Simon Brown LJ and Buxton LJ in the Court of Appeal in *Anderson*, and stated (at paras 68 and 69) that:

> While the Court is not formally bound to follow any of its previous judgments, it is in the interests of legal certainty, foreseeability and equality before the law that it should not depart, without cogent reason, from precedents laid down in previous cases. Since the Convention is first and foremost a system for the protection of human rights, the Court must however have regard to the changing conditions in Contracting States and respond, for example, to any emerging consensus as to the standards to be achieved . . . A failure by the Court to maintain a dynamic and evolutive approach would risk rendering it a bar to reform or improvement.
>
> 69. Similar considerations apply as regards the changing conditions and any emerging consensus discernible within the domestic legal order of the respondent Contracting State. Although there is no material distinction between this and the *Wynne* case, having regard to the significant developments in the domestic sphere, the Court proposes to re-assess 'in the light of present day conditions' what is now the appropriate interpretation and application of the Convention.

The European Court then surveyed the domestic approach to mandatory life sentences, including the reasoning of the Court of Appeal in *Anderson*, and held that the Convention was breached. In *Anderson* in the Lords the same conclusion was reached, Lord Bingham dismissing a submission by the Home Secretary that *Wynne*, not *Stafford*, should be followed in these terms:

> While the duty of the House under s. 2(1)(a) of the Human Rights Act 1998 is to take into account any judgment of the European Court, whose judgments are not strictly binding, the House will not without good reason depart from the principles laid down in a carefully considered judgment of the Court sitting as a Grand Chamber: *R (Alconbury Developments Ltd) v Secretary of State* [2001] 2 WLR 1389 at 1399, para. 26. Here, there is very strong reason to support the decision, since it rests on a clear and accurate understanding of the tariff-fixing process and the Home Secretary's role in it. The Court advanced ample grounds for its change of opinion; among them were the

judgments already referred to in the present case ... In ruling on the rights of the appellant under article 6(1) of the Convention, I am satisfied that the House should, in accordance with the will of Parliament expressed in the Human Rights Act 1998, seek to give effect to the decision of the European Court in *Stafford*.

1.2.3   Interpretation of legislation

Section 3 of the 1998 Act is one of the core provisions. It places a duty on domestic courts, in broad terms, to construe legislation in a way which is compatible with Convention rights. Section 3 is considered further at 1.3.

1.2.4   Declaration of incompatibility

Section 4 is an important part of the overall constitutional settlement. If, despite the duty of interpretation contained in s. 3, it is impossible to read the domestic legislation in a way which accords with the ECHR, the higher courts (defined in s. 4(5)) may make a declaration of incompatibility. The effect of such a declaration is to leave in place the existing legal regime — with the result that acts taken in accordance with it are lawful — but to enable the Government, if it wishes, to take remedial action under s. 10 in order to change the legislative framework to remove the incompatibility. Sections 4, 5 and 10 form a related series of provisions under the Act for dealing with allegedly incompatible statutory provisions. They are discussed further at 1.5.

1.2.5   Public authorities

Section 6 is another core provision of the HRA 1998. It renders it unlawful for a 'public authority' to act in a way which is incompatible with a Convention right (see s. 6(1)). The close relationship between ss. 6 and 3 is revealed by s. 6(2). This provides that the basic rule contained in s. 6(1) does not apply if, in essence, the 'public authority' is compelled to act in the way it did by primary legislation, or by necessarily incompatible subordinate legislation.

   Section 6(3) defines 'public authority' as including courts and tribunals, and 'any person certain of whose functions are functions of a public nature'. Recent case law on this definition is discussed further at 1.4.

1.2.6   Remedies

Sections 7 and 8 provide for the remedies. They are discussed in Chapter Three.

1.2.7 Application of the core provisions

The provisions discussed above are the core of the HRA 1998. The basic structure of the machinery may be illustrated by an example:

A housing authority has an allocation policy under which it allocates a house to Mr X but not to Mr Y. The 1998 Act applies as follows:

(a) A challenge to the decision by Mr Y would take the form of proceedings brought pursuant to s. 7 alleging that the housing authority, as a 'public authority', had acted unlawfully because the action was 'incompatible with a Convention right' (see s. 6(1)).

(b) A court seized of such proceedings has to decide whether the allocation did indeed breach any Convention right. This involves identifying the relevant Articles of the Convention (e.g. Articles 8 and 14); considering issues, that arise under the relevant Articles such as proportionality and the requirement that the action be 'according to law'; together with, of course, the Strasbourg jurisprudence pursuant to s. 2.

(c) If the housing authority claims that the terms of the allocation policy were dictated by legislation, the court has to examine the legislation, in accordance with the duty of interpretation created by s. 3, in order to interpret it so as to comply with the Convention if possible.

(d) If satisfied that the failure to allocate to Mr Y did breach his Convention rights, and was not compelled by primary legislation, the court gives a remedy in accordance with s. 8.

(e) If the terms of the allocation policy are dictated by incompatible primary legislation, the failure to allocate is lawful even if in breach of Convention rights. A higher court can consider whether to make a declaration of incompatibility under s. 4; if it is going to do so, the Crown is entitled to issue a notice in accordance with the terms of s. 5.

1.3 INTERPRETATION OF LEGISLATION

As indicated in the basic outline in 1.2, s. 3 is one of the central pillars of the HRA 1998. Section 3(1) provides:

(i) so far as it is possible to do so, primary and subordinate legislation must be read and given effect in a way which is compatible with the Convention rights.

It is clear that the duty of interpretation created by s. 3 is strong. However, before commencement, many commentators considered that the courts would go to extreme lengths of interpretation to avoid making a declaration of incompatibility. The *Alconbury* litigation highlighted at an early stage a significant disincentive to going down that route. There the Divisional Court made a declaration of incompatibility. There is no doubt that a substantial advantage of that course was that it did not establish as *illegal* large numbers of planning decisions; instead it would have allowed the executive, had it been necessary, to develop a considered new system. In the event, the House of Lords upheld the existing system [2001] 2 WLR 1389). A similar incentive will be in play whenever a finding that existing practice breaches Convention rights will have complex administrative implications.

Nonetheless, s. 3 does create a considerable change in the established approach to statutory interpretation. As Lord Woolf (giving the judgment of the Court) observed in *Poplar Housing and Regeneration Community Association* v *Donoghue* [2002] QB 48:

> It is difficult to overestimate the importance of section 3. It applies to legislation passed both before and after the Human Rights Act 1998 came into force. Subject to the section not requiring the Court to go beyond that which is possible, it is mandatory in its terms. In the case of legislation predating the HRA where the legislation would otherwise conflict with the Convention, section 3 requires the Court now to interpret legislation in a manner which it would not have done before the HRA came into force. When the Court interprets legislation usually its primary task is to identify the intention of Parliament. Now, when section 3 applies, the Courts have to adjust their traditional role in relation to interpretation so as to give effect to the direction contained in section 3. It is as though legislation which predates the HRA and conflicts with the Convention has to be treated as being subsequently amended to incorporate the language of section 3. (para. 75).

He went on to make five points about the use of s. 3:

(a) it could be ignored unless the legislation would otherwise be in breach of the Convention — so the first task was to ascertain whether, absent s. 3, there would be a breach;

(b) if the court had to rely on s. 3 it should limit any extended meaning to that necessary to ensure compatibility;

(c) s. 3 does not entitle the court to *legislate*; its task is still interpretation;

(d) the views of the parties and of the Crown as to whether a 'constructive' approach should be adopted cannot modify the task of the court (if s. 3 applies the court is required to adopt the s. 3 interpretation);

(e) where, despite the strong language of s. 3, it is not possible to achieve a result which is compatible with the Convention, the court is not *required* to grant a declaration of incompatibility and presumably, in exercising its discretion, it will be influenced by the usual considerations which apply to the grant of declarations.

He added:

> The most difficult task which the courts face is distinguishing between legislation and interpretation. Here practical experience of seeking to apply section 3 will be the best guide. However, if it is necessary in order to obtain compliance to radically alter the effect of legislation this will be an indication that more than interpretation is required.

That test would not be passed by the amendment proposed by the tenants in *Donoghue* itself, which would have involved reading into s. 21(4) of the Housing Act 1988, the words 'if it is reasonable to do so'. Lord Woolf commented: 'The amendment may appear modest but its effect would be very wide indeed. It would significantly reduce the ability of landlords to recover possession and would defeat Parliament's original objective of providing certainty. It would involve legislating.'

A similar expression of one limit to the boundaries of a legitimate exercise of the s. 3 duty was articulated by Lord Nicholl in *Re S (Children: Care Order: Implementation of Care Plan)* [2002] AC 291, when he approved the passage from *Donoghue* set out above; referred to Lord Hope's statements in *R v Lambert* [2001] 3 WLR 206, at paras 79–81; and said (at paras 39–41):

> The HRA reserves the amendment of primary legislation to Parliament. By this means the Act seeks to preserve parliamentary sovereignty. The Act maintains the constitutional boundary
>
> The area of real difficulty lies in identifying the limits of interpretation in a particular case . . . For present purposes, it is sufficient to say that a meaning which departs substantially from a fundamental feature of an act of Parliament is likely to have crossed the boundary between interpretation and amendment. This is especially so where the departure has important practical repercussions which the court is not equipped to evaluate. In such a case the overall contextual setting may leave no scope for rendering the statutory provision convention compliant by legitimate use of the process of interpretation.

He also stressed, in para. 41, the importance of the court, if it was ascribing a meaning to legislation pursuant to the obligation under s. 3, identifying clearly the 'particular statutory provision or provisions whose interpretation leads to that result. Apart from anything else this should assist in ensuring that the court does not inadvertently stray outside its interpretation jurisdiction'.

This theme, of a need to identify with care the precise statutory provision that is subject to the s. 3 reading; and (by some means or other) the reading that s. 3 requires, has been the subject of detailed exposition by Lord Hope in two other cases on s. 3 that have reached the House of Lords — *R v A (No. 2)* [2002] 1 AC 45 (see paras 108–110); *R v Lambert* [2001] 3 WLR 206, (see para. 80). As he explained in para. 79 of *Lambert*, he saw the need as closely related to the different functions of legislation and amendment:

> . . . the obligation is one which applies to the interpretation of legislation. This function belongs, as it has always done, to the judges. But it is not for them to legislate. Section 3(1) preserves the sovereignty of Parliament. It does not give power to the judges to overrule decisions which the language of the statute shows to have been taken on the very point at issue by the legislator.

One characteristic of legislation was its ability to achieve certainty by the use of clear and precise language. It followed, said Lord Hope (*Lambert*, para. 80) that:

> So far as possible, judges should seek to achieve the same attention to detail in their use of language to express the effect of applying section 3(1) as the parliamentary drafts-man would have done . . . It ought to be possible for any words that need to be substi-tuted to be fitted into the statute as if they had been inserted there by amendment. If this cannot be done without doing such violence to the statute as to make it unintelligible or unworkable, the use of this technique will not be possible. It will then be necessary to leave it to Parliament to amend the statute . . .

The discussion above shows that the duty created by s. 3 is subject to limits. Two further matters should, however, be noted. The first is that, even on the relatively cautious approach adopted by Lord Hope, it is apparent that normal constraints on statutory construction will be radically changed. At para. 81 of *Lambert*, he made the following points:

(a)   the courts will not be bound by previous authority as to what the statute means;
(b)   a strained or non-literal construction may be adopted;
(c)   words may be read in by way of addition or the words used may be read down to give them a narrower meaning — see para. 4.28 of Clayton and Tomlinson *The Law of Human Rights* (Oxford University Press, 2000);
(d)   words may need to be read in to explain the meaning that must be given to the provision if it is to be compatible — as in *R v A (No. 2)*.

The second point is that in paras 44 and 45 of *R v A (No. 2)* Lord Steyn approached the s. 3 duty on a less cautious basis than that taken by Lord Hope. He said:

> On the other hand, the interpretative obligation under s. 3 . . . is a strong one. It applies even if there is no ambiguity in the language in the sense of the language being capable of two different meanings . . . The draftsman of the HRA had before him the slightly weaker model in section 6 of the New Zealand Bill of Rights Act 1990 but preferred stronger language. Parliament specifically rejected the legislative model of requiring a

reasonable interpretation. Section 3 places a duty on the court to strive to find a possible interpretation compatible with Convention rights . . . The techniques to be used will not only involve the reading down of express language in a statute but also the implication of provisions. A declaration of incompatibility is a measure of last resort. It must be avoided unless it is plainly impossible to do so. If a *clear* limitation on Convention rights is expressed in terms, such an impossibility will arise: *R v Secretary of State for the Home Department, ex parte Simms* [2000] 2 AC 115 at 132A–B.

There are undoubtedly differences of emphasis between this approach and that of Lord Hope but it is not easy to predict what practical difference it will make over time. The s. 3 duty is strong; its boundary may be best expressed by saying that it will not justify a departure from a fundamental feature of the legislation in question, where that fundamental feature can be discerned either from the express words or by truly *necessary* implication (for the meaning of 'necessary implication' see *R v Special Commissioners, ex parte Morgan Grenfell* [2002] 2 WLR 1299 *per* Lord Hobhouse at para. 45). There may be a difference in the application of the duty depending on whether the context is one in which the court is particularly well suited to judge, indeed may be expert — e.g. the requirements of a fair criminal trial — and cases where it is not, such as those concerning social and economic policy. As Moses J put it in *Hooper v Secretary of State for Work and Pensions* [2002] UKHRR 785:

> Such decisions are described as '*polycentric decisions*' by Lon l Fuller in his essay '*The Forms and Limits of Adjudication*' (1978) 92 Harv LR 353. Such decisions require the decision-maker, in considering the impact of adapting legislation, to be in a position to foresee the effects of such adaptation. Parliament is clearly in a better position to do that than the Court in the field of social and economic policy. Such adaptation requires the re-allocation of public funds, a field in which the courts are far less equipped to tread.

For examples of the application of s. 3 see *R v Offen* [2001] 1 WLR 253; *Cachia v Faluyi* [2001] 1 WLR 1966; *O'Hagan v Rea* 2001 SLT (Sc Ct) 30; *Goode v Martin* [2002] 1 WLR 1828.

Lastly, mention should be made of s. 19. This provision applies to Bills going through Parliament. It requires a Minister in charge of any Bill, before second reading, either to make a statement of compatibility or to state that despite his inability to make one, the Government nevertheless wishes the Bill to proceed. The existence of such a statement of compatibility will reinforce the desire of the courts to use s. 3 to find a reading of the legislation that is indeed compatible. This fact has been recognised by Lord Irvine, the former Lord Chancellor. As he said in the Tom Sargeant Memorial Lecture, on 16 December 1997:

> . . . it should be clear from the Parliamentary history, and in particular the Ministerial statement of compatibility which will be required by the Act, that Parliament did not

intend to cut across a Convention right. Ministerial statements of compatibility will inevitably be a strong spur to the courts to find means of construing statutes compatibly with the Convention.

However, in deciding whether legislation is compatible, the statement of the Minister is no more than an expression of opinion, it is not even persuasive authority — see *Re A (No. 2) per* Lord Hope at para. 69.

In *Wilson* v *Secretary of State for Trade and Industry* [2003] HRLR 33 the House of Lords considered whether reference could be made to *Hansard* as background material in deciding whether legislation was compatible (in particular for considering arguments on proportionality). The answer was yes. Such an exercise did not involve any breach of Article 9 of the Bill of Rights. However, care had to be taken in such an exercise. The fundamental principle remained that the will of Parliament is expressed in the language used by it in enactments. Further, one had to remember that 'the proportionality of a statutory measure is not to be judged by the quality of the reasons advanced in support of it, or by the subjective state of mind of individual ministers or members'.

1.4   ACTS OF PUBLIC AUTHORITIES

Section 6 of the HRA 1998, as explained at 1.2.5, is closely related to s. 3 and is another central pillar of the Act. The basic rule is contained in s. 6(1), which provides:

(1)   It is unlawful for a public authority to act in a way which is incompatible with a Convention right.

This is subject to the exception created by s. 6(2):

(2)   Subsection (1) does not apply to an act if —
(a)   as the result of one or more provisions of primary legislation, the authority could not have acted differently; or
(b)   in the case of one or more provisions of, or made under, primary legislation which cannot be read or given effect in a way which is compatible with the Convention rights, the authority was acting so as to give effect to or enforce those provisions.

Section 6(6) should also be noted in this connection. It states:

(6)   'An Act' includes a failure to act but does not include a failure to —
(a)   introduce in, or lay before, Parliament a proposal for legislation; or
(b)   make any primary legislation or remedial order.

The concept of 'public authority', which is central to s. 6, may be of great importance in a local authority context (see s. 6(3), (4) and (5)). In *Donoghue* v *Poplar*

Housing and Regeneration Community Association Ltd [2002] RTR 27, the Court of Appeal considered the position of a housing association, a registered social landlord. It adopted the distinction identified in Clayton and Tomlinson, *The Law of Human Rights* (Oxford University Press, 2000) at para. 5.08, between:

(a)   standard public authorities;
(b)   functional public authorities; and
(c)   courts and tribunals.

Plainly, local planning authorities (and housing authorities) are standard public authorities, with the result that all their acts are acts of public authorities for the purposes of Article 6. In relation to a registered social landlord, such as Poplar Housing, they pointed out that the simple fact that an otherwise private body supplies services at the request of a public body as a mode of discharging that public body's statutory duties does not mean that the private body has become a functional public authority in relation to the services. They said (at para. 58):

> A public body in order to perform its public duties can use the services of a private body. Section 6 should not be applied so that if a private body provides such services, the nature of the functions are inevitably public. If this were to be the position, then when a small hotel provides bed and breakfast accommodation as a temporary measure, at the request of a housing authority that is under a duty to provide that accommodation, the small hotel would be performing public functions and required to comply with the HRA. This is not what the HRA intended . . . Section 6(3) means that hybrid bodies, who have functions of a public or private nature are public authorities, but *not* in relation to acts which are of a private nature. The renting out of accommodation can certainly be of a private nature.
>
> However, the Court finally concluded that Poplar Housing was carrying out public functions in making the particular letting in question. It is plain that in so finding it was heavily influenced, not by the position of housing associations in general, but by the very close relationship between Poplar Housing and Tower Hamlets — it was created to take a transfer of the housing stock; five board members were also members of Tower Hamlets; and it acted under the guidance of Tower Hamlets. As the Court said (at [66]):
>
>> Taking into account all the circumstances, we have come to the conclusion that while activities of housing associations need not involve the performance of public functions in this case, in providing accommodation for the defendant and then seeking possession, the role of Poplar is so closely assimilated to that of Tower Hamlets that it was performing public and not private functions. Poplar is therefore a functional public authority, at least to that extent. We emphasise that this does not mean that all Poplar's functions are public. We do not even decide that the position would be the same if the defendant were a secure tenant.

The decision in *Poplar Housing* established that some registered social landlords could be exercising public functions; the importance of the decision to large-scale transfers of housing stock is obvious. However, the Court of Appeal has subsequently made clear the extent to which the decision depended on the particular relationship with Tower Hamlets. In *R v The Leonard Cheshire Foundation, ex parte Heather* [2002] 2 All ER 936, the subject matter of the judicial review was a decision by the Foundation to close a home. The applicants were long-stay patients who, in common with the majority of the residents in the home, had been placed there and were being funded by the social services department acting under Part III of the National Assistance Act 1948. The Court held that the Foundation was not exercising public functions. Specifically, at para. 35, it held that:

(a)   'in this case except for the resources needed to fund the residents of the different occupants of Le Court, there is no material distinction between the nature of the services LCF has provided for residents funded by a local authority and those provided to residents funded privately';

(b)   's. 26 of the NAA provides statutory authority for the actions of the local authorities but it provides LCF with no powers. LCF is not exercising statutory powers in performing functions for the appellants';

(c)   the appellants argument that if LCF was not exercising public functions they (the appellants) could not rely on Article 8 of the Convention against LCF was circular: 'If LCF was performing a public function, that would mean that the appellants could rely in relation to that function on Article 8, but, if the situation were otherwise, Article 8 cannot change the appropriate classification.'

The Court plainly did have some concern that the approach they had adopted might leave residents exposed to arbitrary closures, and it canvassed, at para. 34, the possibility that residents whose arrangements were made after commencement of the HRA 1998 might be able to insist, against the social services department as a public authority, that those arrangements fully protected their Article 8 rights as a matter of contract between the authority and the home: 'Then not only could the local authority rely on the contract, but possibly the resident could do so also as a person for whose benefit the contract was made. Here this was not a possibility because the . . . residence . . . began long before the HRA came into force'. But on the issue of the definition of public authority, the case establishes (at Court of Appeal level) a clear rule that the provision of services pursuant to arrangements under Part III does not mean that the service provider is a public authority.

That statement is now subject to an important gloss to be found in *R v Partnerships in Care Ltd, ex parte A and others* [2002] 1 WLR 2610. This was an application for judicial review brought by a patient who was compulsorily detained, pursuant to s. 3(1) of the Mental Health Act 1983, in a ward at a private pyschiatric hospital, owned and run by the defendants. On a preliminary issue as to whether the hospital managers were a 'public authority' for the purposes of s. 6, Keith J held that they were. At the time of the hearing, only the first instance judgment (of Stanley Burnton J) in the *Leonard Cheshire* case was available, but it does not appear that the approach of the Court of Appeal would make any difference.

Keith J approached the matter on the basis of recognising (at para. 20) that:

> The decision in *Donoghue's* case has to be seen in the context of a wider debate about the impact of privatisation of public services on public law. To what extent are private providers of public services to be regarded as public authorities and therefore susceptible to judicial review?

He said that that issue had been addressed in two cases — the decision of Moses J in *R v Servite Homes, ex parte Goldsmith* [2001] LGR 55; and the first instance decision in *Leonard Cheshire* (2001) 4 CCL Rep 211. He explained the reasoning of *Servite* as being that:

> . . . the local authority's statutory obligation to provide residential accommodation had ended when the local authority made its arrangements with the housing association. That was because the statutory obligation . . . had been to *make arrangements to provide* residential accommodation, rather than to provide accommodation itself . . . what the housing association did as a result of the arrangements . . . was a matter of private law. (See paras 20 and 21.)

Turning to the facts of the *Partnerships in Care* case, Moses J distinguished this line of reasoning on the basis that, although it might be that the duty of the health authorities ended when the placement with the private home was made, the subsequent question (i.e. whether there were free-standing obligations on the managers which were not derivative from those of the health authority) received an affirmative answer. This was because of the duty placed specifically on them by reg. 12(1) of the Nursing Homes and Mental Nursing Homes Regulations 1984 combined with the compulsory nature of the detention. He commented:

> The public interest in the hospital's care and treatment of its patients is apparent if one remembers that, if as a result of the lack of staff or facilities, patients detained under the Mental Health Act 1983 do not receive the care and treatment which they need, their detention may well be prolonged because they may not recover sufficiently to meet the statutory criteria for their discharge from hospital.

The hospital managers were accordingly a functional public authority in the same manner as the managers of a private prison would be.

1.5　SECTION 6 AND SUBORDINATE LEGISLATION

The application of s. 6 of the HRA 1998 to subordinate legislation requires special consideration. It (and interrelated issues concerning s. 3) raises difficult issues which have not yet been the subject of judicial ruling. They arise in the case of subordinate legislation made before incorporation, under an empowering provision in primary legislation which does not *require* subordinate legislation which breaches a Convention right. In relation to other subordinate legislation, the position is as follows:

(a)　The interpretative duty in s. 3 will apply to any subordinate legislation. Where possible, such subordinate legislation will be construed so as to be compatible. It seems likely that the concerns expressed by, for example, Lord Nicholls in *Re S* (discussed above) about the difficulty of interfering with a central feature of the legislation under the interpretative function of the court will not apply with the same force to delegated legislation made under a wide empowering provision. Parliament will have authorised a wide range of solutions.

(b)　If, after October 2000, subordinate legislation which cannot be construed as compatible is made under a wide empowering provision, that delegated legislation will be *ultra vires*. The empowering provision will be construed, if at all possible, as not authorising non-compatible subordinate legislation. There is a close parallel between this position and the application of the principle of legality discussed in *R* v *Home Secretary, ex parte Simms* [2000] 2 AC 115.

(c)　If, before or after October 2000, delegated legislation is made under an empowering provision which (even after the application of the s. 3 interpretative duty) *requires* non-compliant delegated legislation, that delegated legislation is *intra vires*; the maker of the delegated legislation does not act unlawfully because of s. 6(2). The only solution is a declaration of incompatibility.

The position of delegated legislation made under a wide empowering provision before October 2000 was considered in a joint note produced for the Court of Appeal in *R* v *Lord Chancellor, ex parte Lightfoot*. The note is reproduced at [2000] PL 361; the authors were Robin Allen QC and Phillip Sales, counsel for the applicant and the Lord Chancellor respectively. The note is not mentioned in the Court of Appeal judgment. It is necessarily written on the hypothesis that the Order in the case ('the 1986 Order') was incompatible — a hypothesis not shared by the Lord Chancellor or, ultimately, the Court. Their analysis proceeds on the following lines:

(a) Section 3 does not have retrospective effect; therefore the order in that case (made in 1986) was *intra vires* when made.

(b) 'Section 3 operates by way of imposing an interpretative obligation in relation to existing legislation, *not* by way of repeal of that legislation'; therefore, the continuation in force of the 1986 Order would not be affected by the coming into force of s. 3.

(c) Section 6(1) of the HRA 1998 renders failures to act, as well as acts, unlawful — see s. 6(6); therefore a failure by the Lord Chancellor to introduce compatible legislation in place of the incompatible legislation after commencement of the HRA 1998 would be unlawful.

(d) Moreover (and importantly), an official acting under the 1986 Order who demanded a deposit would be acting unlawfully. He or she would have to give effect to Convention rights. The position of the Court would be the same — it would be obliged to ensure that Convention rights are respected. The position of the official would not be protected by s. 6(2)(b) in the case of this Order, which is not inevitably incompatible.

The solution adopted in the note has practical merit. It preserves a remedy for the victim of non-compliant subordinate legislation without further extensive administrative effects. There must, however, be some doubt about it; both steps (a) and (b) are potentially controversial. Further, in *R v Harlow District Council, ex parte Bono* [2002] 1 WLR 2475, Richards J accepted that the position of the local authority was not protected by s. 6(2)(b) in a sitaution where the regulations in question pre-dated October 2000 and where the empowering provision did not itself require a breach of Convention rights. However, part of his analysis is inconsistent with that of the note. At para. 35 he said:

> If and to the extent that the regulations are incompatible with the Convention by requiring the appointment of a Review Board in breach of the claimants' rights under article 6, then the regulations could themselves be quashed by the court; and if they were quashed, the decision of the Review Board constituted in accordance with them would likewise fall to be quashed. It would however be very surprising if s. 6(2)(b) gave the council a statutory defence unless and until the court formally quashed the material part of the regulations . . .

One reason for taking the course expressed in the note is that an analysis which proceeded on the basis that regulations of this type all became *ultra vires* in October 2000 might create unforeseen consequences in terms of severance and impact on cases affected by the same regulations where no breach of Convention rights was involved. The solution, which would appear to offer the individual applicant as much protection as he or she could reasonably wish whilst avoiding this kind of complication, may therefore stand the test of time.

1.6   DECLARATIONS OF INCOMPATIBILITY

If it is impossible to read primary legislation in a way which is compatible with Convention rights then, as explained at 1.2.4, the High Court and superior courts have jurisdiction to make declarations of incompatibility. The principal effect of such a declaration is that it opens the route to remedial action under s. 10 of the HRA 1998. If a declaration has been made, and rights of appeal have been exhausted (see, for the machinery, the terms of s. 10(1)), a Minister may amend the offending legislation by order under s. 10, if he judges that 'there are compelling reasons for proceeding under this section' (s. 10(2)). Thus use of the s. 10 procedure is not obligatory; if circumstances allow, the Government can address the situation created by a declaration of incompatibility by a slower, more considered series of reforms. This flexibility is important, because clearly there can be more than one Convention-compatible solution. If the decision of the Divisional Court in the *Alconbury* case had stood (see 1.3), with the result that the basic structure of decisions by the Secretary of State in planning would have been found to be incompatible, very considerable care would have been needed in formulating alternative structures. Of course, the basic constitutional settlement created by the Act also allows the Government to choose not to address the situation at all, and to leave in place the incompatible legislation. To do so, however, may force individuals to go to Strasbourg in search of a remedy.

The s. 10 procedure is also available (under s. 10(1)(b)) where:

> it appears to a [Minister or the Privy Council] that, having regard to a finding of the [European Court] made after the coming into force of this section in proceedings against the United Kingdom, a provision of legislation is incompatible with an obligation of the United Kingdom arising from the Convention.

Schedule 2 to the HRA 1998 contains procedural provisions relating to remedial orders.

Mention should also be made of the *obiter* comment of Lord Nicholls in *Re S (Care Order: Implementation of Care Plan)* [2002] 2 AC 291, 322, para. 82, where he suggested that the procedure for making a declaration of incompatibility cannot extend to breaches of *positive* rights. In that case, Lord Nichols considered a potential breach of the right to access to the court under Article 6 in relation to the Children Act 1989.

The Convention violation now under consideration consists of a failure to provide access to a court as guaranteed by Article 6(1). The absence of such provision means that English law may be incompatible with Article 6(1). The United Kingdom may be in breach of its treaty obligations regarding this article. But the absence of such provision from a particular statute does not, in itself, mean that the statute is incompatible with Article 6(1), rather, this signifies at most the existence of a lacuna in the statute. This is the position so far as the failure to comply with Article 6(1) lies in the absence of effective machinery for protecting the civil rights of young children who have no parent or guardian able and willing to act for them. In such cases there is a statutory lacuna, not a statutory incompatibility. (Similar *obiter* comments were made in *R* v *Enfield London Borough, Council, ex parte J* [2002] 2 FLR 1, *per* Elias J; *R* v *Secretary of State for Health, ex parte Rose* [2002] UKHRR 785, *per* Scott Baker J; *Hooper* v *Secretary of State for Work and Pensions* [2002] UKHRR 785, *per* Moses J.)

1.7 RETROSPECTIVE EFFECT OF THE HUMAN RIGHTS ACT 1998

The issue of whether s. 3 applied in relation to events before commencement was addressed by the House of Lords in *Wilson* v *Secretary of State for Trade and Industry* [2003] HRLR 33. It applied the approach to retrospective legislation taken by Staughton LJ in *Secretary of State* v *Tunnicliffe* [1991] 2 All ER 712 and held that, in general, s. 3 should not be applied to causes of action accruing before the section came into force, because 'to apply it in such cases, and thereby change the interpretation and effect of existing legislation, might well produce an unfair result for one party or another. The Human Rights Act was not intended to have this effect' (see *per* Lord Nicholls at para. 20). Application of Staughton LJ's principle might produce different results in some cirumstances, e.g. post-Act criminal trials in respect of pre-Act events. 'The prosecution does not have an accrued or vested right in any relevant sense' (para. 21). As s. 3 had to be read together with s. 4; and as s. 4 could not logically be applied except in cases where the s. 3 duty also arose, this approach meant that declarations of incompatibility equally could not be made (see para. 23).

Wilson recognized that s. 22(4) of the Act created a different position where it legitimately applied, with Lord Nicholls commenting that: 'What is not apparent is why, in respect of pre-Act violations of human rights, victims are given a domestic remedy in this one respect but not more widely, but there it is' (see para. 13).

The interpretation of s. 22(4) in relation to criminal trials which took place before October 2000 has a vexed history. In *R* v *DPP, ex parte Kebilene* [2000] 2 AC 326 Lord Steyn (at 346) argued that s. 22(4) extended the HRA 1998 to trials and to appeals:

> . . . a construction which treats the trial and appeal as parts of one process is more in keeping with the purpose of the Convention and the Act of 1998. It is a sensible and just construction.

It seemed therefore possible for defendants in criminal proceedings to bring appeals after 2 October 2000 based on the retrospective effect of the 1998 Act.

However, superseding *Ex parte Kebilene*, the House of Lords held in *R* v *Lambert* [2001] 3 WLR 206 that the Act did not apply retrospectively to a summing up order made before the Act came into force. The House of Lords adopted the reasoning of the Court of Appeal in *Wilson* v *First County Trust (No. 2)* [2001] 3 WLR 42 and decided that the HRA 1998 did not apply retrospectively to the summing up of a trial heard before that Act came into force. The House of Lords refused to apply Lord Steyn's judgment in *Ex parte Kebilene* (above). Lord Slynn (at para. 6) stated that the Act came into force only on the day appointed by the Secretary of State. There was a presumption against legislation having retrospect effect and it was thus not to be assumed that Convention rights are to be enforced in national courts in respect of past events. However, Lord Hope (at paras 104–107) distinguished a breach of Convention rights by the act of a court from the alleged breach of Convention rights by a prosecuting authority. Thus, retrospective reliance on Convention rights under s. 7(1)(b) is permitted by s. 22(4) at each stage of an appeal.

Contrary to the decision in *R* v *Lambert*, Lord Lloyd at para. 17, Lord Steyn at para. 26, and Lord Hope at para. 72 held in *R* v *Kansal (No. 2)* [2001] 3 WLR 1562 that *Lambert* had been decided unsatisfactorily. Although (with only Lord Hope dissenting) the House of Lords did not depart from the decision of the majority in *Lambert*, it does not appear to have considered criminal cases in which it departed from its own decisions. Also, the effect of the decision in *Lambert* is that criminal convictions arrived at in breach of the United Kingdom's international obligations before October 2000 cannot be reconsidered by the criminal courts.

In *R* v *Lyons* [2002] 3 WLR 1562, the House of Lords decided that the statutory procedure could not be overridden by giving direct effect to the Convention as an international convention.

Further, in *Society of Lloyd's* v *Laws* [2003] EWHC 873, Cooke J held that the HRA 1998 could not be given retrospective effect to interpret the Lloyd's Act 1982. In that case, Laws contended that the Lloyd's Act 1982, s. 14(3) which had granted immunity to the Society of Lloyd's from liability in damages for all claims with the exception of fraudulent misrepresentation was ineffective because of the provisions of the HRA 1998. However, Cooke J decided that the 1998 Act could not be given retrospective effect to interpret the Lloyd's Act 1982 because s. 14(3) of the 1982 Act was clear. This suggests that the HRA 1998 can still have retrospective effect where the meaning of legislation in question before October 2000 is unclear.

Chapter Two

Introduction to the Convention

John Howell QC and David Elvin QC

2.1 INTRODUCTION

As was noted in Chapter One, the HRA 1998 incorporates the majority of the European Convention on Human Rights (ECHR), together with parts of the First and Sixth Protocols, into English domestic law. However, as discussed at 2.2, there may be occasions when reference may be made to those parts of the Convention not specifically incorporated. This chapter deals with the correct approach to the interpretation of the Convention; certain concepts which are common to a number of Articles of that Convention; and, lastly, those Articles which are most likely to be of relevance to matters affecting local government.

The general context of the Convention and its purpose, although not incorporated, are found in Article 1, which aims to 'secure to everyone' within the jurisdiction of the High Contracting Parties 'the rights and freedoms defined in Section I of this Convention'. This emphasizes the universality of the rights to be secured, not limiting their application to nationals of the states or to those possessing legal capacity. This fundamental principle is underlined by the terms of the Preamble to the Convention.

2.2 INTERPRETATION OF THE CONVENTION

2.2.1 General

Since s. 2 of the HRA 1998 imposes a duty on the national courts to 'take account' of the decisions, judgments, etc. of the European Court of Human Rights (see Chapter One at 1.2.2), it seems likely that the approach of those national courts to the interpretation of the ECHR will, even if it does not follow the European Court precisely, be substantially based upon its approach. It is important to note that, if the national courts follow the approach of the European Court, the proper approach to the interpretation of the Convention differs in several important respects from the interpretation of national legislation.

2.2.2 International law principles

The European Court of Human Rights (*Golder* v *UK* (1975) 1 EHRR 524) has adopted the approach to the interpretation of international treaties codified in Articles 31–33 of the Vienna Convention on the Law of Treaties, as applicable to the interpretation of the Convention. However, the very context of the Convention itself and the securing of individual rights may themselves require the application of the Vienna Convention to be viewed with some caution (Jacobs and White, Clarendon Press, 1996, p. 27).

Article 31 of the Vienna Convention requires the interpretation of a treaty to be made in good faith and in accordance with its ordinary meaning, and in the context and in the light of the object and purpose of the treaty. The context of the treaty includes not only its articles but also any preamble and annexes, together with any agreement reacting to the treaty made in connection with its conclusion. Subsequent agreements or practices relating to the treaty are also to be taken into account, together with the relevant principles of international law applicable to the relations between the parties.

Article 32 allows the consideration of supplementary means of interpretation, including preparatory work of the treaty, when the interpretation under the ordinary approach in Article 31 above leaves the meaning 'ambiguous or obscure', or leads to a 'manifestly absurd or unreasonable' result.

Article 33 provides that where there is more than one authenticated text of the treaty, and those texts disclose a difference which the application of Articles 31 and 32 does not remove, the meaning should be adopted which 'best reconciles the texts, having regard to the object and purpose of the treaty'.

2.2.2.1 Ordinary meaning
This principle is commonly used and permits recourse to works such as dictionaries to ascertain the ordinary meaning of words (*Luedicke, Belkacem and Koç* v *Germany* (1978) 2 EHRR 149). However, where the ECHR itself creates special terms or concepts (such as 'civil rights and obligations', or 'necessary in a democratic society') the European Court has adopted its own approach based on the object and purpose of the Convention to determine their scope and meaning. The need to secure a uniform meaning and application of the Convention throughout the contracting states is an influential factor in ascribing meaning where such terminology is used (*König* v *Germany* (1978) 2 EHRR 170).

2.2.2.2 *Context*

As noted above, 'context' requires there to be taken into account not only terms of the Articles of the Convention itself, but also the Preamble ai. the Protocols. The Preamble has not been specifically incorporated by the 1998 Act.

One important question is the extent to which those parts of the Convention and Protocols not incorporated by the HRA 1998 can nonetheless be used as a means of interpretation of the incorporated parts of the Convention. On the assumption that the national courts will generally follow the approach of the European Court in the light of s. 2 of the 1998 Act, there are clear examples of cases where the Court has had regard to matters outside the strict terms of the Convention as applicable to a particular contracting party. Examples include cases where, in order to interpret Convention Articles, the Court has had regard to a Protocol to which a particular state was not a signatory (*Rasmussen v Denmark* (1984) 7 EHRR 372) or which had not been ratified (*Guzzardi v Italy* (1980) 3 EHRR 333). In interpreting the meaning of Convention terms, the European Court has also frequently considered the purpose of the Convention as set out in the Preamble and Article 1 (neither of which is incorporated).

The above strongly suggests that the courts ought to have regard even to those parts of the Convention which have not been specifically incorporated in order to interpret the meaning of the incorporated provisions. To do otherwise would be to proceed inconsistently with the approach of the European Court, would risk the inconsistent application of the Convention, and would divorce it from the very context in which the incorporated provisions were drafted and ratified.

2.2.2.3 *Object and purpose*

As already noted in 2.2.2.2, the Preamble and Article 1 of the Convention, whilst not incorporated, exercise an important influence over the interpretation of the Convention by virtue of their containing important statements as to its object and purpose.

The European Court has stated that the interpretation of the Convention should be objective (*Austria v Italy* (1961) 4 Yearbook 116). Unlike other international treaties, the Convention is not to be approached with a presumption that the provisions should be interpreted restrictively so as to limit their impact on the sovereignty of the contracting parties (*Wemhoff v Germany* (1968) 1 EHRR 55). The Convention should be interpreted 'to realise the aim and achieve the object of the treaty' and not to 'restrict to the greatest possible degree' the parties' obligations under it.

However, since the interpretation of Convention Articles must be 'in harmony with the logic of the Convention' (*Leander v Sweden* (1987) 9 EHRR 433), the use of general provisions cannot be used indirectly to create specific rights not otherwise created by the Convention.

23

as a 'living instrument'

ach to national legislation, the ECHR is not to be inter-
ocial and political circumstances prevailing at the time
ation. The Convention is a 'living instrument' (*Tyrer* v *UK*
1) to be interpreted in 'the light of present day conditions'. In
ue interpretation of the Convention can grow and develop in tandem
changes in social and political attitudes, and not become set in the concepts
of the mid-twentieth century. The decisions of the European Court concerning
the rights of transsexuals (*Goodwin* v *UK* (2002) 35 EHRR 447, paras 89–93),
homosexuals (*Dudgeon* v *UK* (1981) 4 EHRR 149), and illegitimacy (*Marckx* v
Belgium (1979) 2 EHRR 330) provide examples of it reflecting changing
attitudes.

2.2.4 Effectiveness

The European Court of Human Rights has stressed that the ECHR is intended to
provide 'rights that are practical and effective' (*Artico* v *Italy* (1980) 3 EHRR 1),
and has thus emphasized that the Convention should be not be interpreted restrictively but in such a way as to provide the effective protection of those rights
(*Golder* v *UK* (1975) 1 EHRR 524; *R* v *Morrisey* [1997] 2 Cr App R 426;
Goodwin v *UK* (2002) 35 EHRR 447, para. 74).

2.2.5 Other sources of law

The European Court has used other international treaties and instruments when
considering the proper interpretation of the ECHR, both in terms of the scope of
the rights protected and in terms of the scope of any margin of appreciation (see,
for example, *Marckx* v *Belgium* (1979) 2 EHRR 330; *Autronic AG* v *Switzerland*
(1990) 12 EHRR 485; and *Pretto* v *Italy* (1983) 6 EHRR 182).

The European Court may also rely on the domestic laws of the contracting
states, or the law of the European Union, to fortify or assist in the interpretation of
the Convention, especially where there is a common approach to issues (see, e.g.,
Goodwin v *UK* (1996) 22 EHRR 123).

2.2.6 Authenticated language texts

The English and French language texts of the ECHR are equally authentic; and if
they give rise to apparent differences in meaning, that meaning should be adopted
which best fits both versions, in accordance with Article 33 of the Vienna Convention and having regard to the purpose of the Convention (*James* v *UK* (1986) 8
EHRR 123).

2.2.7 Supplementary aids to interpretation — 'travaux préparatoires'

While preparatory work on 'the treaty' is in principle a supplementary aid to interpretation, especially having regard to Article 32 of the Vienna Convention, in the context of the ECHR it provides only limited assistance (*Sigurjonsson* v *Iceland* (1993) 16 EHRR 462). Given the special nature of Convention rights, the preliminary drafts would not seem to be matters which could be relied upon to limit the scope of the Convention provisions.

2.3 COMMON CONCEPTS

The ECHR seeks to strike a fair balance between the demands of the general interest of the community and the requirement to protect an individual's fundamental rights. Accordingly, 'proportionality' in various guises permeates the interpretation of the Convention, both in considering the application of the limitations on the rights conferred by certain of its Articles and in determining the existence and content of certain positive obligations arising from them. Limitations on certain rights also require any interference with them to be 'in accordance with the law', or in a manner 'prescribed by law', and to be 'necessary in a democratic society' (see, e.g., *R* v *Secretary of State for the Environment, Transport and the Regions, ex parte Alconbury Developments Ltd* [2001] 2 WLR 1389, at 1407).

2.3.1 Limitations on rights

Some of the rights secured by the Convention are on their face absolute. For example, Article 3 provides that no one shall be subjected to torture, or to inhuman or degrading treatment or punishment. But in other cases interferences with a Convention right may be justified. To be justified, any such interference must satisfy the requirement of lawfulness; it must pursue a legitimate aim; and it must not involve discrimination infringing Article 14.

2.3.1.1 The requirement of lawfulness
Where the Convention allows an exception to or an interference with some right, the requirement of lawfulness involves not only that the action of the public body must have a basis recognized in national law, but also that certain other requirements are satisfied so as to afford a measure of protection against arbitrary interference by public authorities with the rights safeguarded. As the European Court of Human Rights put it in *Silver* v *UK* (1983) 5 EHRR 347, at paras 86–88, the law must not only be adequately accessible, it must also be formulated with sufficient precision to enable a person to regulate his or her conduct. He or she must be able to foresee, if need be with appropriate advice, the consequences

which a given action may entail to a degree which is reasonable in the circumstances. Thus the degree of foreseeability required will be related to the consequences (see *de Freitas* v *Minister of Agriculture* [1999] AC 69, at 78). Many laws are inevitably couched in terms which are vague, the interpretation and application of which are matters of practice, and some discretion may be left to the authorities. Thus the fact that the outcome may depend on the exercise of a discretion exercised by a public body does not necessarily mean that any interference with a Convention right will fail to satisfy the requirement of lawfulness. According to the European Court in *Malone* v *UK* (1984) 7 EHHR 14, at para. 68:

> The law must indicate the scope of any such discretion conferred on the competent authorities and the manner of its exercise with sufficient clarity, having regard to the legitimate aim of the measure in question, to give the individual adequate protection against arbitrary interference.

In addition to reasonable foreseeability in operation, procedural safeguards against abuse may also be required if any interference is to be in accordance with law. These may include the opportunity to be heard (*W* v *UK* (1987) 10 EHRR 29) and a right to be given reasons for the decision.

2.3.1.2 *The legitimate aims which may justify interference with a Convention right and proportionality*

The legitimate aims which may be pursued are set out in the Articles which permit such interference. As Article 18 states, the restrictions permitted under the Convention shall not be applied for any purpose other than those for which they have been prescribed.

In addition, some provisions of the Convention, such as Articles 8–11, stipulate expressly that any interference must be necessary in a democratic society. Similarly, Article 1 of Protocol 1, prohibits interference with possessions but such interference may occur if it strikes a fair balance between the private rights interfered with and the justification for the interference (see below). That does not mean that the views of the majority must always prevail: a balance must be achieved which ensures fair and proper treatment of minorities and avoids any abuse of a dominant position. In *Derbyshire County Council* v *Times Newspapers Ltd* [1993] AC 534, Lord Keith of Kinkel observed, with reference to Article 10:

> As regards the words 'necessary in a democratic society' in connection with the restrictions on the right to freedom of expression which may properly be prescribed by law, the jurisprudence of the European Court of Human Rights has established that 'necessary' requires the existence of a pressing social need, and that the restrictions should be no more than is proportionate to the legitimate aim pursued.

There must thus be a reasonable relationship of proportionality between the means employed and the legitimate objectives pursued by a public body, assessed by reference to the standards of a democratic society, characterized by pluralism, tolerance and broad-mindedness (*Handyside* v *UK* (1976) 1 EHRR 737, at para. 49 and *R* v *Secretary of State for the Home Department, ex parte Daly* [2001] AC 532, at para. 27). Accordingly the objective must be sufficiently important to justify limiting the right concerned; the means employed must be rationally connected to that objective; and the means adopted must impair the relevant right no more than is necessary to accomplish the objective.

Subsequent domestic cases have tended to prefer, in place of the formulation in terms of 'pressing social need', simply to say that the interference must serve some 'legitimate aim' (generally to be identified by reference to the relevant Article of the Convention) and the interference must strike a fair balance between the rights of the individual and the aim to be served (see, e.g., *Daly* (above), *R (on the application of Samaroo)* v *Secretary of State for the Home Department* [2002] INLR 55, and in particular *R (Pro Life Alliance)* v *BBC* [2003] 2 All ER 977, at 1013). Insofar as this suggests a less stringent test for decision-makers, the context in which the decision is taken, to which the nature of the Convention right in question will be relevant, is of importance. See the discussion of 'deference' at 2.4.2.

Obviously, the more severe the effects of any action on an individual's right and the more important the right which is interfered with, the more important the social need must be if the interference is to be justified, particularly if there is a European consensus which does not involve such interference. Thus freedom of expression and the right to respect for the home require the necessity for any interference to be convincingly established. The protection of rights and freedoms enshrined in the Convention will more easily justify interference with Convention rights, whereas only indisputable imperatives will justify such interference in order to protect other rights and freedoms (*Chassagnou* v *France* (1999) 29 EHRR 615, at para. 113).

For the means employed to be rationally connected to the legitimate objective which may be pursued, they must not be arbitrary, unfair, or based on irrelevant considerations, and they must be capable of achieving their objective. Moreover, the means adopted must impair the relevant right no more than is necessary to accomplish the objective. A restriction which has a scope that is wider than is required would fail this test (see *de Freitas* v *Ministry of Agriculture* [1999] 1 AC 69 at 81). Similarly, where the objective may be achieved in more than one way, the way that is least harmful to Convention rights should be chosen.

Lastly, in this context, proportionality may also require the adoption of procedural safeguards, such as the giving of reasons and judicial supervision (see, e.g., *R* v *Secretary of State for the Home Department, ex parte Wright* [2002] HRLR 1; *Camenzind* v *Switzerland* (1997) 28 EHRR 458, at paras 44–5; and *Funke* v *France* (1993) 16 EHRR 297, paras 56–7.

2.3.2   Wider applications of proportionality

These concepts of necessity and proportionality also have a wider application in relation to the ECHR. Thus, an interference with the implied right of access to a court under Article 6(1) will infringe that Article unless it pursues a legitimate aim and there is a reasonable relationship of proportionality between the means employed and the aim sought to be achieved (*Ashingdane* v *UK* (1985) 7 EHRR 528, at para. 57). So, equally, the scope of implied positive obligations will be influenced by considerations of proportionality. Thus the implied obligation to provide preventative operational measures to safeguard the life of an individual from an immediate threat posed by another identified individual under Article 2, 'must be interpreted in a way which does not impose an impossible or disproportionate burden on the authorities' and which respects the rights of others (*Osman* v *UK* (1998) 29 EHRR 245, at paras 115–116). Similarly, in determining whether there exists any positive obligation — e.g. under Article 8 of the Convention — 'regard must be had to the fair balance that has to be struck between the general interest of the community and the interests of individuals' (*Rees* v *UK* (1986) 9 EHRR 56, para. 37 and see *R* v *Secretary of State for the Home Department, ex parte Wright* [2002] HRLR 1). Lastly, considerations of proportionality are relevant in determining whether a difference of treatment involves a violation of Article 14, requiring the enjoyment of the rights and freedoms set forth in the Convention without discrimination on the grounds of status. There must be an objective and reasonable justification for the difference in treatment, the existence of which, as the European Court stated in the *Belgian Linguistic (No. 2)* (1968) 1 EHHR 252, at para. 10, is to be:

> . . . assessed in relation to the aims and effects of the measure under consideration, regard being had to the principles which normally prevail in democratic societies. A difference in treatment in the exercise of a right laid down in the Convention must not only pursue a legitimate aim: Article 14 is likewise violated when it is clearly established that there is no reasonable relationship of proportionality between the means employed and the aim sought to be realised.

2.4   ESTABLISHING A BREACH OF A CONVENTION RIGHT: THE MARGIN OF APPRECIATION AND DEFERENCE

Subject to limited exceptions, under s. 6(1) of the HRA 1998 it is unlawful for a public authority to act in a way which is incompatible with a Convention right. Thus:

(a)   it is for a victim to show that there has been an infringement of his or her Convention right; but

(b)   it is for the public body to show that there is proper justification for any interference with a prima facie right where any such interference is permissible.

Consequently, it is for the public body to show what its reasons were and that they were relevant and sufficient (*Buckley* v *UK* (1996) 23 EHRR 101, at para. 77).

Behind this second principle, however, there lurk difficult issues concerning the relationship between the judgment made by a public body and the standard of review applied by the court to its actions, which are further complicated by the requirements of Article 6 in relation to administrative proceedings when the determination of civil rights and obligations is involved.

2.4.1   Margin of appreciation

When judging the compatibility of national measures, the European Court of Human Rights has allowed each state a margin of appreciation within the ECHR with which it will not interfere. Such a margin of appreciation is justified on the basis that state authorities may be in a better position to make the relevant judgment than the European Court and that the machinery of protection established by the Convention is subsidiary to national systems for safeguarding human rights (see *Handyside* v *UK* (1976) 1 EHRR 737). For example, this margin of appreciation has been allowed by the European Court in relation to:

(a)   the justification for interference with a Convention right, when establishing the ambit of positive or inherent obligations under the Convention;
(b)   the assessment of what is necessary in a democratic society, and of what constitutes objective and reasonable justification for a difference of treatment under Article 14; and
(c)   compensation terms under Article 1 of the First Protocol.

There are, however, limits to this margin of appreciation allowed to state authorities by the European Court, which varies according to the importance of the right at stake, the seriousness of the interference, the particular purpose pursued by the state, and the degree to which practice varies among Convention states. Differences of view arise even in Strasbourg as to the extent of the margin of appreciation, as can be seen in the differing judgments in *Hatton* v *UK* of the chamber ((2002) 34 EHRR 1) and the Grand Chamber (2003) 37 EHRR 28. Ultimately it is for the European Court in every case to set the limits within which states may act compatibly with the Convention.

Although the margin of appreciation allowed to states by the European Court cannot be of direct applicability in resolving disputes within the domestic legal system about the compatibility of actions by public bodies with Convention rights, it does not follow that the Court will not allow public bodies any margin for judgment, or that it will substitute its own view in all cases. As Lord Hoffman has put it, 'there is no reason why that margin of appreciation should be engrossed by the judicial branch of government rather than the legislature or executive' (*Matedeen* v *Pointu* [1999] 1 AC 98, at 116D and see Dyson LJ in *R* v *Secretary of State for the Home Department, ex parte Samaroo* [2001] UKHRR 1150).

2.4.2 Deference

Whether what has been done is incompatible with a Convention right on the facts found is ultimately a question for a court to determine. But it is likely that, at least in some cases, the court may defer to the opinion of the public body involved on matters relevant to the determination of that question. This is unlikely when the right involved is of particular importance, requiring a high degree of protection; where it is one which is apparently absolute, or where only strictly limited derogations are permitted; or when the courts have any special expertise in the matter or are in the same position to make the relevant judgment as the public body concerned (see, e.g., *R* v *Secretary of State, ex parte Turgut* [2001] 1 All ER 719). Deference is more likely to be shown, for example, when the question turns on the balance to be struck between competing considerations — when the issues require consideration of technical, social, economic or political factors, the raising of taxes and the allocation of resources, or national security or diplomatic relations (see *James* v *UK* (1986) 8 EHRR 123, at para. 46). As Lord Hope put it in *R* v *DPP, ex parte Kebilene* [2000] 2 AC 326, at 348:

> . . . in the hands of the national courts . . . the Convention should be seen as an expression of fundamental principles rather than as a set of mere rules. The questions which the courts will have to decide in the application of these principles will involve questions of balance between competing interests and issues of proportionality. In this area difficult choices may have to be made by the executive or the legislature between the rights of the individual and the needs of society. In some circumstances it will be appropriate for the courts to recognise that there is an area of judgment within which the judiciary will defer, on democratic grounds, to the considered opinion of the elected body or person whose act or decision is said to be incompatible with the Convention . . . the area in which these choices may arise is conveniently and appropriately described as the 'discretionary area of judgment'. It will be easier for such an area of judgment to be recognised where the Convention itself requires a balance to be struck, much less so where the right is stated in terms which are unqualified. It will be easier for it to be recognised where the issues involve questions of social or economic policy, much less so where the rights are of high constitutional importance or are of a kind where the courts are especially well placed to assess the need for protection.

It is now clear that there is a sliding scale on which different factual situations may be located depending on their particular circumstances and the Article of the Convention which applies (for a valuable discussion of this see Lord Walker in *R (Pro Life Alliance)* v *BBC* [2003] 2 All ER 977, at 1011–1015, and see Lord Hoffmann at 998). Articles of the Convention which are stated in terms which are unqualified, most notably Article 3, will allow less scope for deference than those in which the Convention itself requires a balance to be struck. Certain other Articles of the Convention, such as Article 10 and Article 5, may require a high level of scrutiny by the court, whereas it is clear that Article 1 of the First Protocol, at the other end of the scale, requires a high level of deference by the courts to decision-makers (this is partly, although not entirely, a matter of the different wording of the Article). An example of the way in which different factual situations may affect the level of deference required is provided by Article 10, under which it seems there is a higher level of protection afforded to political speech than to commmercial speech. Equally, where a case involves consideration of broad questions of social or economic policy it is almost inevitable that the courts will pay a higher level of deference than in cases that they regard as being within their own competence, such as the liberty of the subject or fair trial rights (although see Lord Walker's reservations about the comments of Laws LJ in *Pro Life Alliance*, at para. 137). At the risk of excessive generalization it will often be the case that the areas of competence of local authorities will tend to involve factual situations which lie towards the end of the scale where a high level of deference is appropriate.

In any event, deference is not the same as immunity from review. Even with such deference as is appropriate in any particular case, the standard of judicial review of the actions of public bodies in relation to Convention rights is likely to be more exacting than has hitherto applied. Members of the Appellate Committee indicated in *R* v *Secretary of State for the Home Department, ex parte Brind* [1991] 1 AC 696, for example, that in considering whether the requirements of proportionality are satisfied, a more stringent approach to the merits would be required of the Court than that warranted by the *Wednesbury* test of unreasonableness. Similarly, in *Smith and Grady* v *UK* (2001) 31 EHRR 24, the Court held that the circumstances in which a court could hold that a policy which interfered with rights under Article 8 was unreasonable, were placed so high that this effectively excluded any consideration of whether the interference with the applicants' rights answered a pressing social need or was proportionate to the national security and public order aims pursued by the Government, so that review on *Wednesbury* grounds failed to provide an 'effective remedy' in that case. This is not to say that judicial review on traditional grounds might never provide an 'effective remedy' in cases involving administrative action, but the *Wednesbury* standard of review will have to be lowered in such cases (see *R* v *Secretary of State, ex parte Turgut* [2001] 1 All ER 719). In *R* v *Secretary of State for the Home Department, ex parte Daly* [2001] AC 532, the House of Lords identified the difference in approach required by the Convention and at common law, acknowledging the overlap between traditional *Wednesbury* grounds and the level of scrutiny required to safeguard Convention rights. Lord Steyn stated (at paras 27 and 28):

> 27. ... I would mention three concrete differences without suggesting that my statement is exhaustive. First, the doctrine of proportionality may require the reviewing court to assess the balance which the decision maker has struck, not merely whether it is within the range of rational or reasonable decisions. Secondly, the proportionality test may go further than the traditional grounds of review inasmuch as it may require attention to be directed to the relative weight accorded to interests and considerations. Thirdly, even the heightened scrutiny test developed in *R v Ministry of Defence, ex parte Smith* [1996] QB 517, 554 is not necessarily appropriate to the protection of human rights. It will be recalled that in Smith the Court of Appeal reluctantly felt compelled to reject a limitation on homosexuals in the army. The challenge based on article 8 of the Convention for the Protection of Human Rights and Fundamental Freedoms (the right to respect for private and family life) foundered on the threshold required even by the anxious scrutiny test. The European Court of Human Rights came to the opposite conclusion ... In other words, the intensity of the review, in similar cases, is guaranteed by the twin requirements that the limitation of the right was necessary in a democratic society, in the sense of meeting a pressing social need, and the question whether the interference was really proportionate to the legitimate aim being pursued.
>
> 28. The differences in approach between the traditional grounds of review and the proportionality approach may therefore sometimes yield different results. It is therefore important that cases involving Convention rights must be analysed in the correct way. This does not mean that there has been a shift to merits review. On the contrary, as Professor Jowell [2000] PL 671, 681 has pointed out the respective roles of judges and administrators are fundamentally distinct and will remain so. To this extent the general tenor of the observations in *Mahmood* [2001] 1 WLR 840 are correct. And Laws LJ rightly emphasised in *Mahmood*, at p 847, para. 18, 'that the intensity of review in a public law case will depend on the subject matter in hand'. That is so even in cases involving Convention rights. In law context is everything.

Whatever may be the general relationship between the judgment made by a public body and the standard of review applied by the Court to its actions, the applicability of Article 6 to administrative decision-making which involves the determination of civil rights and obligations creates particular difficulties. These are discussed at 2.5 in connection with Article 6.

2.5 ARTICLE 6: FAIR TRIAL

Article 6 ECHR is concerned with the right to a fair trial within a reasonable time. Article 6(1) provides:

1. In the determination of his civil rights and obligations or of any criminal charge against him, everyone is entitled to a fair and public hearing within a reasonable time by an independent and impartial tribunal established by law. Judgment shall be pronounced publicly . . .

Article 6(1) also deals with limitations which may be imposed on the public hearing; and Article 6(2) and (3) provide further specific protection for a person charged with a criminal offence, requiring such a person to 'be presumed innocent until proved guilty according to law' and conferring on him or her certain other, specific minimum rights. These are:

(a) to be informed promptly, in a language which he understands and in detail, of the nature and cause of the accusation against him;

(b) to have adequate time and facilities for the preparation of his defence;

(c) to defend himself in person or through legal assistance of his own choosing or, if he has not suffiient means to pay for legal assistance, to be given it free when the interests of justice so require;

(d) to examine or have examined witnesses against him and to obtain the attendance and examination of witnesses on his behalf under the same conditions as witnesses against him;

(e) to have the free assistance of an interpreter if he cannot understand or speak the language used in court.

2.5.1   The applicability of Article 6(1)

The protection which Article 6(1) ECHR affords applies 'in the determination of . . . civil rights and obligations or of any criminal charge'. What constitutes such a right, obligation or charge is not determined merely by any ordinary domestic law classification: the concepts are 'autonomous' under the Convention.

There must be a genuine dispute over a 'civil' right or obligation which can be said (at least on arguable grounds) to be recognized under domestic law, now including Convention rights. Although Article 6(1) ECHR itself does not require any particular substantive content for civil rights or obligations in domestic law, restrictions by way of immunity must not impair the essence of the right of access to a body for the determination of such a right or obligation; they must pursue a legitimate aim and they must bear a reasonable relationship to the aim sought to be achieved (see, e.g., *James* v *UK* (1986) 8 EHRR 123, at para. 81; and *Osman* v *UK* (1998) 29 EHRR 295).

Article 6(1) applies to all proceedings the result of which is directly decisive of private rights and obligations (*Le Compte, Van Leuven and de Meyere* v *Belgium* (1981) 4 EHRR 1, at 15–17, in particular at paras 44, 46 and 47). By contrast, Article 6 does not apply to determinations of rights and obligations under public law. Thus the fact that the outcome may directly affect eligibility to be a member of a public authority does not of itself involve the determination of any civil right (see *Hapsburg-Lothringen* v *Austria* (1989) 64 DR 210; and *Pierre-Bloch* v *France* (1997) 26 EHRR 202 at 233, at para. 50). However, Article 6 can apply to proceedings of a public law character if they are directly decisive of civil rights and obligations. What is significant is the nature of the right or obligation, not the procedure by which or the person by whom it is determined.

For Article 6(1) to apply, the proceedings must be directly decisive of civil rights or obligations. They must be directly affected by and constitute the subject matter of the dispute (see *Fayed* v *UK* (1994) 18 EHRR 393, at 425–428). Accordingly, objectors to licences to carry on certain activities on land must show that those activities will directly affect their rights. Thus objectors could not complain of a breach of Article 6(1) where they could not show that the operation of a nuclear power station exposed them personally to a serious, specific and imminent danger (*Balmer-Schafroth* v *Switzerland* (1997) 25 EHRR 598, at paras 39 and 40 and *R (Vetterlein)* v *Hampshire County Council* [2002] Env LR 198). By contrast, a landowner's appeal against the grant of planning permission for the development of adjoining land involved the determination of her civil rights, since she considered that that development would jeopardize her enjoyment of her own land and reduce its market value (*Ortenberg* v *Austria* (1994) 19 EHRR 524, at para. 28).

What, then, may constitute a civil right or obligation? The determination of pecuniary liabilities often, but not invariably, involves the determination of civil obligations. As the European Court observed in *Schouten and Meldrun* v *Netherlands* (1994) 19 EHRR 432, at 455, it is not:

> . . . in itself sufficient to show that a dispute is 'pecuniary' in nature. There may exist 'pecuniary' obligations *vis-à-vis* the State or its subordinate authorities which, for the purpose of Article 6(1), are to be considered as belonging exclusively to the realm of public law and are accordingly not covered by the notion of 'civil rights and obliga-tions'. Apart from fines imposed by way of 'criminal sanction', this will be the case, in particular, where an obligation which is pecuniary in nature derives from tax legislation or is otherwise part of the normal civic duties in a democratic society.

Similarly, an order to pay the Treasury a sum equivalent to the amount of any excess election campaign expenditure is not a determination to which Article 6 applies, as it forms part of the arrangements for the exercise of the right to stand for election which is not a civil right (*Pierre-Bloch* v *France* (1997) 26 EHRR 202, at 233, para. 51), nor is the mere blighting effect of a planned development scheme, since in that case there was no right under UK law to require an authority to purchase (*Moore* v *UK* (App. No. 40425/98), 15 June 1999, para. 2). By contrast, restitutionary claims which involve the determination of private law rights to quantifiable sums of money (*National and Provincial Building Society* v

UK (1997) 25 EHRR 127) and claims for damages against a public body (e.g. *H* v *France* (1989) 12 EHRR 74) will normally involve the determination of a person's civil rights.

Areas in which civil rights and obligations may be determined include the grant or refusal of permission to develop or exploit private land (*Fredin* v *Sweden* (1991) 13 EHRR 74; *R* v *Secretary of State for the Environment, Transport and the Regions, ex parte Alconbury Developments Ltd* [2001] 2 WLR 1389); the grant, revocation or suspension of licences to carry on business activities (*Pudas* v *Sweden* (1987) 10 EHRR 380 — taxi driver; *Tre Traktörer Aktiebolag* v *Sweden* (1989) 13 EHRR 309 — sale of alcoholic drinks); the expropriation of land; entitlement to benefits and liability to make contributions under social insurance and welfare assistance schemes (*Salesi* v *Italy* (1993) 26 EHRR 187); and access to children in care and adoption proceedings (e.g., *W* v *UK* (1987) 10 EHRR 29).

However, the granting of discretionary benefits, where satisfaction of eligibility criteria does not create an enforceable claim, does not involve the determination of any civil right (see *Masson and van Zon* v *Netherlands* (1995) 22 EHRR 491, at paras 52–3). Similarly, aspects of employment in the public service — such as recruitment, employment, dismissal and retirement — have been treated as not involving the determination of any civil right or obligation, although disputes as to the remuneration or pension payable may do so (see, e.g., *Maillard* v *France* (1999) 27 EHRR 232, at para. 39).

Of some importance in relation to the meaning of 'civil rights' is the approach of the House of Lords in *R* v *Tower Hamlets London Borough Council, ex parte Runa Begum* [2003] 2 WLR 388. The case concerned the administration of a scheme of social welfare, namely the homelessness provisions in the Housing Act 1996. The House proceeded on the basis that Article 6 was indeed engaged because there was a determination of the Appellant's civil rights where a homelessness decision was made, and went on to find that in any event the availability of judicial review satisfied the requirements of Article 6 in an administrative law context. Nevertheless, there was a recognition in the judgments that while the trend in the European Court had been to apply an increasingly broad approach to the concept of civil rights, to hold that the appellant's civil rights were engaged nevertheless went further than the European Court had hitherto been willing to go. Their Lordships therefore expressly reserved their decision on whether the appellant's civil rights were engaged in order that the Secretary of State not be prevented from arguing in some future case that this case did not engage the civil rights of a person in Runa Begum's position. Also of interest is the recognition, particularly by Lord Bingham (see para. 6) and Lord Hoffmann (see paras 34–35) that the question of whether civil rights were engaged in a particular administrative law context was intimately connected with the level of procedural protection required by Article 6. As Lord Hoffmann said (at para. 34), . . . 'it seems to me . . . that an extension of the scope of art 6 into administrative decision-making must be linked to a willingness to accept by way of compliance something less than a full review of the administrator's decision'.

In deciding whether or not a person is charged with any criminal offence, three main factors are of relevance:

(a) the legal classification of the matter under national law;
(b) the nature of the matter in question; and
(c) whether the sanction belongs in general to the criminal sphere by virtue of its nature and its degree of severity.

The treatment of a matter as non-criminal under national law is not conclusive for this purpose and the other factors may also be taken into account (see *Engel* v *Netherlands* (1976) 1 EHRR 647, at 677–679). The second and third criteria are alternative, and not necessarily cumulative, criteria (*Lutz* v *Germany* (1987) 10 EHRR 182, at 198, at para. 55). So far as the third criterion is concerned, as the Court observed in *Lauko* v *Slovakia* (2001) 33 EHRR 40, at paras 58 and 59:

> . . . it suffices that the offence in question . . . should have made the person concerned liable to a sanction which, in its nature and degree of severity, belongs in general to the 'criminal sphere' . . . a punitive character . . . is the customary feature of criminal penalties.

Thus committal to prison for failure to pay a community charge involves a criminal charge (*Benham* v *UK* (1996) 22 EHRR 293). But there may be consequences of disciplinary or professional proceedings for a given group with a special status which lie outside the criminal sphere (see, e.g., *Bendenoun* v *France* (1994) 18 EHRR 54, at 75–76; and *Pierre-Bloch* v *France* (1997) 26 EHRR 202, at 234–235).

2.5.2 The protection afforded by Article 6(1)

The protection afforded by Article 6 ECHR imposes a positive obligation to provide access to a body which satisfies the requirements of Article 6(1) whenever a civil right or obligation, or a criminal charge, falls to be determined (*Golder* v *UK* (1975) 1 EHRR 524). Limitations, such as time limits and immunities, may be imposed on this right provided that they do not impair the essence of the right of access; that they pursue a legitimate aim; and that they bear a reasonable relationship to the aim sought to be achieved.

2.5.2.1 *Independence and impartiality*
Article 6(1) ECHR requires access to a body whose function it is to determine matters on the basis of legal rules following proceedings conducted in

a prescribed manner. The body must be independent both of the executive and of parties to the case. In considering whether a tribunal is independent, regard will be had to its manner of appointment, the term of office of its members, the existence of guarantees against outside pressures and whether it possesses the appearance of independence. Thus, for example, a planning inspector whose appointment can be revoked at any time by the executive is not an independent tribunal (see *Bryan* v *UK* (1995) 21 EHRR 342). Equally, a local authority's rehousing manager is not independent 'simply because she is an administrator and cannot be described as part of the judicial branch of government' (*R* v *London Borough of Tower Hamlets, ex parte Runa Begum* [2003] 2 WLR 388 (HL)).

The body to which there is a right of access under Article 6(1) must also be impartial; this requires the absence of prejudice or bias. It is tested 'subjectively' and 'objectively'. Subjectively, personal impartiality in fact is presumed until there is proof to the contrary. Objectively, the question is whether the tribunal offers guarantees sufficient to exclude any legitimate doubts about its impartiality. While appearances are important, they are not decisive, since misgivings must be capable of being held to be objectively justified (*Kraska* v *Sweden* (1993) 18 EHRR 188, at para. 72). Like the domestic law relating to apparent bias, which is based on a real possibility of bias, the test under the Convention is in some cases more easily stated than applied. Whether the 'real possibility of bias' test differs from the 'objective' test for bias under the Convention, or whether the tests if different would produce different results in the same case, is open to question. However, the European Court did not comment adversely on the real danger of the bias test in *Gregory* v *UK* (1997) 25 EHRR 577, and the application of Convention jurisprudence has led to a further refinement in the common law bias test (*Re Medicaments and Related Classes of Goods (No. 2)* [2001] 1 WLR 700; and *Porter* v *Magill* [2002] 2 AC 358).

2.5.2.2 *Decisions by those who do not satisfy the requirement of independence where those decisions may be reviewed by a body which does*

Some public bodies may well not satisfy the requirement under Article 6(1) ECHR of independence of the executive, and their proceedings may not meet other requirements of that Article. The process will not necessarily involve any infringement of Article 6, however, if the individual can bring his or her case before a court with full jurisdiction in respect of both fact and law. But access to a body which meets the requirements of Article 6(1) but which considers itself bound by findings of fact which are crucial to the dispute which have been made by a body which does not itself meet the requirements of Article 6(1), will not normally satisfy the requirements of this Article (see, e.g., *Terra Woningen* v *Netherlands* (1997) 24 EHRR 456; and *McGonnell* v *UK* [2000] 2 PLR 69). As the Court put it in *Le Compte, Van Leuven and de Maeyre* v *Belgium* (1981) 4 EHRR 1, at para. 51:

Article 6(1) draws no distinction between questions of fact and questions of law. Both categories of question are equally crucial for the outcome of proceedings relating to 'civil rights and obligations'. Hence, the 'right to a court' and the right to a judicial determination of the dispute cover questions of fact as much as questions of law.

It is not the case, however, that the European Court has regarded judicial review of decisions of public bodies which do not satisfy the requirement of independence on the grounds traditionally recognized as being inconsistent in all cases with the requirements of Article 6(1). Some cases may well turn on the absence of any challenge to the primary facts or to inferences drawn from them in those cases. But a restricted role for the European Court in relation to findings of fact may be treated as compatible with Article 6(1) depending on the nature of the rights engaged, where the area of law is specialised, the facts have been established in the course of a quasi-judicial procedure governed by many of the safeguards required by Article 6(1), and the matter involves an area with a high policy content or involving the exercise of discretionary judgment in relation to policy matters (*Zumtobel* v *Austria* (1993) 17 EHRR 116 — an expropriation case; *ISKCON* v *UK* (1994) 18 EHRR CD 133 and *Bryan* v *UK* (1995) 21 EHRR 342 — both planning cases; and *Fischer* v *Austria* (1995) 20 EHRR 349 — revocation of a refuse tip operator's licence on environmental grounds). However, access to a full review of facts and law will be required where the determination involves the imposition of a criminal penalty (*Umlauft* v *Austria* (1996) 22 EHRR 72, at para. 39), or interference with important personal rights such as family life (*W* v *UK* (1987) 10 EHRR 29).

The landmark decision of the House of Lords in *R* v *Secretary of State for the Environment, Transport and the Regions, ex parte Alconbury Developments Ltd* [2001] 2 WLR 1389, concerning the structural compatibility of planning and compulsory purchase procedures, confirmed that in the context of rights concerning the use and enjoyment of property, a 'composite' approach to Article 6 was acceptable (following *Zumtobel* and *Bryan*), namely that the lack of independence of the tribunal (the Secretary of State in those cases) could be cured by the availability of judicial review in the form of statutory rights of appeal on review grounds. *Alconbury* was followed by the Court of Session on appeal in *County Properties* v *Scottish Ministers* 2000 27 SLT 965.

Further, the *Alconbury* decision appears to have the imprimatur of Strasbourg since, in *Holding & Barnes plc* v *UK* (App. No. 2352/02, 12 March 2002), the European Court declared inadmissible the application by one of the *Alconbury* claimants, Holding & Barnes plc, which sought to raise the Article 6 issues decided in *Alconbury*. Referring to the judgment of the House of Lords, the European Court agreed that the case was determined by the approach in *Bryan* and the finding that there were sufficient 'procedural guarantees of fairness' in the proceedings before the Secretary of State.

The contexts in which the 'composite approach' applies extend beyond property and planning rights and include other forms of discretionary administrative decision-making. In *Vilvarajah* v *UK* (1992) 14 EHRR 248, at para. 126, the Court held that the two-stage approach was applicable to asylum cases. In *Stefan* v *General Medical Council* [1999] 1 WLR 1293, at 1299, the Privy Council applied the composite approach in relation to decisions of the Health Committee of the General Medical Council, and their decision was subsequently endorsed by the Commission, which found Stefan's complaint inadmissible ((1997) 25 EHRR CD 130). It was also followed in the context of gaming regulation in *Kingsley* v *UK* (2001) 33 EHRR 13, although Article 6 was breached on the facts because judicial review was ineffective to cure the specific problem in that case.

The *Alconbury* decision has led to consideration of a number of issues, including the extent to which the composite approach in discretionary administrative cases applies where there is some degree of factual dispute and whether a hearing is required before the administrative decision-maker. In general, providing there are sufficient procedural safeguards, it appeared that the composite approach is sufficient and a hearing before the administrative decision-maker is not generally required (see, e.g., *R* v *Hampshire County Council, ex parte Vetterlein* [2002] Env LR 198; *Bovis Homes Ltd* v *New Forest DC* [2002] EWHC 483 (Admin); *R* v *English Nature, ex parte Aggregate Industries* [2003] Env LR 3, paras 101–107; and *Adlard* v *Secretary of State for Transport Local Government and the Regions* [2002] 1 WLR 2515, at paras 31–32). That has now been confirmed by the decision of the House of Lords in *Begum* [2003] 2 WLR 388. According to Lord Hoffman in *Begum*, the procedural safeguards provided by common law requirements of rationality and fairness will generally suffice for the application of the composite approach.

2.5.2.3 A fair hearing
In considering whether there has been a fair hearing, the hearing as a whole falls to be examined. Particular incidents, while obviously relevant to that question, will not be considered in isolation. Accordingly, defects may not be regarded as having undermined the fairness of the proceedings as a whole and they may be cured by a higher tribunal, although Article 6 ECHR does not guarantee any right of appeal.

A fair hearing is regarded as requiring the opportunity to be heard on all important issues, to attend certain hearings, and to know the grounds upon which a decision is based. In addition, it requires access to information necessary to enable the case to be brought effectively, unless there is good reason to deny it (*McGinley and Egan* v *UK* (1998) 27 EHRR 1), and 'equality of arms'.

The principle of 'equality of arms' requires that any party to proceedings must have a reasonable opportunity of presenting his or her case to the court under conditions which do not place him or her at a substantial disadvantage *vis-à-vis* his or her opponent (*Airey* v *Ireland* (1979) 2 EHRR 305; *Dombo Beheer BV* v *Netherlands* (1993) 18 EHRR 213; and *Challenger* v *Secretary of State* [2001] Env LR 209). Article 6 does not require legal aid to be available in all civil cases, and compliance will turn on whether the right of access to a court is 'practical and effective' (*Del Sol* v *France* (2002) 35 EHRR 1281). In *Challenger*, Harrison J rejected an allegation of inequality of arms by unfounded objectors at a public inquiry and took into account the availability of funding under the Access to Justice Act 1999, the nature of public inquiries and the role of inspectors, and the fact that the issues they sought to raise were being raised by other, represented parties. The principle is reflected in the requirement under the Civil Procedure Rules (CPR, Part 1, rule 1.1), that dealing with a case justly includes, so far as practicable, ensuring that the parties are on an equal footing. The principle can be infringed:

(a)   by refusing to inform a person of the reasons for an administrative decision which may enable him or her to challenge it (*Hentrich* v *France* (1994) 18 EHRR 440);

(b)   by refusing to allow a party to adduce evidence, to cross-examine or comment on submissions made; or

(c)   by denying a party the opportunity to influence or comment on an expert report produced as evidence for the determining body.

Article 6 does not require any particular rules of evidence to be adopted, but whatever rules may be chosen must not result in a hearing which is not fair.

2.5.2.4   *Is an oral hearing required?*

A fair hearing does not necessarily require an oral hearing, still less a formal hearing. In many discretionary administrative cases, provided there are sufficient procedural safeguards, consideration of written representations may be sufficient, whether with or without some ability to speak at a local authority meeting (*R* v *Hampshire County Council, ex parte Vetterlein* [2002] Env LR 198; *Begum* v *Tower Hamlets London Borough Council* [2002] 2 All ER 668, at paras 40–3; *R* v *English Nature, ex parte Aggregate Industries* [2003] Env LR 3, at paras 101–107; and *Adlard* v *Secretary of State for Transport Local Government and the Regions* [2002] 1 WLR 2515, at paras 31–32). In *Zumtobel* v *Austria* (1993) 17 EHRR 116, at para. 9, the Court found no breach of Article 6 ECHR even though the only hearing permitted to the claimant whose property was expropriated was the limited opportunity to present reports at the municipal offices in relation to a technical and discretionary area of the law (of which planning provides a prime example). The limited requirement for an oral hearing has now been confirmed by the decision of the House of Lords in *Begum* ([2003] 2 WLR 388).

Begum is also of note in that it clarifies Lord Hoffmann's own remarks in

Alconbury, where he distinguished between matters of 'policy' and 'fact'. In *Begum*, Lord Hoffmann noted the confusion which his remarks had created and held that so long as a decision fell within what could be called 'a classic area of administrative discretion' there would be no need in instances concerning a hearing because 'the relevant decision-making powers may safely be entrusted to administrators' (para. 59). This in turn is seen as a matter primarily for Parliament, so that the courts will be slow to intervene (para. 57).

Even where there is to be a hearing before a proper court, where Article 6 is fully engaged, the European Court has specifically recognized that in the interests of efficiency and economy it may be legitimate to depart from the requirement under Article 6 to hold an oral hearing (*Schuler-Zgraggen* v *Switzerland* (1993) 16 EHRR 405, at para. 58).

2.5.2.5   A hearing within a reasonable time

The right to have a hearing within a reasonable time involves an obligation to secure a system which determines that proceedings be brought within a reasonable time. This obligation does not arise at the date of any offence or any event which gives rise to a dispute about a civil right or obligation, but only with the commencement of the relevant proceedings; and it governs not only the period prior to any trial, but also any appeal. It is not, therefore, a limitation period, neither is it concerned with whether a fair hearing may be had notwithstanding any delay: it provides a separate guarantee from that of a fair hearing (*Porter* v *Magill* [2002] 2 AC 357, at paras 106–15.

Whether the time taken is reasonable will depend on the facts of each case. But shortage of resources is not an acceptable excuse, and the more important the right at stake, the greater the requirement for expedition. Thus, for example, cases involving children, social security, employment, title to land and civil status and capacity may require greater speed of determination. In all cases, however, the complexity of the case and the conduct of those involved and the authorities will be relevant (*Davies* v *UK* (2002) 35 EHRR 720). Moreover, the requirement can require only such expedition as is consistent with the fair determination of the proceedings.

Article 6 ECHR does not prescribe the consequence if the 'reasonable time' requirement is not met. But there is no reason why it should require justice to be denied, even if it is delayed. In *Darmalingum* v *The State* [2001] 1 WLR 2303, the Privy Council held, however, that the normal remedy for a breach of a constitutional requirement for a trial within a reasonable time in the case of a criminal charge, would be to quash the conviction. It is not obvious how this approach (if correct) in relation to criminal proceedings might be transposed to the determination of civil rights and obligations. Indeed, in *Porter* v *Magill* [2002] 2 AC 357, the Court of Appeal would have refused to quash a certificate issued by an auditor even if there had been a breach of a requirement for a hearing within a reasonable

time, although the House of Lords did not consider it appropriate to deal with that
question (see [2002] 2 AC 357, at para. 115).

2.6   ARTICLE 8: RESPECT FOR PRIVATE LIFE AND HOME

Article 8 ECHR (Right to respect for private and family life) provides as follows:

> 1.   Everyone has the right to respect for his private and family life, his home and his
> correspondence.
> 2.   There shall be no interference by a public authority with the exercise of this right
> except such as is in accordance with the law and is necessary in a democratic society in
> the interests of national security, public safety or the economic well-being of the coun-
> try, for the prevention of disorder or crime, for the protection of health or morals, or for
> the protection of the rights and freedoms of others.

Article 8(1) provides that everyone has the right to respect for private and family
life, for the home, and for correspondence. These interests often overlap to a
lesser or greater extent, although the respect for correspondence is not likely to
have significant practical implications for local authorities. Article 8(2) allows the
state to restrict these rights to the extent necessary in a democratic society and
for certain listed public interest purposes, namely public safety, economic
well-being, protection of health, and protection of the rights of others.

These provisions have a considerable impact on local authority functions,
especially in the context of housing, planning, compulsory purchase, and in the
protection of the rights of those with special concerns such as gypsies, where the
concept of 'home' is more complex due to their nomadic habits.

Article 8 imposes both positive and negative obligations on public authorities.
As the European Court held in *Guerra and others* v *Italy* (1998) 26 EHRR 357:

> However, although the object of Article 8 is essentially that of protecting the individual
> against arbitrary interference by the public authorities, it does not merely compel the
> State to abstain from such interference: in addition to this primarily negative undertak-
> ing, there may be positive obligations inherent in effective respect for private or family
> life . . .

On the side of positive obligations, a public authority must take reasonable and
appropriate measures to secure an individual's Article 8 rights, including in
circumstances where those rights are being threatened or infringed by another
individual or company. This in turn may require the use of planning and other
powers in such a way as to protect the rights of individuals under Article 8 from
interferences, whether public or private.

So far as negative obligations are concerned, public authorities must refrain
from action that interferes with an individual's Article 8 rights, unless such action

can be justified in terms of Article 8(2) (*Guerra*). Even then, the action must be proportionate having regard to its objectives and the nature and extent of the interference with the Article 8 rights (see *Buckley* v *UK* (1996) 23 EHRR 101; *Chapman* v *UK* (2001) 33 EHRR 399; and *South Bucks* v *Porter* [2003] 2 WLR 1547 (approving the approach of the Court of Appeal at [2002] 1 WLR 1359)).

2.6.1 Basic concepts

The basic rights protected by Article 8 ECHR are:

(a) the home;
(b) family life;
(c) private life; and
(d) correspondence.

As already noted, these categories are not wholly self-contained and an infringement of Article 8 may affect one or more of these rights (*Re S*; *Re W* [2002] 2 AC 291).

2.6.1.1 Home

'Home' has been broadly interpreted by the European Court, in a way more in keeping with the concept of 'domicile', which has both domestic and business connotations, than a purely domestic notion of 'home'. Thus business premises have been held to be protected under Article 8 ECHR as 'home' whether with living accommodation (*Chappell* v *UK* (1989) 12 EHRR 1) or without (*Niemietz* v *Germany* (1992) 16 EHRR 97).

The key appears to be whether the occupation of the premises, whether business or otherwise, is closely related to the private life of the claimant. Places of work which provide a substantial part of the private life of the claimant fall within the protection of Article 8. These include professional premises, such as the lawyer's office in *Niemietz*, and on that basis, it appears that any person whose workplace forms a substantial part of his or her life will be able to claim Article 8 protection. Protection would thus extend beyond professional offices and might include such premises as the agricultural buildings of a farm, or a private school.

Further, the European Court has not limited 'home' to a lawfully established home (*Buckley*), or to a building in which the claimants intend to live although they have not been able to take up lawful occupation (*Gillow* v *UK* (1986) 11 EHRR 335). In *Buckley*, Mrs Buckley (a gypsy) had purchased land and applied for retrospective planning permission for three caravans. The local planning authority refused planning permission and subsequently took enforcement action. Mrs Buckley successfully argued that this enforcement action constituted a violation of her rights under Article 8. The Court held that the right to respect for the 'home' extended even to cases where that home had been unlawfully occupied or established, and that enforcement action constituted interference by a public authority with Mrs Buckley's right to respect for her home under Article 8(1). By a narrow majority, the Court followed this decision in *Chapman* v *UK* (2001) 33 EHRR 399, but appears to have qualified its stance in *Buckley*. At paras 98 and 99 it held that Article 8 did not guarantee a home, and that a decision by a local authority not to allow gypsies to set up home where they wished was not of itself a violation of Article 8.

Of some importance in this context is the decision of the House of Lords in *Qazi* v *Harrow London Borough Council* [2003] 3 WLR 792. Prior to that case it might be thought that Article 8 had potential relevance to attempts by public landlords to recover possession of property in which a person had established their home. Such a view would have had the support of the Court of Appeal, albeit that whether a person would actually succeed in showing that granting possession would be disproportionate would require strong facts at the least. It is now clear, however, that Article 8 has no application in cases where the ordinary incidents of property law have been met so that possession should be granted under domestic law, and that it will be irrelevant in such cases that the landlord seeking to recover possession is a public body. While the House of Lords accepted that Article 8 could be engaged in such cases, it went on to hold that in such cases Article 8(2) 'is met'. This issue is discussed further in Chapter Nine.

The creation of environmental risks may lead to a violation of Article 8 rights, although not in all cases, and much will turn on the striking of a balance between the rights of the individual and the need of the community for the installation providing the potential source of pollution or disturbance.

The creation of nuisance or risks to health can invoke both the positive and negative aspects of Article 8(1), in that the local authority may find itself in breach by reason both of a failure to act to prevent an infringement and for having authorized an act which infringes Article 8(1) (also demonstrating the overlap between protection of respect for the home and for private life). In *Lopez Ostra* v *Spain* (1994) 20 EHRR 277, Mrs Lopez Ostra successfully alleged a violation of Article 8(1) by the construction and operation of a waste-treatment plant for the leather industry built close to her home. The European Court held that 'severe environmental pollution' was capable of infringing Article 8(1) since it might 'affect individuals' well-being and prevent them from enjoying their homes in such a way as to affect their private and family life adversely', irrespective of whether health was seriously endangered. Further, the European Court held that whether the issue is analysed in terms of a positive duty, to take reasonable and appropriate measures to secure the applicant's rights under Article 8(1), or in terms of an interference by a public authority, to be justified in accordance with Article 8(2), the applicable principles were broadly the same, i.e. that regard must be had to the fair balance that had to be struck between the competing interests of the individual and of the community as a whole. In striking the balance the aims mentioned in Article 8(2), including economic well-being and the rights and freedoms of others, were relevant. The European Court found that a fair balance had not been struck in that case.

Continuing concern for adverse environmental effects also led to a finding of a violation of Article 8(1) in *Guerra and others* v *Italy* (1998) 26 EHRR 357, which involved a chemical plant located close to the claimants' homes. Although the noise caused by Heathrow Airport did not initially lead to the finding of a violation on the facts (*Powell and Rayner* v *UK* (1990) 12 EHRR 355), different results have been reached with regard to the impact of other airports. However, the position has since reversed and the initially more broadly based liability applied by the chamber with regard to night flying at Heathrow Airport in *Hatton* v *UK* (2002) 34 EHRR 1 was rejected by the Grand Chamber of the European Court of Human Rights in its judgment (2003) 37 EHRR 28. In *Hatton* the Grand Chamber rejected the claim under Article 8 (although finding a violation of Article 13) on the basis that the UK was entitled to balance the public interest in the economic benefits of night flying with the impact on Article 8 rights. The Grand Chamber accorded far more weight to the margin of appreciation than had the Chamber. At para. 122 it held:

> The Court must consider whether the Government can be said to have struck a fair balance between those interests and the conflicting interests of the persons affected by noise disturbances, including the applicants. Environmental protection should be taken into consideration by Governments in acting within their margin of appreciation and by the Court in its review of that margin, but it would not be appropriate for the Court to adopt a special approach in this respect by reference to a special status of environmental human rights. In this context the Court must revert to the question of the scope of the margin of appreciation available to the State when taking policy decisions of the kind at issue . . .

Hatton was referred to by all three Law Lords who gave speeches in *Marcic* v *Thames Water Utilities Ltd* [2003] UKHL 66, all of whom indicated that they agreed with the approach of the Grand Chamber. In that case the House of Lords was concerned with an interference with the home caused by 'flooding of a particularly unpleasant kind' from foul water sewers. The defendant water company could have addressed the problem by building more sewers, which would have imposed a larger financial burden on their other customers. Noting that the statutory scheme under which the defendant operated provided limitations on the rights of individual householders to sue sewerage undertakers, but that it did provide a means of redress through the regulator (which had not been pursued by the claimant), the question was whether the scheme was unreasonable, or disproportionate, in the way that it struck the balance between the interests of those householders subjected to flooding, and others. A unanimous House of Lords found that, in cases such as this, the statutory scheme could not be said to be outside the very broad margin of discretion accorded to Parliament in such cases. Lord Hoffmann did, however, state that the regulator would have a duty to compy with Article 8 and that in a particular case, where he exceeded the discretion allowed to him under the Convention, a householder may have a remedy under the HRA 1998.

2.6.1.2   Family life
'Family life' has been widely construed by the European Court and turns very much on the facts of the case. It extends beyond respect for the incidents of married life and 'the mutual enjoyment by parent and child of each other's company' (*W* v *UK* (1988) 10 EHRR 29, at para. 59) to respect for relationships:

(a)   with close relatives other than parents (see *Marckx* v *Belgium* (1979) 2 EHRR 330; and *Boyle* v *UK* (1995) 19 EHRR 179); and

(b)   other than arising from marriage. Relationships giving rise to respect for family life may arise from cohabitation (*Kroon* v *Netherlands* (1995) 19 EHRR 263), and may endure after the termination of the cohabitation or marriage if there are children of the relationship (*Berrehab* v *Netherlands* (1989) 11 EHRR 322). *De facto* family relationships are interpreted broadly (see *X, Y and Z* v *UK* (1997) 24 EHRR 143, where a relationship involving a post-operative transsexual was held to fall within Article 8(1)).

Respect for family life requires proof of a continuing and real tie, although a flexible approach is taken (*Marckx*).

The aspects of family life protected by Article 8 ECHR include not only the fundamentals of a shared family life, including its social, moral and cultural aspects, but also the legal incidents of a family relationship (*Re W and B* [2001] EWCA Civ 757, at paras 52–55 *per* Hale LJ; *Re H (A Child)* [2001] 1 FLR 646; *Re B (A Child)* [2001] 2 FLR 89) including those relating to succession to property on death (*X, Y and Z* v *UK*)

2.6.1.3   Private life
This right, as with the others protected by Article 8(1) ECHR, is approached broadly and includes the protection of 'physical well-being' and freedom from risk to health, from adverse effects on the home, as well as protection of the right to establish and develop relationships with other human beings (*Niemietz* v *Germany* (1992) 16 EHRR 97), including sexual relations (*Dudgeon* v *UK* (1981) 4 EHRR 149), although with limitations (*Lasky, Jaggard and Brown* v *UK* (1997) 24 EHRR 39), and the rights of post-operative transsexuals to have official records amended to record gender change (*Goodwin* v *UK* (2002) 35 EHRR 447).

The width of Article 8 has particular implications for local authority functions with regard to planning, compulsory purchase, public health, and environmental protection (*Lopez Ostra* v *Spain* (1994) 20 EHRR 277; *Hatton* v *UK* (2002) 34 EHRR 1). This aspect also has a considerable overlap with the protection of the home (see 2.6.1.1). These implications will be dealt with under the individual chapter headings.

The respect for private life also includes respect for personal information held or sought by public authorities (*Leander* v *Sweden* (1987) 9 EHRR 43; *Hewitt and Harman* v *UK* (1992) 14 EHRR 657), which includes medical records (*Z* v *Finland* (1997) 25 EHRR 371) and is likely to extend to any form of record containing such information. As with other aspects of Article 8(1), positive as well as negative obligations arise, and an authority may be required to disclose personal information (*Gaston* v *UK* (1990) 12 EHRR 30). Article 8 does not require that that information should be used in a manner which would or might harm the individual concerned; the mere fact of holding the information is sufficient.

The right to respect for a person's private life also has implications for the protection of privacy (*Spencer* v *UK* (1998) 25 EHRR CD 105, *Whiteside* v *UK* (1994) 18 EHRR CD 126), although it seems unlikely that it provides a general right to privacy since there may be factual situations where the protection of privacy may not be justified on 'private life' grounds, such as in the case of major public figures (although see *Douglas and others* v *Hello! Ltd* [2001] 2 All ER 289, at paras 109–12).

While pre-HRA 1998 domestic law does generally require a public authority to have regard to the interests of those affected by the exercise of power (see, e.g., *R* v *Lincolnshire County Council, ex parte Atkinson* (1996) 8 Admin LR 529), the rights protected by Article 8(1) extend much further. For example, the application of Article 8 may require an authority to take action (e.g. where Article 8(2) does not provide a justification for an authority declining to take action) where the lawful discharge of its domestic public law duties may be achieved simply by a careful consideration of the competing interests.

Protection of private life does not apply only in terms of life within the home. Consistently with the broad meaning given to 'home', certain aspects of private life, arising from the right to establish and develop relationships with others, may be protected if they are conducted outside the home, provided that they take place in locations in which the individual is entitled to some degree of quiet enjoyment (*R* v *Worcester City Council, ex parte SW* [2000] HRLR 702, at 717–719). The 'inner circle' referred to in *Niemietz* appears to encompass locations which may be private and even semi-public (such as hotel rooms or private schools; see *Costello-Roberts* v *UK* (1993) 19 EHRR 112), although such rights did not extend to freedom from being photographed by the authorities at a public demonstration (*Friedl* v *Austria* (1995) 21 EHRR 83, by the Commission, at paras 48–51).

In the context of local authority support for asylum seekers, *Anufrijeva* v

London Borough of Southwark [2004] FLR 12, the Court of Appeal found that the Article 8 right to a private life gave rise to a positive duty to provide welfare support in extreme circumstances (which would nevertheless fall short of treatment likely to breach Article 3 as to inhuman and degrading treatment). This would give rise, if the consequences were serious, to a claim for maladministration for a failure to provide such support. The duty to take positive action would be more likely where children were involved, but the standard would nonetheless be high and resources would be relevant in considering the claim. The standard had been reached in one of the cases (*Bernard*). The Court of Appeal also gave comprehensive guidance on claims for damages under s. 8 the HRA 1998. This issue is discussed in detail in Chapter Three.

2.6.1.4　Correspondence

While respect for 'correspondence' has significant implications in the sphere of criminal law and prisons, where there is extensive Strasbourg case law (see, e.g., *Boyle and Rice* v *UK* (1988) 10 EHRR 425; *Campbell* v *UK* (1992) 15 EHRR 137), it also has wider application. Respect for correspondence includes not only written communications, but also telephone calls (*Klass* v *Germany* (1978) 2 EHRR 214), and there is no reason in principle why it should not extend to other means of communication including fax and email (*Amann* v *Switzerland* (2000) 30 EHRR 843). In *R (Nilsen)* v *Secretary of State for the Home Department* [2002] EWHC 668, Crane J held that Article 8 ECHR was engaged with respect to the manuscript of the claimant prisoner's autobiography which was to be sent back to him, but rejected that there had been a breach since it had been taken out of the prison without authority and it was not disproportionate for the prison authority to want to read it before deciding whether to hand it over.

Article 8(1) protects against the interception and surveillance of correspondence (*Halford* v *UK* (1997) 24 EHRR 523) and clearly overlaps substantially with protection of respect for private life.

2.6.2　Restrictions on Article 8 rights

Article 8(2) ECHR contains a number of exceptions to the rights protected by Article 8(1), namely where the interference by the public authority is:

(a)　in accordance with the law;
(b)　necessary in a democratic society; and
(c)　in the interests of national security, public safety or the economic well-being of the country, for the prevention of disorder or crime, for the protection of health or morals, or for the protection of the rights and freedoms of others.

Exceptions (a) and (b) above are discussed at 2.3. The exceptions set out in (c) are to be narrowly construed and they are exhaustive. There is no scope for a wide construction or for inferring additional exceptions (*Sunday Times* v *UK* (1979) 2 EHRR 245; *Golder* v *UK* (1975) 1 EHRR 524). Article 18 of the Convention additionally prohibits the use of the legitimate restrictions in the context of this Article, 'for any purpose other than those for which they have been prescribed'.

2.6.3 General approach to cases with Article 8 implications

Where a case has Article 8 implications, an authority should follow (and preferably be seen to follow) a five-stage approach to the issues (see the classification by headings of the issues in *Niemietz* v *Germany* (1992) 16 EHRR 97, which omits issue (a) for obvious reasons). The five stages are:

(a)   Identification of the Article 8 right, including its positive aspects.

(b)   Has there been an interference with Article 8(1) rights?

(c)   Was the interference 'in accordance with the law'?

(d)   Did the interference have a legitimate aim or aims (i.e. one of those listed in Article 8(2))?

(e)   Was the interference 'necessary in a democratic society'?

This process can usefully be seen in operation in the various stages of the European Court's judgment in *Buckley* v *UK* (1996) 23 EHRR 101, where the Court held, in the context of the enforcement of planning control against the gypsy applicant, that:

(a)   the rights of the applicant to station her caravan on her own land fell within Article 8(1), even though the action was unlawful as a matter of domestic law;

(b)   the enforcement action (both civil and criminal) was a violation of Article 8(1) rights;

(c)   the interference was 'in accordance with the law', since it was accepted that the planning enforcement measures were such and the Court did not disagree;

(d)   the interference pursued 'legitimate aims', namely public safety, the economic well-being of the country, the protection of health and the protection of the rights of others; and

(e)   the interference was 'necessary in a democratic society' since, having regard to the Convention right in issue, its importance for the individual and the nature of the activities concerned, the Court considered that proper regard was had to the applicant's predicament both under the terms of the regulatory framework, which contained adequate procedural safeguards protecting her interest under Article 8, and by the responsible planning authorities when exercising their discretion in relation to the particular circumstances of her case (including objections on planning policy and highway safety grounds).

The authorities arrived at the contested decision after weighing in the balance the various competing interests at issue.

2.7   ARTICLE 10: FREEDOM OF EXPRESSION

Article 10 ECHR (Freedom of expression) provides as follows:

1.   Everyone has the right to freedom of expression. This right shall include freedom to hold opinions and to receive and impart information and ideas without interference by public authority and regardless of frontiers. This Article shall not prevent States from requiring the licensing of broadcasting, television or cinema enterprises.

2.   The exercise of these freedoms, since it carries with it duties and responsibilities, may be subject to such formalities, conditions, restrictions or penalties as are prescribed by law and are necessary in a democratic society, in the interests of national security, territorial integrity or public safety, for the prevention of disorder or crime, for the protection of health or morals, for the protection of the reputation or rights of others, for preventing the disclosure of information received in confidence, or for maintaining the authority and impartiality of the judiciary.

2.7.1   Interpretation of 'freedom of expression'

Article 10 ECHR protects freedom of expression, subject to certain exceptions which must be proportionate and be prescribed by law. Freedom of expression is interpreted widely, covering various forms of expression (*Müller* v *Switzerland* (1988) 13 EHRR 212; *Autronic AG* v *Switzerland* (1990) 12 EHRR 485). The European Court regards Article 10 rights as underpinning the nature of a democratic society and 'affords the opportunity to take part in the public exchange of cultural, political and social information and ideas of all kinds' (*Müller* (above); *Handyside* v *UK* (1976) 1 EHRR 737).

Even pre-incorporation, the English courts accepted that English domestic law embodies rights protected by Article 10 (see *Attorney General* v *Guardian Newspapers Ltd (No. 2)* [1990] 1 AC 109, at 283; *Derbyshire County Council* v *Times Newspapers* [1992] 1 QB 770, at 810H; and *R* v *Secretary of State for Health, ex parte Wagstaff* [2001] 1 WLR 292, DC).

The European Court summarized the principles in its Article 10 jurisprudence in *The Observer and the Guardian* v *UK* (1991) 14 EHRR 153, at 191:

(a)   freedom of expression constitutes one of the essential foundations of a democratic society; subject to paragraph (2) of Article 10, it is applicable not only to 'information' or 'ideas' that are favourably received or regarded as inoffensive or as a matter of indifference but also to those that offend, shock or disturb. Freedom of expression, as enshrined in Article 10, is subject to a number of exceptions which, however, must be narrowly interpreted and the necessity for any restrictions must be convincingly established.

(b) these principles are of particular importance as far as the press is concerned. Whilst it must not overstep the bounds set, *inter alia*, in the 'interests of national security' or for 'maintaining the authority of the judiciary' it is nevertheless incumbent upon it to impart information and ideas on matters of public interest. Not only does the press have the task of imparting such information and ideas: the public also have the right to receive them. Were it otherwise, the press would be unable to play its vital role of 'public watchdog'.

Although it is frequently stated that Article 10 does not embody a general right of access to information, it does protect the right to receive information which others are willing to impart (*Leander* v *Sweden* (1987) 9 EHRR 433; *Gaskin* v *UK* (1989) 12 EHRR 36). In many cases, that right and the willingness of some to impart the information may enlarge the right to receive information even where the public body in question wishes to restrict access (see, e.g., *Autronic* (above); *VDSO* v *Austria* (1994) 20 EHRR 56; and *Ex parte Wagstaff* (above) although see also *R* v *Secretary of State for the Environment, Food and Rural Affairs, ex parte Persey* [2002] 3 WLR 704; *R* v *Secretary of State for Health, ex parte Howard* [2002] 3 WLR 738). In *Wagstaff*, which concerned the lawfulness of the Secretary of State for Health's decision to hold in private the inquiry into the events surrounding the murders perpetrated by Dr Shipman, the willingness of the families and friends of the victims to impart their evidence in public to the press (and the desire of the press to attend the inquiry sittings) led the Divisional Court to hold there to have been a violation of Article 10, which contributed to the decision that the Secretary of State had acted in an unreasonable manner in *Wednesbury* terms. However, the subsequent decisions in *Persey* and *Howard* have established that there is no presumption of openness in all forms of public inquiry nor did Article 10 accord a right of access to information or require the state to facilitate freedom of expression by providing, in addition to existing means of communication, an open forum to achieve a wider dissemination of views. *Wagstaff* appears to be a case which turned on its own special facts.

This does not mean that where the holder of the information is not willing to impart it, Article 10 imposes an obligation to supply the information. The right to 'receive' information under Article 10 is not a right to obtain information whatever the circumstances. Thus in *Gaskin* the European Court held that in the circumstances of that case Article 10 did not embody an obligation on the state to impart the information in question to the individual.

2.7.2 Restrictions on Article 10 rights

As with Article 8 (see 2.6.2), Article 10 ECHR is subject to a number of exceptions:

(a) the rights may be subject to such formalities, conditions, restrictions or penalties as are prescribed by law; and

(b) the exceptions must be necessary in a democratic society; and

(c) the exceptions must be in the interests of national security, territorial integrity or public safety, for the prevention of disorder or crime, for the protection of health or morals, for the protection of the reputation or rights of others, for preventing the disclosure of information received in confidence, or for maintaining the authority and impartiality of the judiciary.

Concepts (a) and (b) are discussed at 2.3. The exceptions set out in (c) are to be narrowly construed and they are exhaustive. There is no scope for a wide construction or for inferring additional exceptions (*Sunday Times* v *UK* (1979) 2 EHRR 245; *Golder* v *UK* (1975) 1 EHRR 524). Article 18 ECHR additionally prohibits the use of the legitimate restrictions in the context of this Article, 'for any purpose other than those for which they have been prescribed'. The principle of proportionality in the context of Article 10 is strictly applied, so that the exceptions may be invoked only in the case of a 'pressing need' (see above). However, this may justify the exclusion of the press, say, from court proceedings where there is a sufficiently strong justification (see the decision of the Commission in *Atkinson, Crook and the Independent* v *UK* (1990) 67 DR 244.

2.8 ARTICLE 14: FREEDOM FROM DISCRIMINATION IN RESPECT OF PROTECTED RIGHTS

The relevant principles in relation to the interpretation and application of Article 14 ECHR (Prohibition of discrimination) are, briefly, as follows:

(a) Article 14 is not a free-standing right but imposes an obligation to secure the non-discriminatory enjoyment of the rights and freedoms protected by the Convention. Thus in relation to rights falling outside the Convention there is no obligation to avoid discrimination.

(b) Despite being an ancillary provision, this does not mean that any allegation that there has been a breach of Article 14 necessarily stands or falls with the claim that there has been a breach of another Article (see the *Belgian Linguistic (No. 2)* (1968) 1 EHRR 252. What must be established is that a claim is within the 'ambit' of one of the other Articles.

(c) The grounds of discrimination listed in Article 14 are broad, e.g. 'property'.

(d) Despite the width of the grounds of discrimination prohibited, there is a need to show that there has been different treatment in a comparable situation. The need for a genuine comparator acts to limit the impact of Article 14. The European Court of Human Rights has taken a restrictive approach to this issue, and outside the classic areas of discrimination (such as sex, race, etc.) it is going to be extremely difficult to find a comparator in a genuinely analogous situation.

(e) Where a prima facie case of discrimination is made out, such treatment may still be permissible if it is shown that any difference in treatment has a 'reasonable and objective justification'.

Article 14 has been raised (unsuccessfully) in a number of gypsy cases (e.g. *Buckley* and *Chapman* (see 2.6.3); *Turner* v *UK* (1997) 23 EHRR CD 81; and *Smith* (see 2.4.2)). It was employed more successfully in the planning context in *Pine Valley Developments Ltd and others* v *Ireland* (1991) 14 EHRR 319, where there had been a refusal to validate a void planning permission, when for others in the same circumstances this had been done.

In *Michalak* v *London Borough of Wandsworth* [2003] 1 WLR 617, at para. 20, Brooke LJ set out the test to be applied in determining whether there has been a violation of Article 14, which consists of four questions:

(a) Do the facts fall within the ambit of one or more of the substantive Convention provisions?

(b) If so, was there different treatment as respects that right between the complainant on the one hand and other persons put forward for comparison ('the chosen comparators') on the other?

(c) Were the chosen comparators in an analogous situation to the complainant's situation?

(d) If so, did the difference in treatment have an objective and reasonable justification: in other words, did it pursue a legitimate aim and did the differential treatment bear a reasonable relationship of proportionality to the aim being sought to be achieved?

Where the discriminatory treatment alleged is based on 'other status', the European Court of Human Rights held that such discriminatory treatment must have 'as its basis or reason a personal characteristic ("status") by which a person or groups of persons are distinguishable from each other' (*Kjeldsen* v *Denmark* (1976) 1 EHRR 711, at para. 56).

In *Southwark London Borough Council* v *St Brice* [2002] 1 WLR 1537, at para. 24, the Court of Appeal rejected the tenant's argument that his landlord's choice of forum of the High Court rather than the county court for a possession action against the claimant was the foundation for a claim of discriminatory treatment under Article 14, since the choice of forum was not based upon any personal characteristic of the tenant. See also *R v Secretary of State for Work and Pensions, ex parte Barber* [2002] 2 FLR 1181 and the first instance decision in *R v Dorset County Council, ex parte Beeson* [2002] HRLR 15 at paras 106–109 ([2003] HRLR 11 for Secretary of State's successful appeal against breach of Article 6) in both of which the Administrative Court held that there was no discrimination since the difference in treatment was not based on a personal characteristic.

However, in *Michalak* (see above), the Court of Appeal (at paras 32–34) rejected the argument that the alleged different treatment between a distant family member under the Housing Act 1985 and under the Rent Act 1977 did not come under Article 14 since it was not based on a personal characteristic, Brooke LJ finding that this narrow test had been superceded by the decisions of the European Court of Human Rights in *Spadea and Scalabrino v Italy* (1995) 21 EHRR 482, *Bullock v UK* (1996) 21 EHRR CD 85 and *Chassagnou v France* (1999) 29 EHRR 615, which had looked favourably on discrimination arguments based on comparators which were not based on a personal characteristic, such as ownership of residential and non-residential buildings.

In *R v Secretary of State for Work and Pensions, ex parte Hooper* [2003] 1 WLR 2623, at paras 91–92, the Court of Appeal followed Brooke LJ's rejection in *Michalak* of the 'personal characteristic' approach, finding that different treatment of applicants in the European Court of Human Rights and in the domestic courts was capable of being discrimination under Article 14 despite this not being a personal characteristic. However, the point was made *obiter* because the applicant did not ultimately rely on this argument in alleging the discrimination in question.

In *Carson v Secretary of State for Work and Pensions* [2003] 3 All ER 577, where it was accepted by the Secretary of State that place of residence came under 'status', the issue was whether circumstances (such as the differences in the economies and social security provisions of South Africa and the United Kingdom) relating to residence were to be taken into account in determining whether a retirement pensioner in the United Kingdom was in an analogous situation to a retirement pensioner in South Africa for the purposes of receiving an annual pension up-rate or whether these were consequences flowing from the 'impugned characteristic' of residence and therefore not to be taken into account. The Court of Appeal, at para. 61, sought to move away from the question of what constituted an 'impugned characteristic' and reformulated the third and fourth of Brooke LJ's questions in *Michalak* into whether the circumstances of X and Y are so similar as to call (in the mind of a rational and fair-minded person) for a positive justification for the less favourable treatment of Y in comparison with X. The Court answered the question in the negative on the basis of the particular economic and benefit provision differences between South Africa and the United Kingdom.

The disagreement as to 'other status' between the *St Brice* line of cases and the *Michalak* approach has not yet been authoritatively resolved; moreover, there has been a move towards 'bundling together' the question of whether discrimination exists and whether it can be objectively justified (see further the decision of the Court of Appeal in *R (on the application of Purja)* v *Ministry of Defence* [2004] 1 WLR 289).

2.9 ARTICLE 1 OF PROTOCOL 1: PROTECTION OF POSSESSIONS

Article 1 of Protocol 1 to the Convention has been broken down into three constituent rules by the European Court of Human Rights in *Sporrong and Lönnroth* v *Sweden* (1982) 5 EHRR 35; *Poiss* v *Austria* (1987) 10 EHRR 231; and *James* v *UK* (1986) 8 EHRR 123:

(1) 'Every natural person or legal person is entitled to the peaceful enjoyment of his possessions'. This is said to be a rule of a general nature enunciating 'the principle of peaceful enjoyment of property'.

(2) 'No one shall be deprived of his possessions except in the public interest and subject to the conditions provided for by law and by the general principles of international law'. The deprivation of possessions is made subject to a number of conditions.

(3) Rules (1) and (2) should not in any way impair the right of a state to enforce such laws as it deems necessary to control the use of property in accordance with the general interest, or to secure the payment of taxes or other contributions or penalties. This derives from the second paragraph of Article 1 of Protocol 1.

The concept of 'possessions' is an autonomous concept under the Convention and is much wider than the equivalent property concepts under the common law. The European Court takes a broad approach to the meaning of 'possessions', including both tangible and intangible rights — generally having a pecuniary value — although its approach is not always easily predictable. Ownership is not the decisive factor under Convention case law and some rights are recognized as 'possessions' which would not be so recognized under national law. 'Possessions' recognized by Strasbourg include:

(a) shares — *Bramelid & Malmstrom* v *Sweden* (1983) 5 EHRR 249;

(b) contributions to private pension funds, at least where there is a right to a portion of the fund, or contractual rights to certain payments — *Müller* v *Austria* 3 DR 25; *Gaygusuz* v *Austria* (1997) 23 EHRR 364;

(c)   business goodwill — *Van Marle* v *Netherlands* (1986) 8 EHRR 491;
(d)   crystallized debt — *Agnessens* v *Belgium* (1988) 58 DR 63;
(e)   intellectual property rights — *Lenzing AG* v *UK* (1999) EHRLR 132;
(f)   Licences to carry out certain activities where there is a legitimate expectation that the licence will continue, and that economic benefits will continue to arise from it — *Tre Traktörer* v *Sweden* (1989) 13 EHRR 309 (liquor licence); *Gudmunsson* v *Iceland* (1996) 21 EHRR CD 42 (taxi licence); and *JS* and *others* v *Netherlands* (1995) 20 EHRR CD 42 (where the claim to renewal of a licence failed due to breach of the licence conditions);
(g)   legitimate expectation as to property — *Pine Valley Developments* v *Ireland* (1991) 14 EHRR 319; *Rowland* v *Environment Agency* [2003] 1 All ER 625, at 647–53; and *Stretch* v *UK*, (App. No. 44277/98) 25 June 2003. In the *Stretch* case, even though an authority had acted *ultra vires*, damages were awarded for both pecuniary and non-pecuniary losses. It appears that while the common law will not permit legitimate expectations to authorize *ultra vires* acts, there may nonetheless be a remedy for breach of Article 1 of Protocol 1.

In terms of the Strasbourg jurisprudence, the deprivation of property is unsurprisingly regarded as inherently more serious than the control of its use where ownership is retained.

It should be noted that successful reliance on Article 1 of Protocol 1 has proved rare in practice. This is indicative of the scope of the possible justifications for interference with the rights protected by that Article. The approach to be taken is similar to that in relation to Article 8 of the Convention (see 2.6.3). The margin of appreciation accorded is especially wide in terms of Article 1 of Protocol 1. In *Sporrong*, the Court said:

> The Court must determine whether a fair balance has been struck between the demands of the general interests of the community and the requirements of the protection of the individual's fundamental rights . . . In an area as complex and difficult as that of the development of large cities, the contracting states should enjoy a wide margin of appreciation in order to implement their town-planning policy.

As with many Convention rights, an interference with possessions may not breach the Convention if the interference strikes a fair balance between the competing private and public interests, i.e. whether it is proportionate.

The right to compensation is not expressly part of Article 1 of Protocol 1. However, the existence of compensation is an important factor in the balancing of the general interest and private rights (see, e.g., *Erkner* v *Austria* (1987) 9 EHRR 464 and *Holy Monasteries* v *Greece* (1994) 20 EHRR 1 for examples of cases in which the absence of compensation was highly material to the finding of a violation). In *James* v *UK* (1986) 8 EHRR 123, the European Court held (at para. 54) that:

> Like the Commission, the Court observes that under the legal systems of the Contracting States, the taking of property in the public interest without payment of compensation is treated as justifiable only in exceptional circumstances not relevant for present purposes. As far as Article 1 (P1⁻1) is concerned, the protection of the right of property it affords would be largely illusory and ineffective in the absence of any equivalent principle. Clearly, compensation terms are material to the assessment whether the contested legislation respects a fair balance between the various interests at stake and, notably, whether it does not impose a disproportionate burden on the applicants (see the above-mentioned *Sporrong and Lönnroth* judgment . . . paras 69 and 73).
>
> The Court further accepts the Commission's conclusion as to the standard of compensation: the taking of property without payment of an amount reasonably related to its value would normally constitute a disproportionate interference which could not be considered justifiable under Article 1 (P1⁻1). Article 1 (P1⁻1) does not, however, guarantee a right to full compensation in all circumstances. Legitimate objectives of 'public interest', such as pursued in measures of economic reform or measures designed to achieve greater social justice, may call for less than reimbursement of the full market value. Furthermore, the Court's power of review is limited to ascertaining whether the choice of compensation terms falls outside the State's wide margin of appreciation in this domain (see para. 46 above).

Attacks on the calculation methods for compensation have been markedly less successful (see, e.g., *Lithgow* v *UK* (1986) 8 EHRR 329). The implication of this is that objectives such as the achievement of greater social justice may call for less than reimbursement at the full market value. In *S* v *UK* (13135/87) 56 DR 254, the Lands Tribunal for Scotland granted about one-sixth of the claimed loss of amenity and future costs of upkeep of fencing, etc. in relation to land expropriated for road widening. The method of assessment was found to be reasonable and the lack of inflation-proofing did not bring it outside the margin of appreciation. In *Howard* v *UK* (see above under Article 8), the European Commission rejected the complaint against a compulsory purchase of a house under Article 8 and Article 1 of Protocol 1. It was noted that:

> In view of the carefully balanced appraisal of the applicant's rights against the advantages to the community of proceeding with the development which are set out in the inspector's report, and the availability of compensation for the value of the property expropriated from the applicants, the Commission finds that the compulsory purchase of their property, which was clearly in the public interest for the purposes of the development plan, was in accordance with the requirements of [Article 1 of Protocol 1].

In *Edgar* v *UK* (App. No. 37683/97) 25 January 2000, a complaint that the Firearms Amendment Act 1997 (following the tragic events in Dunblane), requiring the surrender of high-calibre firearms, infringed Article 1 of Protocol 1, was rejected as inadmissible by the Court in part since compensation was provided and such compensation was based not simply on market value but on such value plus an uplift; and, additionally:

> The Court considers that the applicant is complaining in substance of loss of future income in addition to loss of goodwill and a diminution in value of the company's assets. It concludes that the element of the complaint which is based upon the diminution in value of the business assessed by reference to future income, and which amounts in effect to a claim for loss of future income, falls outside the scope of Article 1 of Protocol No. 1.

2.9.1   Rule (1) — Interference with peaceful enjoyment of property

Like Article 8 ECHR, rule (1) of Article 1 of Protocol 1 ECHR gives rise to the possibility of complaints being made by those affected by impacts on the environment and the construction of development. Article 1 of Protocol 1 is, of course, wider than Article 8, in that the protection offered is not limited to the 'home'. Thus, in cases such as *Powell and Rayner* v *UK* (1990) 12 EHRR 335; *S* v *France* (1990) 65 DR 250; and *Antonetto* v *Italy* (2003) 36 EHRR 10, noise nuisance was the basis of complaints under Article 8 and rule (1) of Article 1 of Protocol 1 (see further above). See also the judgment of the High Court in *Dennis* v *Ministry of Defence* [2003] Env LR 34 (QB), applying Convention principles in the context of a common law noise nuisance claim arising from the flying of military aircraft. The Court recognized that severe noise nuisance, that in turn seriously affected the value of property, could amount to partial expropriation.

Like Article 8, rule (1) is capable of forming the basis for action by a third party objecting to development.

2.9.2   Rule (2) — Deprivation of property

'Deprivation' of property may not only be effected by a specific act of a public authority (such as a compulsory purchase order), but may also be assumed *de facto* from the circumstances. Rule (2) clearly relates to compulsory purchase orders. See *Papamichalopoulos* v *Greece* (1993) 16 EHRR 440, where a naval base was built on the applicant's land without formal expropriation. However, where the interference by a public authority does not amount to 'deprivation', i.e. because ownership or some form of benefit or exploitation remains (such as sale or receipt of rents), it might still amount to an interference with 'peaceful enjoyment' within rule (1).

The relevance of compensation to proportionality has already been referred to above, at 2.9.1.

The European Court of Human Rights has allowed considerable room for manoeuvre as regards expropriations and confiscations. However, in *Sporrong and Lönnroth* v *Sweden* (1982) 5 EHRR 35, the European Court considered expropriation permits which were broadly similar to the blight notice provisions contained in Part IV of the Town and Country Planning Act 1990. The length of the planning blights led the European Court to find the interference with the applicant's property rights not to be justified. This is one of the few examples of a successful application based on Article 1 of Protocol 1.

An argument that a compulsory purchase order breaches rights protected under Article 1 of Protocol 1 must be considered carefully; and if analysed in accordance with the principles set out above, it is unlikely to succeed, especially where compensation is payable, even if the compensation does not represent a precise equivalent to the value of the property taken. It is clear that the protection given to the 'home' under Article 8 is much stronger than the right afforded by Article 1 of Protocol 1. However, for those whose land is not actually compulsorily acquired but which is nonetheless affected, e.g. by the construction of a road, the absence of compensation might be significant. Further, the interests protected by Article 1 of Protocol 1 are much wider than those under Article 8, and the effects of compulsory purchase or road orders on businesses may involve consideration of Article 1 of Protocol 1.

2.9.3   Rule (3) — Control of the use of property

Rule (3) is likely to be the most important rule so far as the exercise of planning powers is concerned. It could apply to development plan decisions (see *Titterrell* v *UK* (App. No. 28911/95)) as well as to development control case work. Here we focus on the latter.

Rule (3) may be invoked by an appellant against the refusal of planning permission, or (even more likely) by an appellant seeking the removal of (or resisting the imposition of) a planning condition. In terms of the refusal of planning permission, it was said in *ISKCON* v *UK* (1994) 76A DR 90:

> As a general principle, the protection of property rights ensured by [Article 1 of Protocol 1] cannot be used as a ground for claiming planning permission to extend permitted use of property.

However, rule (3) may bite with more force in respect of enforcement notice action and the imposition of conditions.

In *Chater* v *UK* (1987) 52 DR 250, it was held by the European Commission that an interference with Article 1 of Protocol 1 had occurred when two enforcement notices prevented an applicant from using his property for vehicle repair and maintenance and for a haulage business. He had not obtained the relevant planning permission. It was held on the facts that a proper balance had been struck between the applicant's personal interest and the general interests, and the application was declared inadmissible.

Further, from *Denev* v *Sweden* (1998) 59 DR 127, it is clear that the control of the use of property covered by rule (3) applies to requirements on individuals to take positive action as well as the imposition of restrictions on their activities. That case involved an obligation to plant trees of a particular species imposed by a Forestry Act (but this would apply equally to conditions). The interference was found to be justified: the Act protected the environment and secured high and valuable timber yield; if the applicant did not wish to cultivate trees, he could use his land for another purpose. However, it is not difficult to imagine planning conditions being attacked by reference to rule (3): consider a condition requiring excessive expenditure, or which rendered the property unsaleable, e.g. an agricultural occupancy condition. Note that in *Herrick* v *UK* (1985) 8 EHRR 66, the restriction on the use of a building as 'an occasional shelter not amounting to a residence' for limited periods was regarded as a restriction of the applicant's rights under rule (1), not rule (3).

2.10   ARTICLE 2 OF PROTOCOL 1: THE RIGHT TO EDUCATION

Article 2 of Protocol 1 ECHR provides that:

> No person shall be denied the right to education. In the exercise of any functions which it assumes in relation to education and to teaching, the State shall respect the right of parents to ensure such education and teaching in conformity with their own religious and philosophical convictions.

The first sentence does not impose any obligation to establish or subsidize education of any particular type, or at any particular level. Parents have no right to insist on the provision of single-sex or selective schools, or that the state should organize or provide resources for education in any particular manner. But the first sentence of Article 2 does confer the right to avail oneself of the means of education existing at any given time and to be given official recognition of studies which have been completed (*Belgian Linguistic (No. 2)* (1968) 1 EHRR 252). The right of access to educational institutions so conferred, however, may be regulated provided that it does not injure the substance of the right or conflict with other Convention rights.

The second sentence of Article 2 aims at safeguarding the possibility of pluralism in education, including the freedom to establish private schools. The state is required to protect parents' religious and philosophical convictions, even where education is provided in private schools. The philosophical 'convictions' so protected, however, are something more than mere opinions. Moreover, they refer only to those convictions worthy of respect in a democratic society, which are not incompatible with human dignity and which do not conflict with the fundamental right of the child to education. They include a parent's convictions on sex education and corporal punishment (see *Campbell and Cosans* v *UK* (1982) 4 EHRR 293; *Kjeldsen* v *Denmark* (1976) 1 EHRR 711); but they do not include a parent's preference as to the language in which education is conducted (*Belgian Linguistic (No. 2)* (1968) 1 EHRR 252) or as to a particular educational programme which should be followed (*T* v *Special Educational Needs Tribunal* [2002] ELR 704). The obligation to respect a parent's convictions is not confined to classes offering religious or philosophical instruction but runs throughout the whole educational programme.

Nonetheless, the state's obligation is only to 'respect', not necessarily to comply with, the rights of parents to ensure that such education and teaching is in conformity with such convictions. It does not prevent schools imparting information of a religious or philosophical kind. But the state must take care to ensure that information or knowledge included in the curriculum is conveyed in an objective, critical and pluralistic manner, avoiding indoctrination that might not respect parents' philosophical or religious convictions. Neither does the second sentence of Article 2 prevent the state requiring that children should be educated and enforcing a duty to ensure that children attend school or receive adequate education at home. Moreover, it should be noted that the United Kingdom accepts the second sentence of Article 2 only insofar as it is compatible with the provision of efficient instruction and training and the avoidance of unreasonable public expenditure (see the HRA 1998, ss. 1(2) and 15(1)(a) and Sch. 3, Part II.

Chapter Three

Remedies and Damages against Local Authorities

Richard Drabble QC

3.1 INTRODUCTION

This chapter is concerned with the availability of remedies and, in particular, damages for breaches of the relevant ECHR Articles. The HRA 1998 contains a set of provisions dealing with remedies. For the most part, these provisions are readily describable and provide a coherent scheme. There are, however, some difficult areas and basic conceptual problems which fall to be addressed.

The most immediately relevant statutory provisions include:

(a)   Section 6. As indicated in Chapter One, this is a central provision of the HRA 1998. It is also the starting point of an examination of the scheme of the 1998 Act as far as remedies are concerned. Section 6(1) provides that it is 'unlawful for a public authority to act in a way which is incompatible with a Convention right'. Section 6(2) contains a set of exemptions to the general rule, including the position where the act in question is the automatic result of a piece of primary legislation.

(b)   Section 7. The drafting assumption of s. 7 is that the individual who claims that his or her Convention rights have been or will be breached, can identify a given public authority whose act is rendered unlawful by s. 6(1). Section 7(1) provides:

> (1) A person who claims that a public authority has acted (or pro-poses to act) in a way which is made unlawful by section 6(1) may —
>
>   (a)   bring proceedings against the authority under this Act in the appropriate court or tribunal, or
>   (b)   rely on the Convention right or rights concerned in any legal proceedings,
>
> but only if he is (or would be) a victim of the unlawful act.

(c)   Section 8. This provision builds on s. 7, which is itself predicated, as we have seen, on the identification of an 'unlawful act' by a given public authority. Section 8(1) authorizes the court to grant such relief or remedy, or make such order, within the powers as it considers just and appropriate. Section 8(2) indicates that damages can be awarded only by a court which has the power to award damages, or to order the payment of compensation, in civil proceedings. Section 8(3) and (4) then proceed to bring into English law the Strasbourg approach to 'just satisfaction'. This is a change of considerable importance, because it opens up the possibility of an award of damages for at least some unlawful acts of local authorities, amending in some cases the previous rule that, short of misfeasance (and leaving to one side the jurisdiction of the Ombudsman), no damages are payable for errors of public law. The material provisions provide:

(3)   No award of damages is to be made unless, taking account of all the circumstances of the case, including —
      (a)   any other relief or remedy granted, or order made, in relation to the act in question (by that or any other court), and
      (b)   the consequences of any decision (of that or any other court) in respect of that act,
      the court is satisfied that the award is necessary to afford just satisfaction to the person in whose favour it is made.

(4)   In determining —
      (a)   whether to award damages, or
      (b)   the amount of an award,
      the court must take account the principles applied by the European Court of Human Rights in relation to the award of compensation under Article 41 of the Convention.

The change made by s. 8(3) and (4) is of great significance. It is not free of conceptual difficulty, because it operates by requiring English courts and tribunals, in awarding 'just satisfaction', to take account of the Strasbourg case law under Article 41 ECHR. The case law has itself been adversely remarked upon by many commentators, because it is difficult to discern in it any systematic approach to the issues involved, and the area of 'just satisfaction' may be one of those where the English courts will develop their own principled approach. However, the decision of the European Court of Human Rights in *Z and others v UK* (App. No. 29392/95) highlights, with stark clarity, the importance of the incorporation of just satisfaction; and the potential for domestic courts to adopt an approach under the HRA 1998 when awarding damages by way of just satisfaction closely modelled on Strasbourg awards under *Z* v *UK* is of considerable importance and is considered in detail at 3.5.4. The importance of *Z* has been underlined by the decision of the Court of Appeal in *JD and others* v *East Berkshire Community Health Trust and others* [2004] 2 WLR 58. But the relative lack of a principled body of case law at the Strasbourg level is not the only problem. Like the 'margin of appreciation', the concept of 'just satisfaction' is fundamentally apt for an international court of last resort. The language of Article 41 ECHR itself makes this clear. Article 41 requires the European Court to afford just satisfaction if 'the internal law . . . allows only partial reparation to be made'. The task of the European Court is thus to examine the overall position in the legal system of the respondent state and to decide whether overall 'just satisfaction' has been awarded. If it has not, the European Court can make good the deficiency. In the context of s. 8(3) and (4) of the HRA 1998, however, the task of the English court will be to award damages, in order to award 'just satisfaction', in respect of an identified act of a public authority (i.e. one component of the English legal system) that is unlawful under s. 6(1) because it has acted 'in a way which is incompatible with a Convention right'. In many cases this will be straightforward. In some cases, however, this will be much more difficult, because examination of whether Convention rights have been breached will involve examination of the way in which different aspects of the English legal system react together. Issues under Article 6 ECHR provide an obvious example of an area where there may be difficulties. These are examined further below.

Mention of Article 6 highlights one aspect of the 'bringing home' of power to award just satisfaction that deserves considerable attention. It is the extent to which it enables damages to be awarded for many breaches of public law where previously domestic law afforded some remedy but no award of damages. It may be that many conventional judicial review cases, which before the commencement of the HRA 1998 led simply to the quashing of the decision, are now capable of being analysed as a breach of a Convention right. If so, the possibility of an award of damages in order to afford just satisfaction arises. This could be a very profound change indeed. Before turning to more detailed consideration of possible awards of damages, however, some other short points on remedies fall to be made.

The Court of Appeal in *Anufrijeva* v *London Borough of Southwark* [2004] Fam Law 12 provides guidance on how to approach damages claims arising from allegations of maladministration in an Article 8 context. It is an important decision which is considered in detail below.

3.2   THE BASIC RULE

The basic rule under s. 7 of the HRA 1998, creates a statutory right of action pursuant to which an individual who complains that a local authority either has acted or proposes to act in a way which breaches ECHR rights, can either take free-standing proceedings against the local authority, or rely on the Convention rights as a defence to action being taken against him or her. This ability does not arise where the breach of Convention rights is the automatic result of primary legislation, in which event the only available remedy is a declaration of incompatibility (see 1.5).

Often, it will be the ability to rely on Convention rights as a defence which is of most significance in cases concerning local authorities. In the planning sphere, for example, arguments that the refusal of planning permission or successful enforcement action would be a disproportionate interference with the right to a home under Article 8 ECHR, fall most naturally to be considered as part of an appeal to an inspector in the normal planning appellate framework (see further 5.5). Similarly, Article 8 ECHR arguments are relevant in many child care cases but naturally form part of the ordinary framework for examining these issues in family courts. If the arguments based on these Convention rights succeed, in the usual case there will be no breach of any such right — the use of the Convention right as a defence, or as an integral part of the case, will have succeeded and no issue of further relief, or damages, will arise.

It is clear from the wording of s. 8(1) of the HRA 1998, and the general scheme of the Act, that a court or tribunal before which an issue concerning an alleged breach of Convention rights has been raised, has available to it the full range of remedies which it normally applies. Thus interim and final injunctions, and declaratory relief, as well as damages, will all be available.

3.3 JUDICIAL REVIEW

Except in cases where points based on ECHR rights are taken as a defence or as an integral part of other proceedings, the most usual way for challenges to be brought against actions or proposed actions of local authorities is judicial review, although once again the dividing line between actions based on Convention rights which must be taken by way of judicial review and actions which can be brought by a free-standing action under s. 7(1)(a) is not free from conceptual difficulty. The particular position of judicial review is recognized in the drafting of the HRA 1998. It is plain that the reference in s. 7(5) dealing with limitations — making the general limitation period of a year 'subject to any rule imposing a stricter time limit in relation to the procedure in question — is intended in part to refer to the strict time limits governing judicial review.

There is one particular and controversial special provision concerning judicial review which received a great deal of attention in the course of Parliamentary proceedings during the passage of the HRA 1998; this is the reference, in s. 7(3), to the standing of the applicant. Section 7(3) provides that:

(3) If the proceedings are brought on an application for judicial review, the

applicant is to be taken to have a sufficient interest in relation to the unlawful act only if he is, or would be, a victim of that act.

Domestic law on standing has now arrived at a state where a large number of pressure groups have been recognized as possessing sufficient standing to bring proceedings for judicial review. Pressure groups whose claim to sufficient standing has been recognized by the courts include the Joint Council for the Welfare of Immigrants, Help the Aged, the Child Poverty Action Group, Greenpeace, Amnesty International, and the World Development Movement. Strasbourg case law does not directly recognize the status of such groups as 'victims'. It insists that in order to be a victim, the person must be actually and directly affected by the act or omission which is the subject of the complaint (see, e.g., *Klass* v *Germany* (1978) 2 EHRR 214, at para. 33). Thus there is a potential problem about a disjunction between the Strasbourg concept of 'victim' and the present, highly developed concept of standing in judicial review.

It is submitted, however, that the number of occasions on which this presents a real practical difficulty to mounting a challenge to the acts of a local authority is small. The role of pressure groups, where what is being alleged is an act affecting the individual rights of a large number of persons, which would be the position where conflict with ECHR rights is being alleged, has often been to remedy a problem that might be described as the 'disappearing claimant'. Thus, in both of the applications brought by the Child Poverty Action Group in the 1980s (e.g. *R* v *Secretary of State for Social Security, ex parte Child Poverty Action Group* [1990] 2 QB 540), any individual applicant or claimant who brought proceedings based either upon delay or upon the failure of the Secretary of Sate to identify his file, promptly found his file identified or his claim determined. The individual grievance disappeared. Thus it was felt to be necessary to litigate the underlying legal issues in the context of an action brought in the name of the Child Poverty Action Group. In other cases brought by pressure groups but involving individual rights, of which the important and successful challenge by the Joint Council for the Welfare of Immigrants to the social security regulations affecting asylum-seekers (*R* v *Secretary of State for Social Security, ex parte JCWI* [1997] 1 WLR 275) is an example, there would be no formal problem about the challenge being brought in the name of an individual claimant who would have been, on commencement, affected by the new regulation. The recognition of the appropriateness of funding test cases on a public interest basis under the Funding Code (*Legal Services Commission Manual*, at 3C–039 *et seq.*) ought positively to assist a challenge brought by an individual applicant, since (in contrast to the position where the challenge is brought by the pressure group itself) an award by the Funding Commission carries a degree of protection against the other side's costs should the application fail.

The approach to standing which brought about the perceived need for the

Child Poverty Action Group to intervene in the 'disappearing claimant' cases may already be outdated. The House of Lords, in *R* v *Secretary of State for the Home Department, ex parte Salem* [1999] 1 AC 450, has expressed a willingness in public law cases to entertain a challenge which by the date of the hearing has become academic for the individual concerned. Scheimann J (as he then was) allowed a judicial review challenge (to the construction adopted by a local authority of some housing benefit regulations) to proceed, despite the fact that the individual claim had been determined to the satisfaction of the claimant, in *R* v *Brent London Borough Council, ex parte Connery* [1990] 2 All ER 355. Thus there is a great deal of scope for arguing, on the existing approach to standing, that an applicant should be allowed to proceed in a challenge to an action or approach of a local authority even if he or she has ceased to have any personal stake in the outcome.

That approach is fortified in the context of the HRA 1998. An individual whose ECHR rights have been breached, is plainly entitled to attempt to receive 'just satisfaction' under s. 8 of the 1998 Act. Even if the court is unwilling to award damages, it should, if its approach is truly to mirror that of the European Court, be willing to grant declaratory relief as part and parcel of the award of 'just satisfaction'. Put another way, the existence of a potential award of damages and/or a declaration makes it less likely that a dispute will be truly academic.

There have, of course, been important examples of judicial reviews brought by pressure groups where the intention was to litigate issues of general principle, not affecting individual rights. A classic example is *R* v *Secretary of State for Foreign and Commonwealth Affairs, ex parte World Development Movement* [1995] 1 WLR 386. However, these cases are inherently less likely to involve Convention rights.

There is the further consideration that in many applications for judicial review brought by pressure groups, the standing of the group could be viewed as representative, i.e. that it had amongst its members individuals who were immediately affected by the allegedly unlawful act complained of. The National Federation of the Self Employed is an example. The Child Poverty Action Group also claimed standing on this basis (having branch members who were social security claimants), although because of the generous overall approach of the courts they never found it necessary to consider that claim. In the context of the HRA 1998, such bodies might be able to claim that they met the test in s. 7(3) on the basis that they were organizations having amongst their members individuals who were 'victims' in the Strasbourg sense.

For all these reasons, it does seem likely that the potential narrowing of the test of standing in judicial review to 'victims' is unlikely to have a significant impact on the ability to mount challenges to local authority action. It is unfortunate, however, that the problem exists at all. There is always the possibility that an appropriate applicant cannot be found, given the fact that he or she may need to be willing to continue with the legal action in circumstances where the individual gain is small or non-existent. There is also the substantial drawback that the court may be forced into hearing elaborate argument about the standing of the particular pressure group it has in front of it (cf. The discussion in Wadham and Mountfield, *The Human Rights Act 1998* (Blackstone Press, 1999), pp. 39–41).

One further issue needs to be mentioned in connection with judicial review. At present, before incorporation, the general approach of the courts is that challenges to public law decisions of local authorities have to be made by way of judicial review, although since the landmark decision of *O'Reilly* v *Mackman* [1983] 2 AC 237, the rigours of this approach have been modified (see, e.g., *Roy* v *Kensington and Chelsea Family Practitioner Committee* [1992] 1 AC 625). The issue arises whether challenges to such decisions on the basis of conflict with the HRA 1998 will need to be brought by way of judicial review, or whether it will be possible to proceed by way of a claim in the county court for damages coupled with a declaration that the act complained of was unlawful because it breached s. 6 of the 1998 Act. In principle this issue could be solved by rules of court made under s. 7(2) of the HRA 1998, but in fact the rules do not provide any answer. The Lord Chancellor's Department Consultation Paper, *Human Rights Act 1998: Rules and Practice Directions* (March 2000), said simply:

> 12. We propose that a free-standing case under Section 7(1)(a) of the Act should be brought in the following ways —
> - using existing judicial review procedures;
> - in the county court or in the High Court where a claim for damages is made (unless this is associated with a claim for judicial review). The normal jurisdictional limits should apply;
> - in the county court or in the High Court following a finding of unlawfulness under Section 7(1)(b) in some other court or tribunal which did not have the power to award damages or compensation. This would cover, for example, actions in respect of a claim for damages in a criminal case arising out of a ruling by a Magistrates' Court or the Crown Court that the prosecution had acted unlawfully.

The rules reflect this approach (see CPR, rule 7.11; PD 7, para. 2.10). The rules thus do not provide any authoritative answer to the question of whether it is effectively possible to challenge the legality of an administrative decision (in terms of its compatibility with s. 6 of the HRA 1998) not by judicial review but rather by an ordinary civil claim for damages coupled with a claim for a declaration. The implications for time limits would be significant, because, as explained at 3.4, the time limit created by s. 7(5) is ordinarily a period of one year, as opposed to the much more stringent approach to judicial review. Of course, in an ordinary claim the remedies specific to judicial review would not be available. In particular, it would not be possible expressly to quash the decision complained of, but this might be of small comfort to a public body whose decision had been ruled by a court to be unlawful because it was in breach of s. 6. Whether or not such a ruling was expressly accompanied by a declaration, or simply formed part of a judgment leading to an award of damages, it would in the present state of the law concerning collateral challenges (see *Crédit Suisse* v *Allerdale Borough Council* [1997] QB 306) create at least some uncertainty about the legal effect of the impugned decision and the extent to which the local authority could rely on it either against the 'victim' who had obtained the ruling, or against third parties. It has also to be said that the possibility of commencing a claim for damages based upon a breach of s. 6, even if an application for judicial review is refused because it has not been made 'promptly' within the ordinary requirements of the judicial review time-limits, may well have a significant effect on the way the court exercises its discretion in connection with issues of delay in judicial review applications. A court in this situation may be faced with the alternatives either of refusing to entertain the application for judicial review, with the result that an alleged threatened breach of Convention rights actually occurs but can found a subsequent application for 'just satisfaction', including damages in an in-time ordinary action; or with accepting a late application for judicial review. Neither alternative is attractive.

Despite these difficulties, the only safe course for an applicant wishing to challenge, and effectively set aside, a decision of a local authority is to assume that the application must be made by judicial review and in accordance with the strict timetable provided for such applications.

The pre-eminent suitability of the judicial review route in cases where damages are sought for maladministration was affirmed by the Court of Appeal in *Anufrijeva* (see above). The decision is considered in detail below. Anyone contemplating a damages claim by a route other than judicial review should consider that decision (especially para. 81) with care.

3.4 TIME LIMITS

As has already been explained at 3.3, the ordinary time limits for judicial review apply to a free-standing application based on judicial review. The specific provision of the HRA 1998 dealing with time limits is s. 7(5). This provides:

> (5) Proceedings under subsection (1)(a) above must be brought before the end of —
> (a) the period of one year beginning with the date on which the act complained of took place; or
> (b) such longer period as the court or tribunal considers equitable having regard to all the circumstances,
>
> but that is subject to any rule imposing a stricter time limit in relation to the procedure in question.

In some contexts, it will clearly be necessary for the claimant to rely on the power to extend time under s. 7(5)(b). For example, where the unlawful act complained of is one of a prosecution in a criminal case (which might well be a local authority in one of its various regulatory functions), the criminal court in which the breach of Convention rights was first established will not have jurisdiction to award damages. In such circumstances, a defendant who wished to obtain just satisfaction would have to commence separate proceedings. Because he or she could not do so until the criminal prosecution had run its course, this might well involve a delay of well over a year from the original unlawful act. In those circumstances, one anticipates that the court would be willing to extend time. Similar factual circumstances might arise in other contexts, where the potential claimant reasonably has to wait for the result of investigations (e.g. a complaints procedure) which cannot themselves result in a damage award.

We have already seen that the concept of a damages claim following as a consequence of a finding by the criminal court that the prosecution had breached Convention rights was expressly addressed in the March 2000 Consultation Paper and is dealt with by the rules (see 3.3). The Paper goes on to state:

> The person seeking a civil remedy should be able to rely upon the finding of unlawfulness at *prima facie* evidence that the defendant authority acted unlawfully. The previous finding of unlawfulness (even if it resulted from a collateral challenge in the earlier proceedings) would be treated, by analogy, in the same way that s. 11 of the Civil Evidence Act 1968 treats a conviction for the purpose of civil proceedings. It would be open to refute the finding on grounds of fact or law using the authority under paragraph 4 of Schedule 1 to the Civil Procedure Act 1997.

Rule 33.9 has been inserted into CPR, Part 33 to achieve this effect.

3.5   JUST SATISFACTION AND DAMAGES

This section is concerned with the principles the courts will apply when confronted with an application for damages by a claimant who is able to establish that his or her ECHR rights have been breached. The subject is potentially of considerable importance for those affected by the actions of local authorities.

3.5.1   Just satisfaction to the injured party

We saw at 3.1 that the HRA 1998, in s. 8(4), requires the court, in deciding whether to award damages and the amount of any award, to take into account the Strasbourg jurisprudence under Article 41 ECHR. It is worth setting out Article 41 in full:

> If the Court finds that there has been a violation of the Convention . . . and if the internal law of the High Contracting Party concerned allows only partial reparation to be made, the Court shall, if necessary afford just satisfaction to the injured party.

Thus the concept that is apparent on the face of Article 41 itself is that the European Court of Human Rights looks at the end result, taking account of domestic law, and if that end result is one of partial reparation only, the position is made good. To an extent, that structure is echoed domestically, because s. 8(3) of the HRA 1998 provides that no award of damages is to be made unless it is necessary in all the circumstances of the case. Section 8(3) expressly provides that the 'circumstances' include other relief granted (by any court), and indeed the consequences of the decision that there has been a breach itself. Thus the basic approach is to provide for a flexible discretionary remedy, of the sort revealed by Strasbourg case law, to be used where the grant of non-monetary relief amounts only to 'partial reparation'. Where damages in any event fall to be awarded as part of existing law (because, say, the breach of Convention rights itself amounts to a tort), it is unlikely that there will be any need to make a further award of damages by way of just satisfaction; although it is possible that even in this situation 'just satisfaction' in respect of certain types of non-pecuniary loss (outraged feelings, distress, anxiety and humiliation) that might not be readily recognized in English tort law may be available.

The problem is in knowing with any degree of certainty when such an award will be required. It has frequently been said that it is difficult to analyse the case law on just satisfaction so as to provide a consistent analysis. Some idea of the range of responses can be gleaned from Karen Reid, *A Practitioner's Guide to the European Convention on Human Rights* (Sweet and Maxwell, 1998) which contains (at pp. 399–425) a survey of recent case law. Critiques of Strasbourg case law can also be found in Mowbray [1997] PL 647 and Harris, O'Boyle and Warbrick, *Law of the European Convention on Human Rights* (Butterworths, 2003), pp. 682–8.

Anufrijeva (see above) now provides comprehensive guidance where damages are sought in respect of maladministration connected with Article 8.

3.5.2 Types of damages

In deciding on the importance of these uncertainties and the direction likely to be taken by the English courts in exercising this jurisdiction, it is sensible to distinguish between:

(a)   damages paid in respect of non-pecuniary loss;
(b)   the availability of exemplary or aggravated damages; and
(c)   damages to be paid in respect of pecuniary loss.

In *Marcic* (see above) HH Judge Harvery ruled that he could make an award of damages in respect of future losses, by analogy with the domestic situation where damages are awarded in lieu of an injunction. He rejected a submission that an award of damages for future losses was not possible. His approach was followed by Buckley J in *Dennis and another* v *MOD* [2003] Env LR 34 at paras 55–63. The case involved the impact of noise from Harrier jets. The main thrust of the judgment was concerned with the domestic law of nuisance, but there is a short reference to the application of human rights principles. The approach taken by the judge allowed the noise to continue but only on the basis that an award of damages was made under s. 8 of the HRA 1998 in respect of Articles 8 and Article 1 Protocol 1 ECHR. Buckley J said:

> Following the implications of *S v France* as identified in *Marcic* and . . . with which I agree, I would hold that a fair balance would not be struck in the absence of compensation. I would hold, as I believe is implicit in the decision in *S v France*, that the public interest is greater than the individual private interests . . . but it is not proportionate to pursue or give effect to the public interest . . .

This line of reasoning does have a difficulty. Damages under s. 8 are only available if the court finds the proposed act to be unlawful; yet the court sanctioned future Harrier flights, presumably holding that they were lawful given the availability of compensation in the form of damages. The reasoning seems circular.

The House of Lords in *Marcic* [2003] 3 WLR 1603 declined to follow either the Court of Appeal (as to the common law of nuisance) or HH Judge Havery, who had held that there was a breach of convention rights. It held that for both it was necessary to examine the statutory scheme in question (here, the Water Industry Act 1991). This provided a mechanism for resolving issues of priorities that arose in the case, the mechanism being enforcement by the director under the scheme. Setting up the statutory scheme was within the area of judgment that should be left to Parliament, and the unfortunate results that had occured in Mr Marcic's case did not cast any doubt on the overall fairness of the scheme. Lord Nicholls commented:

> the malfunctioning of the statutory scheme on this occasion does not cast doubt on its overall fairness as a scheme. A complaint by an individual about his particular case can, and should be, pursued with the Director pursuant to the statutory scheme, with the long stop availability of judicial review. That remedial avenue was not taken in this case.

3.5.2.1   *Damages for non-pecuniary loss*

The uncertainties are at their greatest when it comes to this first category. It is clear that in deciding whether to make awards under this head, the European Court of Human Rights has been heavily influenced by the merits of the individual cases. It has frequently held that the finding of a breach itself is sufficient 'just satisfaction'. It is not possible, however, to find any articulated statement of the circumstances in which this will be the answer. Striking examples of where it has been so held include *McCann and others* v *UK* (1995) 21 EHRR 97 (the terrorists shot on Gibraltar) and *De Wilde, Ooms and Versyp* v *Belgium (No. 2)* (1972) 1 EHRR 438. In the later case, the court held that no monetary compensation should be awarded for the fact that the applicants, who were vagrants, could not challenge the legality of their detention under Article 5(4) ECHR, because even if they had been able to challenge it they would not have been released any earlier. But this approach certainly does not reflect a universal rule.

In areas of direct interest to those concerned with the legality of local authority action, it has been apparent for some time that certain breaches of Convention rights have been held to require fairly substantial awards in respect of non-pecuniary loss. An obvious example is local authority activity in connection with children, e.g. adoption and care proceedings. Here, examination of the case law reveals that there is a real risk that the actions of local authorities create breaches of Convention rights, in particular under Articles 8 and 6 ECHR. To take one example, in *H* v *UK* A 136–B (9 June 1988), a local authority was in part responsible for very significant delays in child-care proceedings by, *inter alia*, the late filing of evidence. The Court in that case plainly thought the delays serious because they were prejudicial to the parent's ability to resist adoption. The European Court held that the overall delays amounted to a breach of Article 6 ECHR and awarded £12,000 damages for non-pecuniary loss. At one level, this amount of damages can be regarded as small. At another level, it introduces into English law a degree of compensation for administrative failure which is not presently available (Ombudsman apart). Other child-care examples include *O* v *UK* (1991) 13 EHRR 578; *Eriksson* v *Sweden* (1990) 12 EHRR 183; *Keegan* v *Ireland* (1994) 18 EHRR 342; and *McMichael* v *UK* (1995) 20 EHRR 205. As awards of 'just satisfaction' go, these are relatively large, no doubt reflecting the context and the degrees of anxiety and feelings that would be engaged. In the *Eriksson* case, for example, the contemporary value of the award would be in the order of £23,000. The underlying complaint was that a mother had been prevented from challenging the equivalent of a care order restricting her contact with her daughter and placing the daughter in a foster home. Social services action that leads to the unlawful detention of the mentally ill is another area in which significant awards might be made. In *Johnson* v *UK* 119/1996/738/937 (unreported), damages of £10,000 were awarded for the unlawful detention of a mental patient.

The existence of potentially large awards of non-pecuniary damages against local authorities in respect of their child-care responsibilities is confirmed by *Z and others* v *UK* (App. No. 29392/95) (see 3.5.4).

3.5.2.2 Decision of the court of appeal in Anufrijeva
Anufrijeva v *London Borough of Southwark* [2003] EWCA Civ 1406 provided the opportunity to examine the appropriate approach in cases where damages are claimed under the HRA 1998 in respect of maladministration engaging Article 8.

There were in fact three appeals heard at the same time. The Court considered the matter under the following headings:

(a)   When does a duty arise under Article 8 to take positive action?

(b)   In what circumstances does maladministration constitute breach of Article 8?

(c)   The nature of a claim for damages under the HRA 1998.

(d)   The Strasbourg principles.

(e)   How should damages be assessed?

(f)   What procedures should be followed to ensure that the costs of obtaining relief are proportionate to that relief?

Some short comments are made on each of these below.

When does a duty arise under Article 8 to take positive action?   This question (and the next) are strictly outside the scope of this chapter, but it raises an issue that will need to be confronted in damages claims where the underlying allegation is maladministration in providing welfare support in one way or another. The Court of Appeal has also had to consider what degree of deprivation would constitute a breach of Article 3 in *R (Q) v Secretary of State for the Home Department* [2004] QB 36 (see paras 59 and 60). In *Anufrijeva* the Court observed that it was easier to envisage a lack of support which would mean that the condition of the alleged victim reached the 'point of Article 3 degradation' than it was to discern some intermediate point which, while not engaging Article 3, did nonetheless breach Article 8 (see para. 37). It concluded that it was 'hard to conceive . . . of a situation of which the position of an individual will be such that Article 8 requires him to be provided with welfare support, where his predicament is not sufficiently severe to engage Article 3'. The position would be different where children were involved, because Article 8 might require the provision of welfare support in a manner which enables family life to continue. The standard would nonetheless be high. In one of the cases (*Bernard*) the standard was reached. The Court of Appeal observed that 'Family life was seriously inhibited by the hideous conditions prevailing in the claimant's home' (see para. 43).

In what circumstances does maladministration constitute breach of article 8?   The Court answered this question in para. 47. It considered that questions of resources were relevant, and that 'maladministration of the type that we are considering here will only infringe article 8 where the consequences are serious'. It was necessary to have regard to both the degree of culpability of the failure to act and the severity of the consequence. Isolated acts of even significant carelessness are unlikely to suffice (see para. 48).

Features of a claim for compensation under the HRA 1998   The Court, in para. 55, listed the following features of a claim for damages under the HRA that could be gleaned from the Act itself:

(a)   The award of damages under the Act. is confined to the class of unlawful acts of public authorities identified by s. 6(1) — see s. 8(1) and (6).

(b)   The court has a discretion as to whether to make an award (it must be 'just and appropriate' to do so) by contrast to the position in relation to common law claims where there is a right to damages.

(c)   The award must be necessary to achieve 'just satisfaction'; language that is distinct from the approach at common law where a claimant is invariably entitled, so far as money can achieve this, to be restored to the position he would have been in.

(d)   The court is required to take into account the different principles applied by European Court of Human Rights.

(e)   Exemplary damages are not awarded; no reasoning is expressed for this conclusion but in practical terms it probably represents the end of a debate considered shortly below.

Drawing on Scorey and Eicke, *Human Rights Damages*, the Court went on to stress the broad discretionary nature of damages awards under the Act. The approach is to determine the 'appropriate' remedy in the light of the particular circumstances of an individual victim, having regard to what would be 'just', not only for that individual victim, but also for the wider public who have an interest in the continued funding of a public service. Damages are not an automatic remedy but a remedy of last resort.

The Strasbourg Principles   The Court recognized, as others have done, the difficulty in extracting general principles from the Strasbourg case law. It recognized that the general principle is *restitutio in integrum*. It follows that where there is significant financial loss flowing from breach of a convention right, this will normally be assessed and awarded (see, for example *Lustig-Prean* v *UK* (2001) 31 EHRR 601 and *Smith and Grady* v *UK* (2001) 31 EHRR 620 (pension rights and loss of earnings following discriminatory discharge from the armed forces in breach of Article 8)).

Turning to cases where this exercise is not possible the Court considered and approved the approach of Stanley Burnton J in an Article 5 case, where he said:

> Thus, even in the case of mentally ill claimants, not every feeling of frustration and distress will justify an award of damages. The frustration and distress must be significant; of such intensity that it would itself justify an award of compensation for non-pecuniary damages. In my judgment, an important touchstone of that intensity in cases such as the present will be that the hospital staff considered it to be sufficiently relevant to the mental state of the patient to warrant its mention in the clinical notes.

The Court observed that this approach could not be applied simply to Article 8 cases, because in line with the general reasoning described above there would be no breach of Article 8 at all where the consequence of delay was no more than distress and frustration. It was, however, necessary to take a broad brush approach. The issue was whether the other remedies that have been granted are enough to vindicate the right that has been infringed. This issue should be decided without an elaborate trial — in many cases it could be done simply on examination of the correspondence and the witness documents.

The gravity of the breach and the circumstances in which it occurred are both relevant (see, for example, the contrasting cases of *Halford* v *UK* (1997) 23 EHRR 523 and *Kopp* v *Switzerland* (1998) 27 EHRR 93, both examples of unauthorized telephone tapping. The complainant in *Halford* was awarded £10,000 by way of just satisfaction because of the circumstances of the breach and the use to which the information was to be put. In *Kopp* the finding of breach was itself sufficient just satisfaction.

How should damages be assessed? The practical approach of the Court was to uphold Sullivan J's reliance (in *Bernard* above) on decisions of the Local Government Ombudsman awarding compensation on behalf of disabled persons deprived of benefits or assistance as a result of maladministration. They were the best comparables when dealing with 'in essence an extreme form of maladministration which had deprived the mother of much needed social service care [suitable accommodation] for a lengthy period'. The resulting award of £10,000 in total was at the top end of the range of Ombudsman awards and, said the Court of Appeal, was at the top end of the range of Human Rights Act damages awards for this type of maladministration engaging Article 8.

What procedures should be followed to ensure that the costs of obtaining relief are proportionate to that relief? The Court was extremely concerned about the potential for complex damages trials in actions were the sums involved would be relatively modest. In para. 81 it gave the following guidance:

(1) the courts should look critically at any attempt to recover damages under the HRA 1998 for maladministration by any procedure other than judicial review in the administrative court;

(2) whilst a claim for damages alone cannot be brought by judicial review, such proceedings should still be brought in the Administrative Court by an ordinary claim;

(3) before giving permission to apply for judicial review, the Administrative Court judge should require the claimant to explain why it would not be more appropriate to use any available internal complaint procedure or take a complaint to the relevant ombudsman, at least in the first instance;

(4) if there is a legitimate claim for other relief, permission should if appropriate be limited to that relief and consideration given to deferring

permission for the damages claim, adjourning or staying that claim until use has been made of ADR, whether by reference to a mediator or an ombudsman or otherwise, or remitting that claim to a district judge or master if the damages claim cannot be dismissed summarily on the grounds that no award is needed to provide just satisfaction; and

(5) the court hoped that in future this type of claim could be determined by the appropriate level of judge in a summary manner by the judge reading the relevant evidence — citing more than three authorities should be specifically justified and the hearing limited to half a day except in exceptional circumstances.

Finally, the Court recognized that other proportionate ways of dealing with these matters might be devised. There was, however, a heavy stress on proportionality.

3.5.2.3 Aggravated or exemplary damages

Turning next to the possibility of awards of either aggravated or exemplary damages, the starting point is that the European Court of Human Rights has not awarded damages under either head in any case to date. As far as aggravated damages are concerned, the very broad nature of the concept of 'just satisfaction' and the European Court's willingness (acting under Article 41 ECHR) to compensate for injured feelings, outrage, helplessness, etc. (see 3.5.1) would appear to make it undesirable to turn to a separate domestic concept of aggravated damages. The courts, in this area, can achieve satisfactory results by applying the broad equitable approach to be found in existing case law under Article 41 ECHR, although no doubt in the hands of English judges a more systematic approach can be expected to evolve in the fullness of time. The change may be not so much to tack a concept of aggravated damages on to the concept of 'just satisfaction' as to force the English courts, when awarding damages for a recognized tort committed in circumstances which also involve a breach of Convention rights, to take a broader view than they might otherwise take to this sort of issue when awarding damages. This general approval is confirmed by *Anufrijeva* (see above) at paras 67–70.

It has been suggested (L. Starmer, *European Human Rights Law*, Legal Action Group, 1999) that English courts might be more willing than the European Court to award exemplary damages if the criteria of 'oppressive, just and unconstitutional' action (to be found in *Rookes v Barnard* [1964] AC 1129) are met. However, it is respectfully submitted that this is unlikely. In a case where the cause of action arises solely under s. 7(1)(a) of the HRA 1998, the court is expressly enjoined by s. 8(3) not to make an award of damages unless the award 'is necessary to afford just satisfaction to the person in whose favour it is made'. As the concept of exemplary damages necessarily goes beyond compensation, awards would seem to be inconsistent with the approach of Article 41 ECHR itself, which requires 'just satisfaction' to be made where the existing 'internal' law of the contracting state affords only 'partial reparation'. An award of exemplary damages would seem be doing more than turning a position of 'partial reparation into full reparation'. No such award has been made — in a number of cases the European Court has simply ignored a request for exemplary damages made to it. The reason may well be the basic structure of Article 41 ECHR.

3.5.2.4   Damages for pecuniary loss

The European Court of Human Rights has not been afraid to award very substantial sums indeed by way of compensation for defined, pecuniary loss. Given the availability of Strasbourg case law to show that such damages can be paid, and in the hands of English judges who might well find it difficult not to make good financial loss flowing from an unlawful act, it would seem likely that damages in respect of pecuniary loss will be regularly awarded wherever a claimant is able to demonstrate causation. This is an area where the desire of the common law to build a coherent, principled approach to comparable situations is likely to be strong. As was remarked at 3.1, the result may be a widespread availability of financial compensation for public law breaches. The acceptance in *Anufrijeva* (see above) that the starting point is *restitutio in integrum* confirms this approach.

One of the most striking examples of a very substantial award of 'just satisfaction' in respect of pecuniary loss is the Irish planning case of *Pine Valley Developments* v *Ireland* (1993) 16 EHRR 379. There the Court awarded I RE £1.2 million where a breach of Convention rights had led to a situation where a company could not develop land in accordance with a planning permission it should (as the Court held) have been able to rely on (for further discussion of this case, see Chapter Two). Indeed, in the property field generally there is scope for high awards of damages by way of 'just satisfaction' in respect of pecuniary loss because of the nature of the issues that arise. In another leading planning case, concerned with blight, *Sporrong and Lönnroth* v *Sweden* (1984) 7 EHRR 256, the Court awarded the equivalent of approximately £100,000 in respect of the period of blight, which had lasted for about 20 years. Once again, this case is discussed further in Chapter Two. The European Court has recognized loss of profit claims, sometimes in circumstances in which it might be thought they had not been proved adequately, e.g. in *Open Door Counselling and Dublin Well Woman* v *Ireland* (1992) 15 EHRR 244, at para. 87.

3.5.3   Just satisfaction where no damages available

We now return to develop a theme hinted at in 3.1, i.e. the extent to which the case law on 'just satisfaction' can be applied to circumstances in which, at present, English public law supplies a remedy but, short of proof of misfeasance, no damages. Some examples might help to crystallize the issues:

(a)   A local planning authority breaches some obligation under domestic law to provide environmental information, e.g. failing to insist on an environmental impact assessment in accordance with EU law in connection with potentially polluting development, or to honour the obligation to provide environmental information under the Environmental Information Regulations. In terms of pure domestic law, there are remedies — the planning permission might be quashed unless issues of delay or prejudice prevent this result; or mandamus might issue to force the information to be revealed. However, the absence of environmental information can, in some circumstances at least, engage Article 8 ECHR, because the state may owe a positive obligation to those potentially affected by pollution in order for them to make decisions about how to order their lives. This approach lies behind the decision in *Guerra* v *Italy* (1998) 26 EHRR 357 (discussed in Chapter Two), where award of 'just satisfaction' in respect of non-pecuniary loss was made. The facts of that case were probably more extreme than might normally be expected in English litigation, but it can readily be seen that the availability of damages makes a significant difference.

(b)   A planning inspector breaches the rules of natural justice, e.g. by holding a conversation with a representative of the planning authority in the absence of a representative of the developer. He refuses planning permission. The existing domestic legislative scheme provides a remedy for this position, because the landowner can use the statutory appeal to the High Court to have the refusal of planning permission quashed. However, the delay in righting the position has caused pecuniary loss, because a contract into which the developer has entered is conditional on obtaining unconditional planning permission. On the face of it (and subject to the difficulty discussed below), this situation can be analysed in terms of a breach of Article 6 ECHR; and as the pecuniary loss is directly caused by the breach, it is difficult to see any defence to a damages claim. In the world of property rights, such claims might be substantial. Similar considerations might apply where the refusal of planning permission is made by a local authority committee including a member who wrongly fails to declare an interest.

(c)   A local authority involved in child care proceedings fails to abide by orders of the court as to the filing of witness statements and the like. The result is that the litigation is unreasonably prolonged. As seen above (at 3.5.2.1) financial 'just satisfaction' has been awarded in this type of situation.

The above examples nevertheless reveal the remaining conceptual difficulty that falls to be discussed. It was indicated at 3.1 that the concept of 'just satisfaction' is apt for an international court of last resort, which judges the performance of the national system as a whole without any need to allocate responsibility to a particular domestic entity. The hypothesis behind the example of the 'biased' planning inspector, for example, is that there will have been a breach of Article 6 ECHR, because the compatibility of the overall system of adjudication in the UK planning system depends on the combination of a quasi-independent inspector with access to a full Article 6 court on a point of law under the statutory appeals procedure (see *Bryan* v *UK* (1995) 21 EHRR 342, discussed further in Chapter 5). Accordingly, so the argument would go, an action by one of the component parts of a composite system which means that that composite system cannot be regarded, on the facts of the individual case, as having produced a result consistent with Article 6, breaches Article 6.

It is submitted that this is the correct analysis and that, in the example at (b), damages would be available against the Inspectorate on the basis that the inspector, as a public authority, had acted 'in a way which is incompatible with a Convention right' (see the wording of s. 6(1) of the HRA 1998). However, this cannot be regarded as certain. The inspector, as *Bryan* itself decides, is not an Article 6 court. There would be no Article 6 problem on the facts of the example if the High Court exercised a fact-finding jurisdiction. The breach of Article 6 ECHR, if such there be at all, arises on the example at (b) from the way the component parts of the English system relate to each other rather than as a necessary consequence of the acts of any one of them. Nonetheless, it is submitted that in the English system, where primary fact-finding is allocated to an administrative body such as the inspector, an action by the inspector which renders the fact-finding indefensible and requires it to be undertaken again, itself breaches Article 6 ECHR and thus creates a right of action under s. 6 of the HRA 1998.

This analysis is supported in particular by the approach of Lord Hoffmann in *R* v *Secretary of State for the Environment, Transport and the Regions, ex parte Alconbury Developments Ltd and others* [2001] 2 WLR 1389, when he rejected the contention of the Lord Advocate to the effect that Article 6 ECHR was not engaged by the ministerial decision at all, but only by a challenge to the legality of that decision made in the High Court. The submission is recorded by Lord Hoffmann in the following terms (at para. 133):

Mr Macdonald submitted that Article 6 has no application to the decision by the Scottish Ministers (or the Secretary of State in England). Their decisions do not involve the determination of anyone's civil rights or obligations. They are simply the exercise of legal powers which affect, perhaps change, civil rights and obligations, but do not determine them within the meaning of Article 6. The point at which rights or obligations are determined is in the proceedings by way of judicial review, which decide whether the exercise of power by the administrator was lawful or not. As that question is decided by a court which is undoubtedly independent and impartial, that is the end of the case.

Lord Hoffmann saw the force of this approach, but ultimately rejected it (see para. 135). It is also supported by the formulation of Lord Clyde in the same case (at para. 150):

> It is thus clear that Article 6(1) is engaged where the decision which is to be given is of an administrative character, that is to say one given in the exercise of a discretionary power, as well as a dispute in a court of law regarding the private rights of the citizen, provided that it directly affects civil rights and obligations and is of a genuine and serious nature. It applies then to the various exercises of discretion which are raised in the present appeals. But while the scope of the article extends to cover such discretionary decisions, the particular character of such decisions cannot be disregarded.

It is further submitted that a similar analysis can be applied to the other examples. On this basis, undue delay by an authority in conducting litigation, in child care cases, is itself action by a local authority 'which is incompatible with a Convention right', namely the Article 6 right to a timeous trial.

3.5.4   *Z and others* v *UK*

This decision of the European Court in *Z and others* v *UK* (App. No. 29392/95) bears considerable, and close, examination as an example of the practical effect the introduction of the concept of 'just satisfaction' into domestic law will have. The case followed on from the decision of the House of Lords in *X* v *Bedfordshire* [1995] 3 All ER 353. It involved complaints by four siblings, Z, A, B and C. To state the outcome first, the European Court awarded:

(a)   £8,000 to Z, £100,000 to A, £80,000 to B, and £4,000 to C in respect of pecuniary damage;

(b)   an identical sum of £32,000 to each applicant for non-pecuniary damage; and

(c)   costs and expenses in a global figure of £32,000.

In making these awards, the European Court rejected submissions made on behalf of the UK Government that the combined pecuniary and non-pecuniary damages for Z should be £20,000; for A, £40,000; for B, £30,000; and for C, £10,000. In doing so, the European Court showed a willingness to engage in an exercise of evaluating individual medical reports for the purpose of deciding on pecuniary as well as non-pecuniary loss. The pecuniary loss figures comprise substantial elements for future medical costs and loss of employment prospects.

The facts of the various cases were fairly extreme. They are set out in the judgment of the Court at paras 9–40.

In order to arrive at the above awards, the reasoning of the European Court took the following steps. First, the Court considered whether there was a breach of Article 3 ECHR. The Commission had unanimously found that there was, before the Court the UK Government did not contest this conclusion. The Court recorded its reasons for accepting the concession that:

> . . . the treatment suffered by the four applicants reached the level of severity prohibited by Article 3 and that the State failed in its positive obligation under the Convention to provide the applicants with adequate protection against inhuman and degrading treatment. (para. 72)

by referring to *A* v *UK* (1998) 27 EHRR 611 and *Osman* v *UK* (1999) 29 EHRR 245, the European Court was effectively spelling out a strong positive obligation contained in the Article 3 ECHR in the social services sphere.

Although uncontroversial by the stage of the court hearing, this finding of a breach of Article 3 ECHR was the foundation of a line of reasoning leading to a substantial damages award that effectively bypassed the difficulties created by *X* v *Bedfordshire* on the one hand and the Strasbourg decision on the other. The reasoning goes as follows.

The European Court (or, to be precise, the majority) revisited its earlier decision in *Osman* (above). In that case, the Court had held that the strike-out proceedings created a breach of Article 6 ECHR. This decision had been heavily criticized, and the reasoning of the majority effectively accepted the criticism. They said:

> The applicants, and the Commission in its report, relied on the Osman case . . . as indicating that the exclusion of liability in negligence . . . acted as a restriction on access to the Court. The Court considers that its reasoning in the Osman judgment was based on an understanding of the law of negligence (see, in particular, paragraphs 138 and 139 of the Osman judgment) which has to be reviewed in the light of the clarifications made subsequently by the domestic courts and notably the House of Lords. The Court is satisfied that the law of negligence is developed in the domestic courts since the case of *Caparo* . . . and as recently analysed in the case of *Barrett* v *Enfield LBC* [1999] 3 WLR 79 includes the fair just and reasonable criterion as an intrinsic element of the duty of care and that the ruling of law concerning that element in this case does not disclose the operation of an immunity. In the present case, the Court is led to the conclusion that the inability to sue the local authority flowed not from the immunity but from the applicable principles governing the substantive right of action in domestic law. There was no restriction on access to court of the kind contemplated in the *Ashingdane* judgment.

Having put the conceptual difficulties of Article 6 ECHR to one side in this manner, the Court returned to Article 3 read together with Article 13, asking itself whether the applicants had an adequate remedy for the now admitted breach of Article 3, as Article 13 would require. It stated:

> Yet the outcome of the domestic proceedings they brought is that they, and any children with complaints such as theirs, cannot sue the local authority in negligence for compensation, however foreseeable — and severe — the harm suffered and however unreasonable the conduct of the local authority in failing to take steps to prevent that harm. The applicants are correct in their assertions that the gap they have identified in domestic law is one that gives rise to an issue under the Convention, but in the Court's view it is an issue under Article 13, not Article 6.1.

The Court went on to hold that there was indeed a breach of Article 13 ECHR. The Government had drawn attention to other remedies — the Criminal Injuries Compensation Board, the Ombudsman, and the complaints procedure under the Children Act 1989 — but once again, by the time of the Strasbourg hearing, had accepted that on the facts of these cases they were not adequate to afford 'just satisfaction' (see para. 107). The Court agreed. It said (at para. 109):

> There should however be available to the victim or the victim's family a mechanism for establishing any liability of State officials or bodies for acts or omissions involving their rights under the Convention. Furthermore, in the case of a breach of Articles 2 and 3 of the Convention, which rank as the most fundamental provisions of the Convention, compensation for non-pecuniary damage flowing from the breach should in principle be available as part of the range of redress.

The Government had already drawn attention (at para. 107) to the fact that after the commencement of the HRA 1998, 'a victim would be able to bring proceedings in the courts against a public authority and the courts would be empowered to award damages.' Thus there is no need now to consider Article 13 ECHR at all. On a repeat of the facts of *Z*, the finding of a breach of Article 3 would itself lead directly to a substantial award of damages by way of 'just satisfaction'. On these facts, there is no difficulty in establishing the public body that is responsible — it is the local social services department.

Attention has already been drawn to the fact that the European Court was willing to consider detailed medical reports when making awards under both the pecuniary and non-pecuniary heads in a manner at least similar to a UK domestic court. It seems highly likely that UK courts will carry this process further. It is to be noted that Lady Justice Arden, who was sitting as an ad hoc judge, dissented from the majority approach to non-pecuniary damages (which was to award all four siblings the same amount without distinction) in favour of a more detailed assessment of the expert evidence. It seems likely that a common law court would be sympathetic to her approach.

In *Z* itself, the case that the UK domestic system would breach Article 13 ECHR if it did not incorporate a remedy including damages was particularly strong because of the importance of the Article breached, as is clear from the passages cited above. However, in *TP and KM* v *UK* (App. No. 28945/95) (a case in which judgment was given on the same day as *Z*), the Court followed a similar approach in a child-care case where the breach involved Article 8 ECHR. At para. 107, it varied the formulation in *Z* to state:

> The Court considers that, where an arguable breach of one or more rights of the Convention is in issue, there should be available to the victim a mechanism for establishing any liability of State officials or bodies for that breach. Furthermore, in appropriate cases, compensation for the pecuniary and non-pecuniary damage flowing from the breach should in principle be available as part of the range of redress.

The Court went on to reject the UK Government's contention that this was a case which did not require compensation. The facts that had led to the finding of breach of Article 8 (summarized in paras 9–28), which concerned a failure to take the initiative in revealing a video relevant to abuse allegations to the parent (see paras 80–3), involved a delay (or a possible delay; see para. 115) in returning the child home. On these facts, the Court said (at para. 108), that the ultimate court order returning the child did not provide an effective remedy:

> It did not provide redress for the psychological damage allegedly flowing from the separation over this period . . . It does not agree with the Government that pecuniary compensation would not provide redress. If, as is alleged, psychiatric damage occurred, there may well have been elements of medical costs as well as significant pain and suffering to be addressed.

The Court ordered payment of £10,000 damages to each applicant.

Once again, there is a short concurring opinion from LJ Arden which differs on the amount of damages. Stating that in the light of the review of domestic damages levels by the Court of Appeal in *Heil* v *Rankin and others* [2000] 2 WLR 1173, reliance could be placed on levels of domestic awards, and that awards of less than £10,000 did not require any increase, she would have awarded £6,000. It is clear that she would have taken into account elements that would not have sounded in a domestic award of damages for psychological injury. Arden LJ said:

> In assessing just satisfaction in this case there are, as explained in the Court's judgment, factors to be taken into account apart from injury to health. They include the loss of an opportunity of an earlier reunion and . . . feelings of frustration and injustice.

3.5.5   The decision of the court of appeal in *JD and others* v *East Berkshire Community Health Trust and others* [2004] 2 WLR 58

These cases actually concerned civil actions arising out of events before commencement of the Human Rights Act 1998. Each case involved accusations of abusing a child made against a parent by the professionals concerned for the welfare of that child. In each case the accusations proved to be unfounded. In these cases a parent claims damages for psychiatric harm alleged to have been caused by the false accusations or their consequences. There was one claim by a child.

Necessarily the claims were pleaded in negligence. The argument that is relevant here was to the effect that the decision *X* v *Bedfordshire* was no longer good law because of the impact of *Z*. The Court also had to consider the impact of domestic decisions in *Barrett* v *Enfield London Borough Council* [2001] 2 AC 550; *S* v *Gloucestershire County Council* [2001] 1 Fam 313 and *Phelps* v *Hillingdon London Borough Council* [2001] 2 AC 619. It summarized its view of their effect in para. 49 of the decision in the following terms: 'Lord Slynn in *Barrett* stated that *Bedfordshire* established that decisions by local authorities whether or not to take a child into care were not reviewable by way of a claim in negligence. We consider that the effect of *Barrett* and the other decisions . . . is to restrict the effect of *Bedfordshire* to that core proposition'.

So the starting point was that there was no domestic duty of care in relation to decisions whether or not to take a child into care. The Court went on to consider the impact of *Z*: *Attorney General* v *Prince* [1998] 1 NZLR 262 and the Privy Council decision in *B and others* (unreported, 16 July 2003), together with the post-*Z* Strasbourg decisions of *E and others* v *UK* [2003] 1 FLR 348; *P, C and S* v *UK* [2002] 35 EHRR 31 and *Venema* v *The Netherlands* [2003] FLR 552. It decided that, as far as the issue of the duty of care owed to a child was concerned, 'the decision in *Bedfordshire* cannot survive the Human Rights Act'. The convention rights of the child might be breached either by a decision to take the child into care or a decision not to do so. Given the scope of potential investigations under the HRA 1998, there was no 'valid reason of policy for preserving a limitation of the common law duty of care which was not otherwise justified. On the contrary, the absence of an alternative remedy for children who were victims of abuse before October 2000 militates in favour of the recognition of a common law duty of care' (see para. 83).

However, the Court did not take the same approach to the existence of a common law duty to the parents, applying similar reasoning to that of the Privy Council in *B* v *Attorney General*. That had included the following statement:

. . . their Lordships consider no common law duty was owed to the father. He stands in a very different position. He was the alleged perpetrator of an abuse. In an enquiry into an abuse allegation the interests of the alleged perpetrator and of the children as the alleged victims are poles apart. Those conducting the inquiry must act in good faith throughout. But to impose a common law duty of care on the department and the individual professionals in favour of the alleged victims . . . and, at one and the same time, in favour of the alleged perpetrator would not be satisfactory.

This conclusion does not exclude the possibility, post-October 2000, of damages under the HRA 1998 payable in favour of the parents (see para. 80 of the Court of Appeal judgment). The facts in an alleged wrongful removal in breach of Article 8 would have to be examined to see whether, on the particular facts, the action was 'necessary in a democratic society'. In neither situation (parent or child) does the action under the Act coincide exactly with any common law action based on a duty of care (see para. 85).

Chapter Four

The Local Authority Administrative and Constitutional Framework and the Human Rights Act 1998

James Maurici and Kate Olley

There are a number of aspects of the administrative and constitutional framework of local authorities that need to be considered in the light of the ECHR and the HRA 1998. For a general account of the legal and administrative framework governing local authorities see chapters 1–5 of Part 1 of the *Encyclopedia of Local Government Law* (Sweet & Maxwell).

The particular matters considered in relation to the ECHR and the HRA 1998 in this chapter are:

(a) local elections;
(b) politically restricted employment;
(c) the Model Codes of Conduct for councillors;
(d) the personal liability of members and councillors;
(e) decision-making; and
(f) powers.

4.1 LOCAL ELECTIONS

It is necessary to consider the applicability of Convention rights in the context of local government elections. Save for the House of Commons, local authorities are the only element of government in England to be the subject of election by universal suffrage.

Under the Local Government Act 1972, individuals have the right to vote in the periodic county and district council elections for the area in which they live, in accordance with the provisions of the Representation of the People Acts. Part IV of the Local Government Act 2000 contains new powers intended to enable the system for elections to local authorities, in particular their timing and frequency, to be rationalized across England and Wales. At present, the timing of the electoral cycle varies according to the type of local authority concerned.

4.1.1   ECHR protection

Article 3 of Protocol 1 ECHR, provides for the right to free elections:

> The High Contracting Parties undertake to hold free elections at reasonable intervals by secret ballot, under conditions which will ensure the free expression of the opinion of the people in the choice of the legislature.

This Article is incorporated in Sch. 1 to the HRA 1998.

The guarantee of free elections held in the manner provided for by Article 3 of Protocol 1 is clearly a matter at the very heart of the democratic system. The European Commission decided the *Greek Case* (1969) 12 Yearbook 1, at 179, in recognition that Article 3 of Protocol 1 presupposes the existence of a representative legislature, elected at reasonable intervals, to be the basis of a democratic society.

The European Court of Human Rights, in *Mathieu-Mohin and Clerfayt* v *Belgium* (1988) 10 EHRR 1, took as a starting point for its interpretation of Article 3 of Protocol 1 ECHR the fact that, according to the Preamble to the ECHR, fundamental rights and freedoms are best maintained by 'an effective political democracy'. Article 3 of Protocol 1 enshrines a 'characteristic principle of democracy' and is 'accordingly of prime importance in the Convention system'. The case of *Mathieu-Mohin* was the first in which the European Court was asked to determine complaints under Article 3 of Protocol 1, and it took the opportunity to indicate the meaning it ascribed to the Article (at paras 46–54). It approved the concept of subjective rights of participation, specifically the right to vote and the right to stand for election to the legislature.

The right in Article 3 of Protocol 1 is phrased in terms of an imposition on states rather than as a right of individuals. In *Mathieu-Mohin*, the European Court recognized that whereas nearly all the other substantive clauses in the ECHR and its Protocols are expressed in individual terms, such as 'Everyone has the right' or 'No one shall', Article 3 of Protocol 1 is different because it uses the phrase 'The High Contracting Parties undertake'. However, the European Court did not consider that it was correct to infer thereby that the Article did not give rise to individual rights and freedoms 'directly secured to anyone' within those parties' jurisdiction but solely to obligations between states. It found that such a restrictive interpretation did not stand up to scrutiny and held, rather, that the 'inter-state colouring' of the wording of the Article does not reflect any difference of substance from the other substantive clauses in the ECHR and its Protocols. The European Court held that the reason for this:

. . . would seem to lie rather in the desire to give greater solemnity to the commitment undertaken and in the fact that the primary obligation in the field concerned is not one of abstention or non-interference, as with the majority of civil and political rights, but one of adoption by the state of positive measures to 'hold' democratic elections.

4.1.2   Extent of the right

The right conferred by Article 3 of Protocol 1 ECHR is not absolute. In *Mathieu-Mohin* the European Court of Human Rights ruled that there was room for implied limitations in the Article and that contracting states had a wide margin of appreciation in this sphere, although it was for the European Court in the last resort to determine whether the requirements of the Article had been complied with. Although contracting states might make rights to vote and to stand for elections subject to conditions, the European Court would have to satisfy itself that the conditions did not curtail the rights in question to such an extent as to impair their very essence and deprive them of their effectiveness. Further, they must be imposed in pursuit of a legitimate aim and the means employed must not be disproportionate. In particular, such conditions must not thwart 'the free expression of the opinion of the people in the choice of the legislature'.

The undertaking of the contracting states in Article 3 of Protocol 1 to hold free elections is taken by the European Court to imply a recognition of universal suffrage. However, as the Court held in *X* v *Germany* (1967) 10 Yearbook 336, it does not follow that the Article accords the right unreservedly to every single individual to take part in elections. It is generally recognized that certain limited groups of individuals may be disqualified from voting. The question is whether such disqualifications affect the 'free expression of the opinion of the people'. The European Court found that restrictions on the right to vote of convicted prisoners serving their sentences did *not* so affect the people's expression. See also *Pearson* v *Secretary of State for the Home Department* [2001] HRLR 39, where the Court found that the disqualification of prisoners from voting at local and general elections was lawful and not in contravention of the ECHR, even in respect of post-tariff discretionary 'lifers'. Although an individual disenfranchisement obviously impaired that individual's right to vote, Article 3 of Protocol 1 was really concerned with 'the wider question of universal franchise.'

The Court held in *Mathieu-Mohin* that Article 3 of Protocol 1 ECHR does not create any obligation to introduce a specific system, such as proportional representation or majority voting with one or two ballots. It recognized that here too the contracting states have a wide margin of appreciation, given that their legislation on the matter varies from place to place and from time to time. For the purposes of Article 3 of Protocol 1, an electoral system must be assessed in the light of the political evolution of the country concerned; features that would be unacceptable in the context of one system may accordingly be justified in the context of another, at least so long as the chosen system provides for the conditions which will ensure the 'free expression of the opinion of the people in the choice of the legislature'. Thus in *Liberal Party, R and P v UK* (1980) 21 DR 211, the applicants contended that when read together with Article 14 ECHR, the United Kingdoms's 'first past the post' electoral system violated Article 3 of Protocol 1 because it tended to favour the two major political parties in the United Kingdom. The European Commission said:

> Article 3 of the First Protocol may not be interpreted as an Article which imposes a particular kind of electoral system which would guarantee that the total number of votes cast for each candidate or group must be reflected in the composition of the legislative assembly. Both the simple majority system and the proportional representation system are, therefore, compatible with this Article.

Article 14 did not protect 'equal voting influence for all voters'.

In the European Court, where the concept of the margin of appreciation is in play, it was clear from the leading cases, such as *Mathieu-Mohin*, that the Court was willing to find a breach of Article 3 of Protocol 1 ECHR only in exceptional cases such as the *Greek Case*, in which the circumstances were that, following a change of government, political parties were prohibited; scheduled elections had been cancelled; and political activities as a whole were prohibited. No elections had been held and parliamentary democracy had been abolished, so that there was at the time no legal basis in Greece for the holding of free elections through which the people could express their opinions in the choice of the legislature.

The United Kingdom was held in breach on just one occasion — *Matthews* v *UK* (1999) 28 EHRR 361 (see 4.1.3). It is likely that domestic courts will adopt a similar approach to the Article.

4.1.3   Applicability

Article 3 of Protocol 1 ECHR applies only to election to bodies that can be defined as a 'legislature', or at least to one of its chambers if it has two or more. (Judge Pinheiro Farinha, in his concurring opinion in *Mathieu-Mohin* (at p. 22), did not think that the wording 'or at least one of its chambers if it has two or more' went far enough. He considered it to be 'inadequate and dangerous': 'As it stands, it would allow of a system at variance with "the opinion of the people in the choice of the legislature" and might even lead to a corporative, elitist or class system which did not respect democracy'. He suggested that the Court should instead have said 'or at least one of its chambers if it has two or more, *on the twofold condition that the majority of the membership of the legislature is elected and that the chamber or chambers whose members are not elected does or do not have greater powers than the chamber that is freely elected by secret ballot*' (emphasis added).

In order to determine the applicability of Article 3 of Protocol 1 ECHR in the local authority context it is necessary to consider the meaning of 'legislature'. The European Court in *Mathieu-Mohin* (and again in *Matthews* v *UK*, below) held that the word 'legislature' does not necessarily mean only the national parliament. It is to be interpreted in the light of the constitutional structure of the state in question. Thus the applicability of Article 3 of Protocol 1 can feasibly extend beyond elections to the national legislature to locally elected bodies.

In *Matthews* v *UK* (1999) 28 EHRR 361, the European Parliament was held to constitute part of the 'legislature' of Gibraltar for the purposes of Article 3 of Protocol 1, so that the United Kingdom was responsible for securing the rights guaranteed by the Article in Gibraltar in respect of elections to the European Parliament as well as purely domestic elections. However, in *X* v *UK* (1972) 6 DR 13, which concerned the cancellation of local elections in Northern Ireland, the European Commission considered the status of local authorities in Northern Ireland and decided that they were not part of the legislature. The Commission took note of the fact that insofar as those authorities had a legislative function, it was confined to the making of by-laws applicable within their areas and those powers were rigidly limited by statute. The authorities had no powers to make rules other than in accordance with the powers conferred by Parliament.

The Commission similarly found in *Edwards* v *UK* (1986) 8 EHRR 96 that the former Greater London Council (GLC) did not form part of the legislature of the United Kingdom, so that the cancellation of elections to it could not raise an issue under Article 3 of Protocol 1. The Commission took into account the fact that the constitutional arrangements of the United Kingdom did not authorize the exercise of legislative powers by subordinate bodies. It found that as a matter of British constitutional law, Parliament, as the elected representative of the British people, could therefore vote to abolish the GLC if that course of action were to recommend itself. The absolute constitutional authority which the British Parliament was able to exercise was indicative of the subordinate and subsidiary nature of the GLC.

The Commission looked at the specific powers enjoyed by the GLC (the main sources of which were the London Government Act 1963 and the Local Government Act (LGA) 1972) and noted that the GLC was a body corporate created by statute and could only do such things as were expressly or impliedly authorized by statute or by subordinate legislation. It was true that the GLC was specifically authorized to do anything calculated to facilitate the discharge of any of its statutory functions, and that it was a repository of extensive powers of a predominantly administrative nature concerning the organization and provision of local services. However, most of those powers were granted by statute or other subordinate legislation which defined closely and restrictively their field of application. Other powers required the approval and consent of a superior executive authority before they might be exercised. Still others could be exercised by the GLC, but such exercise could not become effective until approved by a confirming authority.

Taking into account the powers exercised by the GLC and its relationship to the UK Parliament, the Commission found that, despite the significant scope of its functions, the GLC could not properly be said to form part of the 'legislature' of the United Kingdom. It did not possess an inherent primary rule-making power, and those powers which had been delegated to it by Parliament were exercised subject to Parliament's ultimate control.

These same principles can be seen to have been applied in *Booth-Clibborn* v *UK* (1985) 43 DR 236, the Commission held that English metropolitan county councils could not be considered as legislative bodies. Indeed, the Commission repeated verbatim much of the observation made in *Edwards*. Certain of the Councils' activities required approval or consent. Such powers as they had to make by-laws were derivative and defined by statute or subordinate legislation. They were subject to the doctrine of *ultra vires*. Parliament, having delegated its powers to them, could limit the scope of those powers, and indeed completely abolish the councils themselves. It was not sufficient to constitute a legislature that the councils enjoyed the power to legislate in ways which affected the individuals living in their area.

In *Clerfayt, Legros* v *Belgium* 42 DR 212, the European Commission found that Article 3 of Protocol 1 ECHR was inapplicable because Belgian municipal councils were organs of local authority with power to make rules and by-laws *but not laws*, and so they did not form part of the 'legislature'. The Commission held that '*the power to make by-laws* which is conferred on municipal councils in many countries *is to be distinguished from legislative power* . . . even though legislative power is not restricted to the national parliament alone' (emphasis added).

The test for whether a body constitutes a 'legislature' or part thereof for the purposes of Article 3 of Protocol 1 has two aspects:

(a)   whether the body has an independent (or inherent) power to issue decrees with the force of law; and

(b)   a consideration of the nature of the laws made by the body.

The key is that Article 3 of Protocol 1 does not appear to apply to elected local government bodies in non-federal states. Despite its power to make by-laws, a council is an executive rather than a legislative body. It has no powers other than those conferred by statute (see *Hazell* v *Hammersmith and Fulham London Borough Council* [1992] 2 AC 1. In the UK unitary system of government, with its emphasis on the sovereignty of Parliament, local government bodies, despite being elected by universal suffrage, come under the umbrella of Parliament for the purposes of the right conferred and protected by Article 3 of Protocol 1. By contrast, the powers of the Belgian regional councils are devolved from central government, so that the challenges in *Mathieu-Mohin* and *X, Y and Z* v *Germany*

(1976) 5 DR 90, and in *X* v *Austria* (1976) 6 DR 120 (concerning the German and Austrian *Länder*), were not inadmissible by reason that the bodies did not form part of the legislature. Accordingly, it is arguable that the Scottish Parliament and Northern Ireland Assembly constitute 'legislatures' for ECHR purposes; but the Greater London Authority, for the above reasons, is unlikely to.

It is to be noted that the challenge in *Pearson* v *Secretary of State for the Home Department* [2001] HRLR 39, applied equally to disqualification from voting in local elections as to general elections. However, the focus of the challenge concerned the individual's right to participate, as opposed to participation in elections to a specific body, thus the question of the applicability of Article 3 of Protocol 1 in the local context appears not to have arisen.

4.2   POLITICALLY RESTRICTED APPOINTMENTS

The Local Government and Housing Act 1989 (as amended) provides for restrictions on the political activities of officers holding what are called 'politically restricted posts'. The term 'person holding a politically restricted post' is defined by s. 2(1) of the 1989 Act. It consists of three broad categories of local government officer, as follows:

(a)   Officers who hold certain posts specified in s. 2(1)(a)–(f) of the Act, namely the head of the authority's paid service (s. 2(1)(a)); the chief officers (s. 2(1)(b) and (c)); the deputy chief officers (s. 2(1)(d)); the monitoring officer (s. 2(1)(e)); and assistants for political groups (s. 2(1)(f)). There are an estimated 12,000 officers in this category according to the Government's memorial for the European Court (*Ahmed* v *UK* (2000) 29 EHRR 1).

(b)   Those local government officers whose annual rate of remuneration exceeds a prescribed level and whose posts have not been exempted from the operation of the Local Government Officers (Political Restrictions) Regulations 1990. The Government, in *Ahmed*, estimated that there were approximately 28,000 officers whose salary exceeded the prescribed level. However, in its view, the number of officers who were actually subject to the 1990 Regulations was considerably fewer than 28,000, since a significant number had either been granted an exemption, or would have been entitled to one had they applied.

(c)   As defined by s. 2(2)(c) of the Act, those local government officers whose annual rate of remuneration is less than the prescribed level but whose duties consist in or involve one or both of the duties identified in s. 2(3), namely (i) giving advice on a regular basis to the authority itself, to any committee or sub-committee of the authority or to any joint committee on which the authority is represented; or (ii) speaking on behalf of the authority on a regular basis to journalists or broadcasters. According to the Government's memorial in *Ahmed*, there are an estimated 7,000 officers in this category.

Headmasters and teachers are among those exempt from the operation of the Local Government Officers (Political Restrictions) Regulations 1990 by reason of s. 2(10) of the 1989 Act (note the contrast with the case of *Vogt*, below).

In *Ahmed*, the 1990 Regulations were challenged before the European Court of Human Rights by a number of applicants holding politically restricted posts, who alleged breaches of Articles 10 and 11 ECHR and Article 3 of Protocol 1. Mr Ahmed, a local authority solicitor, was unable to stand as a Labour candidate in municipal elections. The European Court held that although the 1990 Regulations constituted an interference with Article 10 ECHR, this was justified as being in pursuit of the legitimate interests of protecting the rights of others — namely, council members and the electorate — to effective political democracy at the local level, and as being necessary in a democratic society (since the Widdicombe Committee, whose recommendations led to the enactment of the Regulations, had identified a pressing social need to reduce the risk of abuse of power by local government officers). The 1990 Regulations did not represent a disproportionate interference with Mr Ahmed's rights, given the margin of appreciation enjoyed by the state. The European Court referred to the need to maintain the bond of trust between elected members and a permanent corps of local government officers. Its analysis of the 1990 Regulations and the reasons for their introduction is full. It also rejected, for the same reasons that it rejected the challenge under Article 10, the allegation of a violation of Article 11 ECHR.

The European Court unanimously found that there was no breach of Article 3 of Protocol 1. It emphasized that Article 3, Protocol 1 rights were not absolute; that conditions could be imposed on the exercise of such rights; and that restrictions on the right to contest seats at elections were justified as being for the legitimate aim of securing the political impartiality of public servants. In any event the 1990 Regulations only applied so long as a politically restricted post was held.

The European Court has also considered issues relating to politically restricted appointments in another case, *Vogt v Germany* (1996) 21 EHRR 205, in which a teacher was dismissed from her secondary school teaching post on account of her active membership of the German Communist Party. This was considered to be incompatible with her duty as a civil servant to uphold the free democratic constitutional system. The European Court found that it could not but conclude that the interference with Mrs Vogt's Article 10 rights pursued a legitimate aim, as the duty of political loyalty imposed on civil servants was founded on the notion that the civil service was the guarantor of the constitution and democracy. This notion had a special importance in Germany, taking into account its recent history, as the

German constitution was based on the principle of a 'democracy capable of defending itself' (para. 51). However, the Court found overwhelmingly that there had been a violation of Article 10, and by the narrowest of majorities that there had been a violation of Article 11, as the reasons put forward to justify interference with Mrs Vogt's right to freedom of expression were not sufficient to establish convincingly that it was necessary in a democratic society to dismiss her, and her dismissal was found to be disproportionate to the legitimate aim pursued.

4.3   THE MODEL CODES OF CONDUCT

Part III of the Local Government Act (LGA) 2000 provides a new statutory framework governing the conduct of members of local authorities.

Under s. 50(1) of the LGA 2000 the Secretary of State is empowered, by order, to 'issue a model code as regards the conduct which is expected of members . . . of relevant authorities in England'. This model code of conduct was to replace the National Code of Local Government Conduct.

On 5 November 2001, four model codes ('the Model Codes') for the various different local authorities were issued. Section 51 of the LGA 2000 required authorities to adopt a code of conduct which had to incorporate the mandatory provisions of the appropriate Model Code and could also incorporate the optional provisions therein and other provisions consistent with the Model Code. This had to be done within six months of the making of the Model Codes, thus authorities had until 5 May 2002 to adopt a code of conduct, after which date the appropriate Model Code would be automatically applied in the case of those who had not adopted a code (s. 51(5)).

Section 52 required all members, before the end of the period of two months after the authority's adoption of a code, to give to the authority a written undertaking that in performing their functions they would observe the code of conduct, failing which they would cease to be a member at the end of that period.

The Model Codes deal with a number of matters that might be said to touch upon rights protected by the HRA 1998.

The general obligations imposed by the codes include:

(a)   a prohibition on the disclosure of confidential information;

(b)   a requirement that members must not in their official capacity, or in any other circumstance, conduct themselves in a manner which could reasonably be regarded as bringing their office or authority into disrepute;

(c)   a requirement that members do not in their official capacity, or any other circumstance, use their position as a member to improperly confer on or secure for themselves or any other person an advantage or disadvantage.

As regards interests, there is a requirement that personal interests must be disclosed. Personal interests are defined widely in the Model Codes extending to any matter which could reasonably be regarded as affecting the member to a greater extent than others in that area.

There is also a requirement that a member with a prejudicial interest (as defined by the Model Codes) in any matter must:

(a)   withdraw from the room or chamber where a meeting is being held whenever it becomes apparent that the matter is being considered at that meeting, unless he or she has obtained a dispensation from the authority's standard's committee;

(b)   not exercise executive functions in relation to that matter; and

(c)   not seek improperly to influence a decision about that matter.

A prejudicial interest is one which a member of the public with knowledge of the relevant facts would reasonably regard as so significant that it is likely to prejudice the member's judgment of the public interest.

The Queen on the application of Paul Richardson v *North Yorkshire County Council* [2003] 18 EGCS 113 was a challenge by way of judicial review to the requirement under the codes for a member with a prejudicial interest to withdraw from a meeting. The challenge was brought alleging a breach of Articles 6 and 8 ECHR. The case concerned a councillor whose prejudicial interest arose from the location of his property close to the site of a proposed development in respect of which his council was considering an application for planning permission. It was argued on his behalf that on the proper construction of the code of conduct, Mr Richardson was not bound to withdraw even if he had a prejudicial interest, since he was not a member of the decision-making committee and/or he was entitled to attend in his personal capacity to make representations. It was also argued that if, on the proper construction of the code of conduct, he was bound to withdraw, the code was unlawful and in breach of his Convention rights.

Richards J did not need to decide whether Article 6 ECHR conferred relevant rights on Mr Richardson, but found that the application of the code of conduct involved no breach of Convention rights. The material provisions of the code were fully consistent with the aim of ensuring fairness and impartiality in the decision-making process. It was for the Secretary of State to balance the competing interests which are always at stake in that process so as to achieve fairness overall in enacting the provisions of the code, and the result was well within the margin of discretionary judgment allowed to him. The different treatment of the councillor and the developer, who had the opportunity to make oral representations where Mr Richardson did not, was based on the legitimate aim of preserving public confidence in the system, and the restriction placed on Mr Richardson was a proportionate measure. Although it was argued that it was not consistent with the right to respect for Mr Richardson's home under Article 8 to deny him the same chance to be present and to speak at the meeting as others whose homes were affected, Richards J stated that there was no Article 8(1) right to a hearing, and this argument failed in the light of the conclusion reached on the Article 6 argument.

No allegation of a breach of Article 10 ECHR was pursued in *Richardson*. As to the scope for a challenge to the requirement to withdraw based on Article 10, see *Buchner and others* v *Austria* (App. No. 22096/93). The applicants, all members of a community council, complained that they had not been sent in advance the community budget project for that year, even though they had insisted on this after a similar incident in the year before. They requested that the session either be adjourned or the budget item dropped from the agenda, requests which were rejected by majority. The applicants therefore withdrew from discussion what they had claimed was an unlawful decision on the budget project. When they intended to return to participate in the discussion of other items on the agenda the mayor did not re-admit them. The applicants argued that their rights under Articles 10 and 11 had been violated.

The European Commission stated that the mayor's decision not to re-admit the applicants to a particular meeting which they had chosen to leave could not be found to amount to an interference with the rights invoked in circumstances where the applicants had not alleged that before deliberately leaving the meeting they had been arbitrarily prevented from expressing their views on the agenda items nor that at a subsequent meeting they were prevented from expressing their political or other opinions.

It is significant that in *Richardson* Richards J found that it would have been open to Mr Richardson to attend the meeting solely in his personal capacity (although steps would have had to be taken to ensure that the limited basis of his attendance was abundantly clear to all), and the facts of the case were that he was able to arrange for others to put forward any points he wished to make.

One other aspect of the codes which might be objectionable in ECHR terms is the requirement that members must not in their official capacity, or in any other circumstance, conduct themselves in a manner which could reasonably be regarded as bringing their office or authority into disrepute. The extension of the requirement beyond a member's official capacity to private or personal behaviour may well raise issues in relation to Articles 8 and 10. The uncertainty as to what conduct is prohibited may also raise issues.

In *Hashman* v *UK* (2000) 30 EHRR 241, two hunt saboteurs whose appeals against binding-over orders and payment orders of £100 were dismissed, applied to the European Court of Human Rights, complaining that their rights to freedom of expression, as guaranteed under Article 10 ECHR, had been violated. It was contended that the description of their behaviour as being *contra bonos mores* was so broadly defined that it failed to comply with the requirement in Article 10(2) that any interference with freedom of expression must be 'prescribed by law'. The

European Court upheld the complaint, holding that the order by which the applicants were bound over was not legally prescribed as required under Article 10(2). Any interference with the freedom of expression necessitated the utmost scrutiny. The European Court disagreed with the UK Government that the definition of behaviour *contra bonos mores* as 'wrong rather than right in the judgment of the majority of contemporary fellow citizens' contained an objective element equivalent to conduct 'likely to cause annoyance'.

4.4   PERSONAL LIABILITY OF MEMBERS AND COUNCILLORS

Another area in which ECHR issues may arise concerns the statutory procedure of audit and surcharge, which provided for a sanction against senior officers and members of local authorities whose unlawful expenditure or wilful misconduct causes loss to taxpayers.

For many years, provision has been made in local government legislation to protect ratepayers against losses caused by unlawful expenditure or wilful misconduct on the part of members or senior officers of local authorities. Procedures were laid down for the audit of local authority accounts and, in the event of unlawful expenditure or wilful misconduct by a member or senior officer, for the surcharge of that member or officer on a certificate issued by the auditor.

The relevant provisions used to be contained in Part III of the Local Government Finance Act 1982. They were repealed by and re-enacted in the Audit Commission Act 1998, s. 17 of which provided for a power to apply to the court for a declaration that an item of account was unlawful, and s. 18 of the 1998 Act provided for the recovery of unaccounted amounts.

Part V of the LGA 2000 abolishes surcharge and the system of prohibition orders, and provides for a new system of advisory notices to enable auditors to seek a court decision on the legality of a proposed course of action by a local authority (see s. 91 of the LGA 2000, which adds s. 19A to the Audit Commission Act 1998 and revokes ss. 20–23 of that Act).

Section 90 of the LGA 2000 amends the Audit Commission Act 1998 so that the sections which enabled external auditors to recover financial losses incurred by a body subject to an audit are omitted. Section 90 is now in force. First, s. 18 and most of s. 17 of the Audit Commission Act 1998 were disapplied from the day an authority's code of conduct was adopted or applied to it until 27 July 2002 (reg. 4(1) of the Local Authorities (Model Code of Conduct) England Order 2001 (SI 2001/3575)), then s. 90 of the LGA 2000 and the parts of Sch. 6 to the 2000 Act repealing ss. 17 and 18 of the Audit Commission Act 1998 were brought into force on 27 July 2002 (reg. 2 of the Local Government Act 2000 (Commencement Order) (No. 8) 2002 (SI 2002/1718)).

In *Porter* v *Magill* [2002] AC 357, the House of Lords gave consideration to the provisions of the Local Government Finance Act 1982 in the context of a human rights challenge raised by Shirley Porter as part of her legal proceedings, seeking to overturn the auditor's certification of her responsibility (jointly and severally with others) for approximately £31,000,000 as a result of wilful misconduct.

The House of Lords considered that the proceedings were civil not criminal in nature for the purposes of Article 6 ECHR (see paras 83–6 of Lord Hope's speech). The view taken was that proceedings under s. 20 of the Local Government Finance Act 1982 were not punitive in character but compensatory and regulatory, the measure of compensation being the amount of loss suffered. It was noted that there was no provision for a fine or penalty by way of imprisonment and that, therefore, the proceedings before the auditor were civil, and not in the nature of a criminal charge.

The House of Lords went on to hold that:

(a)   on its proper construction, Article 6(1) ECHR created separate, though closely related rights, which required separate consideration;

(b)   although the auditor's role within the context of the Local Government Finance Act 1982 required him to act as investigator, prosecutor and judge, the requirement of the tribunal's independence and impartiality was met by the right of appeal from his decision provided by s. 20(3) by way of a full rehearing by the appellate court; and

(c)   since the Divisional Court's conduct of the appeals satisfied the requirement of independence and impartiality, that element of Porter's rights under Article 6(1) were fully protected.

Finally, in relation to the HRA 1998, it was held by the House of Lords that the right to a determination of a person's civil rights within a reasonable time was, on a proper interpretation of Article 6(1), an independent right which was not to be regarded simply as part of an overriding right to a fair trial and did not require the complainant to show himself prejudiced by the delay. However, having regard to the complexity of the case and the volume of evidence before the Divisional Court, to the immense scope of the auditor's investigations, and to his constant activity in the pursuit of information, the proceedings did not exceed the reasonable time requirement in Article 6(1); and accordingly, Porter's Convention rights were not infringed and they suffered no unfairness at common law.

In *Westminster City Council* v *Porter* [2003] 2 WLR 420, Westminster City Council sought summary judgment in its claim against Porter, for breach of trust. Westminster maintained that as a result of Porter's wilful misconduct the authority had incurred losses of approximately £26 million. Porter argued that it was appropriate to grant a stay of execution pending her application to the European Court of Human Rights. Hart J, rejecting that argument, granted the application for summary judgment. He held that there was no basis for the imposition of a stay pending Porter's application to the European Court since the European Court of Human Rights was not an appellate court in the English jurisdiction, (see *Locabail (UK) Ltd* v *Waldorf Investment Corp (No. 4)* [2000] HRLR 623).

The repeals brought about by the LGA 2000 are prospective, so that if conduct causing loss predates the date of repeal of the surcharge provisions, the prospect of surcharge would apply in such a case.

4.5   DECISION-MAKING

It seems tolerably clear from the Court of Appeal's decision in *Adlard* v *Secretary of State for the Environment, Transport and the Regions* [2002] 1 WLR 2515 that even where a decision to be made by a local authority engages Article 6 ECHR, i.e. it is determinative of someone's civil rights and obligations, it is not ordinarily required to accord a person so affected an oral hearing. *Adlard* was a planning case and is considered further in Chapter Five.

Simon Brown LJ said (at para. 32):

> The remedy of judicial review in my judgment amply enables the court to correct any injustice it perceives in an individual case. If, in short, the court were satisfied that exceptionally, on the facts of a particular case, the local planning authority had acted unfairly or unreasonably in denying an objector any or any sufficient oral hearing, the court would quash the decision and require such a hearing to be given. This presents no difficulties . . .

This recognizes that it is only in exceptional cases that an oral hearing will be required.

Adlard was also cited by Moses J in his judgment in the non-planning case of *R (on the application of Ali, Mohammed and Mohammed)* v *Birmingham City Council and Birmingham City Council Social Services and the Secretary of State for Health* [2002] HLR 51 and by Maurice Kay J in *AFP Westminster City Council* v *Mayor of London* [2003] BLGR 511 in relation to the congestion charging scheme.

There is nothing inconsistent with the HRA 1998 or the ECHR in the delegation of decision-making in accordance with the LGA 1972.

One question that is often asked is to what extent HRA 1998 issues need to be expressly addressed in officer's reports. There is now some guidance on these issues.

In *R (on the application of Malster)* v *Ipswich Borough Council* [2002] PLCR 14 (Sullivan J) and 31 October 2001 (CA) there was a challenge to the grant of planning permission for the redevelopment of the North Stand at Ipswich Town's Portman Road stadium by a local resident. It was alleged that the shadowing effect of the new stand on the Claimant's garden would infringe Article 8(1)

ECHR. Third party objectors had raised Article 8 in their representations to the Borough Council. However, nowhere in the officers report (or elsewhere) were human rights or more specifically Article 8 addressed by the Council. Sullivan J did not consider this to be a problem. He said at para. 88 that Article 8(2):

> . . . required the local planning authority to carry out a balancing exercise between the claimant's interest in the enjoyment of her home (in this particular case her garden) . . . and the public interest in removing an outmoded stand and replacing it with a new one . . . That is precisely what the Council did. There is no suggestion that Mr. Miller's report omitted any relevant impact upon the claimant or that any of her concerns were ignored in the report.

The learned Judge reached a similar conclusion on Article 1, Protocol 1 (para. 89) and the Court of Appeal expressly approved of Sullivan J's approach. Pill LJ rejected the submission that on the facts before the Court the balancing exercise required under planning law did not involve the same considerations as the balancing exercise required by Article 8(2).

Notwithstanding this, it seems to us that it is good practice that where HRA 1998 issues are raised or are otherwise relevant to a decision, this is a matter that should be expressly addressed in the officers report.

4.6 POWERS

There may be circumstances in which a local authority's exercise of its powers pursuant to s. 111 of the LGA 1972 or indeed Part I of the LGA 2000 raises issues under the ECHR. The principal power conferred under Part I of the LGA 2000 is contained in s. 2(1), which provides the authority with the power to do anything which they consider is likely to achieve the promotion or improvement of the economic, social and environmental well-being of their area. The three heads of wellbeing are very wide and give an authority considerable discretion. The powers authorise activities not expressly permitted previously and which in the past local authorities have had to undertake using a variety of mechanisms, including extensive reliance on the incidental powers contained in s. 111 of the LGA 1972.

The case of *R* v *Brentwood Borough Council, ex parte Peck* (1997) *The Times* 18 December, decided before the coming into force of the HRA 1998, concerned an application for judicial review of Brentwood Borough Council's disclosure to local and national media organizations of a film taken on the Council's closed-circuit television (CCTV), installed for the purpose of promoting the prevention of crime. The applicant at the time had been suffering from depression and attempted to kill himself by cutting his wrists with a kitchen knife. He had walked down the High Street in the town centre of Brentwood with a large kitchen knife in his hand and the incident was picked up on Council's CCTV system. The images did not show the attempted suicide but identified the applicant brandishing the knife in a public place.

The Council found its CCTV system to be very successful in reducing crime in the High Street area and decided to have a regular press release informing the public of what the system was achieving. It also decided to co-operate with outside persons and bodies in the preparation of factual programmes concerning the CCTV system. The incident showing the applicant was featured in a press release issued by the Council about its CCTV system. Anglia TV then sought, and were supplied with, footage which was then broadcast in their news programme. At the Council's request, the applicant's face was masked. However, it was later decided by the Independent Television Commission, upon a complaint by the applicant that the news item breached privacy requirements, because the applicant was recognizable to anyone who knew him. A photograph from the footage also appeared in a local free newspaper and the incident was shown on 'Crime Beat' on BBC 1. In the programme the applicant was masked, although not sufficiently for him to be unrecognizable to those who knew him. Advertising trailers for the programme also showed the applicant unmasked, so that he was later recognized by friends and neighbours. This was a BBC error for which it apologized.

The applicant then complained to the Council, which was the first the Council knew of his identity. On a complaint to the Broadcasting Standards Commission, the Commission accepted that it was not evident from the film that the applicant was attempting to commit suicide, but concluded that it was a reasonable inference that his conduct might have been criminal in the same way that of as others shown in the programme.

It was contended on behalf of the applicant in *Peck* that Brentwood Borough Council had no statutory power to distribute footage of its CCTV material to the media for transmission and a declaration was sought that the Council had acted unlawfully. Harrison J held that the Council had power to distribute footage of CCTV film to the media for transmission by virtue of s. 111 of the LGA 1972 in the discharge of its function under s. 163 of the Criminal Justice and Public Order Act 1994. He held:

> I have some sympathy with the applicant who has suffered an invasion of his privacy, as is borne out by the findings of the Independent Television Commission and the Broadcasting Standards Commission. However, if I am right in deciding that the Council does have power to distribute the film footage from its CCTV system, there may on occasions be undesirable invasions of a person's privacy. Unless and until there is a general right of privacy recognised by English law (and the indications are that that may soon be so by incorporation of the European Convention on Human Rights into our law), reliance must be placed on effective guidance being issued by Codes of Practice or otherwise, in order to try and avoid such undesirable invasions of a person's privacy.

The judge noted that the evidence was that CCTV cameras in public places played an important role in both crime prevention and crime detection.

However, in *Peck* v *UK* 13 BHRC 669, it was argued that there had been a breach of Articles 8 and 13 ECHR. The European Court held that there had been no relevant or sufficient reasons which justified the local authority's disclosure. The disclosure had been a disproportionate and unjustified interference with the applicant's private life and infringed his Article 8 rights. The disclosures had not been sufficiently accompanied by safeguards to prevent the disclosure of the applicant's identity. The local authority should have first sought the applicant's consent, masked his identity or ensured that the media had masked his identity. Particular scrutiny and care were required in the context of the crime prevention objective and in the context of disclosures. It was held that later voluntary appearances on television shows by the applicant to discuss the publications of the footage and photographs did not diminish the serious nature of the interference with his right to privacy and the need for care in such disclosure. The applicant's right to an effective remedy under Article 13 ECHR had also been violated, as he did not have an effective remedy in relation to the breach of his Article 8 rights. The European Court found that judicial review was not an effective remedy, that the commissions to which the applicant had complained lacked legal power and could not award damages or prevent the publications or broadcasts, and that no action in breach of confidence had been available at the time as an appropriate remedy.

Chapter Five

Planning and the Environment

Richard Drabble QC and James Maurici

5.1   INTRODUCTION

The exercise by local authorities of planning and environmental powers necessarily involves potential interference with the rights of individuals. A decision to deny an individual the right to build, or to keep a caravan to live in in the open countryside may be denying that individual respect for his or her home (and/or private and family life) and thus raise Article 8 ECHR issues. Planning decisions such as the refusal of permission, or its grant subject to conditions, can also engage Article 1 of Protocol 1, being a control on the use of property. The service of certain notices under the Environmental Protection Act (EPA) 1990 raise similar issues. Furthermore, the same principles will in some cases apply to objectors to the grant of planning permission. A substantial diminution in a person's practical enjoyment of his or her property, brought about by the granting of planning permission to his or her neighbour, is capable of affecting that person's right to enjoy his or her own home and/or property (*Zander* v *Sweden* (1994) 18 EHRR 175; *Ortenburg* v *Austria* (1995) 19 EHRR 524, at para. 28 (see further below).

Planning decisions involve the use of a specialist system of appeals to the Secretary of State and/or inspectors exercising delegated powers, followed by a right of appeal to the High Court on issues of law alone, with planning permission (at least where planning permission is granted on appeal) and enforcement notices being protected by 'ouster' provisions. This specialist system raises a number of issues under Article 6 ECHR which have been considered by the domestic courts in numerous cases since the coming into force of the HRA 1998.

Nor are planning and environmental issues raised solely in civil inquiries and tribunals. Failure to comply with an enforcement notice or a planning contravention notice is a criminal offence, as is the commission of a statutory nuisance under the EPA 1990, with the result that human rights issues relevant to the criminal law may arise here, e.g. the admissibility of material obtained under compulsion (cf. *Saunders* v *UK* (1996) 23 EHRR 313 and *R* v *Hertfordshire*

County Council, ex parte Green Environmental Industries Ltd [1998] Env LR 153 (in the context of ss. 69, 71 and 34(5) of the EPA 1990) and the effectiveness of the 'ouster' provisions in preventing human rights issues being raised by the defence in the criminal courts (cf. *R* v *Wicks* [1998] AC 92 and, more importantly, *R* v *Clarke* [2002] JPL 1372).

Planners and planning lawyers have traditionally considered that the principal matters that have to be considered in making planning decisions and objective land use issues are unrelated to the personal circumstances of the individual. Individual hardship is recognized to be a material planning consideration, but very much as the exception. As Lord Scarman put it in *Westminster City Council* v *Great Portland Estates plc* [1985] AC 661:

> Personal circumstances of an occupier, personal hardship, the difficulties of businesses which are of value to the character of a community are not to be ignored in the administration of planning control. It would be inhuman pedantry to exclude from the control of our environment the human factor. The human factor is always present, of course, indirectly as the background to the consideration of the character of land use.

One more general impact of the coming into effect of the HRA 1998 has been to force the planning system to consider more routinely whether the personal circumstances of the individual have been adequately considered. Certainly, in many contexts (enforcement in a residential context, applications by gypsies and other minority groups to develop in the countryside, and so on) it is necessary for authorities expressly to consider the issues in terms of the approach under Article 8 ECHR. If the rights of the individual are not to prevail, the authority will need to be able to put forward clear reasons in the public interest for overriding them and be able to show that its response is proportionate. See also *Porter* v *South Buckinghamshire District Council* [2004] 1 P & CR 8 on the necessity of full reasons when relying on personal circumstances and Article 8 to override existing planning policies.

It will in many cases be necessary to bear the ECHR in mind when considering cases that arise within an existing statutory framework that is, if properly exercised, capable of producing results that are compatible with the Convention. The exercise of enforcement powers is one such example. A local planning authority may issue an enforcement notice where it appears to the authority that:

(a)   there has been a breach of planning control; and
(b)   it is expedient to issue the notice, having regard to the provisions of the development plan and to any other material considerations.

Subject to any appeal, failure to comply with an enforcement notice gives rise to criminal liability (ss. 172 and 179 of the Town and Country Planning Act (TCPA)

1990). Further, local authorities also have powers to require information in relation to activities on land (ss. 171C and 171D of the TCPA 1990) by way of service of a planning contravention notice, and to issue stop notices and to obtain injunctions restraining breaches of planning control. Under the HRA 1998, each exercise of such powers is vulnerable to challenge unless the authority proposing to take enforcement action can show that it is defensible against the criteria set out in Article 1 of Protocol 1 and Article 8 ECHR where applicable. The service of stop notices, or the seeking of injunctions, by a local planning authority brings these issues into even sharper focus, and the House of Lords has recently confirmed the view of the Court of Appeal that personal circumstances relevant to Article 8 must be taken into account by the Court in considering whether to grant an injunction under s. 187B of the TCPA 1990 (see, e.g., *Porter and others* v *South Buckinghamshire District Council and others* [2003] 2 WLR 1547, considered further below.

In the context of environmental law more generally, similar issues to those mentioned above will arise in respect of the exercise by local authorities of their powers and performance of their duties under the EPA 1990 and other environmental legislation.

Lastly, by way of introduction, the consequences of incorporation into domestic law of the principle of 'just satisfaction' should be mentioned. The right to damages in some situations is examined in Chapter Three. The area of planning is one where there may be relatively large potential damages claims, with the result that it may be sensible for aggrieved parties to formulate their claims as breaches of Convention rights, even if the action of the relevant authority of which they are complaining is unlawful in any event without reference to those rights.

5.2   THE RELEVANT RIGHTS

As is apparent from the brief introduction in 5.1, the most relevant ECHR rights in the context of planning and compulsory purchase will be Article 6 (right to a fair hearing), 8 (right to respect for private and family life and a home), Article 14 (non-discrimination) and Article 1 of Protocol 1 (protection of property) (see further Chapter Two). These Articles are discussed in greater detail at 5.4 to 5.6.

Other Articles may be relevant, although to a less predictable extent. Issues may arise, for example, under Article 3 (inhuman and degrading treatment) and Article 10 (freedom of expression, particularly in the context of environmental information — see *Guerra and others* v *Italy* (1998) 26 EHRR 357 and Chapter Two).

Article 9 (freedom of religion) may also be material in some planning contexts, e.g., in applications for planning permission for places of worship for minority religions. This Article has already been cited (without influencing the result) in a couple of domestic planning cases (see *Ostreicher* v *Secretary of State for the Environment* [1978] 1 All ER 591 (Sir Douglas Frank QC), concerning an adjournment of a planning case sought for religious reasons; and *R v Commissioners of English Heritage, ex parte Chappell* (unreported), 19 June 1986, in which the Court of Appeal held that, as a matter of English law, the right to manifest religion is subject to the reasonable and necessary power of the Secretary of State to close a religious site, and that in this respect there was no material difference between Article 9 ECHR and English law. In *ISKCON v UK* (1994) 76A DR 90, the applicant, who had been served with an enforcement notice in respect of its change of use of a manor in the Metropolitan Green Belt, alleged a violation of Article 9 ECHR. The manor had been used as a residential college for nurses, but ISKCON's frequent attraction to the manor of large numbers of worshippers created traffic problems and disturbance, which damaged the character of the area and inconvenienced local residents. The European Commission found that there had been an interference with ISKCON's Article 9 rights, but that it was justified as being 'necessary in a democratic society'. The Commission noted the detailed consideration given by the inspector to the special circumstances of the case (on the enforcement notice appeal). In holding the application inadmissible, it stated that Article 9 ECHR could not 'be used to circumvent existing planning legislation, provided that in the proceedings under that legislation, adequate weight was given to freedom of religion'.

It is conceivable that in cases raising issues of truly extreme environmental harm, Article 2 ECHR (the right to life) would also come into play. In *Guerra and others v Italy* (1998) 26 EHRR 357 (see 12.3.1.2), two of the judges who concurred in the unanimous judgment that Italy had contravened Article 8 ECHR, also stated that there would have been a breach of Article 2. Yet in this case, the local authority was not the originator of the hazardous situation; it appears to have been sufficient for it either to have had the power to refuse, or to withdraw its previously granted consent to, the project. Thus, an environmental authority which identifies, or ought to identify, a health-threatening activity, but which does not do enough to terminate or contain the threat, may be liable under Article 2 ECHR.

If this analysis is correct then it may provide a route around the current approach which stipulates that a local authority owes no duty of care to a person adversely affected by a polluting or contaminating activity for which it has granted planning permission (see *Lam v Brennan and Torbay Council* [1997] PIQR 448). It will also put pressure on continuous monitoring regimes in all circumstances where consent is granted to processes which are capable of posing a threat to health if their emissions exceed those stipulated in the relevant consent.

In other circumstances, the obligation under Article 2 may extend only to the provision of information. In *LCB v UK* (1998) 4 BHRC 447, the applicant, whose father had served on Christmas Island during nine years of atmospheric testing of nuclear devices, was discovered, in 1970, to have leukemia. The Court held that if the authorities had had available to them, at the time of the testing, information that gave, or reasonably ought to have given, grounds to believe that the applicant's father's exposure to radiation might give rise to a risk to his daughter, then they would be under a duty to furnish such information to the applicant.

However, in reality it is difficult to imagine such extreme cases arising under the HRA 1998 without there being in any event unlawful action measured solely against the existing statutory framework of environmental protection. However, damages issues must also be borne in mind (see Chapter Two).

5.3 'VICTIMS' IN THE PLANNING CONTEXT

Section 7 of the HRA 1998 incorporates the Strasbourg 'victim' test, which is generally said to be narrower than the standing test in judicial review (see Chapter One). The core of the concept of the victim test is that there can be no challenges to law in the abstract: only those directly (or at least indirectly) affected by the matters complained of can be victims. This is wider than it at first appears, allowing as it does those at risk of being affected to be considered victims: (see, e.g., *Open Door Counselling and Dublin Well Woman* v *Ireland* (1993) 15 EHRR 244, where the European Court of Human Rights accepted that two women were victims on the basis that they belonged to a class of women of child-bearing age who might be adversely affected by an injunction prohibiting the distribution of information about abortion services. In some ways this may be broader than the 'sufficient interest' test in English law.

For examples of the 'victim' test in operation in the planning/environmental context, see *Pine Valley Developments Ltd* v *Ireland* (1991) 14 EHRR 319 (considering the effect on the 'victim' status of companies post-dissolution/ insolvency); and *Taurira* v *France* (1995) 83B DR 112 (residents living 1,000 km from a French nuclear test site found not to be 'victims').

Companies as well as individuals may claim to be the victims of infringements of certain (but not all) Convention rights. Article 1 of Protocol 1 protects the rights of 'every natural or legal person', thereby confirming that corporate bodies enjoy rights under the Convention (see *Pine Valley Developments Ltd* v *Ireland*, above). Article 6 ECHR rights can certainly be relied upon by companies. Article 8 ECHR has been given a broad interpretation, and the office of a professional has been treated as a home (*Niemietz* v *Germany* (1992) 16 EHRR 97). However, it seems that Article 8 does not extend to companies (*Open Door and Dublin Well Woman* v *Ireland*, above).

The limitations of the 'victim' test, and in particular the fact that it is narrower than the modern test of standing applied in domestic judicial review, will be felt particularly in the planning context. Where planning issues are concerned, it is often groups rather than individuals that take up the fight, be they local, national or international (see, e.g., *R* v *Secretary of State for the Environment, ex parte*

Rose Theatre Trust Co. [1990] 1 QB 504 and *R* v *HMIP, ex parte Greenpeace* [1994] All ER 329).

Crucially, the Strasbourg jurisprudence does not generally allow representative actions. However, there are some exceptions. Strasbourg case law has allowed representative actions where bodies such as unincorporated associations, professional bodies and trade unions act on behalf of their members who are identified as victims, and where it is shown that there is authority to represent them. Further, in certain circumstances, an unincorporated association could itself be a victim. Representative action might also be taken where the group is really an association of 'victims'. However, public interest groups, *per se*, are unlikely to establish themselves as 'victims' within the Strasbourg case law. To this extent the test is narrower than the sufficient interest test which has allowed public interest litigation by public interest groups (see, *Ex parte Greenpeace*, above).

There is, of course, nothing to prevent public interest groups from funding, assisting or providing representation for individual victims, or even actively seeking out such victims and encouraging them to act as 'test' victims.

The only question that remains is whether a local authority can itself be a 'victim' for the purposes of s. 7 of the HRA 1998. The answer is No. To be a victim, the ECHR requires there to be a 'person, non-governmental organisation or group of individuals' (see Article 34 ECHR). Local authorities and other governmental organizations are thus excluded and have no enforceable Convention rights (see *Ayuntamiento de M* v *Spain* (1991) DR 209). However, there are a number of potential ways around this limitation:

(a)   In the *Alconbury* case (see below), Huntingdonshire District Council was served as an interested party in judicial review proceedings testing the lawfulness and compatibility of the planning appeals system (and the making of orders under the Transport and Works Act 1992) with the HRA 1998. The Council took part in the proceedings before the Divisional Court and the House of Lords, actively arguing that the appeals system was incompatible with the HRA 1998. For procedural purposes Scott Baker J, in giving directions in those cases, ordered that the Council 'stand as a Claimant'. However, it was not conceded that the Council was a victim, or that it could have instigated such proceedings of its own accord. Nevertheless, this illustrates the scope for local authorities to raise human rights arguments in proceedings in which they become involved, albeit not instigated by them.

(b)   Arguably, by virtue of the terms of s. 7 of the HRA 1998, the victim requirement applies only to proceedings under s. 6 alleging unlawfulness, and that would leave it open for local authorities to seek declarations of incompatibility under s. 4 and to otherwise rely on s. 3 in proceedings in which they were involved.

(c)   It could be argued that outside the Convention and the HRA 1998, the parallel common law fundamental rights do apply to local authorities, there being no Article 34-type restriction.

(d)   A local authority could seek out a victim (either a local resident, or a local councilor) and fund litigation by him or her, however, this raises more difficult questions (see, e.g., in a non-HRA 1998 context, *R v Bassetlaw District Council, ex parte Oxby* [1998] PLCR 283 and, more recently, *Corbett v Restormel Borough Council; R v Restormel Borough Council, ex parte Parkyn* [2001] 1 PLR 108 and (2001) 82 P & CR

5.4   ARTICLE 6

The basic requirements of Article 6 ECHR are examined in Chapter Two. Article 6 has been at the forefront of the early post-2 October 2000 challenges to the planning system. Article 6(1) guarantees that in the determination of their civil rights and obligations, everyone is entitled to a fair and public hearing within a reasonable time by an independent and impartial tribunal established by law.

5.4.1   The applicability of Article 6 to planning

The important issue that arose in *Alconbury* [2001] 2 WLR 1389 and was the extent to which the procedural protections of Article 6 ECHR applied in relation to planning decision-making.

Much of the case law of the European Court of Human Rights on this question can be understood only in the light of the principle which it has adopted from an early stage of its history, that the distinction between civil and other rights broadly corresponds to the difference between public and private law. However, the European Court has mitigated the practical effects of this distinction by holding that Article 6(1) ECHR applies to 'all proceedings the result of which is decisive for private rights and obligations', even if they are public law proceedings directed to questions of purely public concern, the effect of which on private law rights is incidental (*Ringeisen v Austria (No. 1)* (1971) EHRR 455, at para. 94; *König v Germany* (1978) 2 EHRR 170, at paras 90–94; *Benthem v Netherlands* (1985) 8 EHRR 1, at para. 32; and *Tre Traktörer AB v Sweden* (1989) 13 EHRR 309, at para. 41).

In planning cases, the relevant private law right potentially affected (albeit in a public law context) is the qualified right to the enjoyment of property, which exists in all Convention states and is protected by Article 1 of Protocol 1. The European Court has consistently held that the right to property is engaged by any state action which substantially restricts the practical use that may be made of it, even if the legal rights of ownership and occupation are undisturbed (*Sporrong and Lönnroth v Sweden* (1983) 5 EHRR 35, at paras 60 and 79).

Article 6(1) ECHR requires not just that civil rights and obligations are in dispute, but also that there is a contestation or dispute as to a civil right or obligation. This is considered further below.

It had been generally assumed, on the basis of Strasbourg case law, that Article 6 ECHR would apply in the UK context to any decision granting or refusing planning permission (conditionally or unconditionally), and to decisions in relation to enforcement proceedings as well as to much of the rest of the planning and environmental legislation in force (*Ringeisen* v *Austria (No. 1)* (1971) 1 EHRR 455 (referred to in the judgments of a number of their Lordships in *Alconbury*); *Zander* v *Sweden* (1994) 18 EHRR 175; *Oerlemans* v *Netherlands* (1991) 15 EHRR 561; *Skarby* v *Sweden* (1991) 13 EHRR 90; *Sporrong and Lönnroth* v *Sweden* (1983) 5 EHRR 35; and *Bryan* v *UK* (1995) 21 EHRR 342). In *Bryan* (still the leading Strasbourg case on Article 6 and the UK planning system), the applicant had been served with an enforcement notice, which required him to demolish certain buildings erected without planning permission. He complained that the review by the High Court of the inspector's decision (upholding the enforcement notice) was insufficient to comply with Article 6(1) ECHR. At para. 31, the European Court noted that the UK Government did not contest (as they had done before the Commission) that the impugned planning proceedings (enforcement action) involved a determination of the applicant's civil rights, and went on to say that on the basis of the established case law it saw no reason to decide otherwise (this concession has been adhered to in later cases — see, e.g., *Chapman* v *UK* (2001) 33 EHRR 18).

In *Alconbury*, before the Divisional Court, the applicability of Article 6 ECHR was a matter of common ground between the parties ([2001] JPL 291, see para. 2 of the Divisional Court's judgment at 296). (It is notable that *Alconbury* involved consideration of the Secretary of State's planning decision-making powers under, *inter alia*, the TCPA 1990 (including call-ins and recovered appeals) and the Transport and Works Act 1992.) The Secretary of State again conceded this point before the House of Lords. However, as this issue had arisen in the context of the appeal in Scotland in *County Properties* v *Scottish Ministers* 2000 SLT 965 (see further 5.4.2.1), the Lord Advocate intervened and argued that on a decision on a called-in application there was no 'contestation', and accordingly Article 6 did not apply at all to the planning determinations in issue.

Lord Slynn (with whom Lord Nolan agreed) concluded (at para. 28) that:

Despite the submissions of the Lord Advocate that a decision on a called in application is not a 'contestation' on the basis of these and a number of other cases it seems to me plain that the dispute is one which involves the determination of 'civil rights' within the meaning of the Convention.

Lord Hoffmann was more attracted to the Lord Advocate's arguments (at para. 74):

Apart from authority, I would have said that a decision as to what the public interest requires is not a 'determination' of civil rights and obligations. It may affect civil rights and obligations but it is not, and ought not to be, a judicial act such as Article 6 has in contemplation. The reason is not simply that it involves the exercise of a discretion, taking many factors into account, which does not give any person affected by the decision the right to any particular outcome . . . [b]ut a decision as to the public interest (what I shall call for short a 'policy decision') is quite different from a determination of right. The administrator may have a duty, in accordance with the rule of law, to behave fairly ('quasi-judicially') in the decision-making procedure. But the decision itself is not a judicial or quasi-judicial act. It does not involve deciding between the rights or interests of particular persons. It is the exercise of a power delegated by the people as a whole to decide what the public interest requires.

Lord Hoffmann gave further consideration to the Lord Advocate's intervention (at para. 135):

. . . it makes little difference whether one says, as in Kaplan, that the administrative act does not fall within Article 6 at all and the question is concerned only with the adequacy and impartiality of the judicial review, or whether one says, as the European Court and Commission have done in other cases, that the administrative act does in theory come within Article 6 but the administrator's lack of impartiality can be cured by an adequate and impartial judicial review. The former seems to me a more elegant analysis, but the latter may be necessary in order to explain, in the context of civilian concepts, why the administrative process can be treated as involving at any stage a determination of civil rights and obligations. So, tempting as it is, I am unable [to] accept Mr Macdonald's short cut.

Lord Clyde also referred to the Lord Advocate's arguments as 'attractive', but similarly rejected them having considered the relevant Strasbourg case law (para. 145). Lord Hutton considered that, in the light of the common law, the Lord Advocate's submissions had 'obvious force' (para. 181). He, like several of the Law Lords, referred in this regard to the Commission's decision in *Kaplan* and the fact that this decision had not been followed in subsequent cases. Lord Hutton was particularly influenced by the European Court's decision in *Bryan* in deciding that 'the determination of a planning application by an official or minister falls within the ambit of Article 6(1)'.

It should be noted that although the Secretary of State accepted before the House of Lords that in many cases, including those before their Lordships, the determination of planning applications will involve a dispute and a 'determination of civil rights and obligations', this acceptance was a qualified one. The Secretary of State's concession was limited in terms of the engagement of Article 6 ECHR where third party objectors are concerned. Where a neighbour complains that a proposed development will affect his or her use and enjoyment of his or her property, this may engage Article 6 (see *Ortenberg*, below) but will not necessarily do so. It will be a question of fact in any particular case whether the third party objector's property rights are so affected by the proposals as to engage Article 6. This may overlap with consideration of the question of 'victim' status under s. 7 of the HRA 1998 (see 5.3).

In any event, there may still be other limits to the scope of Article 6 ECHR. See, e.g., *R v Secretary of State for the Environment, ex parte Slot* 15 July 1996 (unreported), where Hidden J (on appeal, the Court of Appeal found it unnecessary to consider the applicability of Article 6: [1998] 4 PLR 1), in rejecting arguments based on Article 6, held, *inter alia*, that the procedure laid down by Parliament for the diversion of footpaths and the anticipated benefit of diversion did not affect civil rights or obligations (see *contra, R v Secretary of State for Wales, ex parte Emery* [1996] 4 All ER 1, at 17f–19d, in the context of the Wildlife and Countryside Act 1981, s. 53(5) and Sch. 14, para. 4(2) orders modifying the definitive survey map to show a footpath as a public footpath).

5.4.2 The Article 6 issues

With the coming into force of the HRA 1998, planning led the way in terms of the Article 6 ECHR challenges.

5.4.2.1 The role of the Secretary of State

As was widely predicted, the early post-2 October 2000 case law focused on the compatibility with Article 6 of the Secretary of State's powers to determine planning applications and appeals.

These early challenges were systemic — as Lord Hoffmann put it in *Alconbury* (see below) 'the issue . . . is whether it is compatible with the Human Rights Act for Parliament to confer upon the Secretary of State the power to make [planning] decisions . . . [or did Article 6 require] such decisions to be made by independent and impartial tribunals'. (Lord Hoffmann noted that if this was required '[t]his would mean radical amendment to the system by which such decisions have been made for many years' (para. 65)).

The decision of the Lord Macfadyen in *County Properties v The Scottish Ministers* 2000 SLT 965 (delivered on 25 July 2000) sent shock waves through the planning system. *Bryan v UK* (1996) 21 EHRR 342 was distinguished and the Court held that a decision by the Scottish Ministers on a called-in planning application was incompatible with Article 6. Post-*Alconbury* (see below) Lord Mcfadyen's decision was reversed on appeal ([2002] HRLR 11).

The Divisional Court's decision in *Alconbury/Holding & Barnes* in December 2000 ([2001] HRLR 2) sent further shock waves and cast doubt on the future of the Secretary of State's role in the planning system. The Divisional Court granted a declaration of incompatibility, holding that the role of the Secretary of State in the planning system amounted to a breach of Article 6(1) since, in each case, the

Secretary of State as policy-maker was also the decision-maker. *Bryan* v *UK* (1996) 21 EHRR 342 was distinguished. This meant that although decision-making by inspectors under delegated powers was Article 6 compatible, decision-making by the Secretary of State (on call-ins and recovered appeals was not).

However, the role of the Secretary of State in planning (and related CPO/ Highways) decision-making was entirely vindicated by the House of Lords in *Alconbury* ([2001] 2 WLR 1389).

One of the parties in the *Alconbury* case, having lost in the House of Lords, tried to take the case to the European Court of Human Rights. A Chamber of the European Court recently decided that the application was inadmissible:

> . . . the Court does not consider that the present case can, for the purposes of Article 6.1, be distinguished from the . . . *Bryan* case. In particular, as was held by the House of Lords, the fact that in the present case it was the Secretary of State himself rather than (as in the Bryan case) the Inspector who was to take the decision, does not afford a sufficient basis to distinguishing [sic] the decision in that case.

A party can in exceptional cases request that the Grand Chamber of the European Court to consider an application, which has been declared inadmissible. However, it is likely that the end of the road has been reached.

Was this result surprising? The speeches of their Lordships in *Alconbury* placed heavy reliance on a number of Strasbourg authorities where planning decisions of both inspectors *and* the Secretary of State had been unsuccessfully challenged on the basis of a breach of Article 6 (see especially *Bryan, ISKCON* v *UK* 18 EHRR CD 133; *Chapman* v *UK* (2001) 33 EHRR 18; and *Varey* v *UK* (App. No. 26662/95), 27 October 1999). In a sense, the House of Lords in *Alconbury* was doing no more than applying well-established principles of Strasbourg case law.

Thus the first systemic challenge to the planning system failed. The role of the Secretary of State in the planning system was secure.

In *Alconbury* the House of Lords also rejected arguments that the financial interest of the Ministry of Defence in the development precluded in principle a decision being made by the Secretary of State. But Lord Slynn noted (at para. 55) that a specific breach of administrative law might arise on the facts of a particular case, i.e. if the financial interests of the Government were wrongly taken into account by the Secretary of State. This cannot be read literally, however, as financial considerations can be relevant in planning. Lord Nolan said (at para. 64) 'the objection in the Alconbury case based on the ground of [the Secretary of State] having a financial interest in the matter, might if appropriate be raised as objections to the ultimate decision itself. They are insufficient to disqualify him *in limine*'. See also Lord Hoffmann's speech at para. 130. He thought it made no difference that in the *Alconbury* case the 'Ministry of Defence, another emanation of the Crown, has a financial interest in the proposed development', or that in the *Legal and General* case the Secretary of State was deciding whether to confirm his own road improvement scheme. His Lordship noted that judicial review was available if irrelevant matters were taken into account. Similar issues arise in respect of cases involving the local planning authority as landowner or where the local authority otherwise has an interest in the proposed development. This is a matter considered further below.

Thus, in terms of the Secretary of State's role, systemic challenges have been rejected but the possibility of breaches of Article 6 being found in particular cases left open.

5.4.2.2   Local planning authorities

The focus of case law since *Alconbury* has switched to the compatibility of local planning authority decision-making with Article 6 ECHR.

There is much case law on this (see, e.g., *R (on the application of Kathro)* v *Rhondda Cynon Taff CBC* [2002] Env LR 15; *R (on the application of Vetterlein)* v *Hampshire County Council* [2002] Env LR 8; *R (on the application of Malster)* v *Ipswich Borough Council* [2002] PLCR 14; *R (on the application of Friends Provident Life & Pensions Ltd)* v *Secretary of State for Transport, Local Government and the Regions* [2002] 1 WLR 1450; *R (on the application of Cummins)* v *Camden London Borough Council* (unreported 21 December 2001); and *BT plc* v *Gloucester City Council* [2002] JPL 993).

Most of these cases were driven by the emphasis placed by the House of Lords in *Alconbury* on the extensive fact finding 'safeguards' available before an inspector, including an oral hearing, rights of cross-examination and the quasi-judicial nature of the proceedings. Lord Hoffmann, in particular, seemed to indicate that, where one is dealing with the 'finding or evaluation' of facts, those safeguards 'are essential for the acceptance of a limited review of fact by the appellate tribunal'. The consequence has been that in post-*Alconbury* challenges claimants have held up the inspector/Secretary of State decision-making model as the ideal to which local planning authority decision-making should aspire in Article 6 terms — and in several cases argued that as local planning authority decision-making fell short of this ideal (most notably in not providing an inquiry) the Secretary of State was obliged to call in the planning applications in issue to ensure compliance with Article 6. Things had thus come full circle from *County Properties*, where Lord MacFayden expressed the erroneous view that local authorities unlike the Scottish Ministers were an independent and impartial tribunal and that by calling in the application in question County Properties had been denied the opportunity of a hearing before an independent and impartial tribunal, namely the Edinburgh City Council. Although in the recent Court of Appeal decision in *Adlard* (see below) Simon Brown LJ thought it surprising that the local planning authority is not to be regarded as an independent and impartial tribunal (para. 16). However, following the decision of the House of Lords in *R* v *Tower Hamlets London Borough Council, ex parte Runa Begum* [2003] 2 AC 430 this is undoubtedly correct and follows simply from the fact that it 'cannot be described as part of the judicial branch of government'.

The high point of the case-law from the challengers perspective was *Kathro*. This involved a challenge by third party objectors to a major development which the local planning authority was promoting on its own land. The claimants made a pre-emptive challenge to the process before the planning committee was able to make its decision. Although Richards J ultimately rejected the challenge (so the high point for challengers is a defeat) he said:

> 28.   Looking at the overall tenor of the speeches in Alconbury and at the underlying decisions of the Strasbourg court, however, I accept that the finding that the Secretary of State's decision-making process was compatible in principle with article 6 was based to a significant extent on the fact-finding role of the inspector and its attendant procedural safeguards. By contrast, there is no equivalent in the decision-making process of a local planning authority. That process includes a right to make representations and to submit evidence, and persons may be heard orally at a meeting of the relevant committee. But there is nothing like a public inquiry, no opportunity for cross-examination and no formal procedure for evaluating the evidence and making findings of fact. The report of the planning officer to the committee generally contains an exposition of relevant facts, including any areas of factual dispute, but does not serve the same function as an inspector's report. In general there will be no express findings of fact by the committee itself. All of this considerably reduces the scope for effective scrutiny of the planning decision on an application for judicial review. It makes it more difficult, if not impossible, to determine whether the decision has been based on a misunderstanding or ignorance of an established and relevant fact, or has been based on a view of the facts that was not reasonably open on the evidence.
>
> 29.   For those reasons there is in my view a real possibility that, in certain circumstances involving disputed issues of fact, a decision of a local planning authority which is not itself an independent and impartial tribunal might not be subject to sufficient control by the court to ensure compliance with article 6 overall.

Richards J's approach did not find favour in *Friends Provident, Vetterlein,* or *Cummins* or any of the other cases cited above. *Kathro* has been laid to rest by the Court of Appeal in *Adlard* v *Secretary of State for the Environment, Transport and the Regions* [2002] 1 WLR 2515.

In *Adlard* the claimants (who were objectors) contended that because of the Secretary of State's refusal to call in the application for planning permission for a new sports stadium for Fulham Football Club the result was a breach of Article 6. It was said that the failure to allow objectors to make oral representations at the planning committee stage had been a breach of their Article 6 rights that had obliged the Secretary of State to call in. Collins J rejected these arguments relying on the detailed reasons given by Ouseley J in *Cummins* (see above).

The Court of Appeal dismissed the appeal. To understand why, it is necessary to leave planning for a moment and consider the decision of the Court of Appeal in *Begum (Runa)* v *Tower Hamlets London Borough Council* [2002] 2 All ER 668. The Court in *Begum* was concerned with the procedure for a local housing authority's internal review of its decisions on homelessness, such reviews being subject only to appeal in point of law to the county court. Laws LJ said this:

> 40.   As I have shown, the extent to which the first instance process may be relied on to produce fair and reasonable decisions is plainly an important element. But it is not to be viewed in isolation. The matter can only be judged by an examination of the statutory scheme as a whole; that is the necessary setting for any intelligent view as to what is fair and reasonable. Where the scheme's subject-matter generally or systematically involves the resolution of primary fact, the court will incline to look for procedures akin to our conventional mechanisms for finding fact: rights of cross-examination, access to documents, a strictly independent decision-maker. To the extent that procedures of that kind are not given by the first instance process, the court will look to see how far they are given by the appeal or review; and the judicial review jurisdiction (or its equivalent in the shape of a statutory appeal on law) may not suffice. Where however the subject-matter of the scheme generally or systematically requires the application of judgment or the exercise of discretion, especially if it involves weighing of policy issues and regard being had to the interests of others who are not before the decision-maker, then for the purposes of Article 6 the court will incline to be satisfied with a form of inquisition at first instance in which the decision-maker is more of an expert than a judge (I use the term loosely), and the second instance appeal is in the nature of a judicial review. It is inevitable that across the legislative board there will lie instances between these paradigms, sharing in different degrees the characteristics of each. In judging a particular scheme the court, without compromise of its duty to vindicate the Convention rights, will pay a degree of respect on democratic grounds to Parliament as the scheme's author.
>
> . . .
>
> 43.   I should indicate moreover that although there were sharp issues of primary fact falling for determination in the present case, that is not a necessary feature in a s.202 review, and certainly not a systematic one. As often as not there will be no real question of fact, and the decision will turn on the weight to be given to this or that factor against an undisputed background . . . Now, clearly the statutory scheme is either compliant with Article 6 or it is not. Its compliance or otherwise cannot vary case by case, according to the degree of factual dispute arising. That would involve a wholly unsustainable departure from the principle of legal certainty. In my opinion, judged as a whole, this statutory scheme lies towards that end of the spectrum where judgment and discretion, rather than fact-finding, play the predominant part.

In *Adlard* the Court of Appeal placed considerable reliance on the reasoning in *Begum*. One of the judges (Dyson LJ) was common to both decisions.

At para. 17 of his judgment Simon Brown LJ, having set out the passages from *Begum* quoted above said:

What, then, of the planning process? Where in the spectrum does this statutory scheme lie? To my mind there can only be one answer to that question and it is the same answer as *Runa Begum* gave with regard to the homelessness legislation, namely 'towards that end of the spectrum where judgment and discretion, rather than fact-finding, play the predominant part'. Accordingly (see paragraph 40 of *Runa Begum*) 'the court will incline to be satisfied with a form of inquisition at first instance at which the decision-maker is more of an expert than a judge . . . and the second instance appeal is in the nature of a judicial review'.

The Court then went on to consider the main issue which he formulated as follows:

> . . . is the appellants' entitlement to 'a fair and public hearing' by 'an independent and impartial tribunal' satisfied by the English planning system which, in the case of objectors, allows the local planning authority to grant planning permission without having afforded them any opportunity of an oral hearing subject only and always to this court's supervisory jurisdiction on a judicial review application? (para. 15)

The Court held that as planning decisions turned on questions of judgment and discretion rather than findings of fact there was no requirement that a statutory scheme should provide a right to an oral hearing at the initial proceedings. Simon Brown LJ said:

> Quintessentially the decision whether or not to permit this development (and the departure from the development plan which it represents) involves questions of discretion and planning judgment rather than the resolution of primary fact. (para. 32)

His Lordship recognized that planning decisions did involve some fact-finding but this did not affect his judgment overall.

Simon Brown LJ said (at para. 32):

> The remedy of judicial review in my judgment amply enables the court to correct any injustice it perceives in an individual case. If, in short, the court were satisfied that exceptionally, on the facts of a particular case, the local planning authority had acted unfairly or unreasonably in denying an objector any or any sufficient oral hearing, the court would quash the decision and require such a hearing to be given. This presents no difficulties . . .

Thus as in *Alconbury* the systemic challenge failed but the possibility of an Article 6 challenge on a particular set of facts was left open.

The House of Lords refused a petition for leave to appeal in *Adlard*, but recently gave judgment in the appeal in *Begum*. The case undoubtedly supports the *outcome* in *Adlard*. The case is noteworthy, however, for the reduced emphasis placed on the need for 'fact-finding'. In administrative law generally, depending on the context, very little in the way of 'fact-finding' safeguards may be required, notwithstanding that the decision-maker is not 'independent and impartial' in Article 6 terms. It appears that this applies also in the planning sphere. *Bryan* was described by Lord Hoffmann as an exceptional case (para. 54) because the decision of whether there had been a breach of planning control was binding on Mr Byran in any subsequent criminal proceedings. Presumably, therefore, the safeguards noted by the European Court in *Bryan* will not be considered important in ordinary planning appeals where these consequences do not follow.

In any event the importance of a spectrum of decision-making, between those cases where there is a need for findings of primary fact, and those cases where judgment or discretion must be exercised, is now of less importance. All that is required is that the Appeal Court has jurisdiction to deal with the case as the nature of the decision requires, having regard to such matters as the subject matter of the decision appealed against, the manner in which it was arrived at, and the content of the dispute. It may be doubted whether this gives much concrete guidance in specific cases but the decision of the House of Lords undoubtedly indicates a very cautious approach to the application of Article 6 ECHR in public law generally.

Adlard has been applied in a number of more recent cases.

In *Westminster City Council* v *Mayor of London* ('the Congestion Charge judicial review challenge') [2003] BLGR 611, Maurice Kay J considered and applied *Adlard* — see paras 107–109 ('I appreciate that our context is not, in the strictest sense, "the planning process", although it has much in common with it').

In *R* v *Islington London Borough Council and Arsenal FC, ex parte Bedford and Clare* [2003] Env LR 22, a challenge to the Arsenal stadium redevelopment, Ouseley J said:

> It is also quite clear from the decision in *The Queen (on the application of Adlard) v Secretary of State for the Environment, Transport and the Regions* [2002] EWCA Civ 737, paragraphs 31, 32, 39 and 40, that major developments do not by their nature require an inquiry to be held in order for a local authority lawfully to grant planning permission for them.

Adlard was also cited by Moses J in his judgment in the non-planning case of *R (on the application of Ali, Mohammed and Mohammed)* v *Birmingham City Council and Birmingham City Council Social Services and the Secretary of State for Health* [2002] HLR 51.

5.4.2.3 Plan making
In *Bovis Homes Ltd* v *New Forest District Council and Alfred McAlpine Development Ltd* [2002] EWHC 483, Ousley J held that the local plan system was

Article 6 ECHR compliant. He also held that ordinarily local plans do not deter-mine civil rights and obligations such as to even engage Article 6. See also *R v English Nature, ex parte Aggregate Industries UK Ltd* [2003] Env LR 3, where Forbes J applied and upheld Ouseley J's reasoning in this regard: 'However, the learned Judge did say I do not wish to hold however that local plan proposals or designations are never capable of directly affecting civil rights' and gave one example, namely 'the designation of land [in a local plan] for a purpose leading to statutory or non-statutory blight might determine human rights'.

A human rights challenge to the structure plan system was rejected in *Bloor* v *Swindon Borough Council* [2002] PLCR 22 (Ouseley J). The claimants having raised the human rights challenge (in the words of the learned judge) 'fled the field' on these arguments.

5.4.2.4   Other article 6 case law in the planning/ environmental field
Another case referred to by the Court of Appeal in *Adlard* was *R* v *English Nature, ex parte Aggregate Industries UK Ltd* [2003] Env LR 3.

In that case Forbes J considered a challenge by way of judicial review of the decision of the Council of English Nature whereby it confirmed the notification of certain land situated at Bramshill plantation, Hampshire as a Site of Special Scientific Interest (SSSI) pursuant to s. 28 of the Wildlife and Countryside Act 1981 as amended. One of the grounds of challenge was that the Council's decision was made in breach of Article 6 ECHR.

Forbes J rejected the Secretary of State's argument that the designation of an SSSI did not involve a determination of Aggregate Industries' civil rights within Article 6. The learned judge drew attention to a number of ways in which designa-tion of an SSSI removed, diminished and restricted an owner's rights in respect of land within the SSSI. Following SSSI designation, s. 28E of the Wildlife and Countryside Act 1981 requires the owner of land to apply for consent to carry out any of the operations listed within the notification. The Secretary of State had argued that the decisive determination in Article 6 terms came not at the designa-tion stage but later when English Nature (or the Secretary of State on appeal) refused consent for the carrying out of such an operation. The learned judge relied upon the following matters in concluding that Article 6 was engaged:

(a)   the effect of s. 28E of the Wildlife and Countryside Act 1981, which requires the owner or occupier of land to apply for consent to carry out any of the operations listed within the notification, even where such operations are the subject of an existing planning permission or other appropriate licence. (Although it is an offence under s. 28P to carry out relevant works without obtaining English Nature's consent, it is a defence if a person carries out an operation authorized by a planning permission granted under the TCPA 1990); and

(b)   the effect of ss. 28J, 28K, 28L and 28N of the 1981 Act pursuant to which English Nature can, following confirmation of an SSSI, impose a management scheme on the land for the conservation and/or restoration of the SSSI and is empowered to take measures to enforce such a scheme, including the service of a management notice and compulsory acquisition of all or part of the land in question (in relation to this aspect the Secretary of State deployed the same argument as in relation to s. 28E, namely that it was not designation but the later service of a management notice or compulsory purchase order (against which there was a right of appeal to the Secretary of State) that determined civil rights for Article 6 purposes. This was rejected).

Forbes J went on to hold that the SSSI designation process 'comprising [English Nature]'s procedures together with the High Court's power of judicial review (conveniently referred to as the "composite process"), complied with the requirements of Article 6(1)' (see paras 96 *et seq.* of the judgment). Forbes J concluded (at para. 108):

> . . . having regard to the existing procedural safeguards in English Nature's decision-making process and to the nature of the subject matter of the statutory scheme, I have come to the firm conclusion that, in the present case, the High Court did possess "full jurisdiction to deal with the case as the nature of the decision requires" in the exercise of its powers of judicial review . . . English Nature's procedures, when taken together with the High Court's powers of judicial review, did constitute an Article 6(1) compliant determination . . .

The learned judge placed particular reliance upon the Court of Appeal's recent decision in *London Borough of Tower Hamlets* v *Runa Begum* (see above). Forbes J was 'satisfied that English Nature's decision-making process does have a number of procedural safeguards which can be relied upon to produce fair and reasonable decisions' on the basis that:

(a)   the Wildlife and Countryside Act 1981 requires there to be an initial notification of SSSI designation specifying the time within which and the manner in which the representations or objections with respect to notification must be made and imposes a duty upon English Nature to consider any representation or objection duly made when considering whether to confirm the SSSI designation;

(b)   the notification contains a statement of why English Nature has formed an initial view that the site is of special interest, thus enabling informed representations and objections to be made;

(c)   there is prior to confirmation ample opportunity for detailed 'representations and objections to be made by a variety of appropriate means, including experts' reports, detailed correspondence and dedicated meetings with English Nature's officers';

(d) a detailed and comprehensive report, containing details of the various representations and objections and all other relevant information is prepared by officers for use at the meeting at which confirmation of the SSSI is considered and this is made available in advance of the meeting to owners/ occupiers who request it;

(e) the meeting at which confirmation is to be considered is held in public and there is an opportunity for those who wish to make oral representations to do so;

(f) post-confirmation there are further safeguards, such as the right to appeal to the Secretary of State against a refusal of consent; and

(g) if a person affected by an SSSI makes further representations after its confirmation, it is open to English Nature to vary the notification or de-notify.

The Court of Appeal has refused the claimant permission to appeal.

The courts are likely to take a similar approach to any challenge to the system for designating conservation areas. A challenge along these lines was brought in *Blanefield* v *Salisbury District Council* (CO/4366/2000) but was settled on non-HRA 1998 grounds.

In *William Sinclair Holdings Ltd* v *English Nature* [2002] Env LR 4, Turner J quite wrongly granted an interim injunction against English Nature in support of an allegation that the SSSI designation procedure was incompatible with the HRA 1998. This decision was not followed by Newman J in *Aggregate Industries* [2001] EWHC Admin 934.

In *Langton* v *Secretary of State for the Environment, Food and Rural Affairs* [2002] Env LR 20 there was an application for judicial review of decisions to issue and subsequently enforce a notice given under the Animal By-Products Order 1999. The claimant had accumulated a large amount of maggot waste on farmland. The defendant authorities had concluded that the waste presented a hazard to wildlife and was also potentially harmful to public health. A notice was issued requiring the claimant to dispose of the material by incineration but the claimant failed to comply and attempted to plough the waste into the soil. The local authority entered the land and buried the waste in deep trenches. The claimant maintained that the absence of any appeal procedure against the notice deprived him of his right to a fair hearing as guaranteed by Article 6 ECHR. Nigel Pleming QC held that Article 6 was clearly engaged as the decisions affected the claimant's civil rights and obligations. However, the learned judge held that the availability of judicial review as a remedy satisfied the requirements of Article 6 (applying *Alconbury*).

5.4.3   Other Article 6 issues in planning law

5.4.3.1   Funding

Article 6 ECHR requires that there be 'equality of arms' between the parties, i.e. that each party must be given a reasonable opportunity to present his case under conditions that do not place him at a substantial disadvantage in relation to his opponent. This was considered in *R* v *Secretary of State for the Environment, Transport and the Regions, ex parte Challenger and the Cathedral Area Residents' Association* [2001] Env LR 12 (Harrison J). This case concerned the public inquiry into the construction of additional London train links (the Thameslink 2000 inquiry).

At the Thameslink 2000 pre-inquiry meeting it was argued by third party objectors that the issues to be considered in deciding whether to confirm the order were substantial, complex and highly technical and that unless the objectors were given assistance in presenting their case, there would not be equality of arms, rendering the inquiry contrary to Article 6 and hence unlawful. It was said that financial assistance could be given either by the Secretary of State or Railtrack (the latter had refused such a request). The inspector ruled that '[he] and the programming staff will go out of their way to assist those who are unfamiliar with the process, or who are not represented to the same degree as the principal parties. In many cases this will be sufficient to ensure equality of arms'. The inspector also noted that the Legal Services Commission could provide funding for major inquires in certain cases. As regards funding by the Secretary of State the inspector suggested the objectors write to the Chief Planning Inspector. The objectors subsequently failed to secure funding from the Legal Services Commission. No request was made to the Chief Planning Inspector or the Secretary of State directly, however, the judge noted that there was no indication that such a request would have been acceded to.

The applicants sought permission to apply for judicial review of the inspector's ruling. It was contended that the public inquiry would involve a breach of the right to a fair hearing under Article 6(1). Harrison J refused judicial review, holding that even if the HRA 1998 were in force (which at the time it was not), the applicant's submissions based upon the lack of legal aid would not have succeeded given the fact that there was provision in place for such funding and such an application had been considered and rejected. The judge noted that the public inquiry procedure was relatively informal and facilitated lay participation, and that there were in the Thameslink 2000 inquiry other bodies whose views on the project coincided with those of the applicant and who would be presenting detailed expert evidence before the inquiry, thus ensuring that all relevant matters were raised.

See more recently, in *R* v *Secretary of State for Transport, Local Government and the Regions, ex parte Hadfield* [2002] 26 EGCS 137, where the claimant sought to quash the Secretary of State's decision to exercise his power to call in an application for planning permission for the conversion of agricultural buildings to stables and a dwelling, Sullivan J held that the inability to pay for legal representation at an inquiry did not mean that there would be a breach of the claimant's rights under Article 6. Equality of arms was not required in planning inquiries in order to produce a fair hearing. Planning inspectors were experts in their field who were capable of asking appropriate questions if the parties failed to raise any relevant matters. Further, the purpose of an inquiry was to secure planning decisions compatible with the public interest rather than to resolve issues between the parties in a purely adversarial manner.

5.4.3.2 Informal hearings
Alconbury considered planning appeals determined following an inquiry. However, many planning appeals are determined without an inquiry and following an informal hearing. Is this Article 6 compliant? Yes, according to the High Court of Northern Ireland in *R v Planning Appeals Commission, ex parte Stewart* (Gillen J), 26 June 2002. A similar result would be highly likely if a similar challenge were pursued in England and Wales. Further, following *Adlard* (see above), the written representations procedure used in many planning appeals would, it seems, also be held to be Article 6 compliant.

5.4.3.3 Self-incrimination
In deciding whether to take enforcement action, local authorities must ascertain the facts (see Lord Hoffmann's speech in *Alconbury* for a detailed consideration of the enforcement system and the role of fact-finding).

As well as having rights of entry on to land in connection with the service of notices (see, e.g., s. 324 of the TCPA 1990) local authorities can demand information from the occupier of land as to his or her interest (s. 330). Under ss. 171C and 171D of the TCPA 1990, the local planning authority can also serve planning contravention notices. Such a notice, which can be served on an occupier or other person with an interest in the land (s. 171C(2)), may require the recipient to give such information as may be specified in the notice about any operations being carried out on the land; any use of the land, or any other activities being carried out on it; and any matter going to conditions or limitations subject to which planning permission has been granted. Section 173C(3) allows the notice to require the recipient to state whether or not the land is being used for any purpose specified in the notice, or whether any specified operations or activities are or have been carried out on the land; to state when they began; to give names and addresses of any persons known to have so used the land; and to provide information relating to the planning history of the land. Section 171D(1) makes it a criminal offence not to comply with such a notice within 21 days.

As well as raising potential issues under Article 8 ECHR, there are also issues relating to the use of information obtained by such a procedure in any subsequent criminal proceedings. In *Green Environmental Industries Ltd* v *Hertfordshire County Council* [2000] 2 AC 412, a local waste regulation authority discovered a large quantity of clinical waste on Green's land and subsequently served a request for information pursuant to s. 71(2) of the EPA 1990 concerning the source of the waste and Green's business practices. Green, who was not licensed to keep waste on the site, refused to reply without confirmation from the authority that its replies would not be used against it in a prosecution. The authority issued a summons for non-compliance, which was adjourned pending an unsuccessful application for judicial review. Green appealed to the House of Lords. Whilst conceding that s. 71(2) impliedly excluded the privilege against self-incrimination, Green submitted that the 1990 Act had to be interpreted in accordance with Article 6(1) ECHR, which afforded a privilege against self-incrimination. The House of Lords held that the Strasbourg jurisprudence underpinning Article 6(1) was concerned with the fairness of a trial and not with extra-judicial inquiries and that the authority was entitled to request factual information, particularly in view of the urgent need to protect public health from an environmental hazard, even if potentially incriminating, but was not entitled to invite an admission of wrongdoing. Since none of the questions put to Green invited such an admission, Green was obliged to respond to them (see, subsequently, the non-planning decision of the Privy Council in *Stott (Procurator Fiscal)* v *Brown* [2001] 2 WLR 817).

5.4.3.4 Speed of planning decision-making
In *Lafarge Redland Aggregates Ltd* v *Scottish Ministers* 2001 SC 298, a planning application was made in 1991, called in in 1993, and not determined by 1999. In the recent decision of the European Court of Human Rights in *GH* v *Austria* (2002) 34 EHRR 42, the applicant applied for an amendment to planning permission originally granted in 1988. The amendment was granted in 1993 but a neighbour objected and it was not until 1997 that the regional government dismissed that objection, following a referral to the Administrative Court, which remitted the matter back to the regional government. The complaint was (not surprisingly) upheld. See also *Antonetto* v *Italy* (App. No. 15918/89), 20 July 2000, where the Italian authorities failed to take action in respect of an unauthorized development which affected neighbouring properties and which had been in place and unauthorized since 1967. Shorter delays might also give rise to Article 8 issues: (see [2002] JPL 674).

5.4.3.5 Costs of an inquiry
In *Cannell* v *Scottish Ministers* 2002 SLT 634, an allegation that a failure to award costs breached Article 6 ECHR was rejected by the Outer House, which noted that the European Court of Human Rights regarded liability for expenses as a matter exclusively for domestic law.

5.4.3.6　*Time limits/ousters in statutory challenges*

The typical decision-making structure in the planning sphere, consisting of an inquiry and a decision by either an inspector or the Secretary of State, followed by appeal to the High Court, frequently involves strict 'ouster' clauses. Typically, such clauses require the appeal to the High Court to be lodged within six-weeks of the decision complained of. If there is no appeal within the six-week period, the ouster clause will protect the relevant decision from challenge in other court proceedings. On the face of it, and subject to one *caveat*, there does not seem to be anything objectionable in principle to the simple existence of the ouster. It does not, in itself, prevent access to the court. The *caveat* concerns the strict result produced by the interaction of the six-week period and the provisions on service (see *Enterprise Inns plc* v *Secretary of State for the Environment, Transport and the Regions* [2000] 4 PLR 52, where Maurice Kay J held that the enactment of the six-week rule under s. 23(4) of the Acquisition of Land Act 1981 did not constitute a breach of Article 6 ECHR). In *Griffiths* [1983] 2 AC 51, the House of Lords held that the six-week period ran from the date of the decision itself, and not from the date of effective service. Accordingly, it is possible, in the sort of factual circumstance considered in *Griffiths*, for a person directly affected by a decision of an inspector or the Secretary of State to find that time has run out before he or she even knows that the decision has been taken. Given the importance attached in *Bryan* to the role of the High Court in the structure, the result achieved by *Griffiths* may need to be reconsidered.

If the assumption made above (that the ouster clauses are not intrinsically objectionable) is correct, a further issue arises out of the wording of the HRA 1998 itself. In a case where an enforcement notice has been served, appealed to an inspector and upheld by the inspector, does s. 7 of the HRA 1998 allow an individual who is prosecuted for non-compliance with the notice to take a human rights defence in the magistrates' court? The answer is no. A breach of Article 8 ECHR has been ruled out as a statutory defence to a prosecution for breach of an enforcement notice — see *R* v *Clarke* [2002] JPL 1372, where the Criminal Court of Appeal held that *R* v *Beard* [1997] 1 PLR 64 was still applicable. *R* v *Wicks* [1998] AC 92 was also considered and applied.

Another point has arisen in the pre-HRA 1998 cases of *Hughes* v *Secretary of State for the Environment* (1996) 71 P & CR 168, at 171 and 174 (*per* Christopher Lockhart Mummery QC) and *Woolhead* v *Secretary of State for the Environment* (1996) 71 P & CR 419 (*per* Jeremy Sullivan QC). In *Hughes*, one of the reasons for rejecting a challenge to the local plan as being contrary to the Convention (in a s. 287 appeal) was that it was not an issue raised at the planning inquiry and therefore not an appropriate matter for the court to consider, applying *West Cheshire Caravan Co. Ltd* v *Ellesmere Port Borough Council* [1976] 1 EGLR 143. Christopher Lockhart Mummery QC said: 'As a matter of general principle, this court is unwilling to entertain points of a legal or quasi-legal nature which could and should have been raised at the hearing or Inquiry and are raised for the first time in this court.' The judge emphasized the pragmatic reasons for this rule, namely that the matter not having been raised, there was not any evidence before the court to justify the contentions made about the local plan and the Convention (i.e. that it was discriminatory against gypsies and contrary to Article 8(1)). The judge also held that the preclusive provisions found in s. 284 prevented both the whole and part of a development plan from being challenged in proceedings under s. 288 of the TCPA 1990. In *Woolhead* (at 425 *et seq.*), Jeremy Sullivan QC, in the course of a s. 288 appeal, rejected a late application to amend the notice of motion so as to rely on Article 8 ECHR and applied *Hughes*, as 'before [the court] could begin to decide whether there would be a breach of Article 8, the issue would have to be fully argued on the facts'. The place to do that was before the inspector, so that he could report the arguments, the detailed evidence, and his conclusions in respect of that evidence to the Secretary of State.

5.4.3.7 Cases involving the local planning authority as landowner

Under the Town and Country Planning General Regulations 1992 (SI 1992/1492), local authorities are able to grant permission to themselves in respect of their own land, or in respect of development to be carried out by a developer on land which is currently in local authority ownership but which is to be sold for the purposes of the development. The Regulations include safeguards, including consultation procedures, and the possibility of call-in by the Secretary of State is also an important factor. However, the inevitable conflict of interest involved (between the need to determine planning matters objectively in the public interest and a desire to maximize the financial return to the authority) is obvious. It has been the source of considerable disquiet and is a source of a degree of cynicism about the planning system. Advice to authorities requires planning issues and land ownership issues to be considered separately (and by separate committees), but this type of 'chinese wall' requirement cannot remove the conflict completely. (Note that in *Alconbury* the House of Lords was sceptical of the need for chinese walls in central government planning decision-making.)

As explained at 5.4.1, the grant of planning permission may involve the determination of the 'civil rights' of neighbours. Accordingly, the grant of planning permission by a local authority for, say, intensive traffic generating development which might affect a residential area, might be said to involve the determination of the 'civil rights' of those living in the area. No appeal (except by way of judicial review) would lie.

Whatever the position is about the *general* absence of rights of appeal by third parties against the grant of planning permission, there is an argument that there is a breach of Article 6 ECHR where the only evaluation of the facts is by the local authority with a direct financial interest in the outcome of that evaluation. However, such arguments are not assisted by their Lordships' speeches in *Alconbury*.

In the *Alconbury* cases, the House of Lords gave consideration to the financial interest of the Crown in the development of the Ministry of Defence land at Alconbury. The House of Lords also rejected criticisms of the Crown's financial interest in the *Alconbury* case itself. Lord Slynn held (at para. 55):

> I do not consider that the financial interests of the Ministry of Defence automatically preclude a decision on planning grounds by the Secretary of State [or] in principle vitiate the whole process. If of course specific breaches of the administrative law rules are established, as for example if the financial interests of the Government were wrongly taken into account by the Secretary of State, then, specific challenges on those grounds may be possible on judicial review.

Lord Nolan said (at para. 64):

> I would only add that the particular grounds of objection taken by some respondents to the role of the Secretary of State, such as the objection in *Alconbury* based on the ground of his having a financial interest in the matter, might if appropriate be raised as objections to the ultimate decision itself. They are insufficient to disqualify him *in limine*.

Lord Hoffmann stated (at para. 130):

> Nor do I think it makes any difference that in the *Alconbury* case the Ministry of Defence, another emanation of the Crown, has a financial interest in the proposed development. Once again, this is something which might be significant if the Secretary of State was claiming to be an impartial tribunal. But as he is not, the remedy available by way of judicial review to quash a decision on the ground that the Secretary of State has taken irrelevant matters into account is sufficient to satisfy Article 6.

Lord Hutton's view was (at para. 197):

> I am further of opinion that the jurisdiction of the High Court by way of judicial review is sufficient to comply with Article 6(1) in respect of any arguments that the Ministry of Defence has a financial interest in the *Alconbury* development . . .

This seems to indicate a return to the pre-*Alconbury* position, discussed in the Divisional Court's judgment (paras 84 and 85) but not in the House of Lords speeches. This leads to consideration of the law of bias as applied to planning decisions.

The domestic law approach to bias in *R v Gough* [1993] AC 646 broadly accords with that taken in Strasbourg to impartiality under Article 6 ECHR, subject to relatively minor modifications. There must be an objective consideration by the court to determine whether the lack of impartiality is made out on the facts (*Kraska* v *Switzerland* (1993) 18 EHRR 188 (see para. 320); *Gregory* v *UK*

(1997) 25 EHRR 577). In *Gregory*, the Commission referred to the *Gough* test without criticism (para. 32), and the European Court referred to that part of the Commission's view without dissent (para. 48) (see, most recently and importantly, the Court of Appeal's decision in *Re Medicaments and Related Classes of Goods (No. 2)* [2001] 1 WLR 700).

However, in part as an exception to the general approach, the courts have also had to deal with cases where the public body which is by law the decision-taker has had an interest in the decision. A number of English cases have dealt with such financial and other interests in planning decisions (see, e.g., *R v Amber Valley District Council, ex parte Jackson* [1985] 1 WLR 298; *R v St Edmundsbury Borough Council, ex parte Investors in Industry Commercial Properties Ltd* [1985] 1 WLR 298). In these cases the English courts considered situations where planning authorities had made contracts with developers for the exploitation of land which the authorities themselves owned, undertaking to do their best to procure planning permission, to be granted to themselves. The thrust of these decisions is that, notwithstanding such interests, it was acceptable for a decision-maker in the planning context to take such decisions. The potential conflict was built into the legislative system by Parliament. In so holding, the courts followed *R v Sevenoaks District Council, ex parte Terry* [1985] 1 WLR 256 in preference to *Steeples v Derbyshire County Council* [1985] 1 WLR 256. In *Jackson, Investors in Industry* and *Terry* it was held that the authorities had acted fairly and without bias in fact, and that it was irrelevant that a likelihood of bias might reasonably have been suspected. The test was whether the council involved had 'acted in such a way that . . . when it came to consider . . . [the] application for planning permission, it could not exercise a proper discretion'.

The basis for this approach has been variously stated:

(a) the 'reasonable man' test has no application in the case of such decisions (see *Investors in Industry* at 1193–1194 (Stocker J) and Wade and Forsyth, *Administrative Law*, 8th edn (2000), at pp. 450–451; or

(b) that otherwise there would be 'an administrative impasse' (*Terry, per* Glidewell J at 233b) in cases where the planning authority had quite properly become involved in some development.

In short, these cases recognize that the possibility of bias in these regards is built into the legislative system. (It should be noted that, notwithstanding the above, it is clear that if a planning decision-maker becomes too closely involved in a decision, that decision will be liable to be quashed.)

A number of other cases have adopted a similar approach. See *R v Secretary of State for the Environment, ex parte Kirkstall Valley Campaign Ltd* [1996] 3 All ER 304 at 319, where Sedley J (as he then was) noted that the *Terry* approach could be characterized as whether the decision-maker had surrendered its judgment; and while he held that 'structural bias' could 'legitimately be described as a form of bias', it is:

> . . . jurisprudentially a different thing from a disqualifying interest held by a participant in the process. There may well be facets of the statutory set-up which contemplate dealings at less than arm's length between a planning authority and a developer, and these may in turn qualify the questions upon which independent judgment must be brought to bear, and so preserve a decision in which the planning authority has a pecuniary or other interest. But there is a difference of kind and not merely of degree between this situation and the situation of a participant member of a decision-making body who has something personally to gain or lose by the outcome.

Further, in *R* v *Secretary of State for the Environment, ex parte Greenpeace Ltd* [1994] 4 All ER 352, it was unsuccessfully argued that because of the Government's stated support for the THORP, and the state ownership of THORP, Ministers would appear as judges in their own cause unless an inquiry were held. Potts J, notwithstanding the force in the applicant's argument, concluded (at 382):

> . . . Parliament entrusted the ministers with responsibility for making the relevant decisions and gave the Secretary of State a discretion as to whether or not to direct a local inquiry. Provided the Secretary of State applied his mind genuinely and rationally to the issue of whether or not to hold a public inquiry, his decision cannot be impugned.

A similar approach has been taken in Commonwealth jurisdictions, such as New Zealand, e.g. in *Turner* v *Allison* [1971] NZLR 833 and *CREEDNZ Inc.* v *Governor-General* [1981] 1 NZLR 172, where Cooke J stated:

> Realistically, it was clear that the Government had decided that the project was to go ahead — but it was a fallacy to think that because the Government was highly likely to advise in favour of the Order, that they were disqualified from making a determination.

In other words, to do the work entrusted to them, public bodies need to form and express opinions, and to apply a strict impartiality test would make the legislation unworkable and would frustrate the objective which such legislation is designed to achieve (i.e. decision-making in this area by responsive democratic bodies). The true question is whether the public body has addressed itself to the proper statutory criteria and formed the opinion that they were satisfied. Richardson J (in *CREEDNZ*) expressed the view that the rule against bias must be tempered with realism.

The case law indicates that, notwithstanding the modification of the *Gough* test, a local authority's interest in a planning decision may in certain circumstances be so great as to amount to predetermination. One example of this comes again from New Zealand, where in *Anderton* v *Auckland City Council* [1978] 1

NZLR 657, Mahon J held that the council had become so closely associated with the company's attempt to secure planning permission for its project over the six years preceding the hearing of its application that it had completely surrendered its powers of independent judgment as a tribunal and had determined in advance to allow the application (at 692, line 8).

In *Samuel Smith Old Brewery (Tadcaster)* v *City of Edinburgh* (unreported), 3 November 2000 (Outer House), Lord Marnoch held that Article 6 ECHR did not disqualify a planning authority from considering a planning application in relation to land that it owned.

These issues were also touched on in *Friends Provident* (see above).

5.5 ARTICLE 8

Article 8(1) ECHR provides that everyone has the right to respect for private and family life and his or her home (these interests often overlap to a lesser or greater extent). They are all interests which are potentially relevant in the planning/compulsory purchase context.

Article 8(2) allows the state to restrict the rights to respect for the home to the extent necessary in a democratic society and for certain listed public interest purposes, i.e. public safety, economic well-being, protection of health, and protection of the rights of others.

Note that Article 8 ECHR imposes positive and negative obligations on 'public authorities', as defined by the HRA 1998 (i.e. including the Secretary of State and inspectors conducting inquiries, see 5.4 above). The *negative* obligation involves refraining from taking action that interferes with an individual's Article 8 rights (unless such action can be justified in terms of Article 8(2)). The *positive* obligation involves taking reasonable and appropriate measures to secure an individual's Article 8 rights (including in circumstances where those rights are being threatened or infringed by another individual or company). This may require the use of planning and other regulatory powers (such as the power to impose conditions) in such a way as to protect the rights of individuals under Article 8 from interferences, whether public or private.

5.5.1 The rights protected by Article 8

A closer examination of the rights protected by Article 8 ECHR is required at this stage.

5.5.1.1 *Home*

'Home' has been widely defined by Strasbourg case law. Thus, in *Buckley* v *UK* (1996) 23 EHRR 101 (see 5.5.3.2 below), the European Court of Human Rights was satisfied that nothing in Article 8 itself or in the case law limited the concept of 'home' to residences which had been lawfully established. It can also extend to a house which is owned and in which it is intended to live (*Gillow* v *UK* (1986) 11 EHRR 335), and can even (exceptionally) extend to the office of a professional (*Niemietz* v *Germany* (1992) 16 EHRR 97) as well as a business use associated with residential use (*Chappell* v *UK* (1989) 12 EHRR 1).

5.5.1.2   Family life
Clearly this aspect can interrelate with protection of the right to the home and can be of great relevance in the context of minority groups and enforcement action (see further below and see *Chapman* v *UK* (2001) *The Times*, 30 January).

5.5.1.3   Private life
This includes 'physical well-being' and any effect on the home. Note the Commission's consideration of the noise caused by Heathrow Airport in the light of its effect on physical well-being and private life (see, e.g., *Powell and Rayner* v *UK* (1990) 12 EHRR 355).

5.5.2   The five-stage test for application of Article 8

In considering the application of Article 8 ECHR, a five-stage test applies:

(a)   Does a right protected by Article 8 exists?
(b)   Has an interference with that right taken place?

If (a) and (b) are affirmatively answered then Article 8(1) applies, and consideration must be given to the possible justification of the interference under Article 8(2).

(c)   Is the interference in accordance with the law, i.e. is there a legal authorization for the interference?

This must be specific, sufficiently precise and can be derived from domestic statute, common law or international legal regime.

(d)   Does the interference pursue a legitimate aim?

The legitimate aims are listed in Article 8(2): national security, public safety, the economic well-being of the country, the prevention of disorder or crime, the protection of health or morals, or the protection of the rights and freedoms of others. How do these relate to the planning context?

In *Buckley* v *UK* (1996) 23 EHRR 101, a case considering enforcement proceedings against a gypsy requiring her to remove caravans from her land in the context of Article 8, on the issue of 'legitimate aim' the European Court said (at 126, para. 62):

> According to the Government, the measures in question were taken in the enforcement of planning controls aimed at furthering highway safety, the preservation of the environment and public health. The legitimate aims pursued were therefore public safety, the economic well-being of the country, the protection of health and the protection of the rights of others;

In *Miles* v *Secretary of State for the Environment* [2000] JPL 192, Malcolm Spence QC held that 'there is no infringement of Article 8 if the interference is held to be necessary for the preservation of the environment in the interests of the community'.

In the more recent case of *Chapman* v *UK* (a similar case to *Buckley*, see further below) the UK Government submitted that the enforcement of planning controls was 'in the interests of the economic well-being of the country and the preservation of the environment and public health' (at 68, para. 80). However, the European Court considered that 'the interferences in the planning procedures in this case were expressed primarily in terms of environmental policy. In these circumstances, the court finds the measures pursue the legitimate aim of protecting the "rights of others" through the preservation of the environment' and that accordingly it was not necessary to consider whether any other aims were in play. See also the recent decision of Forbes J in *Sabi* v *Secretary of State for Transport, Local Government and the Regions* [2002] EWHC Admin 1515 (preservation or enhancement of conservation area a legitimate aim under Article 8(2) following Chapman).

(e)   Is the interference necessary in a democratic society?

This is of key importance. It involves a crucial balancing exercise as to whether the interference is necessary and proportionate. In *Samaroo* v *Secretary of State for the Home Department* [2001] UKHRR 1150 (a case concerning a challenge to a deportation order) the Court of Appeal suggested that the fifth stage of the test itself involved a two-stage test: at the first stage, the question is: can the objective of the measure be achieved by other means which interfere less with an individual's rights? and, at the second stage, it is assumed that the means employed to achieve the legitimate aim are necessary in the sense that they are the least intrusive of Convention rights that can be devised in order to achieve the aim. The question at this stage of consideration is: does the measure have an excessive or disproportionate effect on the interests of affected persons? Dyson LJ explained that this essentially involved the decision-maker striking 'a fair balance between the legitimate aim on the one hand, and the affected person's convention rights on the other'.

The application of this two-stage test in the planning context has been considered in a number of cases, e.g. *Buckland* v *Secretary of State for the Environment, Transport and the Regions* [2002] JPL 1365 (CA); and *Egan* v *Secretary of State for Transport, Local Government and the Regions* [2002] EWHC 389 (Sullivan J). *Buckland* was expressly approved of by Forbes J in *R* v *Secretary of State for the Environment, Transport and the Regions, ex parte Sabi* [2002] EWHC 1515 and by Elias J in *Gosbee* v *Secretary of State for Transport, Local Government and the Regions* [2003] JPL 1467. *Buckland* was also mentioned in passing and without criticism by the Court of Appeal in *MWH & H Ward Estates Ltd* v *Monmouthshire County Council* [2003] EHLR 10. See also *Lee* v *Secretary of State for Transport, Local Government and the Regions* [2003] EWHC Admin 512 *per* Forbes J.

5.5.3   The application of Article 8 to the planning/environmental context

Article 8 ECHR is most likely to be of importance in the context of:

(a)   enforcement action against unlawfully established homes;
(b)   'third party' complaints against nearby developments.

It is also highly relevant in the context of environmental law more generally.

5.5.3.1   Third parties
'Third party' complaints against nearby proposed developments will typically involve a householder arguing to the local planning authority, or to the Secretary of State on appeal, that any form of environmental nuisance caused by a proposed neighbouring development is an interference with his or her Article 8 rights. The capacity of local residents to run such arguments is illustrated by a number of cases.

The most oft-cited Strasbourg cases in this regard are *Lopez Ostra* v *Spain* (1994) 20 EHRR 277; *Guerra and others* v *Italy* (1998) 26 EHRR 357; and *S* v *France* (1990) 65 DR 250.

In *Lopez Ostra* v *Spain*, a waste-treatment plant for the leather industry in Lorca was built close to Mrs Lopez Ostra's home. Mrs Lopez Ostra brought proceedings on account of the local authority's inactivity in respect of the nuisances and risk caused by the waste-treatment plant. She relied on Article 8 ECHR. The European Court held, unanimously, that there had been a breach. In particular, the European Court held (at para. 51) that 'severe environmental pollution' may infringe the Article 8(1) right to the home (irrespective of whether health is seriously endangered). Further, whether the question was analysed in terms of a positive duty, to take reasonable and appropriate measures to secure the applicant's rights under Article 8(1), or in terms of an interference by a public authority, to be justified in accordance with Article 8(2), the applicable principles were broadly the same, namely, that regard must be had to the fair balance that had to be struck between the competing interests of the individual and of the community as a whole. In striking the balance, the aims mentioned in Article 8(2) (including economic well-being and the rights and freedoms of others) were relevant. However, the European Court concluded (at para. 58) that a fair balance had not been struck between, on the one hand, the interest of the town's economic well-being (that of having a waste-treatment plant where there was a heavy concentration of tanneries) and, on the other hand, Mrs Lopez Ostra's effective enjoyment of her right to respect for her home and her private and family life. There had accordingly been a violation by the authority of Article 8 ECHR. The European Court went on to award damages to Mrs Lopez Ostra in respect of both pecuniary and non-pecuniary loss.

In the more recent case of *Guerra and others* v *Italy* (1998) 26 EHRR 357, the 40 applicants lived in a town approximately one kilometre away from a chemical factory. They complained that the authorities had not taken appropriate action to reduce the risk of pollution by the factory. The European Court held, again unanimously, that Article 8 ECHR had been infringed:

The European Court considers that Italy cannot be said to have 'interfered' with the applicants' private or family life; they complained not of an act by the state but of its failure to act. However, although the object of Article 8 is essentially that of protecting the individual against arbitrary interference by the public authorities, it does not merely compel the state to abstain from such interference. In addition to this primarily negative undertaking, there may be positive obligations inherent in effective respect for private or family life (see the *Airey* v *Ireland* judgment of 9 October 1979, Series A No. 32, at 17 and 32).

In the present case it need only be ascertained whether the national authorities took the necessary steps to ensure effective protection of the applicants' right to respect for their private and family life as guaranteed by Article 8 (see the *Lopez Ostra* v *Spain* judgment of 9 December 1994, Series A No. 303–C, at 55).

The European Court reiterates that severe environmental pollution may affect individuals' well-being and prevent them from enjoying their homes in such a way as to affect their private and family life adversely (see, *mutatis mutandis*, the *Lopez Ostra* judgment cited above, at 54, and 51). In the instant case, the applicants waited, right up until the production of fertilisers ceased in 1994, for essential information that would have enabled them to assess the risks they and their families might run if they continued to live at Manfredonia, a town particularly exposed to danger in the event of an accident at the factory. The Court held, therefore, that the respondent state did not fulfil its obligation to secure the applicants' right to respect for their private and family life, in breach of Article 8 of the Convention. There has consequently been a violation of that provision.

Accordingly it appears that in some circumstances a right to environmental information can arise under Article 8.

In *R (on the application of Furness)* v *Environment Agency* [2002] Env LR 26, the claimant applied for judicial review of a decision of the Environment Agency to grant authorization for the incineration of municipal waste to the interested party under the pollution control regime provided by the EPA 1990. One of the grounds was that the conditions of the authorization were insufficient to protect the claimant's procedural right to information under Article 8. Turner J rejected that ground, holding that the threat to health and property was not of a substantial kind and thus there was no obligation to make the relevant information available prior to it being placed on the public register in accordance with the Environmental Protection (Applications Appeals and Registers) Regulations 1991. The learned judge considered *Guerra* in reaching that decision.

A number of cases have involved noise. *Powell and Rayner* v *UK* (1990) 12 EHRR 335 concerned aircraft noise at Heathrow. The applicants were owners of properties situated near Heathrow. They complained of excessive noise levels in connection with the operation of the airport and the unacceptability of the UK Government's measures aimed at reducing the noise. The European Court held that there was no violation of Article 8(1), whether under its positive or negative head; the UK Government had struck a fair balance between the competing interests of the individual and the community. In particular, the operation of a major airport (even in a densely populated area) was held to pursue a legitimate aim — the increasing use of jet planes had without question become necessary in the interest of the United Kingdom's economic well-being (reference was made to the fact that Heathrow is one of the world's busiest airports and occupies a position of central importance as regards international trade and communications in the UK economy). As regards the action of the UK Government to reduce noise levels, the European Court noted that a number of measures had been introduced to control, abate and compensate for aircraft noise in and around Heathrow (these were listed at para. 42 of the judgment). It also took into account the fact that although s. 76(1) of the Civil Aviation Act 1982 limited the possibilities of legal redress open to an aggrieved person, the exclusion of liability for nuisance was not absolute.

However, the potential for noise to be the basis of an Article 8 argument in relation to a neighbouring development is illustrated by two other cases involving airport noise which have been settled by the UK Government (*Arrondale* v *UK* (1980) 19 DR 186 and DR 26 (F Sett) and *Baggs* v *UK* (1987) 52 DR 29 (F Sett)). In both cases the applicants lived much closer to the airports in question than did the applicants in *Powell*.

Note also the complaints in *S* v *France* (1990) 65 DR 250, where an eighteenth-century house on the Loire was affected by the building of a nuclear power plant. The applicant complained before the French courts of:

(a)   noise nuisance;
(b)   microclimatic changes (including loss of sunlight and increased humidity);
(c)   destruction of the amenities of the site by visual intrusion; and
(d)   industrial lighting at night.

She was awarded compensation under French law in respect of the loss of value caused by noise. The Commission held that the applicant's complaints could constitute infringement of Article 1 of Protocol 1 and/or Article 8 ECHR, the question then being whether a justifiable fair balance had been struck between the general interest and the individual's rights. On the facts the applicant was held to have been reasonably compensated and that there was accordingly no infringement of the Convention.

All of the above cases consider, in Article 8 terms, the adverse effects of and environmental nuisance caused by development which has already taken place. In transposing the principles in these cases into domestic planning law and practice it is the enforcement context that immediately comes to mind. Undoubtedly the effect of an unauthorized development on third parties in Article 8 terms would be a factor that would have to be considered in an enforcement appeal.

However, there is nothing to suggest that the principles involved should not also be brought into play in relation to a proposed interference (i.e. at the planning permission stage). The above case law is thus also potentially of relevance with regard to planning permission. However, one note of caution in this regard — in *Asselbourg and others* v *Luxemburg* (App. No. 29121/95) 29 June 1999, the applicants were complaining of the polluting effects of producing steel from scrap rather than iron ore. The European Court, in declaring the application inadmissible, said:

> It is only in wholly exceptional circumstances that the risk of a future violation may nevertheless confer the status of 'victim' on an individual applicant, and only then if he or she produces reasonable and convincing evidence of the probability of the occurrence of a violation concerning him or her personally: mere suspicions or conjectures are not enough in that respect. In the instant case, the Court considers that the mere mention of the pollution risks inherent in the production of steel from scrap iron is not enough to justify the applicants' assertion that they are the victims of a violation of the Convention. They must be able to assert, arguably and in a detailed manner, that for lack of adequate precautions taken by the authorities the degree of probability of the occurrence of damage is such that it can be considered to constitute a violation, on condition that the consequences of the act complained of are not too remote.

Although the case law considered above shows that Article 8 might involve consideration of a wide range of environmental effects/nuisances caused (or likely to be caused) by existing (or proposed) developments, it is also clear that to constitute unlawful interference under Article 8, the nuisance must be quite severe. Note the failure of the applicants in *Khatun* v *UK* (1998) 26 EHRR CD 212, where complaints about the environmental nuisance caused by the regeneration of Docklands were rejected on the basis that the public good of the redevelopment made the interference justified.

These cases all establish that 'severe environmental pollution may affect individuals' well-being and prevent them from enjoying their homes in such a way as to affect their private and family life adversely, without, however, seriously endangering their health'. Recently, these cases have been considered and applied in the litigation between Marcic and Thames Water.

Marcic sought an injunction and damages against Thames Water, his water and sewerage provider, following the repeated external flooding of his property. Marcic's case was that Thames Water had failed to carry out works to remedy defects in the drainage system and that repeated flooding of his property constituted a nuisance which Thames Water was liable for. It was also contended that Thames Water's failures amounted to a breach of Article 8 and/or Article 1 of Protocol 1.

Following a preliminary hearing ([2001] 3 All ER 698) Judge Richard Havery QC held that Thames Water was not liable in negligence or nuisance for the damage caused by the flooding. However, Thames Water was held to be in contravention of s. 6(1) of the HRA 1998 in that, in failing to carry out the recommended works to the drainage system, it had failed to put an end to the continued infringement of Marcic's Convention rights, *Guerra et al.* were applied. At a subsequent hearing ([2001] 4 All ER 326) damages were awarded. The Court of Appeal decided the case on the basis of nuisance but *obiter* ([2002] 2 WLR 932) indicated that the trial judge's human rights decision was correct. However, the House of Lords [2003] 3 WLR 1603 reversed the decision of the Court of Appeal, both in finding that there was no nuisance and on the human rights issue. The existence of adequate remedy under the statutory scheme under which Thames Water operated, coupled with the high level of deference to be paid to Parliament in cases concerning Article 8, led to the conclusion that there was no breach of the Claimant's human rights. This may have important consequences for the reasoning in other cases where Article 8 has been successfully relied upon.

Dennis v *Ministry of Defence* [2003] Env LR 34 was a nuisance action/ human rights damages claim in respect of aircraft noise caused by harriers operating from RAF Whittering. The claimants successfully relied on Article 8 and Article 1 of Protocol 1. The relevant part of Buckley J's judgment is at paras 55–63.

The *Lopez Osrta/Guerra/S* line of cases has recently been added to in respect of aircraft noise. On the first anniversary of the coming into force of the HRA 1998, the European Court of Human Rights found the increased level of noise caused by aircraft using Heathrow at night since 1993 was a breach of human rights (*Hatton and others* v *UK* (2002) 34 EHRR 1). However, this was overturned by the Grand Chamber of the European Court (2003) 37 EHRR 28.

As was widely predicted, Article 8 ECHR has become part of the armoury of third party objectors — although thus far with limited success.

In *R* v *Leicester City Council, ex parte Blackfordby & Boothcorpe Action Group Ltd* [2000] JPL 1266, Richards J considered a challenge by the residents of Blackfordby and Boothorpe (via a company) to the grant of planning permission for the extraction of coal and clay and for the disposal of 3.9 million tonnes of putrescible waste on a site close to their homes. One of the grounds was that the grant of planning permission involved an interference with the human rights of the residents and that such interference required substantial justification, which was said to be absent on the facts. The human rights point was raised in the context of the common law recognition of the ownership of land as a constitutional right (so as to avoid arguments about the HRA 1998 not being in force). The residents sought to rely on Article 8 and Article 1 of Protocol 1 and on *S* v *France* and pointed to the permitted operations causing increased levels of dust and noise and reducing the value of their properties. The challenge was rejected. Richards J was somewhat doubtful about the level of the adverse effects on the residents but went on to hold that in any event there was substantial justification for the grant of planning permission despite any adverse consequences for the local residents and referred to the substantial benefits to which the permission gave rise as compared to the existing situation. Richards J concluded that the local authority's evaluation of the effects on health and the environment could not be faulted even if the human rights context demanded more by way of justification for the interference with rights. Richards J said (at 1285–1286):

> If Article 8 of the Convention and Article 1 of the First Protocol are engaged at all in those circumstances, the degree of interference with the rights in question does not come high up the scale . . . applying the relevant principles on the assumption that there exists a human rights dimension makes little difference in this case to the analysis and no difference to the outcome. It is plain that substantial justification exists for the grant of planning permission despite the adverse consequences for local residents. I have referred earlier in this judgment to the substantial benefits to which the application gives rise as compared with the existing situation. I have also dealt specifically with the effect of the development on health and the environment. The Council's evaluation of those matters is not arguably irrational even if the issues of health and property values bring into play rights under the Convention or equivalent constitutional rights under domestic law and therefore require correspondingly more by way of justification for interference with such rights. I note too that the arguments advanced by residents in relation to the Convention were taken specifically into account.

In *R (on the application of Vetterlein)* v *Hampshire County Council* [2002] Env LR 8 (Sullivan J), local residents challenged the council's decision to grant planning permission for an energy recovery and waste transfer station. One of the grounds of challenge was that the decision infringed the claimants' Article 8 rights. Sullivan J referred to *Lopez Ostra* as illustrating that 'there may indeed be circumstances where environmental pollution is so severe that it does infringe article 8 rights even though health is not seriously endangered'. However, the learned judge observed that the facts in that case were extreme. Before referring to *Asselbourg* (see above), Sullivan J observed that '[i]n cases concerned with environmental pollution there is bound to be a broad spectrum of actual or potential impact on the quality of life' and that, on the facts before him, the claimants' case was no more than a generalized concern as to the effects of the incinerator in terms of increased nitrogen dioxide emissions, and that such generalized environmental concerns do not engage Article 8, which is concerned with an individual's right to enjoy life in his own home.

In *R (on the application of Malster) v Ipswich Borough Council* [2002] PLCR 14 (Sullivan J) and 31 October 2001 (CA), there was a challenge by a local resident to the grant of planning permission for the redevelopment of the North Stand at Ipswich Town's Portman Road stadium . It was alleged that the shadowing effect of the new stand on the claimant's garden would infringe Article 8(1). Sullivan J (at para. 88) thought it doubtful that this impact crossed the *Lopez Ostra/Guerra* threshold. However, he went on to consider whether, even assuming it *did* cross that threshold, the interference was justified under Article 8(2). Third party objectors had raised Article 8 in their representations to the Borough Council. However, nowhere in the report (or elsewhere) were human rights or, more specifically, Article 8 addressed by the Council. Sullivan J did not consider this to be a problem. He said (at para. 88) that Article 8(2).

> . . . required the local planning authority to carry out a balancing exercise between the claimant's interest in the enjoyment of her home (in this particular case her garden) . . . and the public interest in removing an outmoded stand and replacing it with a new one . . . That is precisely what the Council did. There is no suggestion that Mr Miller's report omitted any relevant impact upon the claimant or that any of her concerns were ignored in the report.

The learned judge reached a similar conclusion on Article 1, Protocol 1 (at para. 89) and the Court of Appeal expressly approved of Sullivan J's approach. Pill LJ rejected the submission that on the facts before the Court the balancing exercise required under planning law did not involve the same considerations as the balancing exercise required by Article 8(2);

In *Cummins v Camden and the Secretary of State for the Environment, Transport and the Regions* [2001] EWHC Admin 1116, Ousley J held:

> It is inconceivable that overshadowing or overlooking of a playground attached to a block of flats could constitute a want of respect for home or family life; a less attractive

view from the windows of one flat cannot do so either. The claim is not made that the effect of the grant of planning permission would be to create some overlooking of the domestic accommodation which would interfere with the normal level of privacy which someone in a central London block of flats could expect to enjoy. Accordingly, no civil rights of the fifth claimant were engaged or determined.

5.5.3.2 Enforcement action against unlawfully established homes

The scope of the right to respect for a person's home was considered by the European Court of Human Rights in *Buckley* v *UK* (1996) 23 EHRR 101.

The more recent decision of the European Court in *Chapman* needs to be considered. *Chapman* was the leading judgment, although separate judgments (along similar lines) were given in a number of other UK gypsy cases on the same day. The judgment contains a detailed and useful analysis of the domestic law relating to gypsies covering the relevant statutory provisions, case law, policies and guidance. The judgment also sets out other relevant international law instruments dealing with gypsies.

The applicant alleged that planning and enforcement measures taken against her in respect of her occupation of her land in her caravans violated her right to respect for home, her family and private life contrary to Article 8 ECHR. She complained that these actions also disclosed an interference with the peaceful enjoyment of her possessions contrary to Article 1 of Protocol 1 to the Convention and that she had no effective access to court to challenge the decisions taken by the planning authorities contrary to Article 6 ECHR. She further complained that she was subject to discrimination as a gypsy contrary to Article 14 of the Convention.

The facts in *Chapman* were somewhat involved. The applicant and her family moved on to land which she had bought and stationed a caravan there. She made various applications for planning permission to station caravans on the land and also to build a bungalow. The district council refused all of these applications. There were two appeals from these refusals of planning permission both of which appeals were dismissed (see further below). Eventually, enforcement proceedings resulted and the applicant and her husband were fined by the magistrates' court on two occasions for non-compliance with an enforcement notice.

Chapman provides a classic example of the application of the 5 stage test:

(a)   The European Court found that rights protected by Article 8 were in play.

(b)   The European Court went on to hold that the decisions of the planning authorities in refusing to allow the applicant to remain on her land in her caravans and the measures of enforcement taken in respect of her continued occupation constituted an interference with her right to respect for her private life, family life and home within the meaning of Article 8 of the Convention. The European Court therefore went on to examine whether this interference was justified under Article 8(2) as being 'in accordance with the law', pursuing a legitimate aim or aims and as being 'necessary in a democratic society' in pursuit of that aim or aims.

(c)   It was not contested by the applicant that the measures to which she was subjected were 'in accordance with the law'.

(d)   The European Court's findings on the legitimate aims pursued are considered above.

(e)   The European Court then gave detailed consideration as to whether the interference was 'necessary in a democratic society' for a legitimate aim.

The European Court noted that the seriousness of what was at stake for this applicant was demonstrated by the facts of this case — the applicant's attempts to try and move away from an itinerant lifestyle had been interfered with by the planning enforcement action taken against her.

On the other hand the European Court observed that:

(a)   Individuals affected by an enforcement notice have in principle, and this applicant had in practice, a full and fair opportunity to put before Planning Inspectors any material which they regard as relevant to their argument and, in this particular case, the applicant's personal financial and other circumstances, her views as to the suitability of alternative sites and the length of time needed to find a suitable alternative site.

(b)   The applicant moved on to her land in her caravans without obtaining the prior planning permission which she knew was necessary to render that occupation lawful (this seems to backtrack from the proposition in *Buckley* that the fact that a home is established unlawfully is of no relevance — the law seems to be that an unlawfully occupied home can still be a home within Article 8(1) but that the fact that it was unlawfully occupied is relevant to the balancing exercise under Article 8(2)).

(c)   The applicant's appeals against refusal of planning permission and enforcement notices were conducted in two public enquiries by inspectors, who were, the European Court noted, 'qualified independent experts. The inspectors in both appeals saw the site themselves and considered the applicant's representations. As is evidenced by the extension of the time period for compliance some notice was taken of the points which the applicant advanced'.

(d)   The inspectors' reasoning gave detailed consideration to the applicant's arguments, both concerning the work that she had done on the site by tidying and planting and concerning the difficulties of finding other sites in the area, and both inspectors weighed those factors against the general interest of preserving the rural character of the countryside and found that the latter prevailed.

(e) The inspectors' reports made clear that there were strong, environmental reasons for the refusal of planning permission and that the applicant's personal circumstances had been taken into account in the decision-making process;

(f) an appeal to the High Court was available insofar as the applicant felt that the inspectors, or the Secretary of State, had not taken into account a relevant consideration or had based the contested decision on irrelevant considerations.

Importantly, the European Court of Human Rights was not persuaded that there were no alternatives available to the applicant besides remaining in occupation on land without planning permission in a green belt area. The European Court (repeating what it had said in *Buckley*) noted that Article 8 did not necessarily go so far as to allow individuals' preferences as to their place of residence to override the general interest and commented that if the applicant's problem arose through lack of money, then she is in the same unfortunate position as many others who are not able to afford to continue to reside on sites or in houses attractive to them.

In all the circumstances, the European Court considered that proper regard was had to the applicant's predicament — under the terms of the regulatory framework, which contained adequate procedural safeguards protecting her interest under Article 8; and by the responsible planning authorities when exercising their discretion in relation to the particular circumstances of her case — the decisions were reached by those authorities after weighing in the balance the various competing interests.

The European Court also reiterated that it was not for it to sit in appeal on the merits of the planning decisions in issue, which were based on reasons which, for the purposes of Article 8, were relevant and sufficient to justify the interferences with the exercise of the applicant's rights.

The judgment made it clear that the humanitarian considerations which might have supported another outcome at national level cannot be used as the basis of a finding by the European Court which would be tantamount to exempting the applicant from the implementation of the national planning laws and obliging governments to ensure that every gypsy family has available for its use accommodation appropriate to its needs. Furthermore, it was held the effect of these decisions could not, on the facts of *Chapman*, be regarded as disproportionate to the legitimate aim being pursued.

One case that was considered by the Commission at the same time as *Chapman* and the other UK gypsy cases was *Varey v UK* (App. No. 26662/95). This case was the subject of a settlement and did not go before the European Court.

The applicants were paid £60,000 by the UK Government in full and final settlement of their Convention complaints (the United Kingdom also paid their costs of £15,500). It should be noted that these were not small sums. In *Varey* the Commission had found a violation of Article 8. On the face of it the only thing that distinguished *Varey* from *Chapman* was, in the later case, the lack of alternative sites to which the applicants could move (see further below).

Chapman has now been considered by the House of Lords in *Porter and others v South Buckinghamshire District Council and others* [2003] 2 AC 558. The case concerned s. 187B of the TCPA 1990 (which gives local planning authorities the power to apply to the court for an injunction to restrain an actual or apprehended breach of planning control whether or not they have exercised or are proposing to exercise any of their other enforcement powers). On such an application the court may grant such an injunction as it thinks appropriate for the purpose of restraining the breach.

Prior to the coming into force of the HRA 1998, the courts' approach to the exercise of discretion to grant an injunction under s. 187B of the TCPA 1990 was to defer to a very great degree to the judgment of the local planning authority as to the necessity or expediency of the injunctive relief sought. Thus in exercising their discretion the courts refused to consider questions of hardship, planning policy or the availability of alternative accommodation.

The central issue for the Court of Appeal in *Porter* was whether the HRA 1998 required the courts to depart from their previous approach to s. 187B of the TCPA 1990 and exercise a greater degree of independent judgment in deciding whether to grant an injunction. It was held that it did and accordingly three of the four appeals were allowed:

(a)   The Court of Appeal, in setting out the new approach to s. 187B, began by confirming that courts are not required or entitled to reach their own independent view of the planning merits of a case — matters such as whether there is an actual or anticipated breach of planning control are still to be taken as decided within the planning process.

(b)   However, in deciding whether to grant an injunction, a court will henceforth have to consider for itself all questions of hardship for the defendant and his or her family if they are required to move, questions of the family's health and education and the availability of alternative sites. These must be balanced with any countervailing considerations, such as the need to enforce planning control in the general interest and the planning history of the site.

(c)   The Court of Appeal was also of the view that in deciding whether or not to grant an injunction a court would be bound to come to some broad view as to the degree of environmental damage resulting form the breach and the urgency or otherwise of bringing it to an end. A court must henceforth be satisfied that the grant of an injunction is proportionate:

Proportionality requires not only that the injunction be appropriate and necessary for the attainment of the public interest objective sought — here the safeguarding of the environment — but also that it does not impose an excessive burden on the individual whose private interests — here the gipsy's private life and home and the retention of his ethnic identity — are at stake.

The Court of Appeal accepted that it will not always be easy in any particular case to strike the necessary balance between competing interests. It also accepted that it would be appropriate for the court to give some weight to the local authority's view, in cases where the authority could show that it had properly considered the proportionality issue, paying proper regard to all materical considerations including any hardship to the defendant.

The House of Lords confirmed the approach taken by the Court of Appeal. Indeed, the guidance offered by Simon Brown LJ at paras 38–42 of his judgment was specifically endorsed by both Lord Bingham and Lord Scott. Their Lordships recognized the same distinction between matters involving planning policy or judgment, where it would never be appropriate for the court to reach its own view, and the broader question of whether the injunction should be granted, on which the court must reach its own view. Questions of hardship are not excluded from that question and the court must reach its own view in striking a balance, although Lord Bingham also recognized that the fact that the local authority has properly considered hardship factors and nevertheless resolved to seek an injunction, would weigh heavily in favour of granting the relief sought.

There have been a number of other cases in the context of enforcement and human rights.

In *Clarke v Secretary of State for the Environment, Transport and the Regions* [2002] JPL 1365, an inspector had dismissed Clarke's appeal against the refusal to grant planning permission in relation to the continued use of certain land for the stationing of a caravan for residential use. The planning decision had involved consideration of the desire and wish of Clarke to live in a caravan, his opposition to living in a conventional home and the obligations of the local authority to apply and enforce planning control. At first instance the judge had found that for the purposes of the HRA 1998 it was necessary for a person to satisfy an inspector that living in conventional housing was contrary to his and his family's cultural values or beliefs. The judge had concluded that it was unclear from the inspector's decision whether Clarke had a 'settled and immutable antipathy to conventional housing' derived from gypsy culture and that accordingly it was necessary to remit the matter back to the inspector. The Court of Appeal dismissed the council's appeal holding that the judge had not erred in his approach, which was entirely consistent with the decision of the European Court of Human Rights in *Chapman* (see above). The Court of Appeal held that where Article 8 ECHR was engaged and it had been shown that a person held certain cultural values or beliefs, such that he was opposed to living in conventional housing, it was not sufficient for a local authority to rely on the fact that conventional housing had been offered but refused; it was necessary that the personal circumstances of the individual concerned be considered and weighed against planning considerations. The Court of Appeal held that the judge, in remitting the case, had correctly directed the inspector to carry out a detailed examination of Clarke's objections to living in conventional housing in order to determine the extent to which Article 8 was engaged.

In *Buckland* v *Secretary of State for the Environment, Transport and the Regions* [2001] 4 PLR 34, Sullivan J considered a challenge to the decision of an inspector, dismissing her appeal against the refusal of planning permission to site caravans on land in the Green Belt. The inspector held that Buckland's needs as a gypsy did not amount to 'very special circumstances' capable of outweighing the need to preserve the Green Belt, and that other suitable sites were available in the locality. It was argued that the inspector had failed to give proper consideration to Buckland's rights under Article 8 ECHR. Sullivan J dismissed the appeal holding that the inspector had properly considered all relevant matters and had reached a decision he was entitled to reach. He had considered Article 8 and had properly weighed up the claimant's rights and needs against the wider policy issues, and it was not necessary or appropriate for the court to go behind that balancing exercise. The learned judge specifically relied on *Chapman*. Sullivan J also held (at para. 52):

> It should come as no surprise that Article 8 does not require that existing policies and procedures for dealing with green belt cases be turned on their head. Our planning system is based on the premise that land owners 'properly expect to be able to use or develop their land as they judge best unless the consequences for the environment or the community would be unacceptable' (see paragraph 36 of PPG1). Or, to use the language of the European Court of Human Rights, planning permission will be granted unless there is a 'pressing social need' for a refusal.

In *Ward* v *London Borough of Hillingdon* [2002] EHLR 4, Stanley Burnton J considered a challenge by a gyspy to a removal order issued by the council under the s. 77 of Criminal Justice and Public Order Act 1994 requiring him to vacate a plot on a designated gypsy caravan site occupied by him and his family. The claimant had occupied the plot after it became vacant without waiting for the plot to be allocated by the council. The claimant argued that the council had failed to make sufficient enquiries regarding his family's needs, that the decision was unreasonable, and that s. 77 was incompatible with several Articles of the Convention including Article 8. The Judge held that the plot the claimant had occupied as a trespasser for about a fortnight could not be said to be his home but his private and family life was affected by the decision; and that in the light of *Chapman* the council's decision was appropriate and proportionate. The council was entitled to evict the claimant and his family having regard to the interests of the claimant and of the travellers already on the site and the existing waiting list:

> The Council had substantial interests to protect: the maintenance of its policy in rela-tion to the management of the site; the avoidance of disorder, if not anarchy, in the allocation of vacant plots; and the interests of those families enjoying higher a priority for the site in accordance with the Council's policy.

In *Egan v Secretary of State for the Transport, Local Government and the Regions* [2002] EWHC 389, Sullivan J considered a s. 288 application (TCPA 1990) challenging the Secretary of State's decision to refuse planning permission for a 12 pitch caravan site. The Secretary of State in considering Article 8 said (at para. 20):

> As the Inspector commented, dismissal of your clients' appeal would result in an interference with your clients' right to a home and private and family life, as protected by Article 8 of the European Convention on Human Rights. However, Article 8 of the Convention is a qualified right. There shall be no interference by a public authority with the exercise of this right, except as is in accordance with the law and necessary in a democratic society in the interests of, amongst other matters, the protection of the rights and freedoms of others. The Inspector considered that the objections to the develop-ment were substantial and that they could not be overcome by the imposition of condi-tions. The considerable public rights carried more weight than your clients' particular needs and the public interest could best be served by dismissing the appeal. The Sec-retary of State shares the Inspector's views. He also accepts that dismissal is necessary and would not place a disproportionate burden on your clients. Like the Inspector he is satisfied that dismissal of the appeal would not result in a violation of their rights under Article 8 of the Convention.

The inspector noted the Council's argument that Egan's needs could be met by existing gypsy sites but did not place significant weight upon that argument. In that context he also concluded that 'there is no essential need for [the appellants] to live on this particular site rather than in the general area'. He also took into account the fact that he had heard no evidence that a search had been undertaken to ascertain whether other more suitable sites existed. However, the inspector was nevertheless prepared to proceed on the basis that was most favourable to the appellants upon the available evidence, namely that 'dismissal of the appeal would be likely to result . . . in all the families having to resort to unauthorised camping on an itinerant basis'. The claimant argued:

(a)   that the decision to dismiss the appeal could only be proportionate if the inspector/Secretary of State had been satisfied that there was an alternative site available — ground 1; and

(b)   that since the result of dismissing the appeal was likely to result in him and his family (including his disabled mother) resorting to unauthorized camping on an itinerant basis it would be wholly disproportionate and hence a breach of Article 8 — ground 2.

Sullivan J refused the application. On ground 1, the judge held that the inspector's approach (with which the Secretary of State agreed) to alternative sites could not be faulted. On ground 2, the learned judge noted that as those issues had been addressed by the inspector and the Secretary of State, in effect the Court was being invited to substitute its own conclusions on the merits as to the proportionality of dismissing the appeal. This the judge refused to do, having undertaken a detailed assessment of the recent case law on the proper approach of the courts in reviewing the assessment of proportionality by a decision-maker (see, e.g., *Samaroo, Mahmood et al.*). The judge concluded (at paras 50 *et seq.*)

> In my judgment, the matters referred to above, in particular the fact that the court does not have expertise in the planning field, that the balancing exercise does involve matters of planning policy, and the court does not have the opportunity of looking at the site and hearing the evidence about special circumstances first hand, all point towards a considerable measure of deference being accorded to the judgment of the decision-taker as to proportionality, it having been established that the necessity threshold has been crossed.

In *Ayres v Secretary of State for the Environment, Transport and the Regions* [2002] EWHC Admin 295, Silber J considered a s. 288 challenge to an inspector's decision refusing to grant permission to Ayres (a Romany gypsy) to use land owned by him as a site for two mobile homes for Ayres and his family. In the decision letter the inspector stated that he appreciated that there appeared to be no available alternative sites while the council had indicated that it would not take immediate eviction action. The inspector considered that the council's actions and that his own actions in dismissing the appeal were not disproportionate and that there would be no violation of human rights under Article 8 ECHR. The inspector had reached that conclusion by balancing the rights of the claimant against the protection of the countryside in the public interest and other development plan considerations and on the basis that there was no proven or indicative evidence of discrimination against the claimant because he was a gypsy so as to amount to a violation of his rights under Article 14 ECHR. The main ground of challenge was that the inspector should have considered imposing a condition for a five-year temporary permission in the light of Article 8. It was said the failure to consider this showed a lack of proportionality under Article 8(2). The imposition of such a condition was mooted but not pursued at the inquiry. A wider lack of proportionality challenge was also pursued.

The judge dismissed the application. He held that the condition, having been mooted but not pursued, the inspector did not have to consider it. The HRA 1998 was not seen as affecting the legal proposition that inspectors need not cast about for conditions not suggested. The judge also rejected any wider proportionality challenge to the decision.

Challenges to the refusal of planning permission by non-gypsy landowners on the basis of Article 8 have also not met with success (*Sabi v Secretary of State for the Environment, Transport and the Regions* [2002] EWHC Admin 1515 (Forbes J); *Gosbee v Secretary of State for the Environment, Transport and the Regions* [2003] JPL 1467 (Elias J)).

For a discussion of the impact of the HRA 1998 on over-enforcement and the *Mansi* principle (*Mansi v Elstree Rural District Council* (1964) 16 P & CR 153), see *R v Secretary of State for the Environment, Transport and the Regions, ex parte Sparkes* [2000] 3 PLR 39. Nigel Macleod QC (sitting as a Deputy High Court Judge) considered Article 1 ECHR of Protocol 1 ECHR and the concept of proportionality in the light of an allegation of over-enforcement (at paras 69 *et seq.*). The challenge was rejected, but the obligation of the Secretary of State to ensure that the terms of the notice do not go beyond what is necessary to remedy the breach of control complained of is reinforced by Convention principles.

5.6   ARTICLE 1 OF PROTOCOL 1

Article 1 of Protocol 1 ECHR is well recognized in Strasbourg case law as containing 'three parts' or, rather, three different classifications of interference with the right to property as protected by this Article. These classifications of interference are:

(a)   an interference in peaceful enjoyment (the first sentence of the first paragraph of Article 1 of Protocol 1);

(b)   a deprivation (the second sentence of the first paragraph of Article 1 of Protocol 1); and

(c)   a control of use (the second paragraph of Article 1 of Protocol 1: see *Sporrong v Sweden* (1983) 5 EHRR 35 [AB2/17], at para. 61: 'This Article comprises three distinct rules'. However, as the European Court of Human Rights said in *Jacobsson v Sweden* (1990) 12 EHRR 56 [AB2/5]:

The three rules are not 'distinct' in the sense of being unconnected: the second and third rules are concerned with particular instances of interference with the right to peaceful enjoyment of property and should therefore be construed in the light of the general principle enunciated in the first rule.

(See also, e.g., *The former King of Greece* v *Greece* (2001) 33 EHRR 21, at para. 50.)

The most serious interference under Article 1 of Protocol 1 is a deprivation, and the least serious is a control of use.

The Strasbourg jurisprudence has held that planning legislation, including the imposition and enforcement of planning and land use restrictions, constitute 'controls of use' (see Simor and Emmerson, *Human Rights Practice* (Sweet & Maxwell) para. 15.028, and the case law cited in footnote 12. This is so notwithstanding the fact that such controls can have the effect of reducing the value of the land significantly. The case law makes it clear that insofar as the land may be used for an alternative purpose and is not rendered worthless, the measures will constitute a control of use and not a deprivation: (see, e.g., *Sporrong* (above), at para. 63; *Pine Valley Developments* v *Ireland* (1992) 14 EHRR 319.

Similarly, environmental measures such as the imposition of reforestation obligations (see *Denev* v *Sweden* (1989) 59 DR 127, at 130), the designation of land as a protected natural site (see *Oerlemans* (1991) 15 EHRR 561 at the Commission stage), and a requirement that landowners allow their land to be used for hunting in the interests of encouraging rational management of game stocks have all been held to constitute controls of use (*Chassagnou* v *France* (1999) 7 BHRC 151). The facts of the last case have a close parallel to this case – with national legislation requiring landowners to allow certain activities on their land without interruption.

Article 1 of Protocol 1 overlaps with Article 8. Article 1 of Protocol 1 is, of course, wider than Article 8 in that the protection offered is not limited to the 'home'. In cases such as *Powell and Rayner* v *UK* (1990) 12 EHRR 335 and *S* v *France* (1990) 65 DR 250 (see above) nuisance was the basis of complaints under Article 8 and rule 1 of Article 1, Protocol 1 (see further above).

Like Article 8, Article 1 of Protocol 1 was widely predicted as likely to be deployed as part of the armoury of a third party objector to development.

In *Malster* (see above), Sullivan J, in considering a third party challenge to the grant of planning permission for a new stand at Ipswich Town's stadium, stated that Article 1 of Protocol 1 'does not take the matter any further, since the Club is equally entitled to the enjoyment of its possessions. It should not be prevented from developing the . . . stand unless there are good reasons for refusing planning permission in the public interest'.

In *Chapman* the European Court rejected the complaint made under Article 1 of Protocol 1 referring to the reasons it had given in respect of Article 8 ECHR.

5.6.1   Rule (1) — interference with peaceful enjoyment of property

Rule (1), like Article 8 ECHR, gives rise to the possibility of complaints being made by those affected by the construction of a nearby development. Article 1 of Protocol 1 is, of course, wider than Article 8 ECHR, in that the protection offered is not limited to the 'home'. Thus in cases such as *Powell and Rayner* v *UK* (1990) 12 EHRR 335 and *S* v *France* (see above), noise nuisance was the basis of complaints under Article 8 ECHR and rule (1) of Article 1 of Protocol 1 (see further at 5.5.3.1). The European Court recognized that severe noise nuisance, that in turn seriously affected the value of property, could amount to partial expropriation.

5.6.2   Rule (2) — deprivation of property

Rule (2) clearly relates to compulsory purchase orders see Chapter Six.

5.6.3   Rule (3) — control of the use of property

Rule (3) is likely to be the most important rule so far as the exercise of planning powers is concerned. In terms of the refusal of planning permission, it was said in *ISKCON* v *UK* (1994) 76–A DR 90: 'As a general principle, the protection of property rights ensured by [Article 1 of Protocol 1] cannot be used as a ground for claiming planning permission to extend permitted use of property.' However, rule (3) may bite with more force in respect of enforcement notice action and the imposition of conditions.

In *Chater* v *UK* 52 DR 250, it was held by the Commission that an interference with Article 1 of Protocol 1 had occurred when two enforcement notices prevented an applicant from using his property for vehicle repair and maintenance and for a haulage business. He had not obtained the relevant planning permission. It was held on the facts that a proper balance had been struck between the applicant's personal interest and the general interests, and the application was declared inadmissible.

Further, from *Denev* v *Sweden* (see above), it is clear that the control of the use of property covered by rule (3) applies to requirements on individuals to take positive action as well as the imposition of restrictions on their activities. That case involved an obligation to plant trees of a particular species imposed by a Forestry Act (but this would apply equally to conditions). The interference was found to be justified: the Act protected the environment and secured high and valuable timber yield; if the applicant did not wish to cultivate trees, he could use his land for another purpose. However, it is not difficult to imagine planning conditions being attacked by reference to rule (3): consider a condition requiring excessive expenditure, or which rendered the property unsaleable, i.e. an agricultural occupancy condition. Note that in *Herrick* v (1986) 8 EHRR 66, the restriction on the use of a building as 'an occasional shelter not amounting to a residence' for limited periods was regarded as a restriction of the applicant's rights under rule (1), not rule (3).

In *Langton* v *Secretary of State for the Environment, Food and Rural Affairs* (see above) it was also argued that decisions to issue and subsequently enforce a notice given under the Animal By-Products Order 1999, article 5(2) breached the right to peaceful enjoyment of his possessions under the Article 1, Protocol 1 and consequently, that there was an entitlement to compensation or damages for the harm caused. Nigel Pleming QC rejected this holding that the works as set out in the notice and enforced by the local authority were proportionate to the interference with rights under Article 1, Protocol 1, as the public interest, in matters of public or animal health, required speedy intervention.

In *R (on the application of Davies)* v *Crawley Borough Council* [2001] 46 EGCS 178, judicial review was sought of the council's decision to adopt a street trading scheme under s. 3 of the Local Government (Miscellaneous Provisions) Act 1982. The claimants each owned a mobile catering van from which they sold food to workers on an industrial estate. There were a number of other catering vans operating on the estate and the council became aware of amenity and traffic congestion problems resulting from the activities of these street traders. Under the scheme, the claimants were required to move their vans to alternative locations and were charged an annual fee. Goldring J rejected a challenge based on Article 1 of Protocol 1.

In *Fisher* v *English Nature* [2003] 4 All ER 366, Lightman J rejected a challenge to SSSI notification on the basis of a breach of Article 1 of Protocol 1.

Chapter Six

Compulsory Purchase

David Elvin QC

6.1 INTRODUCTION

This chapter examines the role of human rights in the compulsory purchase of private property, which, since acquisition must generally be justified by reference to the public interest, on its face directly raises human rights issues. However, an examination of both pre-HRA 1998 law and the developments which have followed its coming into force, suggests that while there are aspects which raise Convention issues, the substance of the pre-Act law appears unlikely to require radical reappraisal, especially in the light of the correspondence between the principles set out in *R v Secretary of State for Transport, ex parte de Rothschild* [1989] 1 All ER 933 and *Chesterfield Properties plc v Secretary of State for the Environment* (1997) 76 P & CR 117 and the principles applied by Strasbourg in the Article 1 of Protocol 1 cases (e.g. *Sporrong and Lönnroth v Sweden* (1983) 5 EHRR 35 and *James v UK* (1986) 8 EHRR 123. In terms of the current procedures, the judgment of the House of Lords in *R v Secretary of State, ex parte Alconbury Development Ltd and others* [2001] 2 WLR 1389 is of considerable importance, since it was held that the current procedure of ministerial compulsory purchase was both lawful and compatible with Article 6 ECHR (contrary to the views of the Divisional Court in [2001] JPL 291 and the Lord Ordinary in *County Properties v Scottish Ministers* 2000 27 SLT 965, also reversed on appeal [2001] 4 PLR 122).

This chapter will consider the issues by reference to the following:

(a)   procedural issues;
(b)   the substantive determination of whether the order ought to be made;
(c)   the relevance of compensation in determining whether to authorize acquisition; and
(d)   specific rules.

6.2 PROCEDURAL ISSUES

The effects of the *Alconbury* litigation have already been considered in earlier chapters. It should be noted that one of the three test cases which reached the House of Lords (*R* v *Secretary of State for the Environment, Transport and the Regions, ex parte Legal and General Assurance Society Ltd*) involved the challenge to a draft ministerial compulsory purchase order promoted by the Highways Agency (an executive agency of the DETR) in order to facilitate road proposals. As with the planning cases, the challenge was to the compatibility *in principle* of the process with Article 6 ECHR rather than issues involving the specific facts of the case (in respect of which the inquiry had not concluded by the time of the hearing). The only fact of importance was the promotion of the order by an arm of the executive, legally part of the department of the confirming minister, which was said, therefore, to give rise to lack of compliance due to absence of both independence and impartiality.

For reasons which are set out elsewhere, the House of Lords held the procedures under consideration compatible with Article 6 ECHR. As Lord Clyde stated (at para. 159):

> As I indicated at the outset, Parliament, democratically elected, has entrusted the making of planning decisions to local authorities and to the Secretary of State with a general power of supervision and control in the latter. Thereby it is intended that some overall coherence and uniformity in national planning can be achieved in the public interest and that major decisions can be taken by a minister answerable to Parliament. Planning matters are essentially matters of policy and expediency, not of law. They are primarily matters for the executive and not for the courts to determine. Moreover as matter of generality the right of access to a court is not absolute. Limitations may be imposed so long as they do not so restrict or reduce the access that the very essence of the right is impaired (*Tinnelly and Sons Ltd* v *United Kingdom* (1998) 27 EHRR 249, para. 72). Moreover the limitation must pursue a legitimate aim and the relationship between the means employed and the aim sought to be achieved must be reasonably proportionate (*Ashingdane* v *United Kingdom* (1985) 7 EHRR 528). In the context of the present cases the aim of reserving to a minister answerable to Parliament the determination of cases which will often be of very considerable public interest and importance is plainly a legitimate one . . . it seems to me that there exists a reasonable balance between the scope of matters left to his decision and the scope of the control possessed by the courts over the exercise of his discretionary power.

The House of Lords did not consider in great detail the differences between compulsory purchase and planning procedures, and applied the same reasoning to both. Indeed, the same issues arise in compulsory purchase order cases (including orders made under the Transport and Works Act 1992) as in planning cases, since:

(a)   In non-ministerial order cases, decisions are made by local authorities applying in many instances their own local policies for regeneration and development. Confirmation of proposed orders where there are unresolved objections is by the Secretary of State for the Environment, Transport and the Regions, who in many cases will apply his own policies in considering whether to make the orders (or to modify them). (See s. 2(2) and Part II of the Acquisition of Land Act 1981 and the Compulsory Purchase by Non-ministerial Acquiring Authorities (Inquiries Procedure) Rules 1990 (SI 1990/512).)

(b) In the case of ministerial orders, the decision is made by the Secretary of State. In highways cases, the order is proposed by the Highways Agency, which is an agency of the DETR. (See s. 2(3) of and Sch. 1 to the Acquisition of Land Act 1981 and the Compulsory Purchase by Ministers (Inquiries Procedure) Rules 1994 (SI 1994/3264).)

(c) As in planning cases, challenges to confirmed orders can be made only by statutory appeal, on judicial review grounds, under s. 23 of the Acquisition of Land Act 1981. This in turn raises the Article 6 issues considered in the *Alconbury* litigation.

On the question of the mechanics of High Court challenges, it should be noted that the six-week time limit in s. 23 of the Acquisition of Land Act 1981 has been held not to be unduly restrictive of access to challenge a decision and is therefore compatible with Article 6 (although decided before 2 October 2000) (see *Enterprise Inns plc v Secretary of State for the Environment, Transport and the Regions* [2000] JPL 1256).

6.3 SUBSTANTIVE DETERMINATION

As far as the making of a compulsory purchase order is concerned, the principally applicable provisions of the ECHR are likely to be Articles 8 and Article 1 of Protocol 1, although in rare cases other Convention Articles may be engaged. The general principles of the Strasbourg case law relating to those provisions are set out in Chapter Two.

Insofar as Article 8 rights are engaged in the compulsory purchase context, it seems most likely that they will be those relating to the 'home', although it is conceivable that issues concerning the rights to private and family life could arise if the effect of the proposed order would interfere with those rights.

6.3.1 General approach

6.3.1.1 Proportionality

The approach of the courts to the determination of the issue whether private rights should be overridden by a compulsory order has undergone some discussion, but currently stands as explained by the Court of Appeal in *R v Secretary of State for Transport, ex parte De Rothschild* [1989] 1 All ER 933 and by Laws J in *Chester-field Properties plc v Secretary of State for the Environment* (1997) 76 P & CR 117. The approach has recently been considered and reaffirmed by Harrison J in *London Borough of Bexley v Secretary of State for the Environment, Transport and the Regions and Sainsbury's Supermarkets Ltd* [2001] JPL 1442. See also *Tesco Stores Ltd v Secretary of State for the Environment, Transport and the Regions* (2000) 80 P & CR 427 (a pre-HRA 1998 case). It is clear that the acquisition, and the overriding of private rights, must be shown to be justified by sufficiently compelling reasons in the public interest.

The pre-HRA 1998 approach to reviewing compulsory purchase orders is set out in *De Rothschild*, where Slade LJ held (at 938–939):

> In answer to counsel's submissions as to 'special rules', I summarise my conclusions thus. First, I do not accept that any special rules beyond the ordinary *Wednesbury/ Ashbridge* rules fall to be applied when the court is considering a challenge to the Secretary of State's confirmation of a compulsory purchase order. Second, however, the Secretary of State, as counsel on his behalf accepted and submitted, must be satisfied that the compulsory purchase order is justified on its merits before he can properly confirm it. He must not exercise his powers capriciously. Given the obvious importance and value to land owners of their property rights, the abrogation of those rights in the exercise of his discretionary power to confirm a compulsory purchase order would, in the absence of what he perceived to be a sufficient justification on the merits, be a course which surely no reasonable Secretary of State would take.

I think that this approach to the matter reconciles the judgments in *Prest v Secretary of State for Wales* ((1981) 81 LGR 193) with the ordinary principles of our law applicable to claims for judicial review. Furthermore, it has the merit of avoiding any reference to onus of proof, which is an expression more appropriate, as counsel for the Secretary of State pointed out, to a *lis inter partes*. As Lord Denning MR observed in *Prest* itself, the Secretary of State's decision certainly is not a *lis inter partes*. As he said (81 LGR 193, at 200):

> It is a public inquiry — at which the acquiring authority and the objectors are present and put forward their cases — but there is an unseen party who is vitally interested and is not represented. It is the public at large. It is the duty of the Secretary of State to have regard to the public interest.
>
> In making his decision, there are a multitude of different factors which the Secretary of State has to take into account. To mention only a few: questions of landscape and other amenity, feasibility, cost and delay. To talk of questions of onus of proof when so many competing factors have to be taken into the balance seems to me not only inappropriate but a somewhat difficult concept.

The clear effect of the above, pre-HRA 1998, was that the judgment of the decision-maker was subject to challenge only on traditional *Wednesbury* grounds. However, the practical application of that approach is not simple since, given the issue of the deprivation of private property rights, the court will look more carefully at the justification put forward for acquisition. This sits comfortably with pre-HRA 1998 principle, in that the intensity of *Wednesbury* scrutiny increases if fundamental human rights are engaged (see, e.g., *R v Ministry of Defence, ex parte Smith* [1996] QB 517, at 554–556 and *R v Lord Saville of Newdigate, ex parte A* [1999] 4 All ER 860, at 872, para. 37 (although see now *R v Home Office, ex parte Daly* [2001] 2 AC 532)). Indeed, in the compulsory purchase context, Laws J stated in *Chesterfield*:

> To some ears it may sound a little eccentric to describe, for example, Kwik Save's ownership of their shop in Stockton as a human right; but it is enough that ownership of land is recognised as a constitutional right, as Lord Denning said it was. The identification of any right as 'constitutional', however, means nothing in the absence of a written constitution unless it is defined by reference to some particular protection which the law affords it. The common law affords such protection by adopting, within *Wednesbury*, a variable standard of review. There is no question of the court exceeding the principle of reasonableness. It means only that reasonableness itself requires in such cases that in ordering the priorities which will drive his decision, the decision-maker must give a high place to the right in question. He cannot treat it merely as something to be taken into account, akin to any other relevant consideration; he must recognise it as a value to be kept, unless in his judgment there is a greater value that justifies its loss. In many arenas of public discretion, the force to be given to all and any factors which the decision-maker must confront is neutral in the eye of the law; he may make of each what he will, and the law will not interfere because the weight he attributes to any of them is for him and not the court. But where a constitutional right is involved, the law presumes it to carry substantial force. Only another interest, a public interest, of greater force may override it. The decision-maker is, of course, the first judge of the question whether in the particular case there exists such an interest which should prevail.

Earlier, Laws J had noted that:

> In the course of argument I suggested to counsel that recent high authority shows that where what may be called a fundamental or constitutional right is threatened by an administrative decision of the state, the court on judicial review will require the public decision-maker to demonstrate that there existed substantial public interest grounds for his interference with the right. I had in mind in particular Lord Bridge's speeches in *Bugdaycay* [1987] AC 514 at 531G and in *Brind* [1991] 1 AC 696 at 748F–749B, and the judgment of Sir Thomas Bingham MR, as he then was, in *ex parte Smith, ex parte* ... As is well known the first dealt with refugees, the second with free expression, and the third with the position of homosexuals in the armed forces: all very far distant from compulsory purchase. I should say at once that the text of these cases was not looked into at the hearing before me; nor was the Strasbourg jurisprudence upon Article 1 of

the First Protocol to the European Convention on Human Rights, to which some reference was also made. But in light of the decision which I have reached, there is no injustice to the respondents in that not having been done.

In the *Bexley* case (above), Harrison J was faced with a direct post-HRA 1998 challenge to a compulsory purchase order based on Convention grounds. He considered both *De Rothschild* and *Chesterfield* and held their approach to be compatible with Article 1 of Protocol 1 jurisprudence.

Hence, even absent direct consideration of the ECHR, scrutiny of the lawfulness of the decision would depend on a careful examination by the decision-maker of the public interest justification for acquisition. While this, pre-HRA 1998, would not involve the court in exercising its own judgment as to the justification, the more intensive approach taken to review where fundamental rights are in issue would be applicable. Even so, there is a close similarity between the approach of the courts applying pre-HRA 1998 principles and the Article 1 of Protocol 1 requirement of 'fair balance'.

Article 8 ECHR may engage in compulsory purchase cases where the proposed order seeks to acquire land which includes a home, or even the broader 'domicile' (see *Niemietz* v *Germany* (1992) 16 EHRR 97). The effect of the deprivation of, or interference with, those rights will have to be justified in Article 8(2) terms, which include economic grounds. The interference will have to be proportionate to the precise interference with the private rights in issue, which again ties in closely with the requirement to show a 'fair balance' under Article 1 of Protocol 1. It is arguable that rights protected specifically by Article 8 ECHR should be accorded greater weight when balanced against the justification for interference, e.g. if the order proposed is to enable a private development to proceed at the expense of private rights. However, it is questionable whether this will differ significantly from the approach taken already (*Chesterfield*), where there is a recognized constitutional right to retain property in the absence of demonstration of weighty grounds for deprivation in the public interest.

Nonetheless, it is possible that greater weight might be attached to such matters now that Convention-based fundamental rights are engaged, and greater scrutiny of the options short of outright acquisition, e.g. the possibility of an agreement with the landowner, may need to be explored fully. Although alternatives short of acquisition fall to be considered at present, in practical terms a landowner may often find that this does not assist greatly if there has been proper consideration of the options open to the authority. He or she may find himself or herself pushed up hard against an inquiry deadline and placed in a difficult bargaining position because there is at least a prima facie case for acquisition and (especially if the proposal is to facilitate a commercial development scheme) an unwilling negotiating party. Convention rights should focus attention more closely on the importance of the rights sought to be expropriated.

Perhaps the principal prospect for adjusting the approach post-HRA 1998 lies in the reviewing court reconsidering for itself the justification for acquisition, namely determining whether the decision is proportionate under Article 8 ECHR or strikes a fair balance in Article 1 of Protocol 1 terms. Since the court is charged under s. 6 of the HRA 1998 to give effect to Convention rights, it must consider the adequacy of the justification.

The extent to which the court will take this duty is unclear and cases such as *Porter* show, at least in some contexts, a greater attention to Article 8 issues. However, the European Court has refused to involve itself in detailed consideration of the merits of policy and planning judgments (in, e.g., *Buckley* v *UK* (1996) 23 EHRR 101; *Chapman* v *UK* (2001) 10 BHRC 48) but the reason for that has been the wide margin of appreciation accorded by an international court to national authorities and the difficult questions of policy and judgment inherent in this area of decision-making. In the context of expropriation, the European Court said in *James* v *UK* (1986) 8 EHRR 123 (at para. 46):

> . . . the decision to enact laws expropriating property will commonly involve consideration of political, economic and social issues on which opinions within a democratic society may reasonably differ widely. The court, finding it natural that the margin of appreciation available to the legislature in implementing social and economic policies should be a wide one, will respect the legislature's judgment as to what is 'in the public interest' unless that judgment be manifestly without reasonable foundation.

More recently (although in the planning context), in paras 91 and 92 of the judgment in *Chapman*, the Court stated:

> 91. In this regard, a margin of appreciation must, inevitably, be left to the national authorities, who by reason of their direct and continuous contact with the vital forces of their countries are in principle better placed than an international court to evaluate local needs and conditions. This margin will vary according to the nature of the Convention right in issue, its importance for the individual and the nature of the activities restricted, as well as the nature of the aim pursued by the restrictions (see the *Dudgeon* v *the United Kingdom judgment* 22 October 1982, Series A No. 45, p. 21, ° 52, and the *Gillow* v *the United Kingdom judgment of* 24 November 1986, Series A No. 109, p. 22, ° 55).
>
> 92. The judgment in any particular case by the national authorities that there are legitimate planning objections to a particular use of a site is one which the Court is not well equipped to challenge. It cannot visit each site to assess the impact of a particular proposal on a particular area in terms of impact on beauty, traffic conditions, sewerage and water facilities, educational facilities, medical facilities, employment opportunities and so on. Because Planning Inspectors visit the site, hear the arguments on all sides and allow examination of witnesses, they are better situated than the Court to weigh the arguments. Hence, as the Court observed in *Buckley* . . . 'insofar as the exercise of discretion involving a multitude of local factors is inherent in the choice and

implementation of planning policies, the national authorities in principle enjoy a wide margin of appreciation', although it remains open to the Court to conclude that there has been a manifest error of appreciation by the national authorities. In these circumstances, the procedural safeguards available to the individual applicant will be especially material in determining whether the respondent State has, when fixing the regulatory framework, remained within its margin of appreciation. In particular, it must examine whether the decision-making process leading to measures of interference was fair and such as to afford due respect to the interests safeguarded to the individual by Article 8 (see the *Buckley* judgment . . . 76–77).

Although there was a substantial dissent on proportionality in *Chapman* (7 out of 17 judges), this was limited to a narrow issue of the existence of a consensus on the rights of gypsies. The familiar position on the margin of appreciation was repeated even by the minority: see the principal dissenting opinion (at para. 3). Moreover, the recent decision of the Grand Chamber in *Hatton v UK*, 5 July 2003, demonstrates the possibility of a wide margin of appreciation in Article 8 cases on public policy and economic grounds.

The Administrative Court dealing with judicial review and statutory reviews has traditionally been unwilling to deal with questions which go to the merits of the case (*Ashbridge Investments Ltd v MHLG* [1965] 1 WLR 1320), whereas determining proportionality and/or 'fair balance' will almost inevitably involve some degree of consideration of the merits. Even within the strict confines of the Strasbourg approach, the European Court would intervene if 'there has been a manifest error of appreciation by the national authorities' or due respect has not been afforded to Article 8 ECHR rights.

The existence of the margin of appreciation within the domestic context has been recognized by the House of Lords in *DPP v Kebeline* [1999] 3 WLR 972, at 993–994, and by Lord Slynn in *Alconbury*, at paras 51 and 52. The margin of appreciation still has some application within the jurisdiction as between the decision-maker and the court, especially where questions of fact or highly fact-specific judgments are involved. As Lord Hope stated in *DPP v Kebeline*:

In this area difficult choices may have to be made by the executive or the legislature between the rights of the individual and the needs of society. In some circumstances it will be appropriate for the courts to recognise that there is an area of judgment within which the judiciary will defer, on democratic grounds, to the considered opinion of the elected body or person whose act or decision is said to be incompatible with the Convention . . . It will be easier for such an area of judgment to be recognised where the Convention itself requires a balance to be struck, much less so where the right is stated in terms which are unqualified. It will be easier for it to be recognised where the issues involve questions of social or economic policy, much less so where the rights are of high constitutional importance or are of a kind where the courts are especially well placed to assess the need for protection.

Lord Slynn in *Alconbury* noted that while there was a difference between the *Wednesbury* approach and the application of proportionality by Strasbourg, the difference 'in practice is not as great as is sometimes supposed'. However, he added that:

> Reference to the Human Rights Act however makes it necessary that the court should ask whether what is done is compatible with Convention rights. That will often require that the question should be asked whether the principle of proportionality has been satisfied . . . This principle does not go as far as to provide for a complete rehearing on the merits of the decision. Judicial control does not need to go so far. It should not do so unless Parliament specifically authorises it in particular areas.

Although those statements recognize that deference should still be accorded to the decision-maker where a judgment has to be struck — as under Article 8 ECHR and Article 1 of Protocol 1 — they do not forbid intervention, and the least which can be said at the moment is that the courts would be justified in taking a more interventionist approach when considering whether the decision is proportionate. At its most basic level, the courts must consider whether there has been a proper appreciation of Convention rights and whether 'due respect' has been given to rights under Article 8 ECHR and Article 1 of Protocol 1. It would therefore be prudent for public authorities, in approaching compulsory acquisitions, to ensure that ECHR rights were fully taken into account and assessed, and that decisions were based on an appreciation of Convention case law on the subject.

However, the approach of the Administrative Court in the *Bexley* case and in *Tesco Stores Ltd* v *Secretary of State for the Environment, Transport and the Regions and Wycombe District Council* (2000) 80 P & CR 427, shows that the existing domestic approach is considered compatible with the approach under the Convention. However, in neither case was attention focused in detail on the extent of the margin of appreciation (and in the case of *Tesco*, the decision pre-dated the HRA 1998) and the issue may warrant further consideration in the light of the above *dicta* from *Kebeline* and *Alconbury*. Given the mandatory requirements of the HRA 1998 and the need to consider compatibility with the Convention, it is difficult to see in any event how the Administrative Court can avoid considerations of whether there has been compliance with Article 8 ECHR and Article 1 of Protocol 1 in an individual case, even if the result does not differ greatly from the position under pre-HRA law. Most recent Government guidance in para. 14 of ODPM Circular 02/03 (*Compulsory Purchase Orders*) integrates ECHR issues with domestic policy:

> A compulsory purchase order should only be made where there is a compelling case in the public interest. An acquiring authority should be sure that the purposes for which it is making a compulsory purchase order sufficiently justify interfering with the human rights of those with an interest in the land affected, having regard, in particular, to the

provisions of Article 1 of Protocol 1 to the ECHR and, in the case of a dwelling, Article 8 ECHR.

6.3.1.2   Alternatives to compulsory purchase

The European Court has stopped short of holding that, where there are alternatives to the act of interference with possession, those alternatives must be pursued first — see *James* v *UK* (1986) 8 EHRR 123, at para. 51:

> The availability of alternative solutions does not in itself render the leasehold reform legislation unjustified; it constitutes one factor, along with others, relevant for determining whether the means chosen could be regarded as reasonable and suited to achieving the legitimate aim being pursued, having regard to the need to strike a 'fair balance'. Provided the legislature remained within these bounds, it is not for the Court to say whether the legislation represented the best solution for dealing with the problem or whether the legislative discretion should have been exercised in another way (see, *mutatis mutandis*, the *Klass and others* judgment of 6 September 1978 . . . para. 49).

Indeed, domestic authority appears already to follow a comparable line. In the recent case of *In the petition of Standard Commercial Property Securities Ltd*, 15 August 2000 (Court of Session), the issue was whether Glasgow City Council had acted unlawfully in approving a compulsory purchase order since it had proceeded on the erroneous basis that to achieve a comprehensive redevelopment, a single developer was required. Lord Nimmo Smith held (at paras 44 and 45 of his opinion):

> 44.   . . . One assumption which underlies the report appears to be that a single comprehensive redevelopment of the whole site, at present occupied by several buildings with different owners, by a single developer is required. It does not necessarily follow that because the whole site requires to be redeveloped a single comprehensive development is required. There is thus no discussion of the possibility of the involvement of more than one developer, or of separate (but mutually compatible) redevelopments of different parts of the site. There is no reference at all to the discussions with Bass about its proposals for redevelopment of the whole site or in any event that part of it occupied by the existing building at the corner of Buchanan Street and Bath Street. There is thus no comparison made between the merits of the proposals of Bass (and later of Standard) and those of Atlas. The committee must be taken to have decided that the corner building required to be compulsorily acquired as part of the CPO site in the belief that its owners were holding the project to ransom, as it was put in the report. Irrespective of what approaches, if any, had been made to Bass by Sears or Atlas, the fact that Bass had proposals of its own and had discussed them with officials of the Council was in my view clearly relevant and material and should have been before the committee in Mr Bennett's report. Moreover, if, as I must assume from counsel's primary submission, the committee took the view that s. 191 had no application for the purposes of deciding whether or not to enter into an agreement with Atlas, it cannot be

said that they took account of the matters which they required to consider under that section.

45. For these reasons in my opinion the committee failed to take account of relevant and material considerations in exercising their discretion under sections 189 and 191 and their decision falls to be quashed . . .

In terms of the ECHR, it seems likely that a similar result would have been reached. By excluding a proper consideration of the alternatives, rather having determined that expropriation was the best option available in the public interest, the decision-maker would have failed to approach the fair balance correctly.

However, as the above case shows, the question of alternatives is not irrelevant to the decision to permit acquisition, and *James* does not make it so. In terms of the Convention, consideration of whether expropriation is proportionate may require the taking up of an alternative short of expropriation, especially if it is practicable. There would have to be consideration then of the extent to which there were compelling reasons in the public interest to justify the pursuit of expropriation rather than pursuing another means to the same end.

For example, where a comprehensive development scheme is proposed by a public authority, perhaps with its own preferred commercial developer, there is bound to be some interplay between the public interest and private commercial concerns. If the landowner has its own plans for development (as in *Standard Commercial Property Securities*), or is willing to participate in the overall redevelopment scheme on a reasonable basis, this will require careful consideration: the public interest cannot legitimately *per se* prefer the commercial interests of the council's developer over the rights of the landowner (whether with or without Article 8 support), and the purpose of the acquisition and public interest will have to be carefully evaluated to determine whether expropriation is proportionate on the facts. It underlines the need for public authorities to act carefully in such cases and ensure that they are able to support by objective means (e.g. by obtaining independent expert advice) the decision to pursue a compulsory purchase scheme in tandem with a preferred developer.

6.3.1.3 *The relevance of compensation*
In terms of the ECHR, the existence of compensation is material to determining whether or not the acquisition amounts to a violation of Article 1 of Protocol 1. This marks a departure from what many authorities still regard as the orthodox position when making compulsory purchase orders, namely that compensation is not relevant at the order stage and is a matter to be left to the Lands Tribunal in the event that the order is confirmed. This can be seen, for example, in the position of the former Department of Transport in *R* v *Secretary of State, ex parte Balchin* [1998] 1 PLR 1, at 5, para. 13 of the Parliamentary Commissioner's report. It is not entirely clear whether this approach would stand up to careful scrutiny in the

case of an individual disadvantaged by the lack or inadequacy of compensation for a compulsory purchase even prior to 2 October 2000, although there were indications to the opposite effect in other contexts (see *R* v *Secretary of State for the Environment, Transport and the Regions, ex parte Alliance against the Birmingham Northern Relief Road* [1999] JPL 426, at 432–433; *Alnwick District Council* v *Secretary of State for the Environment, Transport and the Regions* [1999] 4 PLR 43, at 54–57). However, where, as in compulsory purchase cases, there is a specific requirement to strike a balance, and compensation may be directly relevant to the striking of the balance, it seems open to question whether the approach in those cases can be considered applicable.

In the light of the HRA 1998 and Article 1 of Protocol 1 to ECHR, it appears that to a degree at least compensation must now be regarded as material *in principle* in determining the proportionality of expropriation as against private rights.

The precise level of compensation is not generally a matter with which the European Court will concern itself, although it will be concerned to ensure that it is adequate in broad terms. Indeed, if the compensation is not adequate, this must be a significant factor in determining whether or not a 'fair balance' can be struck and whether compulsory acquisition can be justified in terms of Article 1 of Protocol 1. As the European Court held in *James* v *UK* (1986) 8 EHRR 123 (at para. 54):

> Like the Commission, the Court observes that under the legal systems of the Contracting States, the taking of property in the public interest without payment of compensation is treated as justifiable only in exceptional circumstances not relevant for present purposes. As far as Article 1 is concerned, the protection of the right of property it affords would be largely illusory and ineffective in the absence of any equivalent principle. Clearly, compensation terms are material to the assessment whether the contested legislation respects a fair balance between the various interests at stake and, notably, whether it does not impose a disproportionate burden on the applicants (see the above-mentioned *Sporrong and Lönnroth* judgment . . . paras 69 and 73).
>
> The Court further accepts the Commission's conclusion as to the standard of compensation: the taking of property without payment of an amount reasonably related to its value would normally constitute a disproportionate interference which could not be considered justifiable under Article 1. Article 1 does not, however, guarantee a right to full compensation in all circumstances. Legitimate objectives of 'public interest', such as pursued in measures of economic reform or measures designed to achieve greater social justice, may call for less than reimbursement of the full market value. Furthermore, the Court's power of review is limited to ascertaining whether the choice of compensation terms falls outside the State's wide margin of appreciation in this domain (see para. 46 above).

This approach has been followed subsequently (see, e.g., *Lithgow* v *UK* (1986) 8 EHRR 329, at paras 120–121).

A recent example of the approach of the European Court to compensation, and its unwillingness to look at it except in broad terms, can be seen in the decision declaring inadmissible claims in *London Armoury Ltd and AB Harvey and Son Ltd* (and 156 others) (App. Nos 37666/97 and 37671/97), 26 September 2000, against the United Kingdom arising out of the 1997 Firearms Amendment Acts (see *Steed* v *Home Office* [2000] 1 WLR 1169 for domestic litigation on the same legislation which was brought in following the Dunblane tragedy). The applicants complained that the 1997 Acts deprived them of their possessions without an offer of compensation for the loss of their businesses, since the ban on handguns deprived them of goodwill and business assets. The European Court held as follows:

> The Court further observes that legislative measures introducing controls on the owner-ship or use of particular articles in the interests of public health or safety will inevitably have an adverse financial impact on many categories of business which are dependent to a greater or lesser extent on the continued use of the articles in question, the nature and extent of the impact varying from category to category and from business to business within each category. Because of their direct knowledge of their society and its needs and resources, the national authorities must enjoy a wide margin of appreci-ation in determining not only the necessity of the measure of control concerned but also the types of loss resulting from the measure for which compensation will be made; the legislature's judgment in this connection will in principle be respected unless it is manifestly arbitrary or unreasonable . . .
>
> In adopting the present measures, the legislature determined that the grant of com-pensation, representing the value of the firearms whose possession had been rendered unlawful, should in principle be confined to those who owned the firearms in question, whether as private individuals or as dealers, and should not extend to cover loss of goodwill or other losses sustained by businesses connected with the firearms industry which were to a greater or lesser extent affected by the prohibition on the possession of handguns.
>
> The Court cannot find that in reaching this judgment the United Kingdom upset the fair balance between the demands of the general interest of the community and the requirements of the protection of the applicants' property rights by imposing on the applicants an individual and excessive burden.

The approach in that case was based on the particular balance to be struck there between public safety and full compensation for all losses, and follows *James* and *Lithgow*, but it provides a clear illustration of the difficulties of succeeding in this type of argument where there is a social justification for the expropriation. Indeed, the unsuccessful, though complex and detailed, arguments as to the various possible bases of compensation for nationalisation in *Lithgow* provides another. How far these difficulties extend to cases where the justification, though a public interest one, is not based on social legislation is open to question.

It follows that this approach is unlikely to lead to compulsory purchase order inquiries degenerating into a detailed foreshadowing of arguments in the Lands Tribunal over quantum. However, it should still enable parties who can show that they will not receive adequate compensation to argue that this is a factor to be included in striking the appropriate balance between private rights and public rights. Whether this will be of much practical effect in the majority of cases is open to doubt, given that:

(a)   a long-standing system for compensation at open market value for compulsory acquisition of land and property interests exists for at least the majority of cases (see s. 5 of the Land Compensation Act 1961, which sets out the general rules for assessing compensation for the compulsory purchase); and

(b)   the system of compensation operates on the basis of the 'principle of equivalence', i.e. compensation which reflects the losses suffered (see Lord Nicholls in *Director of Buildings and Lands* v *Shun Fung Ironworks Ltd* [1995] 2 WLR 404, at 411–412).

There are some contexts where compensation is not based on the market value of the interest acquired, such as compensation for disturbance under s. 37 of the Land Compensation Act 1973, where there is no 'compensatable interest' but there are preconditions of entitlement, which include the following:

(a)   the claimant has no interest in the land for the acquisition or extinguishment of which he or she is (or if the acquisition or extinguishment were compulsory, would be) entitled to compensation under any other enactment;

(b)   the claimant must be 'in lawful possession of the land' from which he or she is displaced by the compulsory acquisition; and

(c)   the claimant was displaced from any land in consequence of (amongst other things) the acquisition of the land by an authority possessing compulsory purchase powers.

This presupposes a non-compensatable interest, which includes rights held under licence, such as advertising hoardings. Such rights may, nonetheless, be 'possessions' within Article 1 of Protocol 1 (see Chapter Two) since they have come to an end only because of expropriation, not termination by the licensor. Indeed, this must be so if they are to come within s. 37 of the Land Compensation Act 1973 in any event. It might be the case that if real value could be attributed to the licence itself then there would be a *James* argument that the absence of any compensation for the value of the lost possession should count against expropriation. It would mean that domestic law compensated only for loss of profits and costs of dispossession but provided no compensation for the value of the licence itself. Such a situation would not of itself prevent the making of a compulsory purchase order, but would go to striking the balance between public interest and private rights.

6.3.2 Specific rules

The general approach set out at 6.3.1 may be modified or added to by specific rules in the empowering statute or in terms of policy consideration. These must now be read subject to s. 3(1) of the HRA 1998, so that 'so far as it is possible to do so, primary legislation and subordinate legislation must be read and given effect in a way which is compatible with the Convention rights'.

A familiar example of the specific legislative power is found in s. 226 of the TCPA 1990, which provides (in part):

226. Compulsory acquisition of land for development and other planning purposes

(1)   A local authority to whom this section applies shall, on being authorised to do so by the Secretary of State, have power to acquire compulsorily any land in their area which —

(a)   is suitable for and required in order to secure the carrying out of development, re-development or improvement; or

(b)   is required for a purpose which it is necessary to achieve in the interests of the proper planning of an area in which the land is situated.

(2)   A local authority and the Secretary of State in considering for the purposes of subsection (1)(a) whether land is suitable for development, re-development or improvement shall have regard —

(a)   to the provisions of the development plan, so far as material;

(b)   to whether planning permission for any development on the land is in force; and

(c)   to any other considerations which would be material for the purpose of determining an application for planning permission for development on the land . . .

There should be no difficulty posed by reading this provision consistently with the Convention, given that it is a power which requires a balance to be struck but limits the extent to which the public interest can be invoked to justify the overriding of private rights (see, e.g., *R v Secretary of State, ex parte Leicester City Council* (1987) 55 P & CR 364; *Sharkey v Secretary of State* [1992] 2 PLR 11, at 18–19; and (dealing with the equivalent Scottish legislation) *In the petition of Standard Commercial Property Securities Ltd* (see 6.3.1.2). Although there may be arguments about the precise significance of the language used, the term 'required' imports something more than 'desirable' and is more akin to 'necessary in the circumstances of the case' (see McCowan LJ in *Sharkey*, at 19).

At the time of writing, the Planning and Compulsory Purchase Bill is going through its final stages and it is thought that it will receive Royal Assent in the early part of 2004. The Bill modifies s. 226(1), essentially by substituting for subs. (1)(a) the following: '(a) if the authority think that the acquisition will facilitate the carrying out of development, redevelopment or improvement on or in relation to the land, . . .'.

The existing subs. (2) is to be repealed. This amendment will thus broaden the power to acquire land compulsorily in s. 226, but the exercise of any such power is to be subject to a new subs. (1A), which requires that the new power be exercised by local authorities only for one of three purposes, namely (i) the promotion of the economic well-being of their area, (ii) the promotion or improvement of the social well-being of their area, or (iii) the promotion or improvement of the environmental well-being of their area.

Therefore the amendments, although they extend the power to acquire land compulsorily under s. 226, preserve a need that any such purchase be justified on one of three public interest grounds. There is no alteration to the need for, or the basis for calculation of, compensation. Accordingly it is not thought that the amendments raise any new issues in terms of Article 1 of Protocol 1.

In the case of policy requirements, in general terms as policy there should be no obstacle to applying the relevant legal powers in a manner consistent with the Convention. Moreover, pure policy considerations cannot attract the statutory defences in s. 6(2) of the HRA 1998, which apply only to 'provisions of, or made under, primary legislation'.

Chapter Seven

Housing and the Convention

David Forsdick

7.1 INTRODUCTION

The exercise by local authorities of their housing and associated functions (such as environmental protection and housing benefit) necessarily interrelates with and involves potential interference with the rights of individuals protected under the Convention.

There is no right to be provided with a home under the Convention. However, once housing is provided by a public authority, the Convention will apply to the 'home'. The availability of adequate, safe and secure housing accommodation may be considered to be an essential prerequisite to enjoyment of the other rights and liberties guaranteed, such as security of the person (Article 5), respect for private and family life (Article 8) and the protection of property (Article 1 of Protocol 1). Without such housing, other Convention rights may be incapable of being fulfilled, or may be severely restricted in the extent to which they can be enjoyed. Thus the Convention rights would, in theory, appear to be relevant to the whole range of a local authority's housing functions: from provision of housing at the outset (see Chapter Eight); to the state of that housing; to obtaining possession of the housing; and to protecting that housing from undue environmental interference. How does the Convention add to existing rights and safeguards provided to individuals in those circumstances?

For those who are in accommodation provided by public authorities, issues may arise as to the quality and safety of that accommodation. For example, does the failure of a local authority to repair its housing stock to an acceptable standard constitute a potential breach of Article 8?

Local authorities are major providers either directly or indirectly of residential care for elderly and/or disabled people. Closure of such homes and the forced moving of residents against their will clearly constitutes a potential breach of Article 8, and may raise Article 6 issues relating to the right to a fair hearing. The standard of accommodation provided in residential care homes may in extreme circumstances constitute inhuman or degrading treatment under Article 3. Do these provisions of the Convention add anything to the protection already afforded to such residents by domestic law?

Possession proceedings brought by public authorities against their tenants on the grounds of rent arrears or nuisance potentially involve interference with the Article 8 right of respect for the home. The question may arise as to whether such interference is justified and/or proportionate under Article 8(2).

Introductory tenancies (under s. 124 of the Housing Act 1996) allow tenancies of public sector housing to be terminated in the first year for unspecified reasons relating to the conduct of the tenant. In most cases, the court has no discretion as to whether to order possession. Does this breach Article 6 and/or Article 8 of the Convention? Similarly, do common law rules which act so as to terminate a tenancy infringe Article 8?

Several of the grounds for possession of secure tenancies in the Housing Act 1985 do not require a test of reasonableness to be satisfied, and a possession order can be obtained on the basis that suitable alternative accommodation is available. Does this raise Article 8 issues, on the basis that the public authority may be interfering with the right to the existing home without any assessment of whether such interference is necessary and/or proportionate?

Issues could arise as to whether rent increases which make it impossible for the resident to continue to occupy the home constitute a potential breach of Article 8. For many tenants of local authority and social housing, housing benefit is an essential means of securing continued occupation. Questions may arise as to whether the rent restrictions in the Housing Benefit (General) Regulations 1987 are justified when their impact can be to require long-term residents to move home after short periods of unemployment or ill health because the housing benefit to which they are entitled is artificially limited.

An important question, in the context of local authorities transferring their whole housing stock to registered social landlords (RSLs), is whether (and, if so, in what circumstances) RSLs are public authorities within the meaning of the HRA 1998.

Even for those who rent accommodation in the private sector, questions may arise as to whether the Convention may be used against public authorities to force action against environmental nuisances caused by the landlord, or to prevent outside interference with the occupation of the home such as by excessive noise.

Owners of property may seek to rely on the Convention in compulsory purchase proceedings under the Housing Acts, and in appeals against demolition, closing and repair orders. The making of a compulsory purchase order clearly involves an interference with the right to respect for property under Article 1 of Protocol 1. Thus, in promoting a compulsory purchase order, whether under the housing legislation or otherwise, the local authority or other public body will have to consider whether the public interest said to justify the appropriation of property concerned is of sufficient weight to override the rights of the individual affected (see further, Chapter Six).

From the above illustrations, it is not surprising that prior to the HRA 1998 coming into force commentators and lawyers considered that there were a number of areas in which the Convention could have had implications for local authorities and other public bodies in the exercise of their housing functions. The purpose of this chapter is to consider to what extent the HRA 1998 has, in fact, augmented the rights of, and protection provided to, individuals in some of the areas identified.

The picture, so far, is that the HRA 1998 has not delivered fundamental or far reaching changes in the way local authorities are required to discharge their housing and related functions. There are substantial limitations on the extent of the rights granted by the Convention, and case law under the HRA 1998 has demonstrated that in many respects, the incorporation of the Convention has not resulted in a sea change in the approach taken by the domestic courts. Indeed, as Lord Hope stated in *Harrow London Borough Council* v *Qazi* [2003] 3 WLR 793 at para. 37, none of the challenges to substantive housing provisions that have been made since the coming into force of the HRA 1998 have been successful in the sense that the provisions in question have been declared incompatible or have required the deployment of the special interpretative obligation under s. 3(1) of the HRA 1998.

It is clear, however, from the case law of the European Court — which under s. 2 of the 1998 Act, the UK courts must take into account — that a public authority landlord may be held responsible for breach of Convention rights in a number of ways in relation to housing. This is because a public authority:

(a) in its role as landlord, must not itself act in breach of Convention rights;
(b) in its role as local authority with responsibility for environmental protection, must not act in a way which contributes indirectly towards, or facilitates, a breach of Convention rights (e.g. by permitting industrial activities which create unjustified environmental pollution: see *Lopez Ostra* v *Spain* (1994) 20 EHRR 277); and
(c) in its role as local authority with environmental protection responsibilities, must, in certain limited circumstances, fulfil positive obligations to intervene in relationships between individuals.

7.2 RELEVANT PROVISIONS OF THE CONVENTION

From the above it can be seen that in the housing field, the principal Convention rights which will be relevant are those under Article 8 and Article 1 of Protocol 1.

Article 8 ECHR provides that:

1.　Everyone has the right to respect for his private and family life, his home and his correspondence.

2.　There shall be no interference by a public authority with the exercise of this right except such as is in accordance with the law and is necessary in a democratic society in the interests of national security, public safety or the economic well-being of the country, for the prevention of disorder or crime, for the protection of health or morals, or for the protection of the rights and freedoms of others.

Article 8 imposes positive and negative obligations on local authorities. The negative obligation involves refraining from taking action that interferes with an individual's Article 8 rights (unless such action can be justified in terms of Article 8(2)). The positive obligation involves taking reasonable and appropriate measures to secure an individual's Article 8 rights (including in circumstances where those rights are being threatened or infringed by another individual or company). In the housing field, the positive obligation is only likely to arise in environmental protection situations and is unlikely to arise more generally.

Article 1 of Protocol 1 provides that:

Every natural or legal person is entitled to the peaceful enjoyment of his possessions. No one shall be deprived of his possessions except in the public interest and subject to the conditions provided for by law and by the general principles of international law.

The preceding provisions shall not, however, in any way impair the right of a State to enforce such laws as it deems necessary to control the use of property in accordance with the general interest or to secure the payment of taxes or other contributions or penalties.

Article 1 of Protocol 1 thus:

(a)　protects the peaceful enjoyment of property;
(b)　ensures that the deprivation of property shall only be in accordance with law, and then only subject to conditions — most notably, usually the payment of compensation; and
(c)　provides that the basic rights shall not impair the right of a state to enforce such laws as it deems necessary to control the use of property in accordance with the general interest or to secure the payment of obligations.

It is possible that the exercise of housing functions by public bodies may also give rise to issues relating to inhuman or degrading treatment (Article 3); the right to security (Article 5); and the right to a fair hearing (Article 6). As with all local authority and public decision-making, Article 14 will be applicable, requiring local authorities to ensure that there is no discrimination in the enjoyment of Convention rights on grounds of sex, race, colour, language or religion.

It is conceivable that in extreme cases Article 2, the right to life, could come into play. This may be especially relevant in the context of environmental protection, where the occupation of housing becomes a threat to health by reason of environmental pollution and in circumstances where a person in medical need of a home is destitute. However, in general, domestic law already protects against situations arising where there is a real, discernible threat to life.

Reference should be made to Chapter Five for a more extensive consideration of these Articles.

Before considering the rights which are protected or guaranteed by the Convention, it is necessary to consider the range of bodies which are subject to it and the definition of the 'home''.

7.3 HOUSING BODIES SUBJECT TO THE HUMAN RIGHTS ACT

Section 6(1) of the HRA 1998 provides that it is unlawful for a public authority to act in a way which is incompatible with a Convention right.

Section 1 of the Housing Act 1985 defines 'local housing authority' as meaning a district council, a London Borough Council, the Common Council of the City of London, a Welsh County Council or county borough council and the council of the Isles of Scilly. Such bodies are 'public authorities' and are bound by s. 6(1) of the 1998 Act. Similarly, government departments which hold housing for staff (e.g. the Prison Service of the Home Office) or pending works (the Highways Agency) will be affected, in the exercise of their housing functions, by the Convention.

'Public authority' is defined by s. 6(3) of the HRA 1998 to include any person certain of whose functions are functions of a public nature. In recent years there has been an increasing tendency for local housing authorities to transfer housing stock to RSLs. Indeed, some local authorities now hold no housing stock, and many more are in the process of divesting themselves of most of their council houses. In such circumstances, the local housing authority continues to exist, it retains its nomination rights to social housing and it continues to exercise certain functions which cannot be divested by it. The exercise by it of its remaining housing functions will clearly be subject to the Convention even though it ceases to be a direct provider of accommodation. Further, the housing authority cannot absolve itself of its Convention obligations by delegating the fulfilment of such obligations to private bodies or individuals (see, by analogy, *Costello-Roberts* v *UK* (1993) 19 EHRR 112).

However, for everyday purposes, the local housing authority will in the circumstances described above have a much reduced role, and the occupiers of social housing will be more concerned with the actions of the RSLs. The question therefore becomes the extent to which actions of RSLs are subject to the Convention.

The problem in identifying whether such bodies are subject to s. 6 of the HRA 1998 (and thus the Convention generally) on the basis that their functions are of a public nature, is that there is a huge variety and range of organizations which come under the broad umbrella of RSLs, with wide-ranging roles in the housing field. Indeed, one of the purposes of the Housing Act 1996 was to extend the range of bodies which were involved in the construction, provision, and management of social rented housing, and to open up the sector to new types of landlord, including companies.

Under pre-HRA 1998 domestic law, it appeared that when an RSL (of whatever type) was exercising *statutory* powers, its decisions would be subject to the supervisory jurisdiction of the High Court. In *Boyle v Castlemilk East Housing Co-operative Ltd* (1997) *The Times*, 16 May, the Court had to consider whether a failure of a housing co-operative to make a home loss payment under statutory powers was susceptible to judicial review. The co-operative does not appear to have argued that its actions generally were not susceptible to judicial review, but simply argued that in the circumstances of the particular case judicial review was not appropriate. The Outer House of the Court of Session in Scotland (apparently without considering the wider question as to whether such a co-operative could ever be subject to judicial review) permitted judicial review to proceed on the basis that the making of a home loss payment was the exercise of a statutory function. The correctness of this approach has not been seriously challenged since.

However, in *Peabody Housing Association v Green* (1979) 38 P & CR 644, the exercise of *non-statutory* powers by a housing association (the predecessors of the RSLs under the Housing Act 1996) was held not to be capable of being subjected to judicial review. In that case, the Peabody Housing Association sought possession of a flat. It had a statutory duty to provide housing and was a statutory body, having been incorporated under the Industrial and Provident Societies Act 1965. It was argued by the tenant that the decision to serve notice to quit and to seek possession was *ultra vires* the Housing Association because the decision was based on irrelevant considerations and was perverse. The Court of Appeal held that even assuming that the Housing Association had received public money which it was obliged to spend in a particular way, that did not turn an action that was part of its normal and essential activities into the exercise of a statutory power. The Housing Association had not been acting in pursuance of any statutory power in issuing the notice to quit but had been empowered to issue it simply by its own rules. The decision was therefore a private law decision which was not susceptible to the supervisory jurisdiction of the High Court on judicial review.

The *Peabody* decision probably holds good today on its facts. However, it is clear that the courts are now more concerned with the type of function performed rather than the source of the power, and they have increasingly drawn a distinction between private functions of RSLs and those of a public nature. This follows the analysis of the Court of Appeal in a different context in *R* v *Panel of Takeovers and Mergers, ex parte Datafin* [1987] QB 815. For a full discussion of the distinction between public and private functions, see De Smith, Woolf and Jowell, *Judicial Review of Administrative Action* (Sweet & Maxwell, 1995). The issue therefore, in the context of decisions of RSLs under domestic law, will now be focused on the type of function being exercised rather than the source of the power to exercise the function (statutory or by private agreement).

The question which arises is whether the HRA 1998 changes this basic approach. That issue was first considered by the Court of Appeal in the case of *Donoghue* v *Poplar Housing and Regeneration Community Association Ltd* [2002] QB 84. The appellant was a woman with young children who had been provided with housing by a local authority pending a decision as to whether she was intentionally homeless. As such, she was a weekly, non-secure tenant under Sch. 1, para. 4 to the Housing Act 1985. The property was later transferred to an RSL ('Poplar') and the appellant became a periodic assured shorthold tenant of Poplar. Poplar could not obtain possession of the property without an order of the Court, but the Court was required to make the order if the defendant had a tenancy which was subject to s. 21(4) and the proper notice was served. The Court had no discretion. The appellant argued that s. 21(4) was incompatible with Articles 6 and 8 ECHR, and that to make an order for possession would involve interpreting s. 21(4) in a manner which was not compatible with the HRA 1998. In considering that argument, the Court of Appeal had to examine whether Poplar was a public authority within the meaning of s. 6(3) of the HRA 1998.

The Court of Appeal approached that question by first considering how s. 6(3) should be interpreted and then considering the precise circumstances in which Poplar acted in this case. It approached its consideration of s. 6(3) in the following way:

(a) The definition of who is a public authority and what is a public function for the purposes of s. 6 of the HRA 1998 should be given a 'generous interpretation'.

(b) However, the fact that a body performs an activity which a public body would otherwise be under a duty to perform cannot mean that such performance is necessarily a public function. For example, a hotel which provides bed and breakfast accommodation for homeless people on behalf of a local housing authority would not be exercising a public function for s. 6(3) purposes.

(c) The purpose of s. 6(3) is to deal with hybrid bodies which have both private and public functions. It is not to turn a body which does not have responsibilities to the public into a public body merely because it performs acts on behalf of a public body which would constitute public functions were such acts to be performed by the public body itself (see, e.g., *Costello-Roberts* v *UK* (1993) 19 EHRR 112).

Applying this approach to the situation of RSLs, the Court of Appeal seems to have restricted the circumstances in which an RSL will be a public authority:

(a)　in transferring its housing stock to an RSL, the local housing authority was *not* transferring its primary public duties to the RSL;

(b)　the RSL was no more than the means by which the local housing authority performed those duties;

(c)　the act of providing accommodation to rent — even if that accommodation is provided by a not-for-profit organization to homeless persons — is not *without more* a public function for the purposes of s. 6(3);

(d)　even where the RSL carried out functions which would if exercised by a local housing authority constitute public functions, such acts may — when done by the RSL — remain of a private nature for the purposes of s. 6; and

(e)　what can make an act, which would otherwise be private, public 'is a feature or a combination of features which impose a public character or stamp on the act'.

The Court of Appeal went on to consider (at 65(v)) when this test could be satisfied:

> Statutory authority for what is done can at least help to mark the act as being public; so can the extent of control over the function exercised by another body which is a public authority. The more closely the acts that could be of a private nature are enmeshed in the activities of a public body, the more likely they are to be public. However, the fact that the acts are supervised by a public regulatory body does not necessarily indicate that they are of a public nature.

In the context of the facts of the case, the Court of Appeal took into account the following factors:

(a)　The closeness of the relationship which existed between the local housing authority and Poplar. Poplar was created by the authority to take a transfer of the authority's stock; five of its board members were members of the authority; and Poplar was subject to the guidance of the authority as to the manner in which it acted towards homeless people including the appellant.

(b)　Upon the transfer from the authority to Poplar, it was intended that existing tenants would be treated no better and no worse than they would have been if the transfer had not occurred.

The Court of Appeal went on to hold that:

> . . . there is no clear demarcation line which can be drawn between public and private bodies and functions. In a borderline case such as this the decision is very much one of fact and degree. Taking into account all the circumstances, we have come to the conclusion that while activities of housing associations need not involve the performance of public functions in this case, in providing accommodation for the [appellant] and then seeking possession, the role of Poplar is so closely assimilated to that of [the authority] that it was performing public and not private functions.

It is thus clear that there is no general principle that an RSL is a public authority when providing housing, although on the precise facts it may be.

Factors which may indicate that the RSL is exercising a public function include the following:

(a) it is registered under a statutory scheme and is subject to the regulation of the Housing Corporation;

(b) it receives public funding for the construction and maintenance of housing;

(c) it has close relationships with local housing authorities especially where there have been whole stock transfers; and

(d) in practice, it exercises many of the local housing authority's functions on its behalf and takes nominations for housing from that authority.

These factors indicate that in many cases, subject to the fact and degree test, the activities of the RSLs are likely to be capable of being 'public' in nature. The structure of the Housing Act 1996 supports this inference, with the roles of RSLs closely mirroring, in a number of respects, the previous functions of the local housing authorities.

However, in contrast to local housing authorities, RSLs can and do raise significant funding from the private sector and are governed by different statutory regimes in relation to capital investments. Further, in contrast to the secure tenancies granted by local housing authorities, those granted after 15 January 1989 by what are now RSLs will be assured or assured shorthold tenancies, with different statutory schemes of protection from those afforded to secure (local authority) tenants. These factors indicate that the RSLs are more akin, in some respects, to private landlords than to local housing authorities, and they could be prayed in aid in an appropriate case to show that the balance lies in favour of the particular function in issue not being considered to be public in nature.

Poplar was a case in which the RSL was found, on the particular facts, to be exercising public functions. Nevertheless, its generally restrictive implications were confirmed by the later case of *R v Leonard Cheshire Foundation, ex parte Heather* [2002] HRLR 832, in which Lord Woolf CJ again delivered the judgment of the court.

In the later case, the court relied upon two major factors as indicating that the respondent RSL was not exercising public functions in providing accommodation placed by local authorities under ss. 21 and 26 of the National Assistance Act 1948. First, the respondent provided accommodation both to publicly funded and privately funded residents, and there was no material distinction between the nature of the services provided to each. The degree of funding (most residents were publicly funded) was relevant but not determinative. Secondly, while s. 26 of the 1948 Act provided statutory authority for the actions of local authorities, the respondent itself was exercising no statutory powers in providing accommodation.

Donoghue and *Leonard Cheshire* were applied in a very different context in *R (on the application of A)* v *Partnerships in Care Ltd* [2002] 1 WLR 2610.

Thus, decisions of RSLs in relation to the exercise of statutory functions may be subject to the HRA 1998, but in their relationships with individual tenants RSLs' actions are likely to be 'private'. Thus, for example, in *R v West Dorset Housing Association, ex parte Gerrard* (1994) 27 HLR 150, the apparent concession that the decisions of the Housing Association in respect of allocations of housing under Part III of the Housing Act 1985 (housing the homeless) were susceptible to judicial review was appropriate. It is considered that such decisions of RSLs are likely — depending on the precise nature of the RSL — to be subject to the HRA 1998 as well. A wider concession that the *Peabody* decision was no longer good law, or that the HRA 1998 applied to the sort of decision in that case, would not be justified.

7.4   THE HOME

Article 8 ECHR refers to 'respect for the home'. It is therefore essential to determine, as a starting point for analysis of the extent of Article 8 rights, what is and what is not a 'home'. This can be considered under two separate headings:

(a)   the nature of occupation required; and
(b)   the nature of the premises.

As Lord Hope stated in *Harrow London Borough Council* v *Qazi* [2003] 3 WLR 793:

The word 'home' in article 8(1) has an autonomous meaning in the law relating to

Convention Rights. Its meaning cannot be defined by reference to domestic law. This is because it has to be determined in a way that will enable the expression to be applied uniformly irrespective of the contracting state from which the case comes.

However, in order to demonstrate the areas where the Convention may extend protection to areas not covered by domestic legislation, it is appropriate to consider first what domestic legislation requires to be shown before premises can be subject to the statutory protection of the 'home'.

7.4.1 Domestic case law — 'occupation on a settled basis'

Under domestic security of tenure legislation, the courts have had to consider the ambit of phrases such as 'residence' (s. 2 of the Rent Act 1977), and 'only or principal home' (s. 1(1)(b) of the Housing Act 1988). The case law establishes that a degree of occupation on a settled basis is required before a property becomes a person's home.

In *Herbert* v *Bryne* [1964] 1 All ER 882, CA, Salmon LJ considered that for a building to be someone's home it required 'a substantial degree of regular personal occupation by the tenant of an essentially residential nature'. Lord Denning MR stated:

> In order to be in personal occupation of a house it is not necessary that the tenant should be there himself with his family all the time. A sea captain may be away from his house for months at a time but it is none the less his home . . . Nor does it mean that to gain protection, the tenant must have it as his only home. A man who has a home in the country may also have a home in London spending a couple of nights there a week and yet protected in respect of it . . . Nor does it mean that a man has no home if he is in the course of moving from one home to another. A man on the move may have a home in each place until the move is completed.

It follows that even after a prolonged absence, a house may remain someone's home. Temporary absence is unlikely to mean the premises are no longer the home if the owner/occupier has an intention to return and leaves some visible evidence of that intention (see, e.g., *Wigley* v *Leigh* [1950] 2 KB 305; *Brown* v *Brash and Ambrose* [1948] 2 KB 247).

7.4.2 The approach under the Convention — absences from the home

Direct parallels can be found between the approach in domestic law and that of the European Court of Human Rights. In *Gillow* v *UK* (1986) 11 EHRR 335, a couple were absent from a house they owned in Guernsey for 18 years because the husband's work took them around the world. The claimants had not occupied the house for a substantial period, but the fact that they had left furniture there and had always intended to return meant, in the judgment of the European Court, that the house remained their home (at 349). Thus, the fact that premises are temporarily unoccupied does not necessarily mean that they are not the home for the purposes of Article 8 ECHR.

7.4.3   The approach under the Convention — requirement of 'sufficient and continuous links'

A review of the Strasbourg jurisprudence on the meaning of 'home' was undertaken by the House of Lords in *Harrow London Borough Council* v *Qazi* [2003] 3 WLR 792. Their Lordships approved the European Court's statement in *Buckley* v *UK* (1997) 23 EHRR 101, which required an applicant to show the existence of 'sufficient and continuous links' with the dwelling in question. While this may not be synonymous with the 'settled occupation' test under domestic law, it would seem to be related.

In the case of occupation which is of a temporary and unsettled nature, as, for example, a homeless persons' hostel where people are required to vacate during the day and where room allocations can be varied at short notice, it seems unlikely that Article 8 ECHR would provide additional protection. At most it may be arguable that, in an extreme case, where a person occupies a particular room for a prolonged period, Article 8 may apply. Even in such a case, however, it seems likely that Article 8(2) would allow derogation from the right, bearing in mind the purposes for which such accommodation is provided.

In *O'Rourke* v *UK* (App. No. 39022/97) the applicant complained that his eviction from a hotel room where he had been given temporary accommodation by the local authority was an interference with his right to respect of his home. The European Court of Human Rights dismissed the allegation as manifestly ill-founded. The Court said that it had significant doubts as to whether or not the applicant's links with the hotel room were sufficient and continuous enough to make it his 'home' at the time of his eviction, but even if they were, the eviction was in accordance with law and proportionate in the pursuit of a legitimate aim.

On the other hand, in *Sheffield City Council* v *Smart* [2002], [2002] HLR 34, Laws LJ was satisfied that a non-secure tenancy provided under s. 193 of the Housing Act 1996 was a home for Article 8 purposes.

7.4.4   Two homes cases

In *Gillow* v *UK* (1986) 11 EHRR 335, the European Court of Human Rights was swayed by the concession by the UK Government that the claimants did not have a home in England or elsewhere at the relevant time. The question as to whether a person may have two houses, both of which are his or her home, therefore remained to be determined.

Domestic law has recognized that in certain circumstances a person may have more than one home, and there is no reason to suppose that a different approach would be applied in construing the Convention rights. It would follow that second homes (such as weekend homes) may come within the protection afforded by the ECHR. This would accord with 'two residences' cases under the Rent Act 1977, which show that in genuine cases, where the second dwelling-house is occupied as a home and not for occasional visits, both residences are protected. This has been held to cover situations:

(a)   where the occupier of a country house occupies a town flat for a certain number of nights each week in order to carry out his business (*Langford Properties* v *Tureman* [1949] 1 KB 29);

(b)   where a person owns a town house whilst working and a country house pending retirement (*Elliott* v *Camus* [1949] EGD 261); and

(c)   where a person owns two homes while moving from one to the other.

For a full assessment of these cases, see *Woodfall on Landlord and Tenant* (Sweet & Maxwell). It is considered that the Convention would cover similar situations.

7.4.5   'Let as a separate dwelling'

Domestic legislation imposes an additional test for protection under the security of tenure provisions. Section 1 of the Rent Act 1977 refers to the residence being 'let as a separate dwelling'. Similar provisions are contained in the various Housing and Landlord and Tenant Acts. Such phrases have significantly reduced the scope of certain domestic security of tenure provisions, excluding from their protection situations where a person rents a single room but shares other essential facilities (such as bathrooms and kitchens) with other households in the same building. In such cases the house is not occupied as 'a separate dwelling' and therefore is outside of the scope of much of the domestic legislation. The Convention contains no similar limitation on the meaning of 'home' and there is no evident justification for reading into Article 8 any such restriction on the protection afforded by it. It follows that it is not necessary, for a building to be a person's home, for it to have all the facilities necessary for independent living in a self-contained unit. There does not appear to be any reason in principle why bed-sits and long-term hostels with shared facilities where rooms are allocated on a semi-permanent basis, could not come within Article 8 ECHR.

7.4.6   Business premises

Under domestic legislation, tenancies cannot be secure, assured (Sch. 1, para. 4 to the Housing Act 1988) or protected (s. 24(3) of the Rent Act 1977) tenancies if they relate to business premises (premises to which Part II of the Landlord and Tenant Act 1954 applies). Part II of the 1954 Act applies if the property comprised in the tenancy is or includes premises which are occupied by the tenant and are so occupied for the purposes of a business carried on by him, or for those and other purposes (s. 23(1)). Premises will be occupied for the purposes of a business if it can be said that the business activity is 'a significant purpose' of the occupation. However, the fact that a building is used for business purposes does not mean that it cannot also be a 'home' for the purposes of Article 8 ECHR.

In *Royal Life Savings* v *Page* [1978] 1 WLR 1329, a doctor occasionally saw patients at a maisonette in which he lived. The Court of Appeal considered that the business use was merely incidental to the occupation as the home. In other situations where the dwelling is used for a dual purpose, it may be covered by Part II whilst at the same time being a 'home' attracting the protection afforded by Article 8. In *Cheryl Investments* v *Saldanha* (decided with *Royal Life*), an occupier used the service flat in which he lived for the conduct of an import business. It was held that his tenancy was a business tenancy under Part II of the Landlord and Tenant Act 1954 as opposed to a tenancy under the Rent Act 1977. Nonetheless, the premises were his 'home'.

A similar approach has been taken by the European Court of Human Rights. In *Chappell* v *UK* (1987) 53 DR 241, there was a police search of business premises. The European Commission put emphasis on the finding that the areas searched included a bedroom occupied as a home, with the result that the interference, although directed against business activities, impinged upon the individual's private life and 'the private sphere of items and associations which have the attributes of a home'. It follows that premises used jointly as business premises and as a home will come within the definition of 'home' under the Convention.

In *Niemietz* v *Germany* (1992) 16 EHRR 97, the European Court of Human Rights went considerably further. It held that a lawyer's office (separate from his home) could come within Article 8 ECHR on the basis that interpreting 'home' as including certain professional or business premises is consonant with the object and purpose of Article 8. In that case a lawyer's offices had been searched under a warrant. The applicant alleged that Article 8(1) protected not only the place of residence of an individual against any interference by public authorities, but also business premises such as a lawyer's office, where, in a private sphere, he pursued his profession. The European Court of Justice (ECJ) in *Hoechst* v *Commission* [1989] ECR 2859, at 2924, had held that the fundamental right of inviolability of the home did not extend to business premises. The European Court of Human Rights, however, drew on case law from other contracting states where the protection of the home had been so extended. For example, the word 'domicile' in the French version of the Convention extended to a professional person's office. It followed that not only would a building which was partly used for residential purposes and partly for business uses fall within Article 8(1), but so would a building used solely as an office. It should be noted, however, that the *Niemietz* decision did not purport to extend (and should not be read as extending) Article 8 to all professional premises. Further, whilst the *Niemietz* case was concerned with respecting privacy within the home, it is clear from the approach of Lord Hope in *Qazi* (para. 67) that by analogy with *Khatun* v *UK* (1998) 26 EHRR CD 212, the word should not take on a different meaning according to the nature of the interference which is alleged. The rationale of the *Niemietz* decision was based on the fact that the 'home' of a professional also includes his business premises — the activities in question (as a lawyer) could be carried on at home just as in an office. It is considered that this facet of the professional activity is essential before any Article 8 right could apply to non-residential premises.

In the light of the above case law, it is clear that even where, under domestic legislation, the security of tenure provisions for residential accommodation do not apply, the premises may nonetheless be the person's home for the purposes of Article 8(1); and in some circumstances the premises do not even have to be a 'home' to be entitled to the protection of the Convention. Local housing authorities cannot therefore assume that, just because premises are not within the normal protection of the Housing Acts, the Convention will not apply. This has particular relevance in relation to trespassers and is considered separately in Chapter Nine.

7.4.7 Must the occupation be lawful?

From the case of *Buckley* v *UK* (1996) 23 EHRR 101, it is clear that occupation need not be lawful in order for premises to come within Article 8(1). In that case, the UK Government argued that only a home legally established could attract the protection of Article 8(1). This argument was rejected. There was nothing in the Article which implied that the establishment of the 'home' had to be lawful, and the circumstances were such that Article 8 ECHR was clearly engaged:

> She has lived there almost continuously since 1988 — save for an absence of two weeks, for family reasons in 1993 — and it has not been suggested that she has established, or intends to establish, another residence elsewhere. The case therefore concerns the applicant's right to respect for her 'home'.

In *Chapman* v *UK* (2001) 33 EHRR 18, the Court limited the effect of *Buckley* in a number of respects, although not in relation to the meaning of a home. The *Chapman* case and the position with respect to trespassers is considered in Chapter Nine.

The approach in *Buckley* was endorsed by the House of Lords in *Qazi*.

7.4.8   Limits to the definition of 'home'

There are limits to what may be considered a person's home. In *Loizidou* v *Turkey* (1998) 23 EHRR 513, the applicant owned land in northern Cyprus upon which she had intended to build flats, one of which she would occupy with her family. Construction works had commenced in 1972. Following the Turkish occupation of northern Cyprus she was unable to carry out the development. It was held that there was no breach of Article 8 ECHR because she did not have any home — she merely had the intention to provide a home. Article 8 is therefore engaged only where there is an actual home. This has implications for housing provision (see 7.5).

7.4.9   The *Qazi* decision

Harrow London Borough Council v *Qazi* [2003] 3 WLR 792 is the leading authority on the application of the HRA 1998 to 'the home'. In *Qazi* a house had been let to the defendant and his then wife as joint tenants under a secure tenancy. In 1999, the defendant and his wife separated and she served a notice to quit on the Council. The defendant applied for a sole tenancy but was refused on the basis that he was not entitled, by himself, to family-sized accommodation. His new wife subsequently moved into the house. By operation of common law the Council had a clear right to possession. The defendant resisted an order for possession, however, on the ground that his Article 8 rights were engaged.

The trial judge had decided that the house did not comprise the defendant's 'home' because he had no rights to occupy it. The Court of Appeal reversed his decision and the case went to the House of Lords. In a split decision, the majority held that the house remained the defendant's home even though he had no lawful right to occupy it. *Chapman* and *Buckley* were confirmed and applied.

However, Article 8 could not be relied upon to defeat proprietary or contractual rights and that, therefore, because domestic law gave the Council an unqualified right to immediate possession once the notice to quit had terminated the joint tenancy, meant that there was no infringement of the right to respect for the home, Article 8(1) was not engaged, and there was no need to demonstrate an Article 8(2) justification for the deprivation of the home.

In reaching this conclusion, the House of Lords considered and applied numerous Court of Appeal authorities that had dealt with the application of the HRA 1998 to housing situations, including *Poplar Housing and Regeneration and Community Association Ltd* v *Donoghue*; *R* v *Bracknell Forest District Council, ex parte McLellan* [2002] QB 1129; and *Sheffield City Council* v *Smart* [2002] LGR 467.

The majority of their Lordships considered that there was nothing in Article 8 which required or envisaged the 'rights' granted by it being relied upon to deprive others of their property rights, yet allowing Mr Qazi a defence based on Article 8 would give him a possessory right over the home which he did not have. It would thereby deprive the Council of its rights. It would give Article 8 'an effect it was never intended to have and which it has never been given by the Strasbourg tribunals responsible for implementing the convention' (*per* Lord Scott at para. 151).

Whilst Lord Hope went further, the above chain of logic appears to be central to the analysis of the majority. The contrary analysis (Lord Bingham and Lord Steyn) that prima facie any action by a public authority seeking possession of residential property occupied by a defendant engaged the operation of Article 8 has been rejected.

The approach of the majority was said to arise from the context within which Article 8 was introduced. Lord Hope relied on the passage of Sir Gerald Fitzmaurice in *Marckx* v *Belgium* (1979) 2 EHRR 330:

> . . . the main, if not indeed the sole, object and intended sphere of application of article 8 was that of what I will call the 'domiciliary protection' of the individual. He and his family were not to be subjected to the four o'clock in the monring rat-a-tat on the door; to domestic intrusions, searches and questionings; to examinations, delaying and confiscation of correspondence; to the planting of listening devices (bugging); to restrictions on the use of radio and television; to telephone-tapping or disconnection; to measures of coercion such as cutting off the electricity or water supply; to abominations such as children being required to report upon the activities of their parents . . . in short, the whole gamut of fascist and communist inquisitorial practices such as had scarcely been known, at least in Western Europe, since the eras of religious intolerance and oppression, until (ideology replacing religion) they became prevalent again in most countries between the two world wars and subsequently.

The context, his Lordship held, tended to reinforce the impression that the object of Article 8 is to protect the individual against arbitrary interference by public authorities with his right to privacy and that it is not concerned, as such, with the protection of his right to own or to occupy property. Under this approach, the scope for reliance on Article 8 in the context of normal housing situations is extremely limited.

7.5 HOUSING PROVISION

7.5.1 Provision of housing under domestic law

Domestic legislation gives local authorities and RSLs various powers to provide housing. For example, under s. 8 of the Housing Act 1985, local housing authorities have a general duty to keep under review the need for and condition of housing in their areas, and by s. 9 are empowered to provide 'housing accommodation' by erecting, converting or acquiring houses. However, nothing in the 1985 Act requires a local housing authority to acquire or hold any land for housing purposes. It follows from the decision in *R* v *Lambeth London Borough Council, ex parte A* (1997) 30 HLR 933, that the question whether or not to exercise the powers under s. 9 is for the local housing authority alone, and the courts will interfere only on *Wednesbury* grounds. Thus, domestic law does not oblige local housing authorities to provide social housing themselves even if there is an evident need. Social landlords are similarly empowered to provide accommodation but are not under any enforceable duty to do so. It follows that there is no mechanism, in domestic law, to force the public sector to provide sufficient housing by construction or acquisition to meet all the residential needs placed upon it.

7.5.2 Allocation of housing under domestic law

Part VI of the Housing Act 1996 contains provisions relating to the allocation of existing housing accommodation, and Part VII contains a code relating to homelessness. Only qualifying persons are entitled to be allocated housing and, for example, a person subject to immigration control is not entitled to be placed on a housing register. It follows that under domestic legislation there is no general right to appear on the housing register, or to be allocated a home.

Similarly, in the case of homelessness, domestic legislation does not confer any general right to homeless persons to be housed by the public sector. In particular, certain categories of person may not qualify for any greater assistance than advice to aid them in securing accommodation in the private sector.

7.5.3 Limitations in domestic law as to provision and allocation of housing

It can thus be seen that domestic legislation does not:

(a) impose any general overriding duty on public authorities to provide adequate housing;
(b) give a general right to be allocated housing; or
(c) provide that everybody who is homeless will be entitled to secure public housing.

7.5.4 Position under the Convention

The jurisprudence of the European Court of Human Right shows that none of these fundamental limitations to domestic legislation is likely to be substantially overcome by reliance on Article 8 ECHR.

Cases under Article 8 ECHR have not recognized a positive right to be provided with housing In *Chapman* v *UK* (2001) 33 EHRR 18 the European Court of Human Rights stated:

> It is important to recall that article 8 does not in terms give a right to be provided with a home. Nor does any of the jurisprudence of the court acknowledge such a right. While it is clearly desirable that every human being has a place where he or she can live in dignity and which he or she can call home, there are unfortunately in the contracting states many persons who have no home. Whether the state provides funds to enable everyone to have a home is a matter for political not judicial decision.

This clearly severely limits the ambit of Article 8 in respect of the provision and allocation of housing.

It is doubtful whether the European Court will extend the ambit of Article 8 to impose a positive obligation. The Article was carefully drafted so as to limit its effect. The result of a change in approach by the European Court would be dramatic. It would impose potentially massive obligations of uncertain duration and extent on contracting states, without the limits of such obligations being defined within the Convention itself.

This is supported by *Velosa Barreto* v *Portugal*, 21 November 1995, in which the Court accepted that Article 8 was capable of giving rise to positive obligations on the state but said that this could not extend to a duty to ensure that each family has a home for itself. The applicant landlord wished to obtain possession of a house he owned, in order to move in with his family. Article 8 did not require that he be able to obtain possession in all such circumstances. The facts of the case were not extreme, in that the applicant already had access to other accommodation suitable for his family, but the statement of general principle is of wider application.

In any event the Court of Appeal accepted in *R* v *Royal Borough of Kensington and Chelsea, ex parte O'Sullivan* [2003] 2 PLR 459, that Article 8 was not engaged by an *offer* of a tenancy by a local authority in 1970, albeit that it could be engaged at a later stage once the property had been lived in by the appellant.

In certain extreme circumstances, housing may be so important as to bring into play Article 2 issues — where, for example, a person's health means that he or she is urgently in need of accommodation — but again it is considered that this would more properly be considered an Article 2 issue (not one arising out of Article 8); and in any event it is likely that such circumstances are adequately catered for under domestic legislation (see, for example, s. 21 of the National Assistance Act 1948).

It is possible, too, that in extreme cases (especially where there are children involved) the failure of a local authority to provide housing and to require families to live in extremely poor 'bed-sit' accommodation may constitute a breach of Article 3 but the circumstances are likely to have to be so extreme that the rights of the family in question would be adequately protected under domestic legislation and the supervisory jurisdiction of the High Court on judicial review.

Thus, notwithstanding that European Court jurisprudence is dynamic, it is considered that there is no present basis for concluding that the *Chapman* type approach will be changed in the future.

Whilst it is considered that there is no right to housing provided under the Convention, in deciding whether to allocate housing and, if so, what housing to allocate, a public authority will have to have regard to Article 8 and the implications of its decisions for the family life of the individual concerned.

7.6 RESPECT FOR THE HOME: INTRODUCTION TO GENERAL ARTICLE 8 IMPLICATIONS

Article 8 ECHR guarantees the right of access to and occupation of the home and gives a right not to be expelled or evicted (*Wiggins* v *UK* (1978) 13 DR 40; *Cyprus* v *Turkey* (1976) 4 EHRR 482, at 519). This is fundamental. However, it is considered that this requirement is largely met in domestic law by the Protection from Eviction Act 1977.

The right of access and not to be expelled or evicted under the Convention are not absolute however. Interference in accordance with law is permitted if it is necessary in a democratic society to achieve one of the purposes set out in Article 8(2).

7.6.1 'In accordance with law'

'In accordance with law' requires that there is some specific rule of law (either statutory or common law) which permits the interference in question (*Sunday Times* v *UK* (1979) 2 EHRR 245 — and see *Olsson* v *Sweden* (1988) 11 EHRR 259 for further requirements). So, for example, the taking of possession proceedings on the basis of rent arrears and the enforcement of an order for possession would be in accordance with law. The taking of possession of residential premises without a court order and otherwise than in accordance with s. 3 of the Protection from Eviction Act 1977 would not be.

7.6.2 Necessary in a democratic society

Interference, even if 'in accordance with law', must be 'necessary in a democratic society' to achieve the objectives listed in Article 8(2) (*R* v *Bracknell Forest Borough Council, ex parte McLellan* [2002] QB 1129). While there is a substantial margin of appreciation left to individual member states as to what is and what is not 'necessary' (see, e.g., *W* v *UK* (1988) 10 EHRR 29), the state must be able to demonstrate that the interference is proportionate. It follows that there must be some need for the action taken in order to justify the interference with the right in question.

However, the requirement of proportionality only gets one so far in the context of statutory provisions enacted by Parliament which leave no discretion and which require (rather than simply allow) a court to reach a particular result. In *Donoghue* v *Poplar Housing and Regeneration Community Association Ltd* [2002] QB 48 (see 7.3), the Court of Appeal was asked to rule that the strict wording of s. 21(4) of the Housing Act 1988, which made it obligatory for the court to order possession of an assured shorthold tenancy if the required notices had been served, resulted in a disproportionate interference with the occupier's Article 8 rights because the court was precluded from considering the occupier's family circumstances. The Court of Appeal took a robust line (at 69 and 72):

> There is certainly room for conflicting views as to the social desirability of an RSL being able to grant assured shorthold tenancies which are subject to s. 21(4) of the 1988 Act . . . However, in considering whether Poplar can rely on Article 8(2), the Court has to pay considerable attention to the fact that Parliament intended when enacting s. 21(4) of the 1988 Act to give preference to the needs of those dependent on social housing *as a whole* over those in the position of the Defendant. The economic and other implications of any policy in this area are extremely complex and far reaching. This is an area where in our judgment the court must treat the decisions of Parliament as to what is in the public interest with particular deference. The limited role given to the Court under section 21(4) is a legislative policy decision . . .
>
> We are satisfied that notwithstanding its mandatory terms, s. 21(4) of the 1988 Act does not conflict with the defendant's right to family life. Section 21(4) is certainly necessary in a democratic society insofar as there must be a procedure for recovering possession of property at the end of a tenancy. The question is whether the restricted power of the court is legitimate and proportionate. This is the area of policy where the court should defer to the decision of Parliament.

It can thus be seen that where Parliament has made a policy decision that a particular provision is required in the public interest, the courts will be slow indeed to intervene even if the statutory provision means that the courts considering possession actions do not have a discretion in individual cases.

Qazi further demonstrates that proportionality type arguments do not assist in determining whether Article 8 is engaged in the first place.

7.7 SPECIFIC APPLICATION OF THE GENERAL ARTICLE 8 PRINCIPLES

We have already seen at 7.5 that there is not any right to be housed by public authorities. This is an important starting point for consideration of any particular alleged interference with the right under Article 8 ECHR.

7.7.1 Protection from eviction/deprivation of the home

7.7.1.1 Common law or contractual right to possession

It is clear from the majority view in *Qazi* that Article 8 cannot be relied upon to defeat proprietary or contractual rights to possession even if the landlord is a public authority because the tenant will no longer have 'vis à vis the landlord any right to remain there' (Lord Scott at 134). This approach follows *S v UK* 47 DR 274 and *Di Palma* v *UK* (1988) 10 EHRR 149 where the Commission proceeded on the basis that Article 8 rights could not suffice against an owner of property with an otherwise unimpeachable right to possession.

7.7.1.2 Discretionary statutory grounds for possession

In possession proceedings, domestic courts have a number of discretions. Section 98 and Sch. 15 of the Rent Act 1977, s. 84 and Sch. 12 of the Housing Act 1985, and s. 7 and Sch. 2, the Housing Act 1988, all confer discretions on the court. In claims for possession there is a wide discretion to adjourn on terms, or to stay or suspend orders made. In exercising these discretions, is the role of the Court different under the HRA 1998 than it was previously?

In *Lambeth Borough Council* v *Howard* (2001) 33 HLR 636, CA the Court of Appeal had to consider the implications of the HRA 1998 on the approach to possession orders under Part I of Sch. 2 to the Housing Act 1985. Ground 2 provided a ground for possession based on nuisance or annoyance. By virtue of s. 84(2) the Court had to be satisfied not only that the nuisance had occurred but that it was reasonable to make an order. That involved a consideration of the interests of the landlord and the neighbours (see, e.g., *West Kent Housing Association* v *Davies* (1998) 30 HLR 416, CA). In deciding whether to make an order and in what terms the duty of the judge was to take account of all relevant circumstances as they existed at the date of the hearing in a 'broad, common sense way giving weight as he thinks fit to the various factors in the situation' (*per* Lord Greene MR in *Cumming* v *Danson* [1942] 2 All ER 653, CA).

In *Howard* harassment of a neighbour had been on-going for a number of years. An outright order for possession was granted. The decisiion was appealed on the basis that a suspended order was sufficient given the absence of harassment in the year leading up to the trial. The Court of Appeal refused to intervene. In doing so it held that:

(a) There is nothing in Article 8 which should lead county courts to materially different outcomes from those that they have been arriving at for many years when deciding whether it is reasonable to make an outright or a suspended order for possession.

(b) Making an order for possession involves interfering with a tenant's right to respect for his home. However, the question was whether eviction was 'necessary in a democratic society to prevent disorder or crime or to protect the rights and freedoms of others' and the defendant had denied the neighbour and her daughter one of the most important rights in modern urban society — freedom from fear and the right to live in peace.

(c)   There comes a point at which an antisocial tenant must face the consequences of his actions.

In reaching its conclusion on (a) above, the Court addressed Article 8 in stages:

(1)   there is no arguable incompatibility between Article 8 and the ground for possession — an outright order can be made against a secure tenant if it is reasonable to do so;

(2)   Article 8 was clearly engaged because subject to the Court order the tenant had a right to occupy the premises as his home;

(3)   there may be cases where Parliament has decided that, on certain facts being satisfied, there will be no Article 8(2) balance to be undertaken because it will have been done by the legislature; but

(4)   in discretionary cases such as this the Court had to ask itself not simply whether making an order would be in accordance with law but whether the order was necessary in a democratic society to achieve the Article 8(2) purposes.

This approach is not surprising or novel. A local authority has a number of competing demands on its resources and has to balance the interests of the individual against those of his or her neighbours and the community generally. Where a person fails to pay rent the result is simply that the burden is passed on to others — either through increased rents, or through increased council tax and central taxation. Where a person enjoys loud music, his or her interest in such enjoyment has to be balanced against the interests of his or her neighbours. As the Court stated in *Soering* v *UK* (1989) 11 EHRR 439, 'inherent in the whole of the Convention is a search for a fair balance between the demands of the general interest of the community and the requirements of the protection of fundamental rights'. In general, the balancing exercise is justifiably left to the courts under the test of reasonableness, so long as in applying that test the court considers the implications for the persons sought to be evicted. Given the position under domestic law the conclusion in *Howard* repeated in *Castle Vale Housing Action Trust* v *Gallagher* (2001) 33 HLR 72, 23 February, that Article 8 ECHR was unlikely to make any difference to the way in which the courts have always approached the reasonableness of making possession orders, is now clear.

It can thus be seen that whilst there is logically a separate question of 'necessity', the result will often be the same as under the pre-HRA 1998 approach.

Necessity in this context is not, however, an absolute concept and will have to take account of all surrounding factors. The distinction with the classic approach in *Cumming* v *Danson* may therefore be difficult to discern in practice.

Issues as to how to strike the balance were also considered in *Spadea and Scalabrino* v *Italy* (1995) 21 EHRR 482 and *Scollo* v *Italy* (1995) 22 EHRR 514.

7.7.1.3 Mandatory grounds for possession

In principle, it is clear that Article 8(2) allows legislation to be framed which derogates from the right in Article 8(1) if, for example, such derogation is necessary for the protection of the rights and freedoms of others.

Donoghue v *Poplar Housing and Regeneration Community Association Ltd* [2002] QB 48 concerned the application of s. 21(4) of the Housing Act 1996, which provided a mandatory ground for possession for assured shorthold tenants. In that case the district judge had not allowed an adjournment for a full hearing of the reasons why the occupier claimed that an order for possession under s. 21(4) of the Housing Act 1988 would be inappropriate. He considered the Article 8 issue summarily in the following way:

> If I were to read s. 21(4) in the way in which I am being enjoined to do, this would, in effect, enable people who were intentionally homeless — and that is a finding that has already been made by the local authority, which has been reviewed and has not been challenged, the final decision having been made a year ago in November 1999 — to jump the housing queue, that would impede the human rights of others and that is the proviso to Article 8(2) that I have got in mind, 'the protection of the rights and freedoms of others'.

The Court of Appeal approved of this summary approach. It was not necessary to hold a full trial for the district judge to be able to discern the policy underlying s. 21(4). Nor was it for the Court to rewrite the section. Parliament had struck the balance required under Article 8(2).

However, there were two areas where — at the time of coming into force of the HRA 1998 — it was thought that the current security of tenure provisions would be found to be incompatible with the Convention:

(a)   introductory tenancies; and
(b)   provision of suitable alternative accommodation grounds for possession where reasonableness is not part of the test.

Section 124 of the Housing Act 1996 allows local housing authorities to operate an introductory tenancy regime. Under such tenancies (which last for a year) the local housing authority is entitled to bring the tenancy to an end by obtaining a court order for possession. The court is required by s. 127(2) to make the order if certain notice provisions have been complied with; there is no test of reasonableness or proportionality and no checklist of grounds which the local housing authority has to establish on the balance of probabilities before an order is made (see *Manchester City Council* v *Cochrane* (1999) *The Times*, 12 January).

An introductory tenant is entitled to seek a review of the local housing authority's decision to seek an order for possession before the court hearing, and this may lead to a hearing in front of an officer of the local housing authority; but the tenant has no right to cross-examine complainants and the decision-maker is entitled to rely on hearsay evidence (see Introductory Tenants (Review) Regulations 1997). The only means of challenging a review decision to proceed with an application to the court is by way of judicial review.

The result is that:

(a)   the local housing authority may seek possession on any grounds related to the tenant's conduct;

(b)   the review is not carried out by an independent third party;

(c)   the local housing authority does not have to satisfy a judge that it is reasonable to make the order;

(d)   the judge has no discretion as to whether to make an order;

(e)   the decision to apply for an order would be capable of being challenged only on normal public law and *Wednesbury* grounds; and

(f)   orders can therefore be made without any consideration of the proportionality of the decision to seek to evict, and without any independent assessment of the justification for the eviction.

The argument that this was in breach of the HRA 1998 focused on two flaws which could give rise to challenges under Articles 8 and 6 ECHR. First, under the procedure, the determination of the occupier's civil rights and obligations is not carried out by an independent and impartial tribunal. The determination on the merits of those rights is made by the local housing authority, both initially and on review. The court hearing was considered in effect to be merely a rubber stamp. The avenue of judicial review did not remedy this defect because the *Wednesbury* grounds of challenge did not allow the merits of the decision to be revisited, or proportionality to be considered. Secondly, the provisions were arguably so vague as to infringe the requirement that the interference by public authorities in the right of respect for the home be 'in accordance with law'. The extremely wide discretion to terminate in s. 127 of the Housing Act 1996 is not linked to any particular grounds upon which that discretion can be exercised, and it was therefore thought that this would fall foul of the decision of the Court in *Ollsson* (see 7.6.1). An occupier would simply not know the criteria by which his or her conduct was to be assessed, or the circumstances in which he or she would be considered to have failed to comply with his or her obligations.

However, those arguments were rejected by the Court of Appeal in *R v Brack-nell Forest Borough Council, ex parte McLellan* [2002] QB 1129. Whilst accepting that the review panel did not exhibit the degree of independence required by Article 6 ECHR, in considering the decision-making procedure as a whole, the court could find no reason why the review process could not be conducted fairly. Furthermore, the remedy of judicial review provided an adequate safeguard for those tenants who wished to challenge a decision on the grounds of unfairness or contravention of Convention rights. Secondly, the eviction of a tenant under the scheme was justifiable under Article 8(2) ECHR, as such a course of action was necessary in a democratic society so as to ensure the protection of the rights and freedoms of others. Where a possession order was sought, however, the county court judge has the power to adjourn the hearing to allow for a judicial review application where the reasons given by a local authority were challengeable or where the tenant thought the Article 8(2) exception did not apply.

The second area of concern involved the 'suitable alternative accommodation' ground for possession. Section 84(2)(b) of the Housing Act 1985 allows possession orders to be made on certain grounds where the court is satisfied that suitable alternative accommodation is provided. There is no additional test of reasonableness. For example, all the local housing authority has to establish to gain possession under Ground 10 of Sch. 2 is that it intends, within a reasonable time, to demolish or reconstruct the building or part of the building, and cannot reasonably do so without obtaining possession of the dwelling. There is no additional requirement that the local housing authority's desire to redevelop the building be reasonable, or that the need for the development is proportionate to the impact on the displaced residents.

In such circumstances a person may be deprived of his or her home under domestic legislation where the local housing authority's action is not objectively justified. However, following the analysis in, for example, *Howard* and *Smart*, it now appears that the suitable alternative accommodation ground is a part of the scheme authorized by Parliament and constituting the balance required by Article 8(2).

7.7.1.4　Conditions precedent to seeking possession

In *Sheffield City Council v Smart* [2002] HLR 34, the Council was satisfied that the each defendant was unintentionally homeless and they were therefore provided with non-secure accommodation under s. 193 of the Housing Act 1996. Complaints of nuisance were made against them and they were therefore served with notices to quit by the Council. The defendants asserted that issuing and giving effect to the notices to quit violated their rights under the Convention.

The Court of Appeal held that where Parliament had enacted, in the context of a particular sector in the public housing field, a scheme for the creation and distribution of housing authorities' duties such that the authority was entitled on certain conditions being met, to demand possession of property let to a tenant, Article 8(2) exonerated the housing authority from any liability under Article 8(1) which arose from the tenant's eviction, provided the housing authority had acted fairly and reasonably in conformity with the scheme. Given that s. 193 was predicated on the granting of non-secure tenancies, the policy of the scheme was clearly to allow possession to be obtained by service of a notice to quit. The Court could not take a position which disrupted the day-to-day operation of the scheme and therefore the evictions were justified under Article 8(2).

The Court went on to stress the limited circumstances in which it would intervene to replace its judgement on the facts with those of the housing authority. Laws LJ said:

> 40. I can see that if a tenant sought judicial review upon being served with a notice to quit, the Administrative Court might now look at the case more closely than upon the conventional Wednesbury approach, not least given the recent decision of their Lordships house in *Daly* [2001] 2 WLR 1389, and especially the observations of Lord Cooke of Thorndon. I can see also that at the stage of the trial of the possession proceedings, there might be the rare case where something wholly exceptional has happened since service of the notice to quit, which fundamentally alters the rights and wrongs of the proposed eviction; and the county judge might be obliged to address it in deciding whether or not to make an order for possession. What I am clear the court cannot do is to take a position which disrupts the day-to-day operation of the scheme provided by Parliament in Part VII of Housing Act 1996; and in my judgment, not least given the particular matters relied on by Mr Underwood which I have set out at paragraph 23, that entails the conclusion that the balance of interests arising under Article 8(2) has in all its essentials been struck by the legislature.

An example of a case where it was thought to be appropriate for the court to address the proportionality question can be found in *R v Royal Borough of Kensington and Chelsea, ex parte O'Sullivan* [2003] 2 PLR 459.

7.7.1.5 Closure of residential care homes

In *R v North and East Devon Health Authority, ex parte Coughlan* [2000] 2 WLR 622, the applicant was severely disabled. In 1993 she had been moved with her consent from a hospital which the health authority wished to close, to an NHS facility for the long-term disabled which the health authority assured her would be her home for life. Subsequently, the health authority changed its criteria for eligibility for long-term care and concluded that the applicant no longer qualified. In 1998, following public consultation, the health authority decided to close the NHS facility and to transfer responsibility for the long-term general nursing care of the applicant to the local authority. No alternative residential placement was identified for the applicant. The Court of Appeal quashed the closure decision on the basis, amongst other things, that there was a substantive legitimate expectation that the accommodation would continue to be provided in the NHS facility.

However, the Court of Appeal went on to consider the position under Article 8 ECHR. The decision of the health authority had the effect of evicting the applicant from her home, which had been promised to her for life, in order to make better and more economic use of the premises. The Court held that to consider this issue correctly, the health authority needed to be in a position to compare what the NHS facility offered with what the alternative accommodation would offer. Without carrying out that comparison it was not possible to determine whether the interference with the applicant's right to respect for her home was necessary in a democratic society:

> The saving would be in terms of economic and logistical efficiency in the use respectively of [the NHS facility] and the local authority home. The price of this saving was to be not only the breach of a plain promise made to Miss Coughlan but, perhaps more importantly, the loss of her home and of a purpose built environment which had come to mean even more to her than a home does to most people . . .
>
> . . . the judge was entitled to treat this as a case where the health authority's conduct was in breach of Article 8 and was not justified by the provisions of Article 8(2) . . . By closure of Mardon House the health authority will interfere with what will soon be her right to her home. For the reasons already explained, the health authority would not be justified in law in doing so without providing accommodation which meets her needs. As Sir Thomas Bingham MR said in *R* v *Ministry of Defence, ex parte Smith* [1996] QB 517, 554. 'The more substantial the interference with human rights, the more the court will require by way of justification before it is satisfied that the decision is reasonable . . .' or . . . in a case such as the present, fair.

This approach will need to be adopted for all closure decisions in future. First, the health authority or local authority will have to identify the alternative accommodation and consider its suitability for a particular patient after taking into account the representations of that patient. Secondly, the relevant authority will have to carry out a balancing exercise between the interests of the patient in retention of his or her home and those of economy and efficiency. Thirdly, the courts will require considerable justification of the merits of the interference with the right. Fourthly, the courts will apply a test of fairness.

It is thus clear that there is a significant limitation on the ability of local authorities to close homes provided by them under Part III of the National Assistance Act 1948, which goes beyond the requirements of consultation and the law of legitimate expectation as considered in *R* v *Devon County Council, ex parte Baker* (1995) 91 LGR 479.

7.7.2 Standards of accommodation

7.7.2.1 Standards in residential care homes

It may be arguable that if and to the extent that local social service authorities place residents in insanitary, unhealthy, and/or dangerous residential care homes, they may be subjecting those residents to 'inhuman or degrading treatment' contrary to Article 3 ECHR. However, it is to be noted that under domestic legislation, such residential care homes would be unlikely to retain their registration; and in any event, such placements are likely to be capable of being ultimately challenged on standard judicial review grounds. It is considered that the condition of premises would have to be extremely bad before Article 3 issues would arise; and if those conditions obtained, domestic legislation probably already provides adequate safeguards.

7.7.2.2 Condition of housing provided by local housing authorities

Domestic landlord and tenant law imposes considerable obligations on landlords in relation to the repair and maintenance of dwelling-houses. Section 11 of the Landlord and Tenant Act 1985 implies various covenants into residential leases of less than seven years' duration. Most public housing is let on periodic tenancies and s. 11 would therefore apply. The obligations include:

(a) to keep in repair the structure and exterior of the dwelling-house; and

(b) to keep in repair and proper working order the installations for the supply of water, gas and electricity, and for sanitation.

Section 4 of the Defective Premises Act 1972 imposes a duty on the landlord (where he or she has a repairing obligation) to take such care as is reasonable to see that persons who might reasonably be expected to be affected by defects in the state of the premises are safe from personal injury or from damage to their property caused by a relevant defect. Actions for injunctions and damages lie in default. Local housing authorities and RSLs who ignore tenants' complaints of disrepair do so at their peril.

However, there are significant gaps in the protection afforded by domestic legislation. The most significant is that the landlord's obligations extend to keeping the premises in repair. The cause of action is thus predicated on there being disrepair. Disrepair cannot exist unless the subject matter of the covenant is 'in a condition worse than it was at some earlier time' (*Quick* v *Taff-Ely Borough Council* [1986] QB 809, at 821). Many of the problems faced by tenants of public authorities are not caused by disrepair but by inherent defects in the design or construction of the building. Domestic legislation does not require landlords to remedy problems caused by inherent defects unless either:

(a)   those defects cause other parts of the premises to fall into disrepair; or

(b)   the premises become unfit for human habitation.

In the former case, it is a question of degree whether the works necessary to rectify the damage can fairly be called works of repair. *Woodfall on Landlord and Tenant* (Sweet & Maxwell) shows that where an inherent defect has caused damage and the works required to rectify the damage are works of repair, the landlord may also be required to rectify the cause of the damage (even though it is an inherent defect) if it is proper practice to do so or if it is necessary to do so, in order to do 'the job once and for all' (*Ravenseft Properties* v *Davstone* [1980] QB 12). In the latter case, if the dwelling becomes unfit for habitation the local housing authority has various powers (see s. 604 of the Housing Act 1985 and the options open to local housing authorities — s. 189 repair notice, s. 264 closing order, s. 265 demolition order).

Where neither of these situations applies, the public sector landlord has no obligation to correct inherent defects. Thus, where a house suffers from severe condensation because of an inherent design defect, unless that makes the house unfit for habitation or that condensation causes consequential damage, the tenant has no remedy.

The question which arises is whether in such circumstances a tenant can have recourse to Article 8 rights against local authorities (and against RSLs, to the extent that removing inherent defects may be considered a 'function of a public nature', which is perhaps unlikely). The issue was considered by the Court of Appeal in *Lee* v *Leeds City Council; Ratcliffe* v *Sandwell Metropolitan Borough Council* [2002] 1 WLR 1488. The position in the light of this case may be summarized as follows:

(a)   in principle, a local housing authority has a duty under s. 6 of the HRA 1998 to ensure that the condition of a dwelling-house let for social housing is such that the respect for the home and family life under Article 8(1) is not infringed;

(b)   that in considering in any particular case whether Article 8 has been infringed it is necessary to have due regard to the needs and resources of the community and individuals;

(c)   that in striking a balance between the needs of the individual tenant, and conflicting claims upon the resources of the local housing authority, a degree of deference by the courts to the democratic process in determing those priorities is appropriate and, in particular, to the fact that Parliament has considered the question of substandard housing over a number of years and has declined to impose any obligation on local authorities (see *Southwark London Borough Council* v *Mills* [2001] 1 AC 1, *per* Lord Hoffmann at 9H–10A).

It followed that Article 8 did not impose any general or unqualified obligation on local authorities in relation to the condition of their housing stock. On the facts, which were condensation and consequential mould due to inadequate heating, ventilation, and insulation, there was no breach of Article 8. While the case establishes that Article 8 may be relied upon successfully by a tenant, it is considered that in practice this will only occur in the most extreme cases. The tenor of the judgment, and in particular the emphasis on the need to leave local authorities free to allocate resources and the attitude taken by Parliament to substandard housing, suggest that the courts should be very wary of interfering with the discretion of local housing authorities.

It has been held that local housing authorities cannot use the enforcement procedures in the Housing Act 1985 against themselves (see *R* v *Cardiff City Council, ex parte Cross* (1981) 6 HLR 6). The consequence is that where a local housing authority dwelling is unfit for human habitation, the local housing authority cannot be forced under domestic law to serve repair, closure, or demolition notices. Further, if the unfitness is caused by inherent defects, the local housing authority cannot be forced to carry out works to remedy the defect. There is thus a significant gap in the right of local housing authority tenants. Section 82 of the EPA 1990 permits tenants to take action in the magistrates' court against local housing authorities who fail to remedy an environmental nuisance (see *Sandwell Metropolitan Borough Council* v *Bujok* [1990] 3 All ER 385), but the entitlement to compensation under such proceedings is limited and discretionary. It is therefore considered that s. 82 does not fill the gap in local authority liability identified above. If, as is suggested above, Article 8 ECHR does not give rise to an enforceable right to have accommodation maintained to a specific standard, it is difficult to see how that Article can be relied upon to fill that gap (see also *R (on the application of Erskine)* v *Lambeth London Borough Council*, unreported 14 October 2003).

7.7.3 Affordability of housing

7.7.3.1 Rent increases

It is considered that in extreme circumstances, rent increases by public authorities which have the effect of making continued occupation of the premises impossible by a particular tenant may constitute a breach of Article 8 ECHR. However, in the context of the statutory scheme for assisting tenants with rent payments provided by housing benefit, the restrictions on increases in rent in the various housing legislation, and in the light of cases such as *Wandsworth London Borough Council* v *Winder* [1985] AC 461 (in which it was held that possession proceedings brought by public authorities could in principle be defended on the basis that the rent arrears arose because of unreasonable increases in rent), it is difficult to envisage circumstances in which the Convention will add anything to domestic legislation in relation to limits on rent.

Further, the European Court has held (see *Scollo* v *Italy* (1995) 22 EHRR 514) that there is a wide margin of appreciation left to the national legislature as to what is in the general public interest, and the Court would intervene only if the judgment made is manifestly without reasonable foundation. Given that the gradual relaxation on rent controls has had the policy aim of bringing more private sector accommodation into rented use in the general public interest, it is likely that that policy has a 'reasonable foundation'.

7.7.3.2 *Housing benefit*

Local authorities are responsible for administering housing benefit. Much housing benefit is paid to local authority tenants. Previously the only appeal on the facts against decisions of the local authority on housing benefit questions was to the Housing Benefit Review Board, which was internal to the local authority and on which sat members of the local authority. This clearly raised the possibility of challenge under Article 6(1) ECHR, which occurred in *R (on the application of Bewry)* v *Norwich City Council* [2002] HRLR 2. Moses J reluctantly concluded that the presence on the Review Board of local councillors with a connection to the body resisting entitlement deprived the Review Board of the independence required by Article 6. Moses J placed heavy reliance on the statement of Lord Hoffmann in *R* v *Secretary of State for the Environment, Transport and the Regions, ex parte Alconbury Developments* [2001] 2 WLR 1389, that safeguards will be 'essential' for the acceptance of a limited review of fact by appellate tribunals. The correctness of *Bewry* may therefore be doubted in the light of *R* v *Tower Hamlets London Borough Council, ex parte Runa Begum* [2003] 2 AC, in which Lord Hoffmann confessed that his earlier remarks in *Alconbury* may have been 'incautious' (paras 39–40). In any event the importance of *Bewry* has been much reduced by Sch. 7 to the Child Support, Pensions and Social Security Act 2000. Review Boards have now been replaced by appeal tribunals whose members are chosen from a panel appointed by the Lord Chancellor. There seems no scope for arguing that such tribunals do not comply with Article 6.

There is an element of the housing benefit scheme which was, at the time of the coming into force of the HRA 1998, thought to be susceptible to challenge. The maximum housing benefit which can be paid under the Housing Benefit (General) Regulations is determined by reference to the local reference rent and the property specific rent. Both of these are determined by rent officers. There is no appeal against their decisions.

The regulations on the maximum rent have the potential to make it impossible for tenants to keep up with rent payments (and therefore potentially liable to eviction) without any attention being paid to their specific circumstances (save for the exceptional power of a local authority to pay more than the maximum rent in limited circumstances). A person who has lived in a house for a number of years and who has paid the rent himself or herself throughout that time, may have to have recourse to housing benefit because of either ill-health or redundancy. The maximum rent provisions could mean that he or she was deemed to be occupying a house either which was rented at too high a rent, or which was of too high a standard. In those circumstances, the tenant could find that, after a short period, he or she would be faced with a mandatory ground for possession. It is considered that in such circumstances the local authority would have to pay special regard to the tenant's personal circumstances in determining whether to apply the exceptions to the maximum rent provisions in order to ensure compliance with Article 8 ECHR. It may be that those provisions themselves do not have a reasonable foundation and could be challenged on the basis of their disproportionate impact in such circumstances. Given the approach of the courts to other statutory schemes to do with the provision, maintenance, and repair of public housing, it is considered that the scope for this argument to be deployed has now disappeared.

It was argued in *R (on the application of Painter)* v *Carmarthenshire County Council* [2002] HLR 447, that reg. 7(1)(c)(i) of the Housing Benefit (General) Regulations 1987 (by which a person will not be treated as liable to make payments in respect of a dwelling, and hence be disbarred from entitlement to Housing Benefit, where his liability is to his former partner) involved a breach of Article 8 taken together with Article 14 ECHR. Although Article 8 did not require the payment of housing benefit, it was accepted by the judge that the payment of housing benefit to others demonstrated respect for the protection of the home by the United Kingdom and hence that Article 8, and through it Article 14, were applicable. The question was whether there was discrimination contrary to Article 14 in the exclusion from entitlement on the basis of his former relationship with his landlady. Lightman J found it unnecessary to decide whether this could be a 'status' for the purposes of Article 14, because any discrimination was justified by the need to avoid abuse of the Housing Benefit system. The fact that the claimant himself was not abusing the system did not alter this conclusion, given the absence of any alternative scheme capable of avoiding such abuse.

7.7.4 Conditions in other accommodation

Even if Article 8 ECHR does give rise to rights in respect of disrepair in local housing authority accommodation, it is considered doubtful whether the repair in accommodation provided by RSLs is a function of a public nature. It would follow that disrepair claims against RSLs could not give rise to Article 8 claims.

7.7.5 Injunctions against nuisance behaviour

There are likely to be Convention challenges against applications for injunctions to restrain anti-social behaviour on the basis that they infringe Article 8 or Article

10 ECHR. Clearly, in deciding whether to issue proceedings, the public authority is required to consider whether the taking of the action is necessary in order to achieve one of the objectives set out in Article 8. It is thought that in principle, as long as the public authority considers the impact on the person to be subjected to the injunction and adopts a proportionate response to the problems caused by the behaviour, such challenges are unlikely to be successful.

Conversely, where a person complains to the local authority about intimidation or harassment in the home, the question arises whether such a person can force the local authority to act to protect his or her interests. Notwithstanding the general approach that the Convention does not impose positive obligations, it appears that the local authority could be forced to act against the perpetrator (see, by analogy, *Whiteside v UK* (1994) 76 DR 80, in which the Commission held that there was a positive duty on the Government to provide remedies against harassment).

7.7.6   Protection of the environment related to housing

As indicated at 7.5, there are limited areas in which the ECHR has been held to impose positive obligations on the state under Article 8. This is especially so in the case of environmental protection.

In *Lopez Ostra v Spain* (1995) 20 EHRR 277, a waste treatment plant was built close to the applicant's home in a town which had a heavy concentration of leather industries. The plant began to operate without a licence, releasing fumes and smells which caused health problems to local residents. The applicant alleged breaches of Articles 8 and 3 ECHR, and claimed compensation. It was held that there had been a breach of Article 8 on the following grounds:

(a)   Severe environmental pollution may affect individuals' well-being and prevent them from enjoying their homes in such a way as to affect their private and family life adversely, without, however, seriously endangering their health.

(b)   Whether the question is analysed in terms of a positive duty on the state — to take reasonable and appropriate measures to secure the applicant's rights under Article 8(1) — or in terms of an 'interference by a public authority' to be justified in accordance with Article 8(2), the applicable principles are broadly similar. In both contexts regard must be had to the fair balance that has to be struck between the competing interests of the individual and the community as a whole, and in any case the state enjoys a certain margin of appreciation. Furthermore, even in relation to the positive obligation flowing from Article 8(1), in striking the required balance the aims mentioned in Article 8(2) may be of a certain relevance.

(c)   It is primarily the responsibility of the national authorities, notably the courts, to interpret and apply domestic law. The European Court's task is to establish whether the national authorities took the measures necessary for protecting the applicant's rights to respect for her home and for her private and family life.

(d)   Despite the margin of appreciation, on the facts of this case, Spain had not struck a fair balance between the interest of the town's economic well-being and the applicant's effective enjoyment of her right to respect for her home and her private and family life.

The European Court of Human Rights has reiterated these principles in *Powell and Rayner* v *UK* (1990) 12 EHRR 355, *Guerra* v *Italy* (1998) 26 EHRR 357, and most recently in *Hatton* v *UK*. For recognition of the positive obligation in relation to the environment under Article 8 by the UK courts, see *Marcic* v *Thames Water Utilities Ltd* [2002] QB 929.

Whilst the EPA 1990 and various items of planning legislation in most circumstances ensure that a balance is struck which would be acceptable to the European Court of Human Rights, where a local authority or central government agency declines, as a matter of discretion, to exercise its powers of environmental protection, depending on the severity of the detriment caused to individuals there may be scope for allegations of breaches of Article 8 ECHR (and, in extreme cases, Article 3). Consider a situation where accommodation which is prejudicial to health, and therefore a statutory nuisance under s. 79 of the EPA 1990, is let by a private landlord under an assured tenancy. The local authority is under a duty in such circumstances to serve an abatement notice under s. 80 of the 1990 Act. Any failure by a local authority to serve a notice, or to follow up such action, could be actionable under Article 8 (although it is difficult to see how this adds anything to domestic law).

7.8   DEPRIVATION OF PROPERTY UNDER ARTICLE 1 OF PROTOCOL 1

A tenancy or leasehold interest is property for the purposes of Article 1 of Protocol 1 ECHR. Its loss by action of a public authority can constitute a breach of Article 1 Protocol 1. However, as under Article 8 ECHR, there is a significant margin of appreciation, and the European Court of Human Rights has indicated that the same approach is to be taken generally to whether the action was 'in the public interest' under Article 1 of Protocol 1 as was taken in considering whether the interference was justified under Article 8(2). It is therefore doubted whether Article 1 of Protocol 1 adds anything substantial to the protection afforded to the interests of tenants in normal landlord and tenant situations.

However, it is not only in relation to tenancies that public authorities can deprive persons of their homes. Compulsory acquisition can result in an owner-occupier being deprived of his or her home. In promoting compulsory acquisitions, the public authority will have to consider the implications for those who will lose their homes, in order to ensure compliance with Article 1 of Protocol 1. In *Howard* v *UK* (1985) 52 DR 198, a house was sought to be compulsorily acquired for housing redevelopment. The Government accepted that there had been an interference with the Article 8(1) right but relied on the defence under Article 8(2). The European Court held that the question in such cases was whether the public authority had 'struck a fair balance between the rights of the individual property owners and the rights of the community, in any expropriation of property. A significant factor in any such balance will be the availability of compensation, reflecting the value of the property expropriated'. The same approach applies to Article 1 of Protocol 1

The exercise of compulsory powers in respect of housing is heavily constrained in the United Kingdom. Any proposed compulsory acquisition can be subjected to an independent public inquiry, at which the public authority concerned has to show a justification for the acquisition. As long as the public authority concerned takes into account the needs of the individuals affected in deciding whether or not to pursue a compulsory acquisition, the Convention will not provide any protection additional to that afforded under domestic law.

The case of *Miles* v *Secretary of State for the Environment and the Royal Borough of Kingston upon Thames* [2000] JPL 192 appears to confirm this.

Chapter Eight

Homelessness and Human Rights
Carine Patry

8.1 INTRODUCTION

A local authority's duties in relation to the housing of homeless persons were, until recently, comprehensively set out in Parts VI and VII of the Housing Act 1996. However, the Homelessness Act 2002 received Royal Assent on 26 February 2002. This Act does not replace the 1996 Act provisions, but makes comprehensive changes to the provisions for the assistance of the homeless contained therein. The sections dealing with the amendments to the statutory scheme relating to homelessness came into effect on 31 July 2002 (the text of the Act is available at ⟨www.hmso.gov.uk/acts/acts2002.htm⟩). The delay between Royal Assent and the coming into force of the provisions is to ensure that local authorities have sufficient time to change policies and procedures to take into account the relevant reforms. As such, the substantial changes introduced by the Homelessness Act 2002 fall to be considered.

The Housing Act 1996 can be considered to have had three main policy aims in relation to such duties. These purposes were:

(a)   to prevent homeless persons being moved around between authorities without anyone taking responsibility for them;

(b)   to ensure that the assistance given to homeless persons is no more than necessary, taking into account the amount of housing available to a local authority; and

(c)   to create a category of persons who are ineligible for assistance under the Act.

The Homelessness Act 2002 can be said to have introduced a new policy aim. This is to require local authorities to put greater emphasis on preventing homelessness. As is discussed further below, the policy aim of the 1996 Act, which advocated ensuring that assistance provided is no more than necessary, can be said to have been all but discarded in many areas.

Bearing these purposes in mind, Part VII of the Housing Act 1996 places an obligation on local authorities to secure suitable accommodation to persons who are homeless, in priority need, and who did not become homeless intentionally. Part VI of the 1996 Act contains provisions controlling allocation of long-term, permanent housing.

8.2 RELEVANT HUMAN RIGHTS PROVISIONS

8.2.1 Article 8

The exercise by local authorities of these duties necessarily involves the potential interference with the rights of individuals. In the context of homelessness legislation, the right to respect for one's home is perhaps the most obvious provision which comes to mind. Article 8 ECHR (the requirements of which are dealt with in Chapter Seven) provides that there must, *inter alia*, be respect for a person's home, and family life.

However, it must be noted from the outset that the Strasbourg court has consistently held that the right to respect for the home does not confer any right to be provided with a home, or any positive obligation to provide alternative accommodation of an applicant's choosing (See *X* v *FRG* (1956) 1 Yearbook 202; and more recently, *Burton* v *UK* (1996) 22 EHRR 134; *Buckley* v *UK* (1996) 23 EHRR 101; *Chapman* v *UK* (2001) 10 BHRC 48).

As such, in the context of homelessness legislation, the applicability of Article 8 is mainly of negative effect, i.e. the housing authority will be obliged to refrain from action which constitutes interference with a person's home. Indeed, Article 8 is drafted in such a way as to impose a negative rather than a positive obligation. A person who has no home (i.e. a homeless person) has no existing home by definition, and therefore the respect for such a home cannot be interfered with.

It is thus unlikely that the provisions of Article 8 will have any great effect on the main homelessness provisions. To a large extent, the provisions of the Housing Act 1996, together with the manner in which its provisions have been interpreted by the courts, and the advent of the Homelessness Act 2002, do meet the requirements of the HRA 1998, as will be seen below.

However, even though there is no obligation to provide a home, in deciding whether to allocate housing to an applicant, it is clear that a local housing authority will still have to have regard to the provisions of Article 8 ECHR and the consequences of any decision on both the applicant and their families.

8.2.2 Other Articles

Article 1 of Protocol 1 to the Convention often runs parallel to Article 8, as this Article ensures that every person is entitled to peaceful enjoyment of their possessions, and that no one should be deprived of their possessions except in the public interest. Possessions' have been interpreted to mean all forms of real and other property, including leases, (see *Mellacher* v *Austria* (1989) 12 EHRR 391).

It is also clear that the specialist procedural appeal system in the Housing Act 1996, which provides a right of internal review, followed by an appeal to a county court following an unfavourable decision, may raise issues under Article 6 ECHR. This is discussed at some length below.

It must also be noted that in extreme cases, issues relating to security of the person under Article 5 or the right not to live in inhuman and degrading accommodation under Article 3 may also arise. Article 14 also requires that local housing authorities do not discriminate in the application of ECHR rights on the grounds of race, sex, colour, language or religion.

8.3 HOMELESSNESS, PRIORITY NEED AND INTENTIONAL HOMELESSNESS

In assessing the implications of the HRA 1998 on the homelessness provisions contained in the 1996 and 2002 Acts, it is important to consider the scope and application of those provisions.

8.3.1 The tests: homelessness, priority need, and not intentionally homeless

Section 193 of the Housing Act 1996 provided that if a local authority is satisfied that an applicant is homeless, eligible for assistance, is in priority need, and is not 'intentionally homeless' then they have a duty to accommodate that person (and any relevant persons who are expected to reside with them) for a period of two years. This minimum period has now been abolished, as s. 6 of the Homelessness Act 2002 repeals ss. 193(3) and (4) and 194 of the 1996 Act. In their place, the 2002 Act inserts a new s. 193(3) stating that the duty to secure accommodation for the unintentionally homeless in priority need continues until one of the events specified at s. 193(5)–(8) occurs. However, in practice, this amendment will not change matters to any great extent. Section 193 accommodation will still not be let on a secure or assured tenancy basis and the change in effect merely reduces the bureaucratic burden on local authorities, who previously, at the end of the two-year period, simply moved individuals from the s. 193 duty to the s. 194 power to continue the provision of accommodation. The four tests set out in s. 193 remain the same.

As has already been stated above, Article 8 does not guarantee the right to a home, but instead guarantees the right to respect for one's home, once one has a home. Therefore the decisions made by local authorities in determining whether an applicant meets these tests cannot be challenged as breaches of Article 8, as Article 8 has not been engaged at all at that preliminary stage (see the comments of Pill LJ in *Ekini* v *London Borough of Hackney* [2002] HLR 2, CA, at para. 16).

However, in determining the applications made to them, local authorities must have regard to Article 8 compliance in more indirect respects, as discussed further below under the heading of each of the four relevant tests.

8.3.1.1 Is the applicant homeless?

Part VII of the Housing Act 1996 provides (at s. 175) that a person is considered to be homeless if he has no accommodation available for his occupation (in the United Kingdom or elsewhere) which it is reasonable for him to occupy, or if he does have accommodation but cannot secure access to it, or it consists of a movable structure.

Section 176 provides that accommodation shall only be regarded as 'available' for a person if it is available for occupation by him and any other person who normally resides, or might be reasonably expected to reside, with him as a member of his family (as the existence of family life depends upon the nature of the relationships and not their legal status), thus ensuring compliance with Article 8 in that regard. Family membership is essentially a question of fact, depending upon the real existence of close personal ties (*K* v *UK* (App. No. 11468/85) 50 DR 199).

In order to respect the right to family life under Article 8, the words 'as a member of his family' are to be interpreted according to the definitions developed by the European Court of Human Rights, i.e. as including:

(a)   adopted children (*Widen* v *Sweden* (App. No. 11180/84), 5 March 1986, 43 DR 120; *U and GF* v *Germany* (App. No. 11588/85), 15 May 1986, 50 DR 259);

(b)   illegitimate children (*Marckx* v *Belgium* (1979) 2 EHRR 330);

(c)   aunts and uncles (*Boyle* v *UK* (1994) 19 EHRR 179);

(d)   grandparents and grandchildren (*Marckx* v *Belgium* (above); *Price* v *UK* (App. No. 12402/86), 55 DR 224); and

(e)   cohabitees as well as spouses (*Johnston* v *Ireland* (1986) 9 EHRR 203, at para. 56; *Kroon* v *Netherlands* (1994) 19 EHRR 263, at para. 30).

This is reflected in s. 178 of the 1996 Act, which in fact goes further than the Convention in that 'persons who might reasonably be expected to reside' include persons who have agreed to marry each other, whether or not that agreement has been terminated.

8.3.1.2 Is the applicant in priority need?

It is also clear that no substantive duty to house a person arises if they are not in 'priority need'. Section 192 of the Housing Act 1996 provided that local housing authorities should provide applicants who were not in priority need with advice and such assistance as they considered appropriate in the circumstances. Section 5 of the Homelessness Act 2002 has changed this by inserting a new s. 193(3) into the 1996 Act, which provides a new power (but not a duty) for local authorities to secure accommodation for persons who are unintentionally homeless but not in priority need.

A person has a priority need if they come within any one of the following categories:

(a)   they have dependent children residing with them;

(b)   they are threatened with homelessness as a result of an emergency (fire, flood, disaster of some kind);

(c)   they are, or someone residing with them is, vulnerable because of old age, mental illness, handicap, or physical disability; or

(d)   they are pregnant, or reside with someone who is pregnant.

The definition of 'priority need' has also been extended with the coming into force of the Homelessness (Priority Need for Accommodation) (England) Order 2002. Several new categories of persons are now also considered as persons in priority need. These are:

(a)   a person aged 16 or 17 who is not a 'relevant child' for the purposes of s. 23A of the Children Act 1989 (i.e. was 'looked after, accommodated or fostered');

(b)   a person aged 18 to 21 who is a former 'relevant child' under s. 23A;

(c)   a person who is vulnerable as a result of having been 'looked after, accommodated or fostered';

(d)   a person who is vulnerable as a result of having been a member of the naval, military or armed forces;

(e)   a person who is vulnerable as a result of having served a custodial sentence (within the meaning of s. 76 of the Powers of Criminal Courts (Sentencing) Act 2000) or having been committed for contempt of court or having been remanded in custody (within the meaning of s. 88(1)(b), (c) or (d) of the Powers of Criminal Courts (Sentencing) Act 2000); and

(f)   a person who is vulnerable, as a result of ceasing to occupy accommodation, by reason of violence or threats of violence which are likely to be carried out.

In the recent case of *R (on the application of Morris)* v *Westminster City Council* [2003] EWHC Admin 2266 Keith J held that it was inappropriate for a local housing authority, when deciding whether a homeless person had a priority need for accommodation, to take into account a dependant of that person who was subject to immigration control.

In *Morris* the claimant's application for housing had been refused because although she was found to be homeless and eligible for assistance, she was not in priority need. The claimant had a two-year old daughter, but because her daughter's immigration status was doubtful, the Council held that the claimant was unable to rely on the fact that she had a daughter as giving her a priority need. Keith J held that as the claimant's daughter was a 'person from abroad who was ineligible for housing assistance' within the meaning of s. 185(4) of the 1996 Act, it followed that the Council were correct to disregard her when deciding if the claimant was a person in priority need.

It is important to note that permission to seek judicial review had been granted on the basis that if the reading of s. 185(4) was correct, it would be incompatible with the ECHR. However, Keith J could not make a declaration of incompatibility, as relevant notice had not been given to the court or the Crown. Further consideration of the case was adjourned until notice had been given to the Crown as required by CPR 19.4A.

8.3.1.3   *Is the applicant intentionally homeless?*

The test of 'intentional homelessness' is without doubt the test which has caused the most controversy under the Housing Act 1996. The test remains intact following the coming into force of the Homelessness Act 2002. Therefore, where an authority concludes that a person has become intentionally homeless, its only duty thereafter is to provide the person with temporary accommodation for as long as the authority thinks it reasonable for the person to find their own accommodation and to provide them with advice and such assistance as the authority considers appropriate in the circumstances.

Section 191 of the 1996 Act provides that a person is homeless intentionally if he or she has *deliberately* done or failed to do something in consequence of which they cease to occupy accommodation which is available for their occupation, and which it would have been reasonable for them to continue to occupy. Section 192 goes on to provide that 'an act or omission in good faith on the part of the person who was unaware of any relevant fact shall not be treated as deliberate' for the purposes of establishing intentional homelessness.

What is clear is that even if an applicant is both homeless and in priority need, they will be refused housing if the authority find them to be intentionally homeless. There must therefore be an argument that in certain, but rare, cases, the refusal of housing may constitute a violation of Article 8 ECHR. This argument depends to a large extent on the scope and application of the intentional homelessness test.

The applicant must have *deliberately* done or failed to do something in consequence of which he or she ceased to occupy. In general, this requirement has been fairly leniently interpreted by the courts. The Code of Guidance on Parts VI and VII of the Housing Act 1996 also provides some guidance as to the meaning of 'intentional homelessness' which if followed, goes a large way towards preventing any potential violation of Article 8. In *R v Hillingdon London Borough Council, ex parte Islam* [1983] 1 AC 688, an applicant was found to be intentionally homeless when he left the shared room he was living in because he had deliberately asked his wife and children to come over from Bangladesh and the room could no longer accommodate his needs. The House of Lords held that the room could no longer be said to be 'available for him and his family' and thus he was not intentionally homeless by giving it up.

However, in the case of *R v Brent London Borough Council, ex parte Baruwa* (1997) 29 HLR 915, the local council found Mrs Baruwa to be intentionally homeless because she had spent her money on nursery fees and car maintenance and not her rent, and had been eventually evicted. The Court of Appeal upheld the finding of intentional homelessness.

The point of interest is that the Court of Appeal held that although eviction as a result of rent arrears is not intentional if it is the result of spending assets on the 'necessities of life' it is for an authority and not a court to decide whether a failure to pay rent is deliberate or whether it is due to the tenant having insufficient money to pay for the necessities of life. This thus demonstrates that in many situations it is the authority who will have the only duty to consider its Article 8 duties in such circumstances.

It is therefore theoretically possible that an authority's decision on intentional homelessness could be in violation of Article 8 ECHR. For example, if Mrs Baruwa had seven children in ill-health, was a single parent, was fairly uneducated and simply spent money on the 'wrong things' because of these factors, it may be that the decision to find her intentionally homeless could be disproportionate (even though technically in accordance with the law), especially if she could not afford to pay a private rental deposit, for example, and the consequence of the decision was to render her and her children completely homeless.

In the recent case of *Orejudos v Royal Borough of Kensington and Chelsea* [2003] EWCA 345, the issue of intentional homelessness raised itself in a new context. The claimant was housed in hotel accommodation and was required to sign an agreement to the effect that if he was not going to stay at the hotel, he should contact the respondent to explain his absence, otherwise his booking would be cancelled. The basis of this agreement was that the respondent did not wish to pay for accommodation which remained unused.

In August 2002, the claimant's booking was cancelled, on the basis that he had been absent ten times without explaining his absences. Thereafter, he applied for housing, and the respondents found him to be intentionally homeless. The claimant argued that the condition to stay at the hotel was unduly onerous and breached his Article 8 ECHR rights to a private life. The Court of Appeal held that although a person who was homeless was entitled to the protection of his private space as much as anyone else, the public authority also had an interest in the terms on which he was taking their accommodation. The conditions did not require him to sleep in the room every night, but to give satisfactory reasons if he did not do so. On that basis, the condition was the type of condition which could lawfully be imposed, as the reasons given for the imposition were proportionate in relation to the aim of discharging the statutory obligation of providing accommodation to homeless persons.

8.3.1.4   Is the applicant eligible for assistance?

Three categories of person are ineligible for assistance under the Housing Act 1996 (and still remain so under the Homelessness Act 2002). Persons defined as 'persons from abroad', i.e., persons who are subject to immigration control under the Asylum and Immigration Act 1999. Further, asylum seekers (or dependants of asylum seekers) who do not qualify as 'persons from abroad' are nonetheless ineligible for assistance if they are held to occupy accommodation in the United Kingdom which is 'available for their occupation'.

Such accommodation should only be regarded as 'available' for a person if it is available for occupation by him and any other person who normally resides, or might be reasonably expected to reside, with him as a member of his family, thus ensuring compliance with Article 8 in that regard.

The third category, inserted by Sch. 1, para. 7 to the 2002 Act, which inserts a new subs. 185(2A) into the 1996 Act, is that of persons who are excluded from entitlement to housing benefit by the provisions of the Asylum and Immigration Act 1999. This amendment was made following the case of *Kaya* v *Haringey London Borough Council* [2002] HLR 1, CA.

8.3.2   Failing the tests — internal reviews and appeals

If a housing authority concludes that a person does not meet one of the three tests set out above, then by virtue of s. 202 of the Housing Act 1996, that applicant has a right to request a review of the authority's decision. Such a request for review must be made before the end of the period of 21 days beginning with the day on which the applicant is notified of the authority's decision (or longer, should the authority confirm this in writing). If such a review is requested, the authority is then obliged to carry out a review.

The regulations governing the procedure to be followed in connection with a review under s. 202 are the Allocation of Housing and Homelessness (Review Procedures) Regulations 1999 (SI 1999/71) ('the 1999 Regulations'). Paragraph 2 of the Regulations provides that:

Where the decision of the authority on a review of an original decision made by an officer of the authority is also to be made by an officer, that officer shall be someone who was not involved in the original decision and who is senior to the officer who made the original decision.

Paragraph 6 provides that following a request for a review, the authority must notify the applicant that he or she may make written representations in connection with the review. The reviewer must take into account any representations made (para. 8(1)). Further, if the reviewer considers that there was a deficiency or irregularity in the original decision but is minded nonetheless to make a decision which is against the interests of the applicant, they must notify the applicant of this and that the applicant may make oral or written representations.

Under s. 204 of the Housing Act 1996, if an applicant is dissatisfied with the decision on review, or has not been notified of the decision within 12 weeks of the review being requested, he or she may appeal to the county court on any point of law arising from the decision or, as the case may be, the original decision. This effectively provides judicial review grounds of review by the county court. Such an appeal must be brought within 21 days of being notified (or within 21 days of the date on which the applicant should have been notified).

Under the provisions of the 1996 Act, after the 21-day period had expired, the county court had no jurisdiction to entertain the appeal (see *R* v *Westminster City Council, ex parte Ellioua* (1998) 31 HLR 440). The High Court also held in the same case that it will not entertain any application for judicial review if there has been no appeal to the county court when such an appeal was available. Thus the failure to comply with the 21-day limit was effectively the end of any right of challenge to the review decision.

However, the Homelessness Act 2002 has amended the statutory scheme by inserting a new subs. 204(2A) into the 1996 Act. This provides the county court with the power to give permission for an appeal to be brought after the 21-day deadline has expired. The power will be available if the court is satisfied that there is 'good reason' for:

(a) the applicant being unable to bring the appeal in time, if permission is sought before the end of the 21 days; or

(b) the failure to bring the appeal in time *and* for any delay in applying the permission, where permission is sought after the expiry of the 21 days.

It can be argued that the whole system of internal review and appeal to the county court raises Article 6 issues. Article 6(1) provides, *inter alia*, that in the determination of his civil rights and obligations, everyone is entitled to a fair and public hearing within a reasonable time by an independent and impartial tribunal established by law. Prior to the Homelessness Act 2002, the review/appeal procedure under the 1996 Act could be said to have the following non-compliant aspects:

(a)   the time limit of three weeks within which an appeal must be brought could have been argued to be a prima facie restriction on the right of access to a court. It is correct to state that the right of access to a court is not absolute and the needs and resources of the state must be taken into account (*Golder* v *UK* (1975) 1 EHRR 524, at para. 38). However, any restrictions must be proportionate to a legitimate aim and comply with the principles of proportionality (*Ashingdane* v *UK* (1985) 7 EHRR 528, and more recently, *Stubbings* v *UK* (1996) 23 EHRR 213; and *National and Provincial Building Society* v *UK* (1997) 25 EHRR 127) and legal certainty (see *Société Levage Prestations* v *France* (1996) 24 EHRR 351).

It was certainly arguable that the three-week time limit, with absolutely no discretion to extend that time in exceptional circumstances was disproportionate, given that by definition vulnerable persons are involved. Homeless persons are unlikely to have access to legal representation, and it may be extremely difficult to secure both representation and legal aid before the time limit expires. An applicant is highly unlikely to be able to bring an appeal on a point of law if unrepresented. Added to that, there was no statutory duty on the housing authority to inform the unsuccessful applicant of the three-week deadline.

It has been recognized by the Strasbourg Court that unduly short limitation periods can give rise to a violation of Article 6 (see, e.g., *Perez de Rada Cavanilles* v *Spain* [1999] EHRLR 208). A three-week time limit for an appeal on a point of law, by definition a difficult appeal to bring, when the most vulnerable members of society are at stake, is an extremely short timetable. Compare six-week time limits for statutory appeals in planning cases where informed parties are involved, and three months in normal judicial review proceedings (which can be extended in exceptional circumstances).

However, the new subs. 204(2A) inserted into the 1996 Act has essentially dealt with this problem. Although the new test for extending time can merely be said to have slightly relaxed the rigid time limits contained in the current statutory scheme, the existence of a power to extend time for good reason appears to meet the balance of protecting individual rights whilst maintaining a proportionate and necessary time limit. Only time will tell whether, for example, the court may take into account the substantive merits of the appeal when deciding whether to exercise his power to extend time.

(b)   Article 6 also requires there to be a hearing in front of an independent and impartial tribunal. In a situation where members of the local housing authority both make the decision and review it internally, the review must be open to question as to its compliance with Article 6. It is clear that administrative decisions which are determinate of civil rights may be made by bodies which do not provide all the guarantees of Article 6, provided that there is a right of review or appeal which is sufficient to render the proceedings as a whole compatible with Article 6 (see, e.g., *Bryan* v *UK* (1995) 21 EHRR 342).

It is also clearly the case that the appeal need not provide for a complete re-hearing of matters of law and fact. Where the facts are not in dispute, or have been properly established by a quasi-judicial procedure which includes many of the procedural guarantees of Article 6, then the appeal court's jurisdiction can be properly limited to questions of law (see *Bryan* v *UK* (above), at paras 44–47; *Zumtobel* v *Austria* (1993) 17 EHRR 116, at paras 31 and 32. It may well be that an applicant for accommodation does wish to challenge matters of fact.

However, it must be noted that in determining the sufficiency of review procedures, regard should also be had to the subject matter of the decision, the manner in which the decision was arrived at and the nature of the dispute, including the grounds on which the decision is contested.

In relation to the subject matter, where an assessment of an individual's personal or economic rights are directly determined, the individual must generally be able to challenge that decision before a judicial body which both complies with the guarantees of Article 6 and has full jurisdiction (see *Kaplan* v *UK* (1980) 4 EHRR 64; *Albert and LeCompte* v *Belgium* (1983) 5 EHRR 533). It must be arguable that a determination involving an applicant's right to a home must be a determination of that applicant's fundamental personal rights.

In relation to the manner in which the decision was arrived at, it is clear that where the administrative decision-maker had the benefit of hearing witnesses and representations from both sides, then it is more likely that an appeal on a point of law only may be sufficient to comply with Article 6 (e.g. at a public enquiry, such as in *Bryan* v *UK*). In the present case, however, it is clear that there is not a full hearing and oral representations may only be made if the reviewer believes there to have been a flaw in the original decision but is nevertheless minded to find against the applicant. Does this mean that the statutory scheme is incompatible with Article 6?

In this context, it is important to note the impact of various recent cases. In *R* v *Bracknell Forest District Council, ex parte Johns and another* (2001) 33 HLR 45, two tenants asserted that the introductory tenancy regime (dealt with in Chapter

Seven) was incompatible with Article 6 of the Convention. Longmore J held that the review panel in such cases was neither independent nor impartial, in prima facie violation of Article 6. However, he also held that there was no violation of Article 6 as the remedy of judicial review provided a sufficient right of review to comply with Article 6(1).

Lord Justice Keene granted permission to appeal on 28 February 2001 and directed an expedited hearing. He stated that it was properly arguable that the characteristics of local authority review panels mean that the legislation is not compatible with Article 6. The Court of Appeal gave judgment on 16 October 2001 ([2002] 2 WLR 1448). It upheld the decision of Longmore J, holding that the internal review followed by the right of appeal to the county court on a point of law (essentially on the same basis as for judicial review) would satisfy the requirements of Article 6. The House of Lords granted an application from Nina McLellan seeking leave to appeal in this case. The Appeal Committee made a provisional unanimous decision to grant leave following a consideration of the applicant's petition and invited objections from the respondent on 23 July 2002.

However, this was in the context of introductory tenancies, and a different statutory framework (i.e. the Housing Act 1985). However, in the case of introductory tenancies, a tenant has a right to request an oral hearing, at which he can be represented and he may call witnesses to give evidence and cross-examine other witnesses, in a manner analogous to a public inquiry as in cases such as *Bryan* v *UK* (1995) 21 EHRR 342. None of these safeguards is available as of right to an unsuccessful applicant under the 1996 Act.

These arguments were fully ventilated in the two leading cases on this issue, namely *R (on the application of Adan)* v *London Borough of Newham* [2002] 1 WLR 2120 and *R (on the application of Begum)* v *Tower Hamlets* [2002] 1 WLR 2491, CA [2003] 2 WLR 388 (HL), the latter of which was finally decided by the House of Lords on 13 February 2003.

In *Adan*, it was argued by the claimant that the internal review process, with a subsequent appeal to the county court on a point of law only, was incompatible with Article 6 ECHR. It was conceded by Newham Council that this procedure was 'determinative of civil rights' as required by Article 6. Further, it was common ground that the Council could not constitute an 'independent and impartial tribunal' for the purposes of Article 6 and that 'appeal on a point of law' essentially conferred the same remedies as with judicial review.

The Court of Appeal concerned itself purely with situations where a local authority has to determine issues of primary fact. In all other cases, it held, appeal on a point of law to the county court would be sufficient to guarantee compliance with Article 6. However, where the determination of primary facts was at issue, the argument was that the county court would have simply no power to determine these, given the wording of s. 204 of the Housing Act 1996. All three members of the court agreed that 'appeal on a point of law' could not be interpreted to mean 'appeal on a point of law or fact'.

The Court of Appeal held therefore, that where primary facts were at issue, Article 6 compliance could not be guaranteed, but that in order to avoid this problem, local authorities could use their statutory contracting-out powers to ensure that the internal review was undertaken by someone who did meet the test of an 'independent and impartial tribunal'.

Very soon after this, a differently constituted Court of Appeal decided the case of *Begum*, and essentially reversed (although technically did not, as the judgment in *Adan* was, on the facts of the case, *obiter*) the judgment in *Adan*. The Court of Appeal, deciding exactly the same point and relying heavily on *Johns and McLellan*, held that because the statutory scheme as a whole did not generally or systematically decide questions of fact (and because the scheme required weighing questions of policy into the equation) and the statutory scheme either had to be compliant with Article 6 or not, then on balance, it had to be compliant.

However, the House of Lords granted leave to appeal, and gave judgment on 13 February 2003 ([2003] 2 WLR 388). Their Lordships held that the statutory scheme for appeal against an internal review in the context of the homelessness provisions was sufficient to satisfy Article 6(1) ECHR.

Lord Hoffmann, delivering the leading judgment, assumed without deciding that a dispute between the local housing authority and an applicant to whom it had accepted a duty under the homelessness provisions engaged a civil right. However, following the approach adopted in the case of *Bryan v UK* (1995) EHRR 342, and having regard to the context of the statutory scheme, the need for efficient administration and the margin of appreciation which was to be afforded to Parliament, the subject matter of the decision was the 'suitability of the accommodation'. That decision involved a 'classic exercise of administrative decision-making', and the decision arrived at had been made by virtue of a review process conducted at a senior level of administration, which in itself was subject to statutory provisions which promoted fair decision-making.

In conclusion, Lord Hoffmann held that Article 6 did not require the Appeal Court to have full fact-finding jurisdiction. The county court's jurisdiction under s. 204 (appeal on a point of law), which amounted to that of conventional judicial review, was sufficient.

The precursor to this decision was of course, the decision of the House of Lords in *R v Secretary of State for the Environment, Transport and the Regions, ex parte Alconbury Developments and others* [2001] HRLR 45. In that case (discussed at more length in Chapter 2 of this book), the House of Lords held that the ambit of review afforded to courts (judicial review) was sufficient to remedy the acceptance that the Secretary of State, in planning cases, was not an independent and impartial tribunal.

The basis for this was as in *Bryan*; an applicant in planning cases has the benefit of putting his case orally, and of calling witnesses and cross-examining the respondents' witnesses. Effectively, the House of Lords held that the combination of these factors and the availability of judicial review were sufficient. The specialized subject matter of the appeal and the deference to administrative decision-making also featured heavily in this decision.

Therefore the only Article 6 point which has not been formally decided comes in the shape of some *obiter* comments made by Lord Hoffmann regarding the definition of a 'determination of a civil right or obligation'. Lord Hoffmann commented in *Alconbury* that apart from authority, he would have said that a decision as to what the public interest requires is not a 'determination' of civil rights and obligations, although it may affect them. This point has been conceded in many of the cases discussed above, and in *Begum* Lord Hoffmann assumed this point in the homelessness context rather than deciding it. However, now that the statutory scheme has, in any event, been held to be compatible with Article 6, it is difficult to see why this point would be further argued, in the field of the statutory scheme pertaining to homelessness.

Lord Hoffmann's judgment in *Begum* assumes for the future that a determination as to whether or not someone merits a home under the provisions of the relevant Acts is a determination not merely of what is in the public interest but of that individual's Convention rights. The right to be provided with a home according to set criteria cannot therefore be said to equate with a right to a decision in accordance with what the public interest requires.

8.3.3   Accommodation pending decision

An authority which believes that an applicant may be homeless, eligible for accommodation, and in priority need has a duty, contained in s. 188(1) of the Housing Act 1996, to provide (or at least secure) accommodation pending any decision which they may make as a result of their enquiries. It is clear that such accommodation must be made available for the applicant and any other person who might be reasonably expected to reside with him, as set out at s. 176.

As only a very low standard of 'belief' is required, it is unlikely that Article 8 issues would be raised by any refusal to provide temporary accommodation. However, it is clear that if this accommodation is wholly inadequate, issues under Article 8 or 3 ECHR may be raised. In very extreme cases, e.g. where someone is terminally ill and is in urgent need of accommodation, Article 2 issues may be raised, although to a large extent both of these issues are likely to be adequately dealt with by domestic law in the form of a domestic judicial review application, raising, for example, the National Assistance Act 1948 or other domestic legislation.

8.3.4 Appeals for Accommodation pending appeal to the county court

Section 204(4) of the Housing Act 1996 provided local authorities with a discretion, not a duty, to continue the provision of accommodation pending the making of, or determination of, an appeal to the county court. Previously, applicants wishing to challenge the refusal of the authority to exercise that discretion in their favour had to do so by way of judicial review, and the county court had no jurisdiction to order the council to accommodate pending appeal (*Ali* v *Westminster City Council* [1999] 1 WLR 384, CA). However, s. 11 of the Homelessness Act 2002 inserts a new s. 204A into the 1996 Act, giving an applicant the right to appeal the refusal of the local authority to exercise their discretion in his or her favour. Such appeals are likely to be heard very quickly (and thus potentially in the absence of the local authority) but the Act contains no guidance as to the criteria the court must use in the exercise of their power.

8.3.5 Other relevant changes made by the Homelessness Act 2002

As stated above, one of the keys aims behind the Homelessness Act 2002 was to seek to prevent homelessness. The first four sections of the 2002 Act provide a requirement for local authorities to prepare a 'homelessness review', followed by a full 'homelessness strategy'.

The meaning of a 'homelessness review' is defined in s. 2 of the 2002 Act. Section 2 provides that the local authority must conduct an audit in its own area. This essentially involves gathering statistics about the current homelessness picture in their area, with the aim of ensuring that the authority becomes aware of the problems and the resources they are contending with.

The results of the review form the basis for the authority's homelessness strategy, which is defined by s. 3. The strategy must cover:

(a)   the prevention of homelessness;
(b)   the securing of suitable accommodation for those who are, or may become, homeless; and
(c)   the provision of services to those who are or may become homeless.

It must set out specific objectives and activities for the local housing authority and other public authorities and voluntary organizations and must be kept under review. A local authority's 'homelessness strategy' must essentially be the document which sets out their framework for homelessness prevention. Section 1(5) provides that the local authority is required to have regard to the terms of its homelessness strategy when undertaking any of its other statutory functions. As to timing, s. 1 provides that each authority's homelessness strategy must be published within one year of commencement (i.e. by July 2003) and that new strategies must then be prepared at least every five years.

It is thought that these changes, which seek to prevent homelessness as far as possible, are (as well as the implementation of the Labour Party's election manifesto promises) an attempt to ensure that authorities do comply as far as possible with a positive duty to secure Article 8 rights. Although the European Court of Human Rights has repeatedly emphasized that the aim of Article 8 ECHR is to protect individuals from arbitrary interference by public authorities, there is no doubt that there can be positive obligations upon states to ensure respect for Article 8 rights, subject of course to the general 'margin of appreciation' allowed to states to determine whether respect for Article 8 rights demands positive action in the circumstances. These changes are examples of emerging requirements for the positive prevention of homelessness, and also to provide housing assistance, in order to avoid situations where individuals may suffer as a direct result of a local authority's inaction. In *Marzari v Italy* (1999) 28 EHRR CD 175, a case involving an applicant who suffered ill health but had been evicted from his flat, the European Court of Human Rights held that although Article 8 does not guarantee the right to have one's housing problem solved by the authorities, a refusal of the authorities to provide assistance in this respect might in some circumstances raise an issue under Article 8 because of the impact of such refusal on the private life of the individual.

8.4   PERMANENT HOUSING

The provisions of Part VI of the Housing Act 1996 only apply to the allocation of long-term accommodation. As such, it can be said that the duty to provide an applicant with a permanent home raises issues which are even more fundamental. It is important to note that the allocation provisions of the Homelessness Act 2002 did not come into force until 27 January 2003. However, the provision of permanent housing is fully covered in Chapter Seven.

Chapter Nine

Possession Proceedings by Public Authorities

David Elvin QC

9.1 INTRODUCTION

9.1.1 At common law

The ECHR provides restrictions on the ability of a public authority to bring proceedings for possession in addition to those which already exist as a matter of domestic law.

The applicability of public law principles are focused on those cases where a public law body is involved, whether as claimant or defendant (subject to the extent to which the HRA 1998 has 'horizontal application' through s. 6(3)). Public authorities do not have unfettered powers in respect of the administration and control of their own property (see, e.g., *R* v *Coventry City Airport, ex parte Phoenix Aviation* [1995] 3 All ER 37; *R* v *Somerset County Council, ex parte Fewings* [1995] 1 WLR 1037).

To take the simple example of a public authority terminating a licence to occupy, it may be necessary to consider not simply whether the licensee was given appropriate notice (see *Wandsworth London Borough Council* v *A* [2000] 1 WLR 1246) and proceedings properly constituted but whether the decisions to serve notice and to institute proceedings were lawfully reached having regard to other relevant concerns, including applicable policies, the effect of eviction on the defendant and/or the interaction with statutory duties, and, possibly, whether the decision was proportionate under Article 8 ECHR.

Of the pre-existing common law restrictions, the cases appear to fall into three broad, non-exclusive categories, which overlap to some extent:

(a)   The first category involves the application of rules, both statutory and common law, relating to housing and landlord and tenant matters, which exist to limit the ability of the public sector landlord to terminate rights of occupation or bring proceedings for possession. In addition to purely private law requirements, there exist public law restraints on public authorities to terminate certain rights to occupy (see *Governing Body of Henrietta Barnet School* v *Hampstead Garden Suburb Institute* (1993) 93 LGR 470. Carnwath J held that the Institute could not revoke a licence granted to a school without first giving reasonable notice. 'Reasonable notice' was notice which gave sufficient time to enable practical arrangements to be put in hand to safeguard the public interest. The period stipulated by the Court as reasonable notice took account of the statutory requirements for notice to discontinue a school.

(b)   In the second category are cases arising from the exercise of powers which local authorities may rely upon in order to enter into transactions, e.g. under the LGA 1972. Transactions entered into which are entered into *ultra vires* fall into this category (see, e.g., the interest rates swaps litigation *Hazell* v *Hammersmith and Fulham London Borough Council* [1992] 2 AC 1).

(c)   The third category (overlapping with (b)) includes cases involving the application of more general public law restrictions on the exercise of the ability of an authority to terminate or interfere with an interest, or take action for possession, on the basis of abuse of power (see, e.g., *Wandsworth London Borough Council* v *Winder* [1985] AC 461; *West Glamorgan County Council* v *Rafferty* [1987] 1 WLR 457; and the need to consider matters of 'common humanity' in *R* v *Lincolnshire County Council, ex parte Atkinson* (1996) 8 Admin LR 529; *Wandsworth London Borough Council* v *Ariwodo* (21 December 1999) — although see also *R* v *Brighton and Hove District Council, ex parte Marmont* (1998) 30 HLR 1046).

There are also cases, where although the issue is concerned with the entitlement to obtain property, this arises in a context which makes it clear that it is essentially a public law issue for the Administrative Court, e.g. the compulsory purchase of property and rights to repurchase land acquired under threat of compulsion by central government under the Crichel Down Rules (see, e.g., *R* v *Ministry of Defence, ex parte Wilkins* [2000] 40 EG 180).

In domestic cases, the courts have tended to prefer a procedure whereby public law grounds are raised as a ground for adjournment pending an application for judicial review of the decision to institute proceedings, provided there is the real possibility of a successful judicial review (see *Avon County Council* v *Buscott* [1988] QB 656; and, post-HRA 1998, *Michalak* v *Wandsworth London Borough Council* [2003] 1 WLR 617, at para. 76).

In relatively few cases, a party may be able to raise a public law issue directly in the context of a private law claim, e.g. as a direct defence to a claim. In

Wandsworth v *Winder* (see above), Wandsworth's claim for possession based on arrears of rent failed since the Council's decision to raise the defendant's rent was void for unreasonableness. This collateral challenge to the legality of the Council's decision gave rise to a genuine defence since the effect of the challenge was that there were no arrears of rent. Such defences can properly be raised in the course of ordinary civil proceedings and do not require resort to judicial review. The House of Lords considered that the protection afforded by the judicial review process to public authorities should not take precedence over the preservation of 'the ordinary rights of private citizens to defend themselves against unfounded claims' (Lord Fraser).

In *Wandsworth London Borough Council* v. *A* [2000] 1 WLR 1246, the Court of Appeal (applying *Winder*) held that the relationship between a school managed by a local education authority and the parent of a pupil was governed by public law considerations, so that a headmaster intending to revoke the implied licence which normally allowed a parent to enter the school was required both to warn the parent and also to hear and consider any representations from the parent in respect of the conduct relied upon as justifying exclusion. The failure to meet those requirements could be relied upon in defence to a private law action by the local education authority seeking an injunction (or other relief) against the parent. However, the Court of Appeal (at 1256–1259), perhaps contrary to the trend in other cases (see, e.g., *Rhondda Cynon Taff Borough Council* v *Watkins* [2003] 1 WLR 1864), indicated its reservations as to the use of public law issues as defences, particularly due to the absence of specialized judiciary from most courts in which such issues might arise and the procedural protections afforded by judical review procedure. *Re Hampstead Garden Suburb Institute* appears to fall into this category of case to the extent that the reasonableness of the notice given to terminate a licence is determined by what may be regarded as public interest considerations.

Circumstances in which public law issues can genuinely arise in private law proceedings are likely to be few, but if they give rise to difficulties (whether for the reasons indicated in *Wandsworth* v *A* or otherwise) those difficulties are not insoluble:

(a)   If there is a real need for a specialist administrative court judge, the case can be transferred to the Administrative Court or some other appropriate arrangement made (see *Mercury Communications Ltd* v *Director General of Telecommunications* [1996] 1 WLR 48, at 57; *Trustees of Dennis Rye Pension Fund* v *Sheffield City Council* [1994] 4 All ER 747, at 755; and *Clark* v *University of Lincolnshire and Humberside* [2000] 1 WLR 1988).

(b)   Delay issues can be dealt with as an abuse, as suggested in *Clark* v *University of Lincolnshire and Humberside*, or by adjourning the private law claim to allow the public law issue to be raised in an application for judicial review.

In the light of the House of Lords decision in *Harrow London Borough Council* v *Qazi* [2003] 3 WLR 792, if human rights are to be raised as a ground of challenge where the termination of an interest by a public authority would otherwise be effective, it seems that challenge by way of judicial review will be the only way to raise such issues given the majority view that a case specific balance of interests under Article 8(2) is not required by the court making an order for possession. Lord Millett said at para. 109:

> In the exceptional case where the applicant believes that the local authority is acting unfairly or from improper or ulterior motives, he can apply to the High Court for judicial review. The availability of this remedy, coupled with the fact that an occupier cannot be evicted without a court order, so that the court can consider whether the claimant is entitled as of right to possession, is sufficient to supply the necessary and appropriate degree of respect for the applicant's home.

In any event *Qazi* makes it unlikely that such issues will have any relevance (see further, 9.2).

9.1.2   Under the Convention

Insofar as Convention rights raise issues concerning the termination of tenancies, they are mainly likely to arise under the following provisions, although others may be engaged:

(a)   Article 8;
(b)   Article 1 of Protocol 1; and
(c)   Article 6, with regard to the means of recovery of possession.

Interference with property rights, or the recovery/obtaining of possession, may involve issues combining some or all of these provisions.

In *Sheffield City Council* v *Smart* [2002] HLR 34, at para. 20, Laws LJ explained the impact of the HRA 1998 in terms of its modifying the substantive principles upon which judicial review is now exercised rather than the nature of the process itself:

> For my own part, I would put this matter of the amplitude of the judicial review jurisdiction somewhat more broadly. Before incorporation of the Convention rights there arose from time to time troubling questions in the Strasbourg court whether, in one context or another, judicial review provided a sufficient remedy for the purposes of Article 13 ECHR . . . But it seems to me that the position since 2 October 2000, when

HRA took effect, is necessarily otherwise. This is for reasons of principle which spring from the very nature of the judicial review jurisdiction. As is very well known that jurisdiction exists, and has long existed, as the means by which the exercise of power by any public authority is strictly limited to the scope and purposes of the power's grant, and subjected also to the common law's insistence on rationality and fairness. Before 2 October 2000 the Convention rights did not, at least not directly, measure or confine the scope or purpose of the powers which any public authority enjoyed. But since then, compliance with the Convention rights listed in Part 1 of Schedule 1 to the HRA is a condition of the lawful exercise of power by every public authority, where the Convention's subject matter is involved. It follows in my judgment that the High Court's ancient jurisdiction strictly to keep inferior bodies within the law now requires it (absent an effective alternative judicial remedy) to review the use of power by such bodies for compliance with ECHR. This is not an extension of the jurisdiction. That has not changed. What has changed is the substantive law which governs the actions and omissions of public authorities. In the result (and here I leave aside the possible availability of other remedies which should be exercised first), whereas before 2 October 2000 judicial review's effectiveness as a remedy for ECHR violations was a contingent circumstance, now it is a necessary truth.

Convention issues can be subdivided, in accordance with the analysis adopted by the Court of Appeal in *R* v *Bracknell Forest District Council, ex parte McLellan* [2002] 1 All ER 899, into:

(a) Cases engaging the Convention at the 'macro' level — i.e. where the issue is the broader question of whether Parliament has struck the appropriate proportionality balance in enacting particular legislative provisions (e.g. *Poplar Housing and Regeneration Community Association Ltd* v *Donoghue* [2001] 3 WLR 183), excluding persons from statutory protection (*Somerset* v *Isaacs* [2002] EHLR 18) or setting down particular procedures (e.g. *Alconbury*). As Brooke LJ held in *Michalak* v *Wandsworth London Borough Council* [2003] 1 WLR 617:

> The objective justification for the possession order lies in the statutory arrangements devised by Parliament for identifying who may succeed to successor tenancies and who may not following the death of a secure tenant. There is ample Strasbourg authority for the proposition that appropriate justification may be derived from a statutory scheme, and that it need not always be demonstrated on a case by case basis.

(b) Cases engaging Convention issues at the 'micro' level — i.e. which involve the application of the Convention to the specific facts of the case, in particular where the application of proportionality turns on the individual facts rather than the margin of appreciation afforded to Parliament.

The fact that the principal Convention issue in a case is at the 'macro' level does not itself exclude consideration at the 'micro' level although this is likely to be rare (see Laws LJ in *Sheffield* v *Smart*, at para. 43 and Mance LJ in *Michalak*, at paras 72–76). In *Sheffield* v *Smart*, Laws LJ held:

> ... there might be the rare case where something wholly exceptional has happened since service of the notice to quit, which fundamentally alters the rights and wrongs of the proposed eviction, and the county court might be obliged to address it in deciding whether or not to make an order for possession.

The recent judgment of the House of Lords in *Qazi* reduces yet further the possibility of an exceptional case arising at the 'micro' level (see in particular the passages from the speeches of Lord Millett and Lord Scott set out at 9.2). However, although Lord Hope stated at para. 78 that 'article 8(2) is met where the law affords an unqualified right to possession on proof that the tenancy has been terminated' he nonetheless said at para. 79, having referred to Laws LJ in *Sheffield*:

> I wish to reserve my opinion as to whether it would be open to the tenant, in a wholly exceptional case, to raise these issues in the county court where proceedings for possession were being taken following the service of a notice to quit by the housing authority, bearing in mind as Lord Millett points out that its decision to serve the notice to quit would be judicially reviewable in the High Court so long as the application was made within the relevant time limit.

Whether such wholly exceptional cases can exist, and what may constitute such a case, is discussd further at the end of the next section.

9.2 APPLICATION OF THE HUMAN RIGHTS ACT TO TERMINATION OF RIGHTS TO OCCUPY

This is a difficult issue in respect of which a detailed discussion falls outside the scope of this chapter. However, the recent decision of the House of Lords in *Harrow London Borough Council* v *Qazi* [2003] 3 WLR 792 may provide a short answer in the property context.

The essential question is whether the duty imposed by s. 6 of the HRA 1998 requires the courts to apply Convention principles notwithstanding the lack of 'public' content in the dispute, e.g. in a private dispute between two parties over the entitlement to possession of real property (sometimes referred to as 'horizontal effect') (see Clayton and Tomlinson, *The Law of Human Rights*, at paras 5.80–5.99, 5.114 and 5.115; Grosz, Beatson and Duffy, *Human Rights*, at paras 4-01, and 4-15–4-17; *Douglas and others* v *Hello! Ltd* [2001] 2 WLR 992, at 1025–1026, para. 128 (Sedley LJ).

A distinction can be drawn between the following types of case raising HRA issues:

(a)   Where the Convention will be applicable to the exercise of the court's own discretion or procedure to ensure that in the exercise of the court's own powers, Convention Rights are given due protection, e.g. in the grant of an injunction (see *Douglas* and *others* v *Hello! Ltd* (see above); *Ashdown* v *Telegraph Group Ltd* [2001] 4 All ER 666 (a breach of copyright claim). In Ashdown, at para. 55, Lord Phillips MR pointed out: 'We would add that the implications of the Human Rights Act must always be considered where the discretionary relief of an injunction is sought.'

(b)   Where the Convention issue said to arise does not engage the court's own powers but goes to the application of substantive principles of private law, the Convention would not interfere with the ordinary nature and incidents of private law rights (see, e.g., *Application No. 11949/86 (Di Palma)* v *UK* (1988) 10 EHRR 149 (limitations on the right to obtain relief from forfeiture); *Gustafsson* v *Sweden* (1996) 22 EHRR 409, at para. 60 (government refusal to intervene in labour dispute)). This position has been strongly supported by the majority of the House of Lords in *Harrow London Borough Council* v *Qazi* [2003] 3 WLR 792.

It might be said that these two categories are not distinct since even the exercise of private property rights may be subject to the court's own discretion and hence subject to the court's own duty under the HRA 1998. The minority view in *Qazi*, agreeing with the Court of Appeal, would have lent support to that approach, but the minority view not only supports category (b) but even effectively narrows category (a) as a result of its view that Article 8(2) is complied with when property rights are terminated according to law. Indeed, Lord Millett held at paras 108–109 (see also Lord Scott to similar effect at paras 143–144) that:

> 108.   I would also wish to dissociate myself from the dictum of Waller LJ in *R (McLellan)* v *Bracknell Forest Borough Council* [2002] QB 1129 that, even in a case where a private landlord is seeking possession, the court, as a public authority, must consider whether the order is justified under article 8(2) before making an order. *The fact that a person cannot be evicted without a court order does not mean that the court, as a public authority, is bound in each case to consider whether an order for possession would be disproportionate and infringe article 8 rights. The court is merely the forum for the determination of the civil right in dispute between the parties: see Di Palma v United Kingdom (1988) 10 EHRR 149.* Its task is to resolve the dispute according to law. In doing so it would, of course, have to consider whether the landlord was entitled to possession as a matter of our ordinary domestic law (i.e. apart from the Human Rights Act 1998), taking into account the various statutory provisions which operate in

this field. *But once it concludes that the landlord is entitled to an order for possession, there is nothing further to investigate. The order is necessary to protect the rights of the landlord; and making or enforcing it does not show a want of appropriate respect for the applicant's home.*

109.   I would accordingly endorse the observations of Moses J in *R (Gangera)* v *Hounslow London Borough Council* [2003] EWHC 794 Admin that in proceedings between private parties the court doe not act incompatibly with article 8 by making or enforcing a possession order without considering questions of proportionality. *I also agree with him that it makes no difference that the landlord is a public authority.* (Emphasis added.)

The termination of property rights in accordance with the law, or their own provisions, does not amount to a breach of Article 1 of Protocol 1 (see *JS* v *The Netherlands* (1995) 20 EHRR CD 42; *Gudmundsson* v *Iceland* (1996) 21 EHRR CD 89). Further, interferences resulting from matters of a purely private contractual nature do not fall within the provisions of the ECHR — *Gustafsson* v *Sweden* (see above), at para. 60:

> 60.   Admittedly, the State may be responsible under Article 1 (P1-1) for interferences with peaceful enjoyment of possessions resulting from transactions between private individuals (see the *James and Others* v *United Kingdom* judgment of 21 February 1986 . . . paras 35–36). In the present case, however, not only were the facts complained of not the product of an exercise of governmental authority, but they concerned exclusively relationships of a contractual nature between private individuals, namely the applicant and his suppliers or deliverers.

The same principle was applied in *Di Palma* v *UK*, reported as *Application No. 11949/86* v *UK* (1988) 10 EHHR 149, at 154, where the Commission rejected the claim that the United Kingdom should have taken greater steps to protect the right to relief against forfeiture under the County Courts Act 1984:

> . . . the relations between the applicant and the landlord were regulated by a private contract (the lease) which set out the mutual obligations of the parties. The terms of the lease neither directly prescribed nor amended by legislation, although substantial quantities of legislation regulate the operation of leases in a general way, mainly with a view to protecting the position of tenants. Thus, for example, in order to gain possession of the flat, the landlord had to take proceedings before the courts to obtain a possession order, without which eviction of the applicant would have been unlawful. In view of the exclusively private law relationship between the parties to the lease the Commission considers that the respondent Government cannot be responsible by the mere fact that the landlord by its agents, who were private individuals, brought the applicant's lease to an end in accordance with the terms of that lease, which set out the agreement between the applicant and the company . . . It is true that the landlord issued proceedings in the domestic courts in order to forfeit the applicant's lease. This fact alone is not however

sufficient to engage State responsibility in respect of the applicant's rights to property, since the public authority in the shape of the County Court merely provided a forum for the determination of the civil right in dispute between the parties. In contending that State responsibility for an interference with rights protected by the Convention arises in respect of this complaint, the applicant seeks to demand that a State be subject to a positive obligation to protect the property rights of an individual in the context of his dispute with another private individual . . . In the present case the applicant and the landlord had entered into contractual arrangements set out in the lease which expressly provided for the applicant's tenancy to terminate if rent remained unpaid once demanded.

However, it should be noted that:

(a)   s. 6(3) of the HRA 1998 now imposes an obligation on the courts not 'to act in a way which is incompatible with a Convention right'; and

(b)   the case was one where the right to relief was limited by statute, and was not a general power exercisable by the court.

In the light of the House of Lords decision in *Harrow London Borough Council* v *Qazi* [2003] 3 WLR 792 these distinctions cease to matter. The Court of Appeal had held that a former tenant whose tenancy had come to an end by operation of law could still have a right to a home within Article 8 ECHR, relying on the Strasbourg view (see *Buckley* and *Chapman* below) that an unlawful occupier may nonetheless have Article 8 rights. A local authority tenancy had been terminated by Mr Qazi's wife giving notice to quit (as she was entitled to do under the tenancy agreement), subsequent to which they were divorced and Mr Qazi remarried and his new wife moved into the premises. On the basis of *Hammersmith* v *Monk* [1992] 1 AC 478 there would be no question as a matter of private law that the tenancy had been properly determined, but it was alleged that the Council was in breach of Article 8 in seeking to recover possession. The Court was only asked to consider whether Article 8 was engaged in principle, and was not asked to consider the facts of how Article 8(2) might apply, it appearing to be common ground that if the Court found Article 8 to be engaged then the matter should be remitted to the county court.

The Court of Appeal's decision in *Qazi* was referred to without criticism in later Court of Appeal cases, but it was overturned by the House of Lords by a three to two majority decision (Lords Bingham and Steyn dissenting on the need to apply Article 8(2) to the decision of the Court) on the basis that, whilst Article 8 was engaged, the Court was not required to carry out a balancing process under Article 8(2) and the order for possession had rightly been made by the county court.

In summary it was held that:

(a)   'home' has an autonomous meaning under the Convention not dependent on the provisions of domestic law, but determined by a consideration of the 'factual circumstances, namely the existence of sufficient and continous links', applying *Buckley* v *UK* (1996) 23 EHRR 101;

(b)   Article 8 protects respect for the home, but does not guarentee a right to a home;

(c)   a home may exist for Article 8 purposes even if it is occupied unlawfully;

(d)   issues of proportionality and Article 8(2) will almost never be relevant at the stage of ordering possession — the Convention rights will be satisfied provided that the rules of the substantive law of property have been observed in terminating the interest and that any discretions applicable under statute or domestic law have been properly exercised;

(e)   the court's duty under s. 6(2) does not require it to consider further the issue of proportionality once it has discharged the requirements of UK domestic law;

(f)   there is no difference in result whether the possession action involves a public or a private landowner (paras 78, 80, 108–109, 143–144);

(g)   it does not appear to matter whether the basis of the action is terminated by an interest created or protected by a statutory scheme or at common law; and

(h)   if any Convention points are to be taken, the proper approach is to seek judicial review of the landowner's (who would necessarily have to be a public sector landowner) decision to terminate the interest or seek possession.

The result was put bluntly by Lord Scott at paras 144 and 146:

> 144.   . . . If article 8 does not vest in the home-occupier any contractual or propriretary right that he would not otherwise have, and does not diminish or detract from the contractual or proprietary rights of the owner who is seeking possession, the problem identified by Waller LJ does not arise. The fate of every possession application will be determined by the respective contractual and proprietary rights of the parties. Article 8 can never constitute an answer. In my opinion the *McClellan* case, like the *Donoghue* case [2002] QB 48, was correctly decided but for the wrong reason.
>
> . . .
>
> 146.   . . . In my opinion, the jurisprudence has shown, in effect, that article 8 has no relevance to these landlord/tenant possession cases.

The majority clearly presents a stark answer to attempts to invoke Article 8 in property cases other than by way of judicial reviw. Indeed, it drew criticisms from the powerful minority judgments of Lord Bingham and Lord Steyn. Lord Steyn stated at para. 27:

27. It would be surprising if the views of the majority on the interpretation and application of article 8 of the European Convention on Human Rights, as incorporated into our legal system by the Human Rights Act 1998, withstood European scrutiny. It is contrary to a purposive interpretation of article 8 read against the structure of the Convention. It is inconsistent with the general thrust of the decisions of the European Court of Human Rights, and of the commission. It is contrary to the position adopted by the United Kingdom government on more than one occasion before the European Court of Human Rights. It does not accord to individuals 'the full measure of the [protection] referred to': *Minister of Home Affairs* v *Fisher* [1980] AC 319, 328. On the contrary, it empties article 8(1) of any or virtually any meaningful content. The basic fallacy in the approach is that it allows domestic notions of title, legal and equitable rights, and interests, to colour the interpretation of article 8(1). The decision of today does not fit into the new landscape created by the Human Rights Act 1998.

It is not impossible therefore that the issue will come back. Nevertheless, for the present, it is clear that judicial review, where it applies, is the only route by which human rights can be raised in order to defeat claims to possession or similar claims based on the ordinary incidents of real property.

Furthermore, even raising these issues by way of judicial review could only be successful in the most exceptional of cases. *Qazi* has now been further considered by two separate divisions of the Court of Appeal, both of which gave their judgments on 9 December 2003, in *London Borough of Newham* v *Amrana Kibata* [2003] EWCA 1785 and *Bradney* v *Birmingham City Council* [2003] EWCA 1783. Insofar as Article 8 may be relied upon at all, it is made clear that (a) it will only be by way of judicial review and (b) it will only be in the 'wholly exceptional' case that Article 8 may have any relevance. Thus, it will not be enough that the Council may have procured a notice to quit from one of two joint tenants in circumstances that would defeat the wishes of both that the other tenant would be protected. In *Bradney* Lord Phillips MR described the wholly exceptional case as follows (echoing Laws LJ in *Sheffield* v *Smart*, see 9.1.2):

29. This is not a 'wholly exceptional' case where, for example, something has happened since the service of the notice to quit, which has fundamentally altered the rights and wrongs of the proposed eviction and the Council might be required to justify its claim to override the article 8 right (see *Qazi* at paragraph 79).

In practical terms, however, it will generally not be possible to raise Article 8(2) issues on the facts.

9.3 SECURITY OF TENURE

Protection of the home also includes considerations of security of tenure. In *Gillow* v *UK* (1986) 11 EHRR 335, the restrictions on occupation imposed by

Jersey laws regulating rent were held to amount to a violation of Article 8(1) ECHR, since they excluded the claimants from permanent occupation of their former home (from which they had been absent for a number of years) due to a change in the qualifying conditions for permanent occupation which had occurred after they had vacated the building for a period abroad.

The statutory conferring of limited security of tenure and the specifying of mandatory grounds of possession do not violate Article 8. In *Donoghue v Poplar Housing and Regeneration Community Association Ltd* [2002] QB 48, the Court of Appeal considered whether the assured shorthold provisions of the Housing Act 1988, with their mandatory ground for possession, violated the Article. Lord Woolf CJ, giving the judgment of the Court, held that they did not:

> 72.   We are satisfied, that notwithstanding its mandatory terms, s. 21(4) of the 1988 Act does not conflict with the defendant's right to family life. Section 21(4) is certainly necessary in a democratic society insofar as there must be a procedure for recovering possession of property at the end of a tenancy. The question is whether the restricted power of the court is legitimate and proportionate. This is the area of policy where the court should defer to the decision of Parliament.

The exclusion of persons from the extent of statutory protection was considered in *Somerset County Council v Isaacs* [2002] EHLR 18, and the exclusion of gipsies from security of tenure by virtue of s. 4(6) of the Caravan Sites Act 1968 and s. 5 of the Mobile Homes Act 1983 was compatible with the Convention on the basis of 'macro' considerations and was proportionate under Article 8(2), having regard to the decisions in *Donoghue* and *Sheffield v Smart*. A challenge under Article 14 also failed (see also *Smith v Barking and Dagenham London Borough Council* [2002] 48 EGCS 141). However, the potentially discriminatory application of Rent Act succession provisions to exclude same sex couples has been resolved by reading down the relevant provisions to allow such succession and to prevent a breach of Article 14 (*Fitzpatrick v Sterling Housing Association* [2001] 1 AC 27; *Mendoza v Ghaidan* [2003] Ch 380).

9.4   TRESPASSERS *AB INITIO*

Where action is taken against trespassers *ab initio*, the discretion of the courts under pre-HRA 1998 law is severely limited. This is relevant not only in cases of residential trespass but also has particular ramifications in the case of the eviction of gypsies from, say, highway land, where there is in any event also government policy requiring consideration of 'toleration' (see Department of the Environment Circular 18/94) and of the 'considerations of common humanity' referred to in *R v Lincolnshire County Council, ex parte Atkinson* (see 9.1). In *McPhail v Persons Unknown* [1973] Ch 447 the Court of Appeal held that there was no jurisdiction to postpone or suspend a possession order against trespassers *ab initio*. That result derived from a consideration of historic principles, i.e. judge-made law. As the Master of the Rolls held, at 457 (see also Lawton LJ at 461–462):

> Seeing that the owner could take possession at once without the help of the courts, it is plain that, when he does come to the courts, he should not be in any worse position. The courts should give him possession at once, else he would be tempted to do it himself. So the courts of common law never suspended the order for possession.

The question is whether the courts, in the exercise of their power to order to possession, ought to take a wider view of the impact of a possession order even on trespassers who may have rights under Article 8 notwithstanding that they are trespassers (see *Buckley* v *UK* (1996) 23 EHRR 101; *Chapman* v *UK* (2001) 33 EHRR 18; *Sheffield* v *Smart* [2002] HLR 34). The European Court qualified the Article 8 rights somewhat in *Chapman* (at para. 101) without departing radically from *Buckley*:

> . . . if the establishment of a home in a particular place was unlawful, the position of the individual objecting to an order to move is less strong. The Court will be slow to grant protection to those who, in conscious defiance of the prohibitions of the law, establish a home on an environmentally protected site. For the Court to do otherwise would be to encourage illegal action to the detriment of the protection of the environmental rights of other people in the community.

The Court of Appeal in *Michalak* v *Wandsworth London Borough Council* [2003] 1 WLR 617 considered that this issue was covered by the consideration of the issues in that case and in *Sheffield* v *Smart*. Mance LJ held (at para. 77):

> 77. The judgment in *Sheffield CC v Smart* does not refer to the line of cases establishing the court's duty at common law, prior to the Human Rights Act, to make a possession order against a trespasser with no defence: cf *Sheffield Corp v Luxford, Jones v Savory* and *McPhail v Persons Unknown* . . . or to the statutory restrictions on the right to suspend a possession order once made. The effect of *Sheffield CC v Smart* is, however, to preserve the relevance and operation of both.

This view presents a number of difficulties since it was based on a consideration of the statutory origin of possession powers under housing legislation rather than the judge-made law in McPhail. The distinction is that in the former cases, where possession is sought under statute, Parliament may be considered to have struck the balance between public and private interests necessary to establish proportionality under Article 8(2), as was indeed the case in *Donaghue, McLellan* and *Smart*. However, in the case of judge-made law it is not only unclear whether the appropriate opposing considerations which are required for Article 8(2) purposes have been taken into account, but it is also an area where the courts have the ability to review the restraints imposed on their powers by their own decision. It is, after all, the exercise of the court's own power which is in issue (see *Wilson* v *First County Trust Ltd (No. 2)* [2002] QB 74, at paras 15–22).

However, the answer given in *Qazi* in the House of Lords is that Article 8 should not influence the ordinary incidents of property law or the exercise of rights under the substantive law. Since no distinction appears to be drawn between public and private landowners, or between statutory schemes and the general law, it seems clear that the landowner's right to evict trespassers and to obtain immediate orders for possession remains undisturbed. In the words of Lord Scott:

> 151. ... If Mr Qazi has no contractual or proprietary right under the ordinary law to resist the council's claim for possession, and it is accepted he has not, the acceptance by the court of a defence based on article 8 would give him a possessory right over 31 Hutton Lane that he would not otherwise have. It would deprive the council of its right under the ordinary law to immediate possession. It would constitute an amendment of the domestic social housing legislation. It would give article 8 an effect that it was never intended to have and which it has never been given by the Strasbourg tribunals responsible for implementing the Convention ...

If Lord Steyn is correct, there may be more mileage in this issue, especially if the House of Lords was wrong to adopt a blanket approach to Article 8 and possession proceedings — what if there were a breach of Article 8 notwithstanding compliance with the substantive law? There seems at least a basis for questioning whether judge-made law (such as the *McPhail* rule) and common law remedies do lie outside the scope of proportionality even in property cases, given they may not have been regulated by Parliament and may be subject to adjustment in any event as principles develop. Such issues are, however, unlikely to trouble the possession lists in the county courts at present.

9.5 'SELF-HELP' REMEDIES

Self-help raises difficult issues. English common law rules still retain some vestiges of the ability to recover possession by means of 'self-help', although the extent to which these may be used in practice by public authorities is unclear. Principle examples of self-help are the use of reasonable force to eject a trespasser from property (subject principally to restrictions contained in the Criminal Law Act 1977); distress for rent; and the forfeiture of a lease by peaceable re-entry. The question is to what extent the ability to obtain a remedy by such means can be regarded as consistent with Article 6 or 8 ECHR where no tribunal (independent or otherwise) has adjudicated prior to enforcement.

On one hand, it can be said there is inherent in certain rights to occupy the means of their determination or enforcement, e.g. in a lease by peaceable re-entry (see above). Such an ability to determine is, in any event, severely circumscribed by the protections afforded by statutory provisions limiting forcible entry (see the Criminal Law Act 1977) and conferring security on occupiers requiring the bringing of legal proceedings to recover possession. However, these matters do not overcome the problem that, in the case of re-entry, it is the physical act which not only determines the right (however limited) to occupy but also achieves the recovery of possession, avoiding the need for legal proceedings. There is no question here of the court adjusting its remedies to accord with Convention principles since the court is only likely to become seised of the issue once the action has been taken.

In any event, there remain doubts whether self-help is consistent with Article 6 where an authority relies on self-help other than with the assistance of any independent and impartial tribunal. Indeed, it is the act of the interested public body itself which determines the interest. Proportionality may be difficult to demonstrate given that well-established procedures exist for the recovery of possession including the ability to get a case before the courts at very short notice in appropriate cases of urgency, particularly in cases of trespass (see, e.g., CPR Part 55, rules 55.2(1)(b), 55.5(2), 55.6, 55.7(2), and 55.8). Whilst it is open to argument that procedures for reinstatement and compensation in cases of unlawful eviction exist, it remains uncertain where this is sufficient for the purposes of Article 6, although it may provide an answer to a challenge under Article 1 of Protocol 1.

Such measures only apply *ex post facto*, after the determination has occurred and occupation has been lost (or the distress levied), even if only for a limited period of time until the position is redressed by the court. There also remain Article 8(1) problems, since the act of self-help may have already violated respect to the home and/or private life. Difficult questions remain as to whether the use of self-help and consequent violations of Articles 6 and 8 can be proportionate to the aims to be achieved unless there exist genuinely exceptional circumstances.

One sign of judicial discontent is the warning issued with regard to the exercise of the right to distrain by Lightman J (albeit *obiter*) in *Fuller* v *Happy Shopper Markets Ltd* [2001] 1 WLR 1681 (at 1692, para. 27):

> . . . a landlord is bound to take the greatest care before levying distress that there are no claims on the part of the tenant which may be available by way of equitable set off to be offset against and satisfy the rent outstanding. In any ordinary case he would be well advised to give notice of his intention and invite the tenant to agree what is owing and to inform him whether there are any cross-claims and (if so) to identify them. The ancient (and perhaps an anachronistic) self help remedy of distress involves a serious interference with the right of the tenant under Article 8 of the European Convention on Human Rights to respect for his privacy and home and under Article 1 of the First Protocol to the peaceful enjoyment of his possessions. The human rights implications of levying distress must be in the forefront of the mind of the landlord before he takes this step and he must fully satisfy himself that taking this action is in accordance with the law.

However, this issue may require further consideration in the light of *Qazi*. Lightman J's analysis may not stand if the view that Article 8 does not interfere with the ordinary incidents of property law applies more widely than possession proceedings.

Chapter Ten

Social Services

Ben Rayment

10.1 INTRODUCTION

The general framework of local authority social service provision is governed by the Local Authority and Social Services Act 1970. The list of functions is set out in Sch. 1 to the 1970 Act and includes responsibilities under various Acts for children and families, mental health patients, the elderly, and the disabled. The responsibility of the state for such a vulnerable cross-section of people, and its involvement in intimate and important areas of their lives, may be expected to raise questions involving individual rights. This chapter sets out some of those questions and some possible answers as to the likely relevance of the Convention rights to the work of local authority social services departments in these areas.

The courts have already emphasized that the ECHR is a set of principles rather than a set of detailed rules (*R* v *DPP, ex parte Kebilene* [1999] 3 WLR 972, HL). The flexibility of approach when combined with the heavily discretionary nature of much social services law suggests that the effect of the HRA 1998 will be more likely to raise questions of emphasis and interpretation about the extent and exercise of that discretion rather than the discovery that extensive legislative amendments are necessary to ensure compatibility with the Convention. The unsurprising conclusion that s. 3 of the HRA 1998 is likely to be far more frequently invoked than the declaration of incompatibility, does not diminish the potentially significant effects of the strong adjuration to interpret existing legislation in accordance with Convention rights insofar as it is possible to do so.

10.2 CHILD CARE AND ADOPTION

Local authority social services departments have extensive duties 'to safeguard and promote the welfare of children within their area who are in need' and 'so far as is consistent with that duty, to promote the upbringing of such children by their families'. These duties are principally contained in Parts III, IV and V of the

Children Act 1989. Social services departments also have responsibility for adoptions in their area under the Adoption Act 1976. Under both Acts, responsibilities are carefully divided between the local authority and the courts. At the time of writing, adoption law was about to undergo a radical transformation with the enactment of the Adoption and Children Act 2002, which repeals the entire Adoption Act 1976 except for its Part 4 and para. 6 of Sch. 2. The Act received the Royal Assent on 7 November 2002 but the majority of its provisions were not yet in force at the time of writing. The Act was expected to be implemented gradually and to be fully in force in 2004.

In determining applications relating to the upbringing of children under the Children Act 1989, the 'welfare' of the child concerned, as defined in s. 1 of the Act, is 'paramount'. In adoption proceedings, the welfare of the child shall be the court's 'first consideration' (s. 6 of the Adoption Act 1976). However, the language of the new Adoption and Children Act 2002 mirrors that of the Children Act 1989 — pursuant to section 1(2), 'The paramount consideration of the court or adoption agency [in coming to a decision relating to the adoption of a child] must be the child's welfare, throughout his life'. A fundamental issue of approach is posed by the extent to which the rights-based approach under the Convention may be reconciled with the paramountcy principle of the 1989 Act. In child care law as it is practised in England, the only 'rights' referred to as a matter of practice are those of the child. In fact the Children Act 1989 itself does not refer to 'rights' at all, only to the fact that parental responsibility must be exercised in order to maximize a child's welfare.

Many child care practitioners appear to take the view that there is little difference in practical terms between the two approaches. This may be so in the sense that the outcome of many cases decided after the coming into force of the HRA 1998 is unlikely to be any different to that of cases decided prior to the coming into force of that Act. Nevertheless, on a theoretical level there is a significant difference in approach, and it remains to be seen what changes this produces. Under the ECHR, disputes are resolved by an analysis of the competing rights of all the parties involved, with no priority being given initially to any one party. In cases not involving the Children Act 1989, it has already been acknowledged that, for the purposes of Article 8 ECHR, the scales are initially evenly balanced, with no preference being given to the welfare of the child (see *R v Secretary of State for the Home Department, ex parte Gangadeen and Khan* [1998] 1 FLR 762, *per* Hirst LJ). In *BCC v L* [2002] EWHC 2327 Fam, at para. 57, Charles J drew attention to 'the overlap between the purposes that underlie Article 8 and the Children Act' as identified by Hale LJ in *Re W and B (Re W Care Plan)* [2001] 2 FLR 582. More specifically, at para. 44, he held that the threshold set by s. 31(2) of the Children Act 1989 for the making of care and supervision orders 'accords with the essential object of Article 8 of protecting the individual against arbitrary interference by public authorities'. With regard to the making of care orders and

s. 31 of the Children Act 1989, the Adoption and Children Act 2002 amends s. 31 of the 1989 Act and introduces a new s. 31A to provide that a court may not make a care order until a care plan has been prepared by the local authority and considered by the court.

The significance of this theoretical difference is liable, in the majority of cases, to be hidden because, as already mentioned, the rights of all the parties will be unlikely to compel any different result than in a case decided by applying the welfare principle. However, not every case will fall into this category, and it may be here that a rights-based approach could have an impact.

While many would argue that a rights-based analysis of a case helps to clarify the issues at stake, it does not necessarily make their resolution any easier, and in some cases may even make this harder. The possibility and difficulties of conflict arising between the equally held rights of two children can be seen in *Re A (Conjoined Twins: Medical Treatment)* [2001] UKHRR 1, CA.

Articles 6 and 8 ECHR will be most frequently invoked in children cases. They are considered first, followed by other rights which may also be brought into play in this area.

10.2.1 Relationship between Articles 6 and 8

It is important at the outset to look at some of the considerations that underlie the relationship between Articles 6 and 8 ECHR. The primary focus of Article 6 is on the procedural requirements that attach to a fair and effective hearing. Article 8, on the other hand, is primarily concerned with defining the scope of the substantive right to respect for, amongst other things, private and family life. However, it is well established in ECHR jurisprudence that there are inherent in Article 8 ECHR certain procedural requirements, entitling parents to be involved in any decision-making process concerning the care of their children to a degree sufficient to provide them with the requisite protection of their interests (*W v UK*, 8 July 1987, Series A No. 121-A, 28–29, paras 62 and 64). The different focus of the two articles may, depending on the circumstances of the particular case, justify an examination of the same set of facts under both articles (see, e.g., *McMichael v UK*, 24 February 1995, Series A No. 307-B, 57, para. 91; *TP and KM v UK* (App. No. 28945/95); *P, C and S v UK*, 16 July 2002 (App. No. 5647/00); *BCC v L* [2002] EWHC 2327 Fam).

Thus in the McMichael case the failure to provide access to certain documents was found to have had an impact not only on the conduct of the judicial proceedings but also on a fundamental element of the family life of the applicants. Another example is provided by the case of *P, C and S*. In that case the main procedural failing alleged was the fact that S's parents were not legally represented at the hearing of the local authority's application for a care order or on the local authority's application for freeing and an adoption order which followed shortly after the care proceedings. This was held to be not only a breach of Article 6(1) ECHR but also a breach of Article 8 ECHR. This appears to have been founded on the fact that legal representation in the period following the making of a care order might have made a difference on the decision taken to free S for adoption and on the decision relating to continuing contact between S and her parents prior to and after her adoption. The passage in *P, C and S* (para. 119) which set out the requirement of fairness and respect for the interests safeguarded by Article 8 in the decision-making process was approved in *BCC* v *L* (at paras 72–74). In that case, it was held that at the heart of the court's decision-making process in deciding whether to seek further evidence before making a court order on the basis of a proposed care plan, was the question of whether the court could conclude on the existing evidence that it had sufficient information to make a properly informed and procedurally fair decision as to what order would best promote the medium- to long-term welfare of the child (para. 71). What constitutes fairness will depend on the subject matter of the relevant decision-making process (para. 74).

In the specific circumstances of proceedings under the Children Act 1989, it has been held that unfairness at any stage of the litigation process may involve breach of both Article 8 and Article 6. In this regard the litigation process is wider than the purely judicial part of the proceedings. This is important because although Article 8 is wider in scope than Article 6, which only applies to the litigation process, unlike Article 8, Article 6 is an unqualified right and cannot be balanced against other rights and interests (*Re C* [2002] 2 FCR 673).

10.2.2   Article 6

10.2.2.1   *Determination of civil rights and obligations?*

Only when civil rights and obligations are being determined do the procedural guarantees contained in Article 6 ECHR apply. In the Convention's early jurisprudence, 'civil rights' were referred to in contradistinction to public law rights. Rights to receive social security benefits are often categorized as public law rights in domestic legal systems but that is not determinative under the Convention (see 10.3.2.4). Article 6 has been held applicable to determinations involving the right to respect for family life under Article 8 ECHR in cases concerned with the placing of children in public care (*Olsson* v *Sweden (No. 1)* (1988) 11 EHRR 259), adoption (*Keegan* v *Ireland* (1994) 18 EHRR 342) and fostering. (*Eriksson* v *Sweden* (1989) 12 EHRR 183). In UK domestic law it has been suggested that civil rights and obligations in this area are probably coterminous with such rights as may be enjoyed under Article 8 (see Lord Nicholls in *Re S and others* [2002] 2 AC 291).

Once the civil right or obligation in question has been identified, the next question that arises is when the right to respect for family life is actually being determined. Civil rights and obligations are not determined where proceedings are merely at a preliminary and/or investigative stage (see *Fayed* v *UK* (1994) 18 EHRR 393). The test as applied by the European Court of Human Rights has been to ask whether the determination is 'directly decisive' of a person's civil rights before Article 6 is brought into play (see *Le Compte, Van Leuven and De Meyere* v *Belgium* (1981) 4 EHRR 1). Inclusion on the Department of Health's consultancy index of people unsuited to work with children does not amount to a determination of a person's right to work in his chosen profession given that the index was simply to enable a prospective employer to be put in touch with a previous employer for the purpose of obtaining a reference. There was therefore no right under Article 6 to challenge a registration before an independent tribunal (see *R* v *Secretary of State for Health, ex parte C* [1999] 1 FLR 1073, *per* Richards J; on appeal, the Court of Appeal did not express a view on the compatibility of the index with the Convention ([2000] 1 FLR 627)). Parity of reasoning would suggest that inclusion on other types of registers maintained by local authorities equally does not involve a determination of civil rights. However, common law principles of administrative law may require a person to be given an opportunity to make representations before his or her name, or a child's name, is entered on a register (see *R* v *Norfolk County Council, ex parte M* [1989] QB 619, DC). Although no specific reference was made to Article 6 ECHR, the case of *R* v *Wokingham District Council, ex parte J* [1999] 2 FLR 1136, provides another illustration of this principle in the social services context. The court held that, while it was desirable that an adoption panel should allow a parent to make oral or written representations to it, there was no decision affecting the mother's final rights when the panel recommended that the adoption agency make an application dispensing with her consent to adoption. The mother's remedy was to challenge the appropriateness of the recommendation in the course of the adoption proceedings.

Local authorities are equipped with a number of significant powers for use in the interim investigative and assessment stage of proceedings before a 'final' order or determination is made. The applicability of Convention rights has been widely mooted in relation to the exercise of these powers. The police have powers under the Children Act 1989 to take a child into their protection for 72 hours (see s. 46). The courts have powers to grant emergency protection orders which may, in the first instance, involve the removal of a child from his or her carer for up to a maximum of eight days. In certain circumstances such orders may be made without notice. In addition, s. 45(9) provides that there may be no appeal against the making of such an order or any direction contained in it for a period of up to 72 hours. An emergency protection order confers parental responsibility on the applicant, although it should only 'take such action in meeting its parental responsibility as is reasonably required to safeguard or promote the welfare of the child (having particular regard to the duration of the order)' (s. 44(5)). Accordingly, a parent may not be able to be present at some of these hearings and so be unable to call witnesses or challenge the evidence put forward by the local authority. However, even if such an application does involve a determination of civil rights and obligations (which may be doubted, as the actual removal does not constitute a determination of rights as such), it may be argued that Article 6 is not breached, as the ability of the parents to present their case in accordance with the standards required by Article 6 is only delayed for a relatively short period and not precluded. Under Article 8, such measures will nevertheless require close justification (see 10.2.4)

Support for this proposition may be derived from observations of the House of Lords in *R* v *DPP, ex parte Kebilene* [1999] 3 WLR 972, which makes clear that English courts retain an 'area of discretion' in deciding how precisely Convention rights, which are to be applied as a set of principles, should apply to local conditions (see, in particular, the speech of Lord Hope). This 'discretionary area of judgment' exists in relation to both qualified and unqualified rights such as Article 6.

It is important to note that the question of whether civil rights and obligations are being determined is not necessarily simply a question of whether or not the decision in question is, formally speaking, legally revocable. Where the actions of a local authority are such that if incapable of challenge they would lead to a *de facto* determination of a person's rights then Article 6 is likely to apply.

However, local authority decisions in relation to children, although of considerable importance to the persons concerned by them, will frequently not be determinative of rights for the purposes of Article 6. Day-to-day decisions by a local authority as to where a child will live under a care order are not determinations of the civil rights and obligations of either parents or child according to the House of Lords in *Re S and others*, at para. 78. In the case of a parent, the right to take such decisions was determined not by the local authority but by the court which made the care order conferring parental responsibility and control over such matters on the local authority. In the case of a child, such decisions are normally and inevitably determined by those with parental responsibility for the child. Where Article 6 requires judicial control of such decisions this will, in the absence of any other legal remedy, be satisfied by judicial review.

More important decisions about the level of contact between a child and its parents will involve determinations of civil rights and obligations and the Children Act 1989 makes provision for judicial determination of such disputes. But there are other important decisions for which the Children Act makes no provision for court intervention. Lord Nicholls in *Re S* gave as an example a decision by a local authority under s. 33(3)(b) of the Children Act 1989 that a parent shall not meet certain of his parental responsibilities for a child (at para. 79). He also referred to the fundamental questions as to a child's future that may remain to be decided following the making of a care order, such as whether rehabilitation remains a possibility. Where such a situation arose he doubted that judicial review would provide a sufficient remedy for the purposes Article 6, even applying the heightened level of scrutiny that is required in cases involving fundamental rights as discussed in *R* v *Secretary of State for the Home Department, ex parte Daly* [2001] 2 WLR 1622.

Thus where the challenge turns on disputed questions of fact then it may be necessary to commence proceedings under s. 7 of the HRA 1998 to establish that a local authority's conduct is unlawful in terms of s. 6 of the HRA 1998. This power was exercised in *Re M* (unreported) 29 June 2001. In that case a local authority reviewed its care plan and ruled out any further prospect of the child returning to live with either of its parents. The decision was set aside in proceedings brought under ss. 7 and 8 of the HRA 1998 on the basis that the process in reaching that decision was unfair and had not involved the parents to a sufficient degree to protect their rights under Article 8. The House of Lords approved this approach in *Re S*, at para. 46.

A difficulty remains in respect of children who do not have a person able to question a local authority's care decision on their behalf. Such children may have no practical way of bringing the situation that affects their civil rights before the court. Where this is the case this may give rise to a breach of Article 6 in the shape of the child's lack of access, in any practical sense, to the courts (*Re S*, at para. 82). However, the absence of provisions in the Children Act dealing with such a situation may mean that, while the United Kingdom is in breach of its international obligations under the ECHR, there is nevertheless no specific provision of the Children Act that can be said to infringe or be incompatible with the ECHR under the HRA 1989 (see *Re S*, at paras 85 and 86). Interestingly, in *R* v *Enfield Borough Council, ex parte J* [2002] 2 FLR 1, Elias J suggested, without having to decide the matter that in a similar 'lacuna' case he would be inclined simply to make a declaration of incompatibility to the effect that a 'gap' in the legislation existed leaving it to the executive to decide how to fill it (at para. 69).

10.2.2.2 *A fair hearing and 'equality of arms'*

The European Court of Human Rights has held that the right to a fair hearing includes the concept of 'equality of arms' (see *Neumeister* v *Austria* (1968) 1 EHRR 91). The concept has been summarized by the European Court as follows:

> . . . equality of arms implies that each party must be afforded a reasonable opportunity to present his case — including his evidence — under conditions that do not place him at a substantial disadvantage *vis-à-vis* his opponent'. (*Dombo Beheer BV* v *Netherlands* (1993) 18 EHRR 213, at para. 33)

This principle has implications for the ability of parties to call evidence of their choosing. The rule in family proceedings is that all expert evidence should be disclosed to the other parties. This duty applies whether or not the evidence is favourable to the party seeking it. This is at variance with the rule in ordinary civil litigation in common law systems, namely, that legal privilege applies to protect reports prepared in connection with litigation from disclosure (see *Re L (A Minor) (Police Investigation: Privilege)* [1996] 2 FCR 145, HL). Litigation privilege was recognized by the European Court in *Niemietz* v *Germany* (1992) 16 EHRR 97, in the context of non-family proceedings. However the Court has declared L's complaint on this ground inadmissible. It stated that since L had been able to obtain further evidence on this point and attack the credibility or weight to be attached to that adverse evidence, it had not been demonstrated that she had been deprived of an adequate or proper opportunity to present her case. The European Court also referred to the fact that these conditions applied to all the parties to the proceedings, and L was therefore not placed in any worse position than that of the other parties (*L* v *UK* [2000] 2 FCR 145). The principle in *Re L* — that litigation privilege is essentially a creature of adversarial proceedings and cannot exist in the context of non-adversarial proceedings — has been reaffirmed more recently by the Court of Appeal in *Three Rivers District Council* v *Bank of England* [2003] QB 1556.

The principle of 'equality of arms' also has potential implications for rules or practices which restrict the ability of parties to be able to call and cross-examine witnesses. Courts should, in the light of this principle, be extremely slow to exercise their discretion to decide cases summarily, as set out in *Re B (Minors)* [1994] 2 FLR 1, CA ('Applications for . . . committal to the care of the local authority . . . are likely to be decided on full oral evidence, but not invariably.'). To allow the court under domestic law such a discretion does not itself infringe Article 6 (see *H* v *France* (1989) 12 EHRR 74, at paras 60 and 61; *Eriksson* v *Sweden* (1989) 12 EHRR 183, at paras 74 and 75). Whether the discretion is as limited under the ECHR as was suggested (but rejected) by the domestic courts in *W* v *Ealing London Borough Council* [1993] 1 FLR 463, remains to be seen (it was argued that only if the relevant test for striking out a claim in civil proceedings was met should a party to care proceedings be deprived of a full trial). The Court of Appeal has confirmed the breadth of the spectrum of permissible procedures and the generous extent of judges' discretion in deciding how to proceed in individual cases in Children Act proceedings (*Re Y and K (Children)* [2003] 2 FLR 273).

Failure to disclose documents to the parents in a care case, even if the substance of those documents is made known to them, may in appropriate circumstances amount to an infringement of Articles 6 and 8 (see *McMichael* v *UK* (1995) 20 EHRR 205, at para. 80 — the documents in question were confidential medical and social services records). Where advice for the protection of children by a local authority was not provided to the applicant but was provided to his lawyer, and the European Court was satisfied that the contents of that advice were well known to the applicant, there was held to be no breach of his Article 6 rights as the presentation of his case was not affected (see *Hendricks v Netherlands* (1983) 5 EHRR 223, at para. 144).

Where a jointly instructed or other sole expert's report, though not binding on the court is 'likely to have a preponderant influence on the facts by [the] court' there may be a breach of Article 6 if a litigant is denied the opportunity, before the expert produces his report:

(a) to examine and comment on the documents being considered by the expert; and

(b) to cross-examine witnesses interviewed by the expert and on whose evidence the report is based;

in short to participate effectively in the process by which the report is produced (see *Mantovanelli v France* (1997) 24 EHRR 370). Whether or not the opportunity to comment on the report to the trial court is sufficient to ensure the fairness of the proceedings will depend on the particular facts of the case. In *Mantovanelli* and in *Buchberger v Austria* [2001] ECHR (App. No. 328/99) the opportunity was insufficient, in *Sahin and others v Germany* [2002] 1 FLR 119 it was sufficient. In *Re C* it was pointed out that Mantovanelli's case concerned private law proceedings and that those principles applied *a fortiori* to public law child care proceedings.

Public interest immunity applications may also have an effect on a party's ability to present his or her case. The entitlement to relevant evidence has been held not to be an absolute right in the context of criminal proceedings (see *Jasper v UK* (App. No. 27052/95). However, if such evidence does exist and is not to be disclosed then it must be strongly arguable in criminal proceedings that it would be unfair to allow a prosecution to continue. In care proceedings, it may be difficult to argue that it would be appropriate to withdraw such proceedings if it was the local authority's case, based on other cogent evidence, that the child had suffered or was likely to suffer significant harm and that a care order was necessary.

The 'adversarial' nature of a fair trial is taken to mean that under the Convention, 'all evidence must be produced in the presence of the party with a view to adversarial argument'. Not only does this have implications for the conduct of a hearing, but it also indicates that it should be conducted in the party's presence (see *Barbera, Messegue and Jabardo v Spain* (1988) 11 EHRR 360, at para. 78). This contrasts with the position under domestic law which holds care proceedings to be essentially non-adversarial (see *Re L (A Minor) (Police Investigation: Privilege)* [1996] 2 FCR 145, HL). This has not so far led to any finding that the position in domestic law on litigation privilege infringes the ECHR.

Article 6(1) may also assist litigants who were made the subject of adverse findings in other proceedings which are sought to be relied upon in subsequent proceedings. For example, that they abused a child, where they may not have had an opportunity properly to contest those allegations (see *Re B (Children Act Proceedings) (Issue Estoppel)* [1997] 1 FLR 285, Hale J). Merely inviting a person who is not a party to the proceedings to intervene just for the purposes of those aspects of the case which might lead to adverse findings against him or her, may not be enough to ensure that person has had a fair trial (see *Re S (Child Case: Intervener)* [1997] 2 FCR 272 (step-father alleged to be an abuser but not a party to the proceedings); *sub nom Re S (Care: Residence: Intervener)* [1997] 1 FLR 497, CA).

A 'McKenzie friend' describes a person who may be allowed to assist a person in presenting their case in court proceedings although they do not do so in a representative capacity as would be the case when a lawyer is formally instructed. As far as 'McKenzie' friends are concerned, in family proceedings the common law has been held not to infringe Article 6(1) (see *R v Bow County Court, ex parte Pelling* [1999] 2 FLR 149 (the Convention argument was referred to only at first instance); [1999] 2 FLR 1126, CA). There is no right to a McKenzie friend, and accordingly there is no right in the McKenzie friend to act once he or she is appointed by a litigant in person; the court in deciding such an issue is solely concerned with the position of the litigant in person and the issues of fairness and justice. The complexity of the proceedings is a relevant consideration. However, a McKenzie friend should generally be allowed to act in proceedings held in public unless fairness and the interests of justice dictate otherwise. In proceedings in private, the reasons for holding the proceedings in private may make it undesirable in the interests of justice for a McKenzie friend to assist. The question of whether family proceedings should be held in private is discussed at 10.2.2.3. In the future the judge's discretion falls to be exercised in accordance with Article 6 ECHR.

'Equality of arms' may also raise issues of legal funding, although there is here again an overlap with effective access to a court (see 10.2.2.6).

10.2.2.3   A public hearing and public pronouncement of judgment

Rule 4.16(7) of the Family Proceedings Rules 1991 provides that: 'Unless the court otherwise directs, a hearing of, or directions appointment in, proceedings to which this Part applies shall be in chambers.' Rules 4.23 and 10.20(3) impose restrictions on the disclosure of documents filed in court in respect of family proceedings. In *Re PB (A Minor) (Hearing in Private)* [1996] 3 FCR 705, the Court of Appeal considered that the state of affairs produced by these rules was compatible with Article 6(1) ECHR on the basis that the Article itself refers to the interests of minors as a legitimate reason for holding a hearing in private, and also for excluding the press and public. Cases involving children are commonly held in private in other European jurisdictions, but this is not universally the case. In Scotland the presumption is that proceedings will be held in public.

The European Court of Human Rights held admissible a complaint from PB's father against the United Kingdom on the basis of the Court of Appeal's judgment in the case (see *B* v *UK* [2000] 2 FCR 97). The Court also held admissible a complaint that s. 12(1) of the Administration of Justice Act 1960 (which makes the publication of any information in relation to child proceedings automatically a contempt of court) infringes Article 10 ECHR (right to freedom of expression). Also in issue in *Re PB* was the domestic practice of pronouncing judgment in open court, subject to questions of identification, only when there is some point of public interest contained in the decision.

The complaints raised in *Re PB* have now been dismissed by the full European Court in *B and P* v *UK* (App. Nos 00036337/97, 00035974/97). In both cases the relevant county court judges had exercised their discretion to refuse to hold the proceedings in public in the interests of the children concerned. Although the general rule expressed in Article 6(1) ECHR was that proceedings should be held in public, it was not inconsistent with this provision for a state to designate an entire class of cases as an exception to the general rule where considered necessary in the interests of juveniles or for the protection of the private life of the parties and the interests of justice, provided the need for such a measure was subject to the control of a court which could consider whether to exercise its discretion in particular cases where such a request was made. This legitimate protection afforded to children by Article 6(1) could not be undermined by the public pronouncement of judgment, even though Article 6(1) narrowly construed appeared to be absolute in its terms. Those with a relevant interest, e.g. the press, would not be precluded from applying for permission to obtain access to any judgment, and the judgments on points of public interest of first instance courts and the Court of Appeal were routinely published. As the limitations in these particular cases were justifiable in the interest of juveniles, the private life of the parties and the interests of justice, it was not necessary to consider Article 10.

The ECHR has increased the prominence of children's views in proceedings which concern them, by highlighting the desirable role of a guardian to represent children in private law proceedings where there exists a significant conflict of interest between them and their parents (see *In Re A (A Child) (Contact: Separate Representation)* [2001] 1 FLR 715. A guardian is routinely appointed to represent the views of the child in public law proceedings. However, these developments implicitly raise the issue of whether this aspect of Article 6 ECHR will lead to an increase in the number of occasions when children may insist on being present during care proceedings and giving evidence to the court. This currently happens very rarely.

10.2.2.4 A hearing within a reasonable time

Raising delay as a complaint under the ECHR is particularly dependent on the circumstances of the case. Time does not necessarily start to run from the point at which proceedings are issued, but may start from when the decision to initiate care proceedings was taken (see *H* v *UK* (1987) 10 EHRR 95).

A number of complaints have been made to the European Court of Human Rights in the context of family proceedings on this ground. Proceedings lasting one year, nine months were not a violation of Article 6(1) ECHR regard to the complexity of the proceedings in *Johansen* v *Norway* (1996) 23 EHRR 33. In *H* v *UK*, however, where proceedings lasted two years, seven months, there was held to have been a breach of Article 6 on this ground. Five months' delay was the direct responsibility of the local authority and this had prejudiced the applicant's application. In *Paulsen-Medalen and Svenson* v *Sweden* (1998) 26 EHRR 260, proceedings which lasted three years, three months were in breach of Article 6(1). The assessment of the reasonableness of the length of the proceedings must have regard to the complexity of the proceedings and the conduct of the applicant and the local authority. *Dicta* in *H* v *UK* were repeated, to the effect that authorities are required to act with exceptional diligence in ensuring the progress of proceedings involving children because of the danger that procedural delay will result in the *de facto* determination of the issue.

Care proceedings in English courts take between 22 and 112 weeks to complete. The average length of proceedings in 2000 was 45.7 weeks and is a matter of continuing concern (see [2000] Fam Law 230).

10.2.2.5 Impartiality and independence

The overlapping concepts of impartiality and independence have particular importance in the context of administrative decision-making. When a person's civil rights are determined then such a determination must be by an independent and impartial tribunal such as a court. In those cases when an administrative body, such as a social services department, actually determines a person's civil rights itself, then there must be recourse to an independent and impartial tribunal of full jurisdiction within the meaning of Article 6 ECHR. Thus where a social services decision determines a persons' civil rights and obligations, e.g. whether to approve foster parents or prospective adopters, then there must be access to a court or tribunal of 'full' jurisdiction. In most cases judicial review or, where provided for, proceedings under the Children Act, will provide an independent and impartial tribunal with a sufficiently full jurisdiction to ensure compliance with Article 6 (see *R* v *Secretary of State for the Environment, Transport and the Regions, ex parte Alconbury Developments Ltd* [2001] 2 WLR 1389). It was previously thought that judicial review might not be sufficient where the determination of the issue involved disputed issues of fact and there were insufficient procedural safeguards before the primary decision-maker, including possibly an oral hearing. The scope for such an argument has, however, been considerably reduced by the decision of the House of Lords in *Runa Begum* v *Tower Hamlets London Borough Council* [2003] 2 WLR 388. It would appear that the main issue is no longer whether there are disputed issues of primary fact but simply whether the decision is or is not one that involves 'the classic exercise of an administrative discretion'. This seems to turn primarily on whether it has traditionally been seen as such and the court will pay a generous discretion to Parliament in deciding whether this is necessary. It is therefore unlikely that an oral hearing will be required in circumstances where an oral hearing was not previously thought necessary under domestic law but the court must nevertheless consider whether, in all the circumstances, the decision is one that can be 'entrusted to administrators'.

10.2.2.6   Access to justice: effective access to a court

As far as the provision of legal aid is necessary to ensure effective access to a court much depends, unsurprisingly, on the particular circumstances of the case. In *Airey* v *Ireland* (1979) 2 EHRR 305, the applicant was seeking a decree of judicial separation. The absence of legal aid was not automatically a breach of Article 6 ECHR, but here absence of legal aid removed right of effective access. Article 8 ECHR was also held to have been violated. The European Court of Human Rights stated (at para. 24):

> The Convention is intended to guarantee not rights that are theoretical or illusory but rights that are practical and effective. This is particularly so of the right of access to the courts in view of the prominent place held in a democratic society by the right to a fair trial. It must therefore be ascertained whether the applicant's appearance before the High Court without the assistance of a lawyer would be effective, in the sense of whether she would be able to present her case properly and satisfactorily.

In *Winer* v *UK* (1987) 52 DR 158, the Commission noted that, 'unlike Article 6(3)(c) which expressly provides for legal aid in criminal cases where necessary, the Convention does not guarantee such a right of assistance in civil cases' (at 171). *Munro* v *UK* (1987) 52 DR 158, concerned the unavailability of legal aid in defamation proceedings. The Commission distinguished *Airey* and *Winer*. In doing so it contrasted the 'general nature' of defamation proceedings with the intimate nature of judicial separation proceedings, which regulate the legal relationship between two people and 'may have serious consequences for children of the family'. This may assist those who do not qualify for automatic legal aid in respect of care proceedings. If a case is straightforward and uncomplicated then this has an important bearing on the question of the need for legal funding to ensure effective access to a court. The case of *Webb* v *UK* (1984) 6 EHRR 120 involved affiliation proceedings. Given the nature of the case there was held to be no violation even though there was no legal aid. In the case of *P, C and S* v *UK*, the discharge of the mother's legal aid certificate in care and adoption proceedings was held to involve a breach of Article 6.

In considering questions of effective access to a court, it important to remember that Article 6 is primarily only concerned with procedural rights. The substantive rights to which the procedural guarantees attach are principally a matter for domestic law or consideration under one of the substantive ECHR rights such as Article 8. Accordingly the content of national rules will not infringe Article 6 unless they are such as to reduce the individual's access to a court in such a way as to impair the very essence of the right (*Ashingdane* v *UK* (1985) 7 EHRR 528).

Thus in *Stubbings* v *UK* (1996) 23 EHRR 213, it was held by the European Court that by imposing a limitation period in respect of civil damages claims, the state did not automatically impair the substance of the right claimed by the adult claimants who had suffered sexual abuse in their childhood.

A direct way in which a litigant may be denied access to a court is by an order preventing any further applications with respect to a child under s. 91(14) of the Children Act 1989. The Court of Appeal currently takes the view that there is generally no infringement of Article 6(1) in such cases, because there is no real denial of access to a court but only a restriction on obtaining an immediate or notice hearing (see *Re P (Section 91(14) Guidelines) (Residence and Religious Heritage)* [1999] 2 FLR 573, CA). However, the procedure for the hearing of such an application for an on notice hearing should be informed by the requirements of Article 6 as to the calling of evidence in the same way that the Article applies to situations in which a litigant may need to obtain leave to bring proceedings under s. 10 of the Children Act 1989.

The principle that Article 6 does not itself guarantee any particular content of civil rights and obligations has arisen in the context of actions against local authorities for negligence in failing to protect children within their area of responsibility against abuse. In this regard the European Court has held that the mere non-existence of a cause of action in tort does not amount to an exclusionary rule or immunity depriving a person of effective access to a court (see *Z* v *UK* [2001] 2 FLR 612, (2002) 34 EHRR 97; *DP and JC* v *UK* [2003] 1 FLR 50, (2003) 36 EHRR 14). However, as was held in *DP and JC* this state of affairs may violate other substantive rights under the ECHR such as Article 13 (right to an effective remedy) taken in conjunction with Article 8.

10.2.2.7 Presumption of innocence and freedom from self-incrimination
Freedom from self-incrimination is recognized by the European Court of Human Rights as an important component of Article 6 ECHR even though not specifically mentioned in the text of the Convention (*Funke* v *France* (1993) 16 EHRR 297; *Saunders* v *UK* (1996) 23 EHRR 313; *IJL, GMR and AKP* v *UK* (2000) *The*

Times, 13 October). This freedom under English law is not expressed as a right but as the 'privilege' against self-incrimination.

Under s. 98(1) of the Children Act 1989, a witness shall not be excused from answering any question in the course of his or her evidence on the basis that to do so would incriminate him or her or his or her spouse, of an offence. However, the rigours of this provision are mitigated to the extent that s. 98(2) prevents such evidence from being admissible in criminal proceedings.

It should also be noted that applications are also regularly made by the police for disclosure of medical evidence filed in care proceedings to assist them with any criminal investigation that may be ongoing. The House of Lords has concluded that where a party has voluntarily initiated a process that led to the preparation and filing of an expert report, he or she may be said to have waived privilege against self-incrimination and the report may properly be disclosed to the police (*Re L (Police Investigation: Privilege)* [1996] 1 FLR 731, HL). (A further complaint by L to the European Court was rejected in *L* v *UK* (see 10.2.2.2 above).)

The relevant factors for determining such applications are set out in *Re EC (Disclosure of Material)* [1996] 2 FLR 725, CA:

(a) the welfare and interest of the child concerned and of other children generally;
(b) the interest in the public administration of justice and the prosecution of serious crime;
(c) the seriousness of the offence(s) alleged and the probative value of the evidence concerned;
(d) the importance of encouraging frankness in cases involving children and the relevance of confidentiality in achieving that end;
(e) the importance of encouraging inter-agency co-operation;
(f) 'fairness' to the person incriminated by the material and/or others who would be affected by disclosure of it;
(g) previous disclosure in the same case.

The view has been expressed that the current interpretation of the protection offered by s. 98(2) of the Children Act 1989 may infringe a party's right to a fair trial on the basis that giving evidence in the care proceedings may prejudice him or her in any later criminal proceedings (see *Re L (Care: Confidentiality)* [1999] 1 FLR 165) (local authority pressing ahead to seek findings in civil proceedings may infringe parents' right to a fair trial contrary to Article 6 on the basis that it may incriminate them in criminal proceedings on the present interpretation of s. 98(2), *per* Johnson J). However, it may be considered that such an argument is premature at that stage and that the correct time for it is in front of the judge in the criminal proceedings, provided that he has the power to rule such evidence inadmissible if to admit would infringe a defendant's rights under Article 6.

As far as the position in relation to expert evidence is concerned, there appears to be no argument based on legal privilege and/or privilege against self-incrimination which will successfully prevent disclosure to the police. It will merely be a balancing exercise by the court of the factors set out in *Re EC* (above). This position is supported under the ECHR as a result of *L v UK* (above), which confirms that, in relation to expert evidence, there is no objection to disclosure of an expert report on the grounds of the risk of self-incrimination in possible criminal proceedings. However, on the facts of *L*, the expert in question had not interviewed the mother and had not passed on any of her confidences. The report was the result of conclusions which were not dependent on the mother's admissions but on a medical analysis of hospital notes about her use of methadone. The argument that transcripts of such evidence ought not to be disclosed to the police where a report did contain an admission was rejected in *Re AB (Care proceedings: disclosure of medical evidence to the police)* [2003] 1 FLR 579.

However, the question arises at what point an infringement of the Convention is in issue. It is arguable that to disclose this evidence would not infringe a person's right not to incriminate himself or herself until it was actually used as evidence in any criminal trial. This casts the duty to protect the relevant party's right on the criminal trial judge, by ensuring that s. 78 of the Police and Criminal Evidence Act 1984 is interpreted in such a way as to produce a result compatible with Article 6. A case raising similar issues (and a similar result) in the environmental context was *R v Hertfordshire County Council, ex parte Green Environmental Industries Ltd* [2000] 2 WLR 373, HL (in which *Saunders* (above) was considered), where Lord Hoffman undertook a survey of the Convention jurisprudence in this area.

What is less clear is the extent to which a prosecuting authority may use admissions made under compulsion in order to investigate and gather its own 'independent' but (as it is sometimes called) derivative evidence concerning the allegations. This point was not decided by the House of Lords in *Ex parte Green Environmental Industries*. The Privy Council has held, in *Stott (Procurator Fiscal, Dunfermline) and another v Brown* (2000) *The Times*, 6 December, that where the criminal law compels an admission from a suspect, the question to be asked is whether the legislative scheme in question represents a disproportionate legislative response to the problem, and whether the balance between the interests of the community at large and the interests of the individual are struck in a manner unduly prejudicial to the individual. Such a balancing exercise in the context of child care law is likely to be considerably more complicated than in relation to maintaining road safety. Other jurisdictions appear to take a strict approach to the admission of so-called 'derivative' evidence (see, e.g., *British Columbia Securities Commission v Branch et al.* (1995) 123 DLR (4th) 462, Sup Ct Can).

There may be separate arguments against disclosure under Article 8 ECHR, including ones on behalf of the relevant child.

10.2.3 Article 8

Article 8(1) ECHR provides: 'Everyone has the right to respect for his private and family life, his home and his correspondence.'

There is a vast jurisprudence on Article 8 ECHR, covering as it does an enormous range of human activity which includes, but is by no means restricted to, an individual's family life. Some of this jurisprudence will be relevant to issues arising in cases involving local authorities. In the paragraphs which follow, a general outline of the interests covered by Article 8 most relevant to child care is followed by consideration in greater detail of the crucial question of justifying interferences with the right to respect for family life (see 10.2.4 below).

10.2.3.1 Positive or negative right?

> [Article 8] does not merely compel the State to abstain from . . . interference; in add-
> ition to this primarily negative undertaking, there may be positive obligations inherent
> in an effective respect for private and family life . . . These obligations may involve the
> adoption of measures designed to secure respect for private life even in the sphere of the
> relations of individuals between themselves.

(*X and Y* v *Netherlands* (1985) 8 EHRR 235, at para. 23; see also *Marckx* v *Belgium* (1979) 2 EHRR 330, at para. 31.)

This positive obligation includes the provision of a regulatory framework of adjudicatory and enforcement machinery protecting individuals' rights, and the implementation, where appropriate, of specific steps (see the European Court cases *G* v *UK (Minors: Right of Contact)* (2000) *The Times*, 1 November, and *Nuutinen* v *Finland*, 27 June 2000).

However, as the European Court of Human Rights itself has held, the boundaries between a state's negative and positive obligations under Article 8 do not lend themselves to 'precise definition' (see *Stjerna* v *Finland* (1994) 24 EHRR 194). Thus one may conclude that while the state is under some positive duty to foster private and family relationships, there is some uncertainty as to the extent to which this is required under the Convention. In relation to the enforcement of a contact order, for example, the establishment of contact might not be able to take place immediately and might require preparatory or phased measures. The co-operation and understanding of all concerned is an important ingredient. While national authorities must do their utmost to facilitate such co-operation, any obligation to apply coercion is limited as the interests of the child and his or her rights under Article 8 (see *G* v *UK* (above)). In *G* v *UK* the European Court recalled that the principal obstacle to the applicant's contact with his children was the opposition of the mother, and that this factor had to be balanced against the danger of harming the children through the use of coercive orders.

In *Re W and B and W (Children) (Care Plan)* [2001] 2 FLR 582, Hale LJ explained (at paras 55 and 59) that the positive obligation imposed by Article 8 meant that it could be 'readily inferred' that local authorities would be in breach of this duty by failing to take adequate steps to secure for a child who has been deprived of a life with his family of birth, a life with a new family who can become his new 'family life'.

The extent of the state's positive obligation is particularly unclear when the right in issue would involve significant questions regarding the expenditure and distribution of resources by the state. For example, to what extent might Article 8 support an argument in favour of a court directing a local authority to expend resources on particular work with a family? What if, following *W and B and W*, a care plan breaks down because a local authority does not provide the resources that it said it would — can a local authority plead poverty to escape its obligations; and what of the legitimate expectations of the parents or child? (See generally 10.3.2.4 on the application of Convention rights to questions of resources.)

More promising areas involve the notion of fair procedure in the process of taking children into care, with sufficient involvement of parents in decision-making during care proceedings. There is an overlap here with Article 6 ECHR, which is more specifically concerned with procedure, but in such cases there has also been held to be an infringement of Article 8 (see 10.2).

10.2.3.2   Private life
This aspect of Article 8 ECHR includes the right to develop one's own personality, but also to develop relationships with other human beings. Such relationships which are not protected as a matter of 'family life' may nevertheless be covered by Article 8 as a matter of 'private life'.

10.2.3.3   Family life
The existence of family life is a question of fact (see *K* v *UK* (1986) 50 DR 199). In *X, Y and Z* v *UK* [1997] 2 FLR 892, at 900, potentially relevant factors were listed as including whether the couple live together, the length of the relationship, and whether they have demonstrated commitment to each other by having children together or by any other means. In *Keegan* v *Ireland* (1994) 18 EHRR 342, at para. 44, the European Court of Human Rights held that:

> . . . the notion of 'the family' . . . is not confined solely to marriage-based relationships and may encompass other *de facto* 'family' where the parties are living together outside of marriage. A child born out of such a relationship is *ipso iure* part of that 'family' unit from the moment of his birth and by the very fact of it. There thus exists between the child and his parents a bond amounting to family life even if at the time of his or her birth the parents are no longer cohabiting or if their relationship has then ended.

Once the family relationship is established, it is the state's duty to respect that relationship in the particular form it takes.

Illegitimacy should have no bearing on the existence or otherwise of a family relationship. However, the fact of a blood or genetic link by itself may not be enough to establish a right to family life, e.g. in the case of a sperm donor. The European Court has held that biological and sociological reality should prevail over legal presumptions (*Kroon* v *Netherlands* (1994) 19 EHRR 263 — is the relationship of 'sufficient constancy'). *Keegan* and *Kroon* were considered in *Re H* and *Re G (A Child) (Adoption: Disclosure)* (2001) *The Times*, 5 January. Butler-Sloss LJ held that whether Article 8 ECHR was engaged, depended on the facts and upon the real existence in practice of close family ties. Thus it was not necessarily an interference with the right to family life not to consult a birth father over the adoption or freeing of his child under ss. 16 and 18 of the Adoption Act 1976. The father in G's case should be notified, and if he wished to take part in the proceedings he should be joined. In H's case, the basis for refusing to notify the father was that the relationship lacked sufficient constancy to put family life in issue, even though it appears that the child's existence was concealed from the father. It is clear that the Court was influenced by the fact that it considered that at the most the father could only make a Children Act application, and that even this was improbable given his circumstances. Her Ladyship noted that where in a case it was subsequently found that an unmarried father without parental responsibility did enjoy a right to family life with a child then Article 6 might also apply, raising the difficult question of the impact of the rights of other parties under Article 8 and the welfare principle on the right to a fair trial. The court expressed its concern about the acceptance of the mother's refusal to disclose the identity of the father. Issues such as notification should be dealt with at an early stage in the proceedings to avoid the difficulties noted by Butler-Sloss LJ.

The promotion of family life has led the Commission to reject a complaint by a natural father who sought to establish his paternity of a child by blood testing, on the basis that the family in which the child was settled would be disrupted (*MB* v *UK* (App. No. 22920/93)). It has been doubted that the ability of a person with 'care and control' of a child to refuse consent for paternity testing to take place, under Part III of the Family Law Reform Act 1969, is compliant with the ECHR (*Re O; Re J (Blood Tests: Constraint)* [2000] 2 All ER 29, Wall J). But this may not be a breach in every case having regard to *Re H* and *Re G (A Child) (Adoption: Disclosure)* (above).

The parent-child relationship remains the central and 'fundamental' element of family life. Interference with it by the state will amount to an automatic interference with family life: see *B* v *UK* (1988) 10 EHRR 87. However, the less favourable treatment of unmarried fathers under English law, in that they do not acquire parental responsibility automatically, does not infringe Article 8 ECHR (*McMichael* v *UK* (1995) 20 EHRR 205 (position in Scotland); and *Re W; Re B (Child Abduction: Unmarried Fathers)* [1998] 2 FLR 146, Hale J). Other problems faced by an unmarried father are that he will have no rights to refuse consent to the removal of the child from the jurisdiction without applying to a court, or to be notified of or joined to adoption or freeing proceedings (see *Re H and Re G*).

'Family life' has also been held to include the ties between grandparents and grandchildren as these relationships may play a considerable part in family life. Respect in this context implies an obligation for the state to act in a manner calculated to allow these ties to develop 'normally' (see *Marckx* v *Belgium* (1979) 2 EHRR 330; see also *Hokkanen* v *Finland* (1994) 19 EHRR 139, at paras 63 and 64). The status of grandparent does not automatically lead to a conclusion that family life exists, and each case has been scrutinized by the Commission to establish that such a relationship exists in fact. Unlike the case of the parental relationship, intervention by the state amounts to an interference requiring justification under Article 8(2) only where it actually interferes with the relationship in such a way as to affect a normal grandparent-grandchild relationship.

The ECHR has also been held to protect the relationship between siblings (see *Moustaquim* v *Belgium* (1991) 13 EHRR 802, at para. 36); and that between an uncle and nephew (see *Boyle* v *UK* (1994) 19 EHRR 179, at paras 41–46).

Family life may cover the relationship between a foster parent and a foster child, although the European Court stated that this may depend on the nature of the fostering arrangements — see implicitly *Gaskin* v *UK* (1989) 12 EHRR 36, at para. 49, where the lack of consent from the applicant's foster parents for him to obtain access to social work records was insufficient to displace his right to receive this information about his family life. In *Rieme* v *Sweden* (1992) 16 EHRR 155, as in *Eriksson* v *Sweden* (1989) 12 EHRR 183, the views of the child and the foster parents were important in establishing the existence of 'family life'.

Transsexual and homosexual unions may be recognized as *de facto* family life, but it has been held that there is no obligation on the state to recognize the parental role of a transsexual father (see *S* v *UK* (1986) 47 DR 274; *X* v *UK* (1997) 24 EHRR 143). In *Fitzpatrick* v *Stirling Housing Association Ltd* [2001] 1 AC 27, it was held that a gay man could succeed to a protected tenancy under the Rent Act 1977 by virtue of being a member of the deceased's 'family'. In *Fretté* v *France* (App. No. 36515/97) the European Court noted that the right to respect for family life presupposed the existence of family life, accordingly the complainant, a homosexual man had no right to start a family through adoption. The European Court was divided over whether discrimination against homosexual adopters was sufficient to engage Article 8 itself, indicating a difference of view amongst contracting states and members of the Court.

10.2.3.4 Home

'Home' has been defined as a continuous residence with no intention to establish a home elsewhere (see *Buckley* v *UK* (1996) 23 EHRR 101). There is an overlap between the concepts of 'home' and 'family' and 'private life'. A domestic violence injunction could well involve an interference with all three of these rights, although it seems very likely that under Part IV of the Family Law Act 1996, the balancing exercise that ss. 33–40 require the court to carry out would be justified under Article 8(2). For local authorities, similar issues may arise in relation to the inclusion of 'exclusion' orders in interim care orders, especially where this may affect contact between a child and the excluded person.

In *McLeod* v *UK* [1998] 2 FLR 1048, it was held that although a wife was in contempt of court for failing to deliver up certain chattels to her husband, when the husband entered her house with police officers to collect the items, this was disproportionate to the legitimate aim of preventing a breach of the peace.

The concept of the 'home' is discussed in detail in Chapter Seven at 7.4.

10.2.3.5 Correspondence

The right to respect for one's correspondence is a right to uninterrupted and uncensored communication with others. Cases in this area have involved phone-tapping by the state and interference with prisoners' correspondence (see *Malone* v *UK* (1984) 7 EHRR 14; *Halford* v *UK* (1997) 24 EHRR 523 (both phone-tapping cases); *Golder* v *UK* (1975) 1 EHRR 524; *Silver* v *UK* (1983) 5 EHRR 347 (both prisoner cases).

There are public law cases in which it has been directed that indirect letter contact between a parent and a child in a foster placement should be censored by a local authority. Such action will have to be strictly justified as necessary under Article 8(2).

10.2.4   Justifiable interferences under Article 8(2)

Article 8(2) ECHR provides:

> There shall be no interference by a public authority with the exercise of this right except such as is in accordance with the law and is necessary in a democratic society in the interests of national security, public safety or the economic well-being of the country, for the prevention of disorder or crime, for the protection of health or morals, or for the protection of the rights and freedoms of others.

10.2.4.1   Care proceedings

Taking a child into care prima facie involves an interference with the right to family life in Article 8 ECHR. Children and adults both have a right to family life under the ECHR, and tensions between these rights will therefore arise. Under the Children Act 1989 and the Adoption Act 1976, the focus in cases involving Article 8 will generally be on whether or not the interference complained of is justified or proportionate in terms of Article 8(2).

In *Olsson* v *Sweden (No. 2)* (1992) 17 EHRR 134, it was said that 'the interests, as well as the rights and freedoms of all concerned, must be taken into account, notably the children's best interests and their rights under Article 8 of the Convention'. In *Johansen* v *Norway* (1996) 23 EHRR 33, the European Court said that 'particular weight should be attached to the best interests of the child'. In *Scott* v *UK* [2000] 1 FLR 958, the European Court stated: 'Undoubtedly, consideration of what is in the best interests of the child is always of crucial importance.' The view has been expressed in the House of Lords that there is nothing in the Convention which requires the courts to act otherwise than in accordance with the interests of the child (see *Dawson* v *Wearmouth* [1999] 1 FLR 1167, *per* Lord Hobhouse at 973H (change of child's surname; parental rights not in issue)).

As already mentioned, most interferences by the state in public law proceedings will amount to an interference with Article 8(1) and will require justification as being necessary under Article 8(2). Decisions of the European Court of Human Rights in cases involving the public care of children have emphasized the following general considerations in deciding whether state action which interferes with Article 8(1) may be justified under Article 8(2) (the principles in the Court's case law are conveniently recalled in the *Johansen* decision (above)):

(a) The taking of a child into care should normally be regarded as a temporary measure to be discontinued as soon as possible.

(b) The European Court recognizes that national authorities enjoy a wide margin of appreciation in assessing the necessity for taking a child into care.

(c) The aim of the care system is to reunite children and families, and interim measures (such as contact) should be designed to facilitate this end. This requires strict scrutiny of limitations such as restrictions placed by authorities on parental rights and access, or on the legal safeguards designed to secure that relationships between parents and a young child are not curtailed (*Johansen* v *Norway*, at paras 65–85; *Scott* v *UK*). However, where there is no question of rehabilitation and adoptive placements are urgently required, it is not contrary to Articles 6 or 8 ECHR to give leave to a local authority to terminate contact between parent and child under s. 34 of the Children Act 1989 (see *Re F (Minors) (Care proceedings: Contact)* (2000) *The Times*, 8 June, Wall J).

(d) In achieving this aim, a fair balance has to be struck between the interests of the child in remaining in public care and those of the parents in being reunited with the child.

(e) In carrying out this balancing exercise, the court must attach particular importance to the best interests of the child which, depending upon their seriousness and cogency, may override those of the parent. In particular, the parent cannot be entitled to have such measures taken as would harm the child's health and development (see *Johansen* v *Norway* (above)).

The wishes of the child may have a greater bearing on the ability to justify certain interferences with his or her Article 8 rights, e.g. as to the amount of contact between a parent and a child, or as regards medical treatment.

The duty to take the least interventionist approach in public law proceedings under the Children Act 1989 has been reinforced by Article 8. In *Re O (A Child) (Supervision Order)* (2001) *The Times*, 20 February, Hale LJ held that where a local authority sought a care order in respect of an infant child through fear of abuse or harm by its parents, it was appropriate to make a supervision order instead of a care order to give effect to jurisprudence under the HRA 1998. Cases decided before the 1998 Act might not be appropriate to post-1998 Act care order applications.

In relation to emergency procedures taken in the context of care proceedings, while it may be that no determination has taken place in order to engage Article 6 ECHR (see 10.2.2.1) close justification will be required under Article 8(2) ECHR of such measures which clearly amount to an interference with family life. That said, the question of justification must be considered in the light of the particular circumstances in which such powers are normally exercised. 'Questions of emergency care measures are, by their nature, decided on a highly provisional basis and on an assessment of risk to the child reached on the basis of the information, inevitably incomplete, available at the time' (see *P, C and S v UK*, 16 July 2002 (App No. 56547/00), at para. 128). This has led the European Court to conclude in one case that even where a removal had been based on a factual error there was no violation of Article 8 (see *TP and KM v UK*). However, despite making due allowance for the circumstances in which such legitimate powers may be exercised, the European Court has held that it is for the respondent state to establish that a careful assessment of the impact of the proposed care measure on the parents and the child, as well as the possible alternatives to taking the child into public care, have been considered prior to the implementation of the measure (see *K and T v Finland* (App. No. 25702/94), at para. 166; *P, C and S v UK*, above). In both *K and T* and *P, C and S* the European Court found violations by the respondent states, as those cases involved the removal of babies from their mothers at birth, a step which requires 'exceptional justification'. In those cases relevant and sufficient reasons to justify such an interference with Article 8(1) rights were lacking.

Of particular importance in justifying steps taken by social services in the lives of children and families will be whether or not those concerned have been sufficiently involved in the local authority's planning and decision-making.

Although rejecting the argument on the facts, in *Johansen v Sweden*, the European Court referred to the complainant's argument, without critical comment, that Article 8 rights were capable of being violated by the failure to involve her to a sufficient degree to provide her with the requisite protection of her interests. In *Scott v UK* [2000] FLR 958, the European Court rejected an argument on the facts that the local authority had failed, in breach of the applicant's Article 8 rights, to involve her sufficiently in non-judicial decisions which had made the making of an adoption order inevitable. The European Court noted that the decision to abandon rehabilitation with the mother was not 'legally irrevocable' and that she had had ample opportunity to attempt to change the course of events by making appropriate representations to the local authority and/or by resort to the domestic court seised of the matter.

While the European Court relied on the fact that the procedure followed by the local authority was not 'legally irrevocable' as a reason for rejecting the complaint in *Scott*, it has in other instances warned of the particular dangers in child care proceedings of a *de facto* resolution of cases. This concern has arisen principally in relation to delay. However, there are other ways in which the outcome of child care proceedings may be determined, sometimes decisively, by the decisions taken by local authorities which are extremely difficult in practice for parents to challenge at a later stage, whether before or, in some cases, after a final order is made.

These issues are potentially raised by the way in which responsibility for children is divided under the Children Act 1989 between the courts and local authorities (*Manchester City Council v F* [1993] 1 FLR 419; *Re T (A Minor) (Care Order: Conditions)* [1994] 2 FLR 423; *Re J (Minors) (Care Plan)* [1994] 1 FLR 253; *Re L (Sexual Abuse: Standard of Proof)* [1996] 1 FLR 116). The notable feature of that division of functions is that once a care order is made the court's supervision of the way in which that care plan is carried out by the local authority is very limited.

The House of Lords considered this issue in *Re S* (considered at 10.2.2.1 in the context of Article 6). In that case the Court of Appeal (at paras 79–80) decided that, in order to ensure the Article 8 rights of children in respect of whom care orders had been made, it was necessary to introduce a 'starring' system in respect of fundamental elements of the care plan which if not fulfilled would result in a real risk of a breach of ECHR rights. Where there was a real reason to fear that such starred elements might not be fulfilled then it was justifiable, using s. 3 of the HRA 1998, to read into the Children Act a power in the court to require a report on progress either to itself or to the Children and Family Court Advisory and Support Service (CAFCASS) which could then decide whether it was appropriate to return the matter to court.

The House of Lords rejected this innovation by the Court of Appeal as impermissible judicial legislation beyond the powers of interpretation conferred by s. 3 of the HRA 1998. The starring system devised by the Court of Appeal was inconsistent with the scheme of the Children Act in its allocation of responsibilities between the courts and local authorities. It raised a number of issues that could only be properly and legitimately dealt with by legislation (*per* Lord Nicholls at para. 43) (although the House of Lords expressed the hope that consideration of these matters would be undertaken by Parliament). Nor did the House of Lords consider that it was appropriate to make a declaration of incompatibility under s. 4 of the HRA 1998. Where local authority decisions such as the failure to involve parents during the formulation of the care plan, or changes in an interim care plan threatened their Article 8 rights, they had in most cases an adequate remedy by way of judicial review proceedings or proceedings brought under s. 7 of the HRA 1998 (see 10.2.2.5).

As to the making of interim care orders, the House of Lords in *Re S* merely observed that Article 8 would not be infringed where a court maintained an appropriate balance between the need to satisfy itself as to the appropriateness of the care plan and the avoidance of 'over-zealous investigation into matters which are properly within the administrative discretion of the local authority' (at para. 102, approving Wall J in *Re J* [1994] 1 FLR 253, at 262).

Children's and parents' rights to respect for private and family life may be bolstered by other rights, e.g. the right to freedom of religion (Article 9), or the right of parents to have their children educated in conformity with their religious and philosophical convictions (Article 2 of Protocol 1) (see 10.2.7).

10.2.4.2 Adoption

Adoption is a particularly drastic interference with family life and cuts across the general principle that the aim of taking children into public care is to reunite them with their families. Consequently, adoption requires particularly close justification under Article 8(2) ECHR. In serious and appropriate cases there is no doubt that adoption may be justified under the Convention as a mechanism for providing needy children with stability over and above that offered by long-term foster care. However, while adoption itself may be justified under Article 8(2) where this is an 'overriding requirement' in the interests of the child (see *Johansen* at 10.2.4.1), the procedures and conditions under which an adoption takes place will require close scrutiny under Article 8(2).

As noted above, at the time of writing the law and practice of adoption was about to undergo a fundamental and radical overhaul with the introduction of the Adoption and Children Act 2002. The commentary which follows deals principally with the state of the law under the Adoption Act 1976. Significant provisions in the 2002 Act with regard to adoption include, in particular, the linguistic shift towards 'paramountcy' rather than 'first consideration' (s. 1, thus aligning the status of the child's welfare with the Children Act 1989), the possibility of adoption by same sex and unmarried couples (ss. 50 and 144) and by single individuals (s. 51), the abolition of the freeing process and its replacement with new measures for placement for adoption with consent and placement orders (ss. 18–29), and new provisions relating to advertising (ss. 123–124) and inter-country adoptions (ss. 83–91).

In English adoption law the practice of freeing a child for adoption under s. 16

of the Adoption Act 1976 before an alternative adoptive placement has been identified and the prevailing practice of 'closed' adoptions are likely to be two particularly controversial areas in terms of justification under Article 8(2).

Freeing exposes a child to considerable uncertainty, and may deprive him or her of any family for the time that it takes to find adopters. Freeing also affects the legal status of the child concerned, leaving him or her legally severed from his or her birth family before an adoption order establishes a link with an adoptive family. The Adoption and Children Act 2002 abolishes the practice of freeing by virtue of the provisions on placing children with parental consent and placement orders (ss. 18–29).

The practice of closed adoption, where ties between birth family and a child are completely severed subject only to the right of the child to obtain details of his or her birth family when he or she reaches the age of majority, may be the subject of challenges under Article 8. Section 12(6) of the Adoption Act 1976 allows the court to attach such terms and conditions to an adoption order as it thinks fit, which includes an order for contact. In *Re C (A Minor) (Adoption: Conditions)* [1988] 1 All ER 705, HL, such directions were described as 'exceptional' and would never be imposed on adopters who were not prepared to submit to such a condition.

Understanding of adoption is, however, evolving. The Convention itself is a 'living instrument', the interpretation of which falls to be reconsidered from time to time in the light of changing social values (*Tyrer* v *UK* (1978) 2 EHRR 1). In this respect it is worth noting that in many European legal systems closed adoptions, although not unknown, are much less prevalent than in England and Wales. Evidence that UK law is significantly out of line with that in other signatories to the ECHR may be relevant to the question of justification.

The evolving interpretation of a child's or birth parent's right to family life may make it more difficult to justify terminating contact between a child and his or her birth family where open adoption is identified as in the child's interests. This issue was raised in a case settled by the UK Government (*Clark* v *UK* (App. No. 23387/94). Where this is so, it may be increasingly difficult for a local authority to justify seeking a closed adoption because proposed adopters are unlikely to accept post-adoption contact with the birth family. Instead, the local authority may be required to do more to find or persuade adopters to accept some degree of post-adoption contact.

In *P, C and S* v *UK*, the applicants successfully argued that a lack of access to legal advice between the making of a care order and the subsequent freeing and adoption proceedings had unjustifiably deprived the applicants of the opportunity to put forward those factors that militated in favour of a further assessment of a possible rehabilitation and for their viewpoints on the possible alternatives to adoption and the continuation of contact even after adoption to be put forward at the appropriate time for consideration by the court. The parents were thus insufficiently involved to provide them with the requisite protection of their interests and it could not be ruled out that those disadvantages had had an effect on the outcome of the case (paras 136–137).

Further difficulties are created from the perspective of a right to family life where a family comprising several children is split up, with a plan for an elder child to be in permanent foster care with greater contact with his or her natural parent, while younger siblings are to be adopted with no contact with their mother and perhaps little contact with their sibling in foster care. Legally, children in this position have their status as relations terminated with each other as well as with their parents, which represents a major interference with their right to respect for their family life.

It remains to be seen whether, as some have suggested, the ECHR will force local authorities to a greater level of concurrent planning involving adoption and rehabilitation options, by placing children with people who will, if rehabilitation proves impossible, provide a permanent substitute family as part of a local authority's obligations under Article 8. Such an approach must not be allowed to interfere with the primary objective under the Convention when taking children into public care, which is their reunion with their families.

Post-adoption, only the adoptee has a right under the Adoption Act 1976 to apply to the Registrar General for such information as is necessary for him or her to be able to obtain a copy of his or her birth records (s. 51), subject to various arrangements about counselling having been complied with (see, in the Adoption and Children Act 2002, the requirements in Sch. 1). There is equally the potential for an application to be made to the court under rule 53(4) of the Adoption Rules 1984 (SI 1984/265), for disclosure of the case papers. However, the position is very different in respect of natural parents or siblings who wish to obtain information in order to try to contact an adopted relative. Leave may be granted by the High Court to the Registrar to disclose details of an adoptee's birth records (s. 50(5)), but the grant of leave must be underpinned by more than a strong desire to know how the adoptee's life has progressed; a need or benefit relating to the adoptee must be established (see *Re H (Adoption: Disclosure of Information)* [1995] 1 FLR 236). The court's discretion to grant leave should be exercised very sparingly and only in exceptional circumstances (*D* v *Registrar General* [1997] 1 FLR 715, CA.

An Adoption Contact Register was set up under the Children Act 1989, providing a method by which natural parents or siblings may leave their details, which will be sent to the adoptee so that he or she may get in contact if he or she wishes (s. 51A). This will mitigate in many cases, but not all, the need to seek disclosure from the Registrar.

However, there are cases in which an application for disclosure may be the only way in which an adopted child may ever learn that he or she is in fact adopted. An intermediary may be appointed in such situations to approach the

ɛd person, while the adoptee's anonymity is retained until he or she decides
.........er he or she wishes to have contact with a birth family. Arguably in terms of
both parties' right to 'family life', the judicial imposition of the test of
'exceptional circumstances' in respect of s. 50(5) is disproportionate given the
ways in which the use of the disclosed information can be managed so as to
mitigate the disruption to the life of the adoptee. Such applications would nevertheless require careful scrutiny, as the effect on the life of the adoptee may be
considerable.

Even more unusual is the case where an adoptee's access to information about
his or her birth mother is restricted on public policy grounds on the basis that
identification might put the mother's physical safety at risk (*R* v *Registrar General, ex parte Smith* [1991] QB 393; [1991] 1 FLR 255, CA). In such a case,
Article 8 may be likely to add little to such an application, as English law recognizes as extremely important the right of the adoptee to have access to information about his or her birth family save in the exceptional circumstances of *Ex
parte Smith*. *Ex parte Smith* was recognized in *R (Crown Prosecution Service)* v
Registrar General [2003] 2 WLR 504, as being 'a case with very special facts'
(*per* Waller LJ at 513G, para. 13). As such, it was a case where public policy
justified an absolute duty being limited so as not to be used to facilitate the
commission of a crime.

10.2.5   Article 3

Article 3 ECHR (prohibition of torture or inhuman or degrading treatment or
punishment) is a relatively infrequent source of complaints against the United
Kingdom, and the social services field is no exception. However, in *Z and others* v
UK, (2002) 34 EHRR 97, it was held that the failure of the UK authorities to
provide children with appropriate protection against serious long-term neglect
and abuse amounted to an infringement of the prohibition on inhuman and
degrading treatment in Article 3. Equally, the European Court of Human Rights
held that the applicants had not been afforded an effective remedy to establish the
liability of public officials as guaranteed by Article 13 of the Convention. The
case arose out of *X* v *Bedfordshire County Council* [1995] 2 AC 633, where the
House of Lords held that it was against public policy to allow litigants to sue local
authorities for negligence in the performance of their statutory child care duties.
English law on this issue had already been reconsidered in *Barrett and others* v
Enfield Borough Council [1999] 2 FCR 434, as a result of *Osman* v *UK* (2000) 29
EHRR 245, which found that a similar immunity for actions against the police
was a breach of Article 6 ECHR. However, the European Court in *Z* subsequently
revisited the Article 6 point and held that the non-existence of a particular right of
action did not have the same effect as an immunity from suit in negligence (see
10.2.6). *X* was applied in *MAK* v *Dewsbury Healthcare NHS Trust* [2003] Lloyd's

Rep Med 13, in the context of an allegation of negligence against a local authority social services department carrying out investigations into child abuse following an incorrect provisional diagnosis of possible child abuse by a consultant paediatrician. It was held that the local authority could not be held liable in negligence since each of its employees involved in the investigation was a potential witness in possible criminal or child protection proceedings. No one acting in that capacity should be open to a claim in negligence. The *X* litigation has now finally drawn to a close; *Keating* v *Bromley London Borough Council* [2003] ELR 590 was the trial of the remaining issues, namely the question of the vicarious liability of a local authority for the negligence of its employees. The claim was dismissed.

10.2.6 Article 5

Under Article 5 ECHR, no person shall be deprived of his or her liberty save in the circumstances set out in Article 5(1)(a)–(f). The majority of these exceptions concern detention in connection with criminal proceedings. In addition, detention may be legitimate in relation to those of unsound mind, or who are alcoholics or drug addicts (Article 5(1)(e)). Detention of a minor will be legitimate under a lawful order for the purpose of educational supervision, or for the purpose of bringing him or her before the competent legal authority (Article 5(1)(d)).

None of these identified purposes of detention may be easily reconciled with the purpose of secure accommodation orders set out in s. 25 of the Children Act 1989. However, the Court of Appeal has stated, relying on *Koniarska* v *UK* (App. No. 33670/96) that 'educational supervision' was not to be equated rigidly with notions of classroom teaching but, particularly in a care context, should embrace many aspects of the exercise by the local authority of parental rights for the benefit and protection of the child concerned including the making of an order under s. 25 of the Children Act 1989 (*Re K (A Child) (Secure Accommodation Order: Right to Liberty)* [2001] 2 All ER 719). This argument was foreshadowed in *Campbell and Cosans* v *UK* (1982) 4 EHRR 293, where it was held that 'educational supervision' could extend to include more general aspects of a child's 'upbringing' ('the whole process whereby in any society, adults endeavour to transmit their beliefs, culture and other values to the young'). In *Campbell*, the European Court accepted that the refusal by parents to send their child to a school in which corporal punishment was practised, was justified as part of their right to have their child educated in conformity with their own religious and philosophical convictions. Education connoted the inclusion of discipline. The current Children (Secure Accommodation) Regulations 1991 were introduced in response to the case of *Abbott* v *UK* (1990) DR 290.

10.2.7   Article 9 and Article 2 of Protocol 1

The right to freedom of thought, conscience and religion has given rise to few complaints to the European Court of Human Rights. In the English courts, in private child law proceedings, it has been held that the question of religion could only ever be one factor, albeit in some cases a weighty one, among a range of factors to be taken into account in determining a child's welfare under s. 1(3) of the Children Act 1989. In *Re P (Section 91(14) Guidelines) (Residence and Religious Heritage)* [1999] 2 FLR 573, CA, Ward LJ held, relying on *Hoffmann* v *Austria* (1994) 17 EHRR 293, that 'in the jurisprudence of human rights, the right to practise one's religion is subservient to the need in a democratic society to put welfare first'. Similar reasoning led the Court of Appeal to reject an application for a specific issue order by a Muslim father that his five-year-old son should be circumcised (*Re J (Specific Issue Orders: Muslim Upbringing and Circumcision*) [2000] 1 FLR 571. In *Re P* the point was made that it was not the court's (i.e. the relevant public body's) fault that the child concerned had not, for the majority of her life, grown up in the Jewish tradition; the omission was due to illness and the rejection by her parents of some Jewish foster parents who had earlier been put forward as potential carers.

The above highlights the fact that Article 9 ECHR imposes only a negative duty on a public authority to avoid infringing the right, unlike Article 8, which is capable of imposing positive obligations on public authorities. However, both Article 8 and Article 2 of Protocol 1 (right to respect for education and teaching in conformity with the religious and philosophical convictions of parents) may require more positive steps to be taken by the local authority. Article 2 of Protocol 1 is limited in this respect in its application in the United Kingdom, in relation to the obligation to ensure education in accordance with the convictions of the parents, by a reservation preserved by s. 15 of the HRA 1998. The principle that children should be educated in accordance with their parents' philosophical and religious convictions applies only insofar as it is compatible with the provision of 'efficient instruction and training and the avoidance of unreasonable public expenditure' (see Part II of Sch. 3 to the HRA 1998). It has been held that the right to education does not guarantee a particular standard of education, but it does imply a right to reasonable enjoyment of existing institutions within any country without unjustified discrimination (see *R* v *Secretary of State for the Home Department, ex parte Holub* (unreported), 8 October 1999, *per* Carnwath J — but see below as to the possibility of a guarantee of a minimum level of social provision which could include education). The decision was upheld on appeal ([2001] 1 WLR 1359). The right was not a right to education in a particular country, and did not confer the right to enter the United Kingdom for that purpose. In the case of Article 2 of Protocol 1, only parental views that reach a certain level of cogency, seriousness, cohesion, and importance should be recognized (*Campbell and Cosans* v *UK* (1982) 4 EHRR 293).

It should be noted that the duty to 'respect' in Article 2 of Protocol 1 applies only to the local authorities' functions in relation to education and religion. However, where a local authority has assumed parental responsibility in respect of a child, it may be argued that it has assumed responsibility over these matters connected as they are with a child's development. In *Olsson* v *Sweden (No. 1)* (1988) 11 EHRR 259, the parents, who were non-religious, complained that their children being placed with a religious foster family constituted an infringement of their Article 8 rights. This argument was raised only late in the day and was not supported by the evidence, but the European Court did not reject the parents' argument as being unable to form a valid complaint on the basis of Article 8 ECHR (see also *Karnell and Hardt* v *Sweden* (1971) 14 Yearbook 664).

The right to determine education has been held to be an integral part of custody, and where custody is removed then so is the right to determine education (see *X* v *Sweden* (1978) 12 DR 192). Given that parental responsibility would give a father a say in this question, it would appear that the Children Act 1989 has overtaken this decision. In a similar vein, where a child has been adopted, then it has been held that parental rights in respect of the educational and religious upbringing of a child cease (see *X* v *UK* (1978) 11 DR 160).

In *Kjeldsen, Busk, Madsen and Pedersen* v *Denmark* (1976) 1 EHRR 711, compulsory sex education at school did not infringe the parents' rights (or implicitly the children's) under any of the potentially relevant Convention Articles. In *Kjeldsen*, it was a particular feature of the case that there were other schools at which sex education was not compulsory. The topics on the school curriculum were of a general nature, in the public interest and did not entail indoctrination based on any particular moral outlook in a way that might have infringed the ECHR. Parents remained free to guide their children in accordance with their own convictions. This decision may be contrasted with that in *Campbell and Cosans* (see above), because in that case not only were there no alternative schools available at which corporal punishment did not take place, but also the nature of the infringement was such that the parental intervention afterwards could not have mitigated the effect of the conduct complained of in the way that parental tutelage could have in the case of *Kjeldsen*. In any event, subsequent cases concerning corporal punishment have been brought as a complaint by the child under Article 3 ECHR, which is arguably more appropriate (*Costello-Roberts* v *UK* (1993) 19 EHRR 112; *A* v *UK* (1999) 27 EHRR 611), although for punishment to be inhuman or degrading, it must reach a certain level of severity (*R* v *Lichniak* [2003] 1 AC 903; *R (Bernard)* v *Enfield London Borough Council* [2003] HRLR 4). Conversely, however, in *R (Williamson)* v *Secretary of State for Education and Employment* [2003] QB 1300, a case concerning teachers at, and parents who sent their children to, schools where discipline was enforced by the use of corporal punishment, the Court of Appeal held that the prohibition on corporal punishment did not constitute a breach of Article 9. As regards Article 3, the Court in *Williamson* found that it was unclear at what point reasonable chastisement becomes criminal assault, nor at what point the state should intervene to prevent the commission of such an offence. As such, the extent of parents' 'rights' in this respect was unclear.

10.2.8   Article 10

Article 10 ECHR provides:

> 1.   Everyone has the right to freedom of expression. This right shall include freedom to hold opinions and to receive and impart information and ideas without interference by public authority and regardless of frontiers. This article shall not prevent states from requiring the licensing of broadcasting, television or cinema enterprises.

Limitations are placed on the exercise of these freedoms by Article 10(2), such as are prescribed by law and are necessary in a democratic society:

> ... in the interests of national security, territorial integrity or public safety, for the prevention of disorder or crime, for the protection of health or morals, for the protection of the reputation or rights of others, for preventing the disclosure of information received in confidence, or for maintaining the authority and impartiality of the judiciary.

Article 10 was not considered by the European Court of Human Rights in the case of *P and B* v *UK* (above). However, in rejecting the complaint under Article 6 ECHR the European Court held in those particular cases that hearings in private were permissible under that Article, and in those circumstances Article 10 added no additional weight to the complainants' arguments.

In *Re H (Minors) (Injunction: Public Interest)* [1994] 1 FLR 519, the Court, with the support of a local authority, approved of young children remaining in the care of a parent who was a transsexual. The Court of Appeal rejected the submission that the terms of an injunction designed to prevent publicity concerning the case should be determined solely on the grounds of the paramountcy of the welfare of the children; both Article 10 and Article 8 were in issue:

> The public may know the facts but public interest turns to public curiosity as soon as information is sought as to the identity of the parties. When that becomes the focus of attention, then the public interest in the protection of the children concerned becomes the greater public interest and the interest of the particular child becomes the more important factor.

See also *Re Z (A Minor) (Identification: Restrictions on Publication)* [1997] Fam 1 and *Re G (Minors) (Celebrities: Publicity)* [1999] 3 FCR 181. The complaint in *Re Z* was found to be manifestly ill-founded (see (1997) 25 EHRR CD 159). As already mentioned, in *Re PB* (at 10.2.2.3) it was the automatic holding of family proceedings in private and the automatic contempt which attaches to the publication of material generated in the course of the hearing which was alleged to infringe Article 10. On the approach of both Article 10 and *Re H*, certain properly tailored restrictions will not infringe Article 10.

10.3 OTHER DUTIES OF LOCAL AUTHORITIES

10.3.1 General responsibilities to children

Under Part III of the Children Act 1989, local authorities have responsibilities for all children in their area, whether or not they are on a child abuse register or the subject of proceedings. In *Re V, Re L (Sexual Abuse: Disclosure)* [1999] 1 FLR 267, CA, two local authorities argued unsuccessfully that their duties to children in their area, under ss. 17 and 47 of the Children Act 1989, required them to disclose civil findings made in care proceedings of child abuse to a football club and another local authority. In the context of these cases there were no pending investigations by the police or any other agency in respect of which the information sought might have assisted with their inquiries. (Contrast this situation with the one in which there is an ongoing criminal investigation and disclosure is sought by the police (*Re EC (Disclosure of Material)* [1996] 2 FLR 725, CA, which influenced the court in *Re V*).) It should be noted that the Court of Appeal was able to reach this conclusion by its interpretation of s. 17 of the Children Act 1989, without referring to Article 8 ECHR. However, Butler-Sloss LJ reinforced her conclusion against disclosure by reference to the test laid down in *R v Chief Constable of North Wales, ex parte Thorpe* (below), which did address the problem in terms of Article 8.

Even where a person has been convicted of an offence against a child, it will only be if there is a 'pressing need' for disclosure of that information that the holder of the information may disclose it to members of the public (see *R v Chief Constable of North Wales, ex parte Thorpe* [1998] 3 FLR 57, CA). In this case the police were permitted to notify a campsite owner of the fact that an abuser had moved on to the site. Such disclosure was a justified interference with Article 8 ECHR on the particular facts of this case. Further consideration was given to the practical application of these principles to the disclosure of unproved allegations of abuse to another local authority in *R v Local Authority and Police Authority in the Midlands, ex parte LM* [2000] 1 FLR 612, *per* Dyson J. LM had lost previously held employment as a result of past disclosures of the allegations. In refusing disclosure, the Court held that a court was more likely to find a 'pressing need' for disclosure to another local authority than to members of the public. The distinction between disclosure to the public and disclosure to another public body in pursuit of its statutory functions was drawn in *R* v *Chief Constables of C and D, ex parte A* (2000) *The Times*, 7 November, *per* Turner J. Here an inter-police force transfer of information had no immediate, or even indirect, consequence for the applicant, and it was clearly arguable that the doctrine of procedural fairness was not engaged at all. In addition, the Court held that a local authority which requires sensitive 'non-conviction' information as an individual's prospective employer has a 'pressing need' to receive such information. Issues under Article 8 may arise in other cases as to whether the 'pressing need' test applies to transfers between bodies pursuing a law enforcement or statutory child protection function. However, the thrust of *Ex parte A* is that this is unlikely.

For the position on the maintenance of registers, see the discussion at 10.2.2.1.

10.3.2   Mental health functions

Under the Mental Health Act (MHA) 1983, responsibilities for mental health patients are shared between the Secretary of State, NHS trusts and local authority social services. In addition, Part V of the MHA 1983 provides for the system of independent mental health review tribunals, which offers an important safeguard against the powers of detention or control under guardianship of patients under the Act. In this area the ECHR has had, and is likely to continue to have, an impact. As far as local authority social services are concerned, the effects are likely to be significant in certain specific areas that require their involvement in the care of those with mental health problems.

The only specific reference to mental health patients under the Convention is contained in Article 5, which guarantees the liberty and security of the person, although other rights may be important, such as those contained in Articles 8 and 6 and, to a lesser extent, Articles 9, 10 and 3.

10.3.2.1   Detention and discharge
The social services department may be involved initially in the detention of a mental health patient either by being requested to find accommodation for a patient who has been detained under police powers for up to 72 hours (s. 136 of the MHA 1983), or by deciding to make an application for a compulsory admission.

The criteria for compulsory detention were considered by the European Court of Human Rights in *Winterwerp* v *Netherlands* (1979) 2 EHRR 387:

(a)   the detention should be based on objective medical expertise;
(b)   the disorder must be such that compulsory confinement is warranted; and
(c)   the detention should endure only as long as this is warranted.

Generally, on these criteria there is little in the MHA 1983 which is liable to infringe the Convention. However, as far as the Secretary of State's power to order a recall of a conditionally discharged restricted patient pursuant to s. 42(3) without further medical evidence is concerned, this does infringe Article 5 ECHR (*Kay* v *UK* (1998) 40 BMLR 20, European Commission on Human Rights).

Winterwerp requires that where the grounds for detention cease to exist, the patient must be released. In this regard there is a difference between unrestricted and restricted patients. The former are entitled to be released as soon as the registered medical officer concludes that the grounds for detention no longer exist. In the case of restricted patients, they are not entitled under the MHA 1983 to immediate release when the medical opinion is that they should be released but only after the approval of the Secretary of State or tribunal.

While this state of affairs suggests some incompatibility with the last limb of the *Wintwerp* test, the European Court has since held, in *Johnson* v *UK* (1997) 40 BMLR 1, that a finding that a patient is no longer suffering from the mental disorder which led to his or her confinement need not inevitably lead to an immediate discharge. The patient's discharge may be made subject to conditions such as residence in a hostel. In Johnson's case, he was conditionally discharged in 1989, but was not released because no hostel could be found which was prepared to accommodate him before he was absolutely discharged in 1993. His rights under Article 5 ECHR were held to have been violated. While *Johnson* is an extreme case, it highlights the fact that problems in finding accommodation must not be allowed significantly to interfere with a patient's conditional release. A delay, following a decision to transfer a patient from a secure psychiatric hospital to less restrictive conditions, was rejected in *Ashingdane* v *UK* (1985) 7 EHRR 528. Here there was no question of the patient regaining his liberty, as he would have continued to remain in detention in the second institution.

Concerns have also arisen as to whether or not informal patients who are compliant and being treated in hospital, but who are unable, though lack of capacity, to consent to treatment, are effectively being 'detained', albeit without the procedural safeguards for challenging detention which accompany compulsory detention under s. 3 of the MHA 1983 (see *R* v *Bournewood Community NHS Trust, ex parte L* [1999] 1 AC 458, HL).

10.3.2.2 *Nearest relatives*

The patient's nearest relative is an important safeguard for those who are admitted for compulsory treatment. The patient's nearest relative must be consulted and must approve of the admission under s. 3 of the MHA 1983. Nearest relatives are statutorily defined in s. 26. The result of this is that persons who may not know the patient, or whom the patient mistrusts, may become his or her nearest relative with the function of protecting the patient's interests. Hitherto, the 1983 Act has not provided a remedy by which the patient may advance reasonable objections in order to replace the nearest relative with someone the patient would like to exercise that function on his or her behalf. In JT v UK [2000] 1 FLR 909, a friendly settlement was reached regarding a complaint that this state of affairs infringes a patient's Article 8 rights. The MHA 1983 would be amended to allow a detained patient to object to a person acting in the capacity of nearest relative and to exclude certain persons from assuming that function. Subsequently, in *R (M)* v *SSH* [2003] UKHRR 746, a declaration of incompatibility was made in respect of ss 26 and 29 of the MHA. Parliament had failed to deal with the infringement identified in JT. That it intended to do so was not a reason for refusing a declaration.

In another case the same sex partner of a person detained under the MHA 1983 wanted to be treated as her 'nearest relative' for the purposes of the Act. The case was settled on the basis that, having regard to s. 3 of the HRA 1998, such a person could be regarded as falling within the definition of a person living with the patient as the patient's husband or wife (*R (JSG)* v *Liverpool City Council and the Secretary of State for Health* (Admin Court Order of 22 October 2002)).

A further issue arises in relation to the ability of the local authority to apply to the county court under s. 29 of the MHA 1983 to displace a nearest relative and have his or her function performed by an approved social worker on the grounds in s. 29(3). These grounds are essentially that the nearest relative either is unable to exercise that function or has exercised, or is proposing to exercise, that function without due regard for the interests of the patient or the public. As English domestic law stands, it may be arguable in certain cases that Article 8 (and possibly Article 6) is infringed in that no provision is made for the patient to take part in such proceedings to remove his or her nearest relative.

10.3.2.3 *Compulsory treatment*

Social services will not be directly involved in the treatment of detained patients. However, faced with the refusal to undergo treatment by a client, they will have to consider what may be achieved if they apply for compulsory admission.

Treatment under the MHA 1983 without the patient's consent relates only to treatment for the client's mental health. Nevertheless, this will cover a wide range of conditions including, for example, anorexia nervosa (see *B* v *Croydon Health Authority* [1995] 1 All ER 683). Treatment for one disorder, which alone does not merit detention, is capable of being ancillary to treatment for another disorder, which alone does merit detention (*R (B)* v *Ashworth Health Authority* [2003] 1 WLR 1886. Refusal of consent to a Caesarian section should not be overridden under the 1983 Act (see *St George's Healthcare NHS Trust* v *S* [1999] Fam 26, CA). However, there is little in the Convention jurisprudence to indicate what level of assistance may be derived from Article 8 in this situation. Levels or standards of treatment are unlikely to be challengeable under Article 5. A successful challenge would be likely to require levels of service to infringe the person's rights under Article 2 or 3, but these would be unusual and extreme cases. In *Herczegfalvy* v *Austria* (1992) 15 EHRR 437, where a mentally ill patient was handcuffed to a security bed, the European Court held that there had been no breach of Article 3 ECHR. In *R (N)* v *M* [2003] 1 WLR 562, the Court of Appeal decided that the trial judge had been correct to apply the *Herczegfalvy* best interests and medical necessity tests, instead of the *Bolam* tests.

10.3.2.4 Community care

The rights and obligations that arise under community care law are contained in a confusing patchwork of legislation much of which originated in private members' bills (for an outstanding specialist work on this area see Clements, *Community Care and the Law* (Legal Action Group, 2000)).

Domestic law rights in issue in this area may involve difficult issues of classification under the Convention. Insofar as such rights are economic and social in nature they are not the primary focus of the Convention. Separate Council of Europe treaties govern economic and social rights. Legally, the effect of those treaties is simply to bind their signatories as a matter of public international law and there is no mechanism for individual enforcement of them as there is under the ECHR. Nor, it should be remembered, does the Convention generally guarantee any specific level of content in the rights it protects, merely the enjoyment of what is provided under the domestic law in question (see, e.g., the right to education referred to at 10.2.7).

However, this is not to suggest that Convention rights are of no relevance in this area. While the allocation of resources to its welfare priorities is essentially a matter for particular states and their public authorities, there may nevertheless be circumstances in which a right guaranteed by the Convention would be meaningless unless some action is taken to create conditions under which that right can be exercised. Thus although domestic legislation may, in compliance with Article 2 of the Convention, protect on its face the right to life, the state concerned will nevertheless violate Article 2 if at least some basic measures are not taken to give that protection some value. The closure of residential care homes may involve the relocation and resettlement of very frail elderly people who may have been in residence for a considerable period. While it is to be hoped that any genuine threat to their lives from such a proposal would lead to it being postponed by the relevant authority, the example does illustrate the relevance Convention rights may have in this area.

Article 8 ECHR is on its face most specific in this regard as it may require positive action connoted by the right to *respect* for private and family life. However, in considering Article 8, a court must also take into account the need to strike a fair balance between the general interest and the interest of the individual. For example, under domestic law, local authorities may take resources into account when assessing or reassessing needs under s. 2(1) of the Chronically Sick and Disabled Persons Act 1970 (*R* v *Gloucestershire County Council, ex parte Barry* [1997] 2 WLR 459). This means that service provision under domestic community care legislation generally only becomes susceptible to challenge when provision falls below what may be considered 'reasonable' on familiar judicial review grounds of challenge. The question then arises whether in a particular case the right to 'respect' for private and family life requires a greater guarantee in this context, given the discretion that states are accorded under the Convention to strike a fair balance in deploying their resources (cf. the United Kingdom's reservation to Article 2 of Protocol 1, at 10.2.7). That is likely to be a difficult argument on which to establish a violation of Convention rights in many, if not most, cases.

In *R* v *North and East Devon Health Authority, ex parte Coughlan* [1999] 2 CCL Rep 27, [2001] QB 213, it was held that the respondents had unjustifiably infringed the applicant's Article 8 rights by their decision to close homes maintained by them under Part III of the National Assistance Act 1948. The respondents had promised the applicant a 'home for life'. However, the impact of the case is limited, because by their representation or promise the respondents had effectively elevated the applicant's entitlement above that of the general class of people to whom such duties are owed. Where there is no specific legitimate expectation of a particular level of benefit, as in *Coughlan*, the guaranteed substantive content of the rights of the general class of recipients is likely to be subject to a much greater degree of discretion to allocate resources as the local authority sees fit, as discussed above. This has proved to be the approach adopted by the courts post-*Coughlan*. In *R* v *St Helens Council, ex parte Haggerty* [2003] HLR 69, a local authority's decision not to meet the increased care fees of a care home, which resulted in the closing down of the home, and the residents having to move to alternative homes, was not a breach of the residents' Article 8 rights. Furthermore, in *R* v *East Sussex County Council, ex parte Dudley* [2003] ACD 86, Maurice Kay J, in deciding that there had been no breach of either consultation requirements or Article 8 on the decision to close down a care home, doubted the applicability of Article 8 in the particular case because of the absence of a *Coughlan*-style 'home for life' promise (see also *McKellar* v *Hounslow London Borough Council*, QBD, HHJ Keppel Q 28 October 2003).

In *R* v *Enfield London Borough Council, ex parte J* [2002] 2 FLR 1, Elias J, held that while the local authority had no power under s. 17 of the Children Act 1989 to provide financial assistance to a mother and her child in order to secure accommodation, he made a declaration that where a failure to exercise the powers under s. 2 of the LGA 2000 to provide such financial assistance would infringe the Article 8 rights of the mother and her daughter, the power to do so became a duty so to act.

Chapter Eleven

Education

Natalie Lieven

11.1 INTRODUCTION

Article 2 of Protocol 1 to the Convention provides that:

> No person shall be denied the right to education. In the exercise of any functions which it assumes in relation to education and to teaching, the State shall respect the right of parents to ensure such education and teaching in conformity with their own religious and philosophical convictions.

Issues relating to education will also arise under other Articles of the ECHR, in particular Article 6 (right to fair hearing in determination of civil rights), Article 8 (right to family life) and Article 14 (the prohibition on discrimination). These will be considered in relation to the particular educational issues dealt with below.

Article 2 of Protocol 1 was the subject of considerable debate at the drafting stage, and a number of states entered reservations because of concerns about the onerous nature of the obligations which might be imposed (see Harris, O'Boyle and Warbrick, *Law of the European Convention on Human Rights* (Butterworths, 1995). The text was altered in draft from a positive duty to the negative wording. The UK Government still entered a reservation in the following terms:

> . . . in view of certain provisions of the Education Acts in the United Kingdom, the principle affirmed in the second sentence of Article 2 is accepted by the United Kingdom only in so far as it is compatible with the provision of efficient instruction and training, and the avoidance of unreasonable public expenditure.

Under s. 1(2) of the HRA 1998, this reservation has effect in domestic law. The reservation closely follows s. 9 of the Education Act 1996.

Article 2 of Protocol 1 contains a separate duty in each sentence, but the two sentences must be read together. The right to respect for parental views is subject to the limitations which have been placed on the scope of the first sentence. This means that parental convictions cannot lead to more extensive duties on the state than have been found to exist by reason of the obligation not to deny the right to education.

There is relatively little case law on this Article, either from the European Court of Human Rights or from the Commission, and only a few cases have arisen so far in the domestic courts. Both Court and Commission have taken a rather restrictive approach to the scope of the duties under Article 2 of Protocol 1 following the leading case of *Belgian Linguistic (No. 2)* (1968) 1 EHRR 252. The European Court has not been prepared to accept arguments that the negative terms of the Article can incorporate situations where a person is effectively excluded from meaningful education, whether because of the type of education being offered or the cost. However, there is considerable potential to rely on Article 2 of Protocol 1, and it may be that the domestic courts will take a more positive approach to the state's duty in the realm of education. The European Court is obviously constrained by the fact that the education systems and resources of member states vary considerably, whereas the domestic courts do not have this constraint. Thus arguments, for instance, about higher or further education being a right may be easier to advance under the HRA 1998 than was the case before incorporation. Some of the opportunities for taking arguments beyond the current Strasbourg jurisprudence are referred to below.

However, it has to be said that in the relatively short time since the HRA 1998 came into effect, the domestic courts have taken a very cautious approach to Article 2 of Protocol 1 and have followed the spirit of the *Belgian Linguistic* case closely (see, in particular, *Holub v Secretary of State for the Home Department* [2002] EWHC 2388.

11.2   EXTENT OF THE RIGHT TO EDUCATION

The scope of the right in Article 2 of Protocol 1 was considered in the leading case, *Belgian Linguistic (No. 2)* (1968) 1 EHRR 252. The European Court held that Article 2 did enshrine a right, but the extent of the right was severely circumscribed. The right was not to a particular form or quality of education, but only a right of access to the education which was already available in the particular state. The Court said (at 280):

> The negative formulation indicates, as is confirmed by the preparatory work, that the Contracting Parties do not recognise such a right to education as would require them to establish at their own expense, or to subsidise, education of any particular type or at any particular level.

The Court held that what was guaranteed to individuals was a 'right in principle, to avail themselves of the means of instruction existing at a given time' (at 281).

The *Belgian Linguistic* case established the following rights:

(a)   access to educational establishments existing at the time;
(b)   the right to an effective education;
(c)   education in the national language;
(d)   recognition of any qualifications obtained.

There was no right to education in the language of the parent's choice, or in their own language.

As can be seen from the above quotation, the European Court lied on the preparatory works of the Convention in applying this rather restrictive approach. Generally the preparatory works have rarely been used by the European Court (see Harris, O'Boyle and Warbrick, op. cit., at 17), partly because of the dynamic approach to interpretation of the ECHR. It could therefore be argued that the strict adherence to the signatories' original intentions should no longer lead courts to limiting the duty to provide education to what is already in existence.

The European Court found in *Belgian Linguistic* that the state has no duty to provide a particular form of education but merely to guarantee access to what is already provided. There is no guarantee as to the quality of education to be provided, but it was said in *Belgian Linguistic* that the pupil should be able to profit from that education. This comment was made in the context of recognition of qualifications, but could be applied by analogy to the quality of the education being provided. If, for instance, in the field of special education, it could be said that the education being provided was of no benefit to the pupil because it was totally ill-suited to his or her needs, this could amount to a denial of access to education within the terms of the first sentence of Article 2 of Protocol 1. The Commission has been reluctant to become involved in arguments about the standard of education that is being offered (see *P* v *UK* [1997] ERLR 287, which concerned the question whether the schools involved had properly provided for the child's special needs).

In the only English case which has considered the scope of Article 2 of Protocol 1 in any detail, *Holub* v *Secretary of State for the Home Department* [2002] EWHC 2388, the Court of Appeal accepted the submission that the right to education must encompass the provision of an effective education (see para. 23 of the judgment). It went on to approve a passage from *Lester and Pannick on Human Rights Law* (1st edn, Butterworths, 1999), where it is suggested that the general right to education encompasses, amongst other things, the right of access to such educational establishments as exist and a right to effective (but not the most effective) education. The Court of Appeal then said:

> As regards the right to an effective education, for the right to education to be meaningful the quality of the education must reach a minimum standard.

But we do not think that the right is more extensive than this. If Mr Luba's submission that there is a right to an 'appropriate' education means something more than an effective education in the sense described above we do not accept it. There is nothing in the authorities or the literature to which we have been referred which supports such a submission. The Convention does not confer a right to education in any particular country and so does not invite comparison between educational systems.

The relatively restrictive approach to the right to education may be affected in any particular case by the duty not to discriminate contained in Article 14 ECHR (see 11.7).

11.3   MEANING OF 'EDUCATION'

Apart from the level of education, the word 'education' has been given a very broad meaning, different from mere 'teaching' or 'instruction'. In *Campbell and Cosans* v *UK* (1982) 4 EHRR 293, the European Court of Human Rights said:

> ... the education of children is the whole process whereby in any society, adults endeavour to transmit their beliefs, culture and other values to the young, whereas teaching or instruction refers in particular to the transmission of knowledge and to intellectual development.

Campbell and Cosans concerned the use of corporal punishment in schools in the United Kingdom. The European Court held that discipline within schools was an aspect of education. This would suggest that many elements of the way schools are run outside the classroom have the potential to fall within the definition of 'education' and therefore within the ambit of the second sentence of Article 2 of Protocol 1. Thus policies about what pupils wear, or how they behave outside class, will all be matters which fall within the meaning of 'education' for these purposes. The approach of the European Court in *Campbell and Cosans* also seems to support a wide scope to the form of education, such as adult or vocational training, although (as will be seen below) this has not yet been followed through.

There has been some debate about whether Article 2 of Protocol 1 is restricted to elementary education. In cases subsequent to *Belgian Linguistic*, the Commission has stated that the Article is primarily concerned with elementary education and not advanced studies (*X* v *UK* (1975) 2 DR 50) (see also *Valasinas* v *Lithuania* (App. No. 44558/98). The distinction appears to be between primary/secondary education and higher education. However, it is not entirely clear why this distinction should be maintained, particularly in the light of the wide definition of 'education' which the European Court and Commission have adopted. The Court itself has not indicated that Article 2 of Protocol 1 has no application to higher education. In *Eren* v *Turkey* the Commission, in an admissibility decision, said that the Article referred to all levels of education. The position appears to be that the right to education in Article 2 of Protocol 1 is primarily engaged in respect of elementary education, but that higher and further education can fall within its scope for the purpose of arguing that there has been discrimination in the field of access to education within Article 14 ECHR. It has certainly been the European Court's approach to apply more rigorous standards in terms of protecting rights in respect of education at elementary level, and this is likely to be continued.

The distinction between elementary and higher education is important in arguments about financial assistance to students in higher education. In *O'Connor v Chief Adjudication Officer* [1999] 1 FLR 1200, the Court of Appeal rejected an argument that there was a breach of Article 2 of Protocol 1 and Article 14 ECHR, where a student was denied benefits which would have allowed her to continue her university course. This was partly on the basis of Article 2's primary concern being school-level education, and partly on the basis of the lack of a positive duty to provide funding.

11.4 SCOPE OF THE STATE'S DUTY TO PROVIDE EDUCATION

As has been seen at 11.3, there is no duty on the state to provide a particular form of education. In *X* v *UK* (1978) 14 DR 179, a challenge was brought to the UK Government's failure to provide funding for non-denominational schools in Northern Ireland. The Commission stated that there was no duty to provide such funding on the basis of the *Belgian Linguistic* case. Equally, in *Verein Gemeinsam Lernen* v *Austria* (1995) 82A DR 41, the Commission said that there was no positive obligation on the member state to subsidize a particular form of education.

In *W and DM and M and HI* v *UK* (1984) 37 DR 96, the applicants' children were refused places in local grammar schools on the grounds that to admit pupils would be contrary to efficient education. They were thus required to attend comprehensive schools. The Commission found that the complaint was inadmissible because there was no breach of the parents' role in education, the transmission of their values or philosophical beliefs.

There has been found to be a right to establish private schools; and, subject to certain limitations, a denial of this right could be a breach of the first sentence of Article 2 of Protocol 1 (*Jordebo* v *Sweden* (1987) 51 DR 125). The existence of such schools has been one way in which the court has found that the parental rights in the second sentence of Article 2 of Protocol 1 have been protected because they have alternatives in the private sector. It is difficult to see how this approach can be supported if the private schools are outside the financial reach of the parents involved. In the United Kingdom, private education is unlikely to be considered as an alternative unless it is being funded by a local education authority, for instance in a special education case. The right to establish private schools is subject to the state regulation of such schools, for instance in respect of the quality of education provided.

Challenges have been brought arguing that states should establish particular schools because the existing schools fail to respect the parents' religious or philosophical beliefs contrary to the second sentence of Article 2 of Protocol 1. The European Court and Commission have refused to impose any obligation on states to establish particular types of schools to accord with parental beliefs.

There is no case law on the denial of the right to education through its financial cost. This is doubtless because the European Court has concentrated on elementary education where there is universal state provision. However, if domestic courts are prepared to accept that Article 2 of Protocol 1 applies to higher education then issues arise around the fees charged, the grants paid and social security benefits which are available to students. If, for instance, a student has to give up a course because neither a student loan nor benefits are available, this might amount to a denial of education contrary to Article 2 of Protocol 1. This is an area in which domestic courts may be more prepared to become involved than the European Court, which has had to consider the very different educational provision across all the signatory states. In *O'Connor* v *Chief Adjudication Officer* [1999] 1 FLR 1200, the Court of Appeal did not give any support to this argument. However, in *R (on the application of Mitchell)* v *Coventry University* [2001] ELR 594, a case concerning fees for overseas students, Collins J said: 'one can envisage circumstances where to require the payment of fees across the board might mean that certain people would be unable because of poverty to have access to the institutions that exist and such persons might be able to complain that they were denied a right of education'. However, on the facts of the case the situation did not arise.

In *X* v *UK* (1980) 23 DR 228, the Commission held that access to higher education could be restricted by reference to academic attainments. However, this would seem to be justifiable in any event, in relation to particular educational institutions, and probably would not turn on any distinction between the levels of education concerned, unless there was no alternative elementary education. It was held in the same case that Article 2 of Protocol 1 did not apply to vocational training. Again, this distinction may be difficult to uphold in the future.

It follows from these cases that the state can regulate access to educational institutions and to particular courses or lessons. This was confirmed by Richards J in *R (on the application of Roberts) and Governors of Cwmflinfach Primary School* (unreported), 22 March 2001. That case concerned the school's policy of stopping pupils from wearing earrings. Unsurprisingly, the court held that this was a legitimate policy and there was no breach of the ECHR.

11.5   RESPECT FOR RELIGIOUS AND PHILOSOPHICAL BELIEFS

The second sentence of Article 2 of Protocol 1 requires the state to respect parents' religious or philosophical beliefs in the exercise of any functions relating to education. The second sentence must be read together with the first, and it is the fundamental right to education to which the parental rights are attached. In *Kjeldsen, Busk Madsen and Pedersen* v *Denmark* (1976) 1 EHRR 711, the European Court said:

> The right set out in the second sentence of Article 2 is an adjunct to this fundamental right to education. It is in the discharge of a natural duty towards their children — parents being primarily responsible for the 'education and teaching' of their children — that parents may require the state to respect their religious and philosophical convictions. Their right thus corresponds to a responsibility closely linked to the enjoyment and the exercise of the right to education.

In *Campbell and Cosans* v *UK* (1982) 4 EHRR 294, the European Court said that 'respect' for parental views meant more than merely acknowledging them. The parents had challenged the use of corporal punishment in their children's schools. The UK Government argued that it had sought to strike a balance between the views of parents in favour of and opposed to corporal punishment, and it had thereby acknowledged the parental beliefs. However, the European Court held that this did not amount to respect for those beliefs. The parents' philosophical beliefs could not be overridden by the state seeking to strike a balance between such beliefs. In these circumstances the Court held that there was a breach of the first sentence of Article 2 of Protocol 1, because the child could return to school only if the parents acted contrary to their philosophical beliefs.

In *Valsamis* v *Greece* (1982) 4 EHRR 293, the parents, who were Jehovah's Witnesses, challenged the requirement for their daughter to take part in a school parade on the grounds that it was contrary to their religious and philosophical beliefs. The European Court found that there was nothing in the parade which could offend the parents' beliefs and dismissed the application. Therefore, the question whether parental beliefs had been offended became a question for the Court, and one of objective judgment. Two members of the Court dissented on this point and said that the parents' perception had to be accepted unless it was obviously unfounded or unreasonable. In practice, s. 389 of the Education Act 1996 allows a child to be wholly or partly exempted from religious instruction if his or her parent so wishes, and this is likely to accord with the duties in Article 2 of Protocol 1.

So long as religious education is either voluntary or subject to exemptions, there is no reason why this should not comply with the rights in Article 2 of Protocol 1 as well as with those in Article 9 ECHR (freedom of thought, conscience and religion). In *Angelini* v *Sweden* (1986) 51 DR 41, participation in religious instruction was compulsory in state schools, but the applicant was exempted from large parts of that instruction. There was held to be no breach of Article 9 ECHR.

The contrast between *Valsamis* and *Campbell and Cosans* is noteworthy, and may rest on the fact that *Campbell and Cosans* involved corporal punishment, which came close to being a breach of Article 5 ECHR, whereas the Court in *Valsamis* clearly thought that there was justification for the school parade. Further, the penalty on the child in *Valsamis* was slight, whereas in *Campbell and Cosans* the effect of refusing to accept corporal punishment was that the child could no longer attend the school. In practice, courts will balance their assessment of the importance of the belief in question against the consequences of the school's actions. If the outcome is that the child cannot attend the school then this is more likely to lead to the court's intervention.

The meaning of 'philosophical convictions' was considered in *Campbell and Cosans*, where the European Court said that it meant 'such convictions as are worthy of respect in a "democratic society" . . . and are not incompatible with human dignity; in addition, they must not conflict with the fundamental right of a child to education'.

The substance of the parental right in the second sentence of Article 2 of Protocol 1 is not that parental beliefs cannot be countered. In *Kjeldsen, Busk Madsen and Pedersen* v *Denmark* (1976) 1 EHRR 711, the European Court said:

> . . . The state, in fulfilling the functions assumed by it in regard to education and teaching, must take care that information or knowledge included in the curriculum is conveyed in an objective, critical and pluralistic manner. The State is forbidden to pursue an aim of indoctrination that might be considered as not respecting parents' religious and philosophical convictions. That is the limit that must not be exceeded.

Kjeldsen concerned the teaching of sex education in Danish schools. The European Court found that the teaching in question did not overstep the bounds of what a democratic state could regard as being in the public interest. With respect to sex education, parents have a similar right to that on religions education in s. 405 of the Education Act 1996, unless the sex education in question is contained within the National Curriculum.

Therefore the court will have to make a judgment, first, whether the parental beliefs have been offended (see *Valsamis*) and, secondly, whether such 'offence' is acceptable in the public interest. In *Kjeldsen*, the Court quite closely considered the content of the education in issue in order to decide whether it was justified in the circumstances. Domestic courts will have to consider the substance of the education in issue, the strengths of parents' views and their justification in order to reach a conclusion as to the importance of the educational content which is being disputed.

The importance of religious beliefs has been emphasized by Collins J in *R (K)* v *London Borough of Newham* [2002] ELR 390, where he found that the local education authority had to take on board such beliefs in its admission policies. In that case the issue arose because a Muslim girl did not gain a place in a single sex school, contrary to the religious beliefs of her parents. Collins J found the HRA 1998 gave an extra onus to the issue, over and above that which existed in the School Standards and Framework Act 1998.

In *R (Williamson)* v *Secretary of State for Education and Employment* [2002] ELR 214, a group of parents, teachers and headteachers argued that the law preventing them from inflicting physical chastisement upon children in school was in breach of their human rights under Article 9 or Article 2 of Protocol 1, as being contrary to their religious beliefs. This argument was rejected on a number of grounds, including that as the law protected physical integrity a stronger case was required to justify the infliction of physical injury. It was also held that a support for corporal punishment was not itself the manifestation of a belief.

11.6 CONTENTS OF CURRICULUM

In principle, the content of the curriculum is at the discretion of the state. However, it can be seen from 11.5 that the state must not be guilty of indoctrination and must convey information in a 'pluralistic manner'. In theory this would suggest that courts will scrutinize the detail of the curriculum to ensure 'objectivity' and 'pluralism'; in practice this seems somewhat unlikely. Subject to the broad requirements of *Kjeldsen* (see 11.5 and below) and the need for there to be a proper education, the state has been given a wide margin of appreciation in the setting of the curriculum. It seems fairly unlikely that there would be a breach of the ECHR in this regard.

In *Kjeldsen, Busk Madsen and Pedersen* v *Denmark* (1976) 1 EHRR 711, the European Court placed some reliance on the fact that parents who wished to disassociate themselves from the integrated sex education within the state curriculum could send their children to private schools where the content of sex education was different. In that case those private schools were heavily subsidized by the state, as were the non-denominational schools in *X* v *UK* (1978) 14 DR 179, where similar arguments were raised about religious education. It is unclear whether the existence of private schools which were beyond the financial reach of many parents would be considered in the same way.

11.7 DUTY NOT TO DISCRIMINATE

Closely linked to the requirement for respect of parental views (see 11.5) is the duty not to discriminate under Article 14 ECHR, unless such discrimination is found to be justifiable. It is important to remember that discrimination in Article

14, unlike the European Union law, is not limited to fixed categories (see Chapter 2). In the *Belgian Linguistic* case (see 11.2), the fact that there was different treatment of French and Dutch-speaking children, which was apparently less favourable to French speakers, was generally acceptable because it was in pursuit of a legitimate policy, namely the promotion of unilingual areas. It has certainly been the preferred approach of the UK courts to pass by the issue of whether there has been discrimination in any particular case and go directly to the question of whether the discrimination, if any, has been justified.

There may be some tension between the limited application of the first sentence of Article 2 of Protocol 1, as found in the *Belgian Linguistic* case, and the requirement not to discriminate. There has been found to be no duty to establish particular types of schools under Article 2 of Protocol 1 — the right is merely to have access to education which currently exists. However, it could be argued that the financing and support by the state of certain religious schools but not others is discriminatory, subject to any justification put forward by the state. The most obvious area of relevance in the United Kingdom is the financing of Muslim schools. It may be difficult for the UK Government to justify the financial support of Christian or Jewish schools in certain areas but not of Muslim schools. However, in *Verein Gemeinsam Lernen* v *Austria* (1995) 82A DR 41, the Commission stated that there was no positive obligation on a state to subsidize any particular form of school. In that case, a secular school was refused a subsidy which would have been available to a church school. The argument put forward by the Austrian Government, and accepted by the Commission, was that church schools were so widespread that it would be a great financial burden if the state had to take them over. The case therefore partly turned on lack of a positive obligation to provide particular schools, and partly on justification for the different treatment.

Another potential area for arguments about discrimination is in the admissions policies of particular schools. Under s. 91 of the School Standards and Framework Act 1998, certain schools can seek to preserve their character through admission processes, thereby, for instance, keeping a certain proportion of pupils from a particular religion. This must potentially discriminate against children of a different religious persuasion and thus will turn on justification. If a challenge to such an admission policy is brought, it will be for the school or local education authority to show that the discrimination is objectively and reasonably justified. Matters such as the history of the school, the religious and social make-up of the area, and the school's particular educational philosophy could all be relevant.

Admission criteria may give rise to a number of arguments about discrimination between pupils. The existence of catchment areas for schools may itself discriminate against certain racial or religious groups, or indeed social groups. Parents from a wider area may argue that children from outside the catchment should also be considered for entry. To counter such an argument, local education authorities and governors will have to show that the admission criteria are justified in administrative and educational terms. The standard which the courts will apply in deciding whether a particular decision is justified is dealt with in Chapter 2. It is important to bear in mind that discrimination is not limited to race, sex or disability, but covers any discrimination on 'on any ground' including 'other status', (see Article 14). In *R v School Admissions Panel for Hounslow, ex parte Hounslow London Borough Council* [2002] ELR 402, it was argued that there was unlawful discrimination between siblings. The argument succeeded to the degree that there was found to be inadequate reasoning in the Panel's decision on the matter.

11.8 ADMISSION PROCEDURES

The degree to which the fairness of admission procedures, and indeed expulsions and suspensions, fall within the protection of the Convention is not clear. If there is no right to a particular form of education (see *Belgian Linguistic*) then it is possible to argue that there is no right to any particular admission which can be protected. So long as there is alternative education available, which must be the case under UK domestic law for school age education, then there would be no breach of the first sentence of Article 2 of Protocol 1. However, it could still be argued that the refusal to admit a particular pupil was discriminatory and thus in breach of Article 14 ECHR. Therefore, the decision of the local authority would be unlawful under s. 6 of the HRA 1998. Nevertheless, the mere refusal to admit a pupil to a particular school is unlikely to raise any arguable breaches under the ECHR.

It seems that 'the right to education', so far as it exists, is not a right which itself gives rise to any rights under Article 6 ECHR (right to a fair trial, etc.). For Article 6 to arise, the 'right' in issue must itself be a 'civil right' within the meaning of the European Court's jurisprudence. For consideration of what is a 'civil right', see Chapter Ten, at 10.2.2.1. In *Simpson v UK* (1989) 64 DR 188, the Commission considered an application by the parent of a child with special education needs (SENs). The child's mother wanted him to be placed in a private specialist school, but his SEN statement named a large comprehensive school with some specialist facilities. One of the complaints was that the SEN procedure, under the old internal local authority appeal system, was a breach of Article 6. The Commission held that the right in question was not a 'civil right' within the meaning of Article 6 because it fell within the domain of public law, and had no private law analogy and no repercussions on private rights or obligations. A similar conclusion was reached in *App. No. 10193/82 Germany* (1984) 7 EHRR 141, where the Commission decided that university admissions fell outside Article 6 because there was no determination of a 'civil right'. This approach was supported in the Divisional Court in *R(B) v Head Teacher of Alperton Community School and others* [2001] ELR 359, where following *Simpson* it was held that

Article 2 of Protocol 1 constituted a public rather than a civil right and therefore Article 6 did not apply in an exclusion appeal.

These cases do leave open the question of whether an exclusion from a fee-paying school would give rise to a potential breach of Article 6 ECHR, because there would be a contract between the parties which would give rise to a 'civil right'. However, even this argument would not arise for cases involving admission to schools, because there would not yet be any contract. For the purposes of local education authorities, this is likely to be of any relevance only in the context of placements for children with SENs.

11.9   SUSPENSION OR EXCLUSION

In all disciplinary matters the school and state have considerable discretion. Suspension or exclusion are not themselves a denial of the right to education, although they can amount to such (see *Campbell and Cosans* v *UK* (1982) 4 EHRR 294). There has been found to be no breach of the first sentence of Article 2 of Protocol 1 if the pupil can enrol in another educational establishment (*Yanasik* v *Turkey* (1993) 74 DR 14). Equally, there is no breach where the pupil is expelled and excluded from other establishments if there are good grounds for doing so and the principle of proportionality has been followed (see *Sulak* v *Turkey* (1996) 84A DR 98). However, that case might have been considered differently if elementary education had been in issue rather than higher education.

In practice, in the United Kingdom the duty on local education authorities in s. 14 of the Education Act 1996 is to provide sufficient schools to educate all school age children in their area, and the rights of appeal against exclusion or suspension would normally ensure that there would be no breach of the ECHR. The only obvious problem areas are either where the authority has failed to provide sufficient school places, or where a child has been excluded and no alternative provision has been made. In certain cases such rights of appeal are removed (see s. 95 of the School Standards and Framework Act 1998) if the pupil has been expelled twice before. It seems likely that such a provision is justifiable and proportionate, but that will of course depend on the facts of the individual case. In cases where the authority has simply failed to provide a place for a child, there will be a breach of Article 2 of Protocol 1 but there would be a breach of statutory duty in any event. The relevance of the Convention in these circumstances is merely that it would be a potential route for a claim for damages.

In *R P* v *NUSMUWT* [2001] ELR 607 it was held that the exclusion of a child from class where arrangements were made to teach him separately did not amount to an infringement of his right to education.

11.10   SPECIAL EDUCATIONAL NEEDS

Particular issues are likely to arise in respect of children with special educational needs (SENs). The views of the parents of the children in question should be taken into account, but there is no right to parity of access with other children (see *Simpson* v *UK* (1989) 64 DR 188). If the parents wish to have the child educated in a mainstream school, but the local education authority has named a special school as being the suitable school, the parents may argue that such a placement would be contrary to their philosophical beliefs. Such an argument would often be countered by the authority saying that it was contrary to efficient education to place the child in a mainstream school. This is made directly relevant by reason of the UK Government's reservation, referred to at 11.1.

In other cases the parents may feel that the most appropriate school is a special school, while the authority wishes to place the child in a mainstream school with certain support. In *Klerk* v *Netherlands* (1995) 82A DR 129, a deaf child was being required to transfer to a school for the hard of hearing. It was held that even if the parents' philosophical convictions were in issue, Article 2 of Protocol 1 did not require a place to be provided in a mainstream school with the additional expense that that could require. The same conclusion was reached in *PD and LD* v *UK* (1989) 62 DR 292 and *Graeme* v *UK* (1990) 64 DR 158.

The general approach to such arguments was considered by the Commission in *Simpson* v *UK* (above), where the commission stated:

> The Commission notes that the United Kingdom Government provides special education for disabled children either in normal mainstream schools with special departments, or in specialised segregated institutions. In keeping with current educational trends section 2 of the Education Act 1981 provides that children with special educational needs should be educated in an ordinary school with normal children of their own age if that is compatible with the special education that the former require, the provision of efficient education for other children at the school and the efficient use of resources. The Commission recognises that there must be a wide measure of discretion left to the appropriate authorities as to how to make the best use possible of the resources available to them in the interests of disabled children generally. While these authorities must place weight on parents' and pupils' views, it cannot be said that the first sentence of Article 2 of Protocol No. 1 requires the placing of a dyslexic child in a private specialised school with the fees paid by the State, when a place is available in an ordinary State school which has special teaching facilities for disabled children.

In extreme cases the parents may be able to argue that the child would be denied education by such a placement, because she or he would be unable to derive benefit from it. Some support for this can be drawn from *Holub* v *Secretary of State for the Home Department* (see 11.2), through the comments that the quality of education must reach a minimum standard. As in all aspects of Article 2 of

Protocol 1, it is likely that the Court will give considerable discretion to the education authorities.

11.11   ARTICLE 8

There may be cases where education issues raise arguments under Article 8 ECHR, the right to family life. Two examples that have arisen in domestic cases are the naming of a boarding school in an SEN statement in *CB* v *Merton London Borough Council* [2002] ELR 441. The Court rejected the argument in respect of the particular case, but did say that in a case which concerned a school attendance order, Article 8 might be engaged. Secondly, in the *Hounslow School Admissions Panel* case (see above) it was argued that not having a policy which allowed siblings to be educated together was contrary to Article 8.

11.12   CONCLUSION

There are some interesting potential issues under Article 2 of Protocol 1. However, the European Court of Human Rights has taken a fairly restrictive approach to challenges brought under this Article. So far the domestic courts have not indicated much willingness to step outside the limitations on the Article set in Strasbourg. Possibly the most fruitful area of challenge will be by linking Article 2 of Protocol 1 with discrimination claims under Article 14 ECHR. Even here it will be necessary to think very clearly about the justification arguments which are likely to be raised by defendants, whether schools, local education authorities or the Secretary of State.

Chapter Twelve

Local Authority Licensing

Daniel Kolinsky

12.1 CONTEXT

Some of the leading judicial review cases arise in the context of local authority licensing. For example, *Associated Provincial Picture House* v *Wednesbury Corporation* [1948] 1 KB 233, CA, concerned a challenge to the exercise of a local authority's cinematography powers.

The range of local authority licensing powers is vast, including, for example, tattoo parlours, street entertainment, street trading, theatres and waste management. For a convenient overview of this (and registration powers), the reader is referred to Cross, *Local Government* (Sweet & Maxwell), at Appendix D; and Arden, *Local Government Constitutional and Administrative Law* (Sweet & Maxwell), at 78–139.

The specific statutory scheme for each of the local authorities' licensing functions informs the scope of their powers. That said, common principles have emerged in licensing cases, and these form the backdrop for assessing the impact of the HRA 1998. The common principles may be summarized as:

(a) the applicability of principles of natural justice (see, in particular, *R* v *Barnsley Metropolitan Borough Council, ex parte Hook* [1976] 1 WLR 1052, CA; *R* v *Huntingdon District Council, ex parte Cowan* [1984] 1 WLR 501);

(b) the application of *British Oxygen Co. Ltd* v *Board of Trade* [1971] AC 610, that policies (governing entitlement to licences) must be applied with regard to the individual circumstances of the particular case;

(c) the ground of judicial review that irrelevant considerations must not be taken into account, applied, for example, in *R* v *Liverpool City Council, ex parte Luxury Leisure Ltd* (1998) 1 LGLR 222, where it was held that misinformed local views could not be taken into account when considering the grounds of opposition to an application for an amusement centre under the Gaming Act 1968, s. 34 and Sch. 9, and the Lotteries and Amusements Act 1976, s. 16 and Sch. 3;

(d)   Discretionary powers, such as the powers to impose conditions, must be exercised within the scope of the statute and not in such a manner that no reasonable authority would impose such conditions (see *Waynesburg,* above);

(e)   the licensing authority must not act for an improper purpose, such as levying fees for general revenue-raising purposes (see, e.g., *R* v *Manchester City Council, ex parte King* (1981) 89 LGR 696).

12.2   HUMAN RIGHTS AND LICENSING: OVERVIEW

The most directly relevant articles of the ECHR are Article 6 (right to a fair trial) and Article 1 of Protocol 1 (the right to property) which arise across the spectrum of licensing decisions. This chapter therefore deals with those articles in detail.

Further, as local authority licensing powers cover such a wide range of social and economic activity, there is considerable potential for other substantive Convention rights to arise (depending on the particular context of the licensing powers). This chapter does not attempt to provide an exhaustive checklist of all such issues. Rather, it seeks to illustrate the range of issues which may occur in the licensing context. The message is that the full range of Convention rights may be relevant, and local authorities will need to examine the particular context in which licensing decisions are being made in order to spot potential human rights issues.

12.3   ARTICLE 6(1): THE RIGHT TO A FAIR TRIAL

Article 6 ECHR, so far as it is material for present purposes, provides as follows:

> 1.   In the determination of his civil rights and obligations . . . everyone is entitled to a fair and public hearing within a reasonable time by an independent and impartial tribunal established by law . . .

The European Court of Human Rights and the Commission have adopted broad approaches to the key concepts of 'civil rights' and 'determination' within the scope of Article 6. As such, it may be concluded that the grant, revocation, refusal, and suspension of licences are likely to be characterized as involving the determination of civil rights (see, e.g., *Tree Traktörer Atkiebolag* v *Sweden* (1989) 13 EHRR 309, the withdrawal of an alcohol licence from a restaurant, *Pudas* v *Sweden* (1987) 10 EHRR 380, the revocation of a public service transport licence from a private passenger carrier; *Benthem* v *Netherlands* (1985) 8 EHRR 1 — the decision whether to grant a licence to a petrol filling station). This approach is consistent with that taken by the House of Lords in *R* v *Secretary of State for the Environment, Transport and the Regions, ex parte Alconbury Developments and others* [2001] 2 WLR 1389, at para. 28, to the construction of 'civil rights and obligations'.

The fact that the local authority has discretion whether or not to grant the licence and as to the terms imposed, is not a bar to the applicability of Article 6 (*Pudas*, at para. 34, concerning the revocation of a public transport licence in the exercise of the licensing authority's discretion).

The real focus in licensing cases is likely to be on whether the fair trial requirements of Article 6 have been satisfied, not on the question of whether Article 6 is engaged at all. The decision of the House of Lords in *Alconbury*, as applied in the Court of Appeal decisions of *Begum (Runa)* v *Tower Hamlets* [2002] 1 WLR 2491 and *R* v *Secretary of State for Transport, Local Government and the Regions, ex parte Adlard* [2002] 1 WLR 2515, provide the starting point for evaluating whether the requirements of Article 6 are satisfied in the particular licensing context under consideration. *Runa Begum* has now been considered by the House of Lords ([2003] 2 WLR 388), which affirmed the Court of Appeal's view that there was no breach of Article 6.

A great many local authority licensing bodies will not themselves satisfy the requirement imposed by Article 6 for the decision-making tribunal to be independent of the executive and the parties (*Reingeisen* v *Austria (No. 1)* (1971) 1 EHRR 455, at para. 95). However, the focus is on the whole decision-making process; not simply the initial decision-making before the local authority itself. What needs to be considered is whether the composite decision-making process (i.e. (a) the decision-making by the local authority plus an appeal process or (b) the decision-making before a local authority together with the supervisory jurisdiction of the High Court) is compatible with Article 6. A valid appeal system is capable of curing non-compliance with Article 6 requirements at the initial decision-making stage. In the licensing context, a key issue is whether full jurisdiction (to review factual findings) is required, or whether supervisory jurisdiction is sufficient.

In a number of licensing contexts legislation provides rights of appeal to courts in respect of the refusal or revocation of licences, in which case Article 6 issues are unlikely to arise. However, there are a number of cases where no legislative provision is made for an appeal to a court in respect of a local authority's decision either not to grant, or even to revoke a licence or registration, e.g. in the context of a door supervisor who is refused registration or has it revoked. In this situation, judicial review is the only remedy open, and whether it meets the requirements of Article 6 may well depend on the context and nature of the matters in issue.

In *Alconbury*, the House of Lords decided that judicial review of the Secretary of State's decision on a planning application, which he had called in for his own determination under s. 77 of the TCPA 1990, was sufficient to satisfy the requirements of Article 6 even though the Secretary of State was not himself an independent tribunal. In *Alconbury*, the following factors were stressed by the House of Lords:

(a)   The House of Lords emphasized the existence of 'uncontested safe-guards' in the administrative decision-making process under scrutiny, particularly the fact that the applicants enjoyed the protection afforded by a public inquiry before an inspector (see paras 46 (*per* Lord Slynn), 128 (*per* Lord Hoffmann) and 152 (*per* Lord Clyde)). The level of safe-guards that do exist in the particular licensing context under consider-ation is a factor of considerable significance in determining whether the remedy of judicial review is sufficient to satisfy the requirements of Article 6.

(b)   The points at issue in *Alconbury* were considered to be points of expedi-ency and policy, not disputes of fact. At para. 117, Lord Hoffmann emphasized that the safeguards referred to in (a) above were essential for the acceptance of a limited review of fact by the appellant tribunal where disputes as to the finding or evaluation of facts were concerned. In the licensing context, therefore, it may well make a difference whether the decision applies a general policy or involves specific factual findings. The latter are more likely to give rise to the need for a full review of those factual findings, particularly when the findings imply an adverse judgment as to an individual's suitability for a particular role. Further-more, the actual grounds of challenge put forward may be of importance in evaluating the adequacy of the review (e.g. is there a genuine dispute as to an important factual issue?).

(c)   The extent to which the original decision-making body has particular specialist knowledge and whether this is a relevant factor may well vary depending on the particular licensing context under scrutiny. The more specialist the original decision-making body, the more willing the court is to forgo the requirement of factual review (see *Bryan* v *UK* (1995) 21 EHRR 342, at paras 44–47, and the emphasis on the specialist nature of planning in *Alconbury*). Accordingly, specialists' decisions as to whether a licence holder has sufficient skills may well be treated differently from broad judgments as to a licence holder's character.

However, the emphasis apparently placed by Lord Hoffmann on the need for more extensive review where there are disputed questions of primary fact has come to have less importance in the light of Lord Hoffmann's own remarks in the later case of *Qazi*. In that case Lord Hoffmann said that his comments in *Alconbury* may have been 'incautious'. The importance of the fact finding mechanisms in *Bryan* v *UK* were explained by the fact that there was a possibility of criminal proceedings arising out of the findings made in an enforcement inquiry, and that factual findings made in the earlier proceedings would not be open to challenge in those later criminal proceedings. In the absence of such special circumstances it seems that a limited review may well suffice for Article 6 purposes even where issues of primary fact fall to be determined by the decision-making body.

Whether or not more is needed will now depend on whether the case is one in which the decision-making is acting in the 'classic area of an administrative discretion'. Little guidance is offered in *Runa Begum* as to how to recognize such cases but Lord Hoffmann makes clear that deference or a margin or appreciaton should be allowed to take account of the extent to which national traditions as to which areas are to be allotted to such administrative discretion will vary, and the courts will be 'slow to conclude that Parliament has produced an administrative scheme which does not comply with constitutional principles'. In practice, therefore, it is now unlikely that there would be found to be a breach of Article 6 in a licensing case because judicial review is likely to be enough to satisfy the requirements of Article 6.

Also emphasized in *Begum* as relevant in determining whether the limited scope of supervisory review will suffice is whether there is a genuine justification for a limited review such as the interests of administrative expediency (see *Zumbotel* v *Austria* (1994) 17 EHRR 116, at para. 32, 'regard being had to the respect which must be accorded to decisions taken by administrative authorities on grounds of expedience').

A case which does not fit neatly in with the approach set out in *Alconbury, Begum* and *Adlard* is *Kingsley* v *UK* (2001) 33 EHHR 13, in which the failure to give reasons for a revocation decision was specifically identified as a factor compounding the lack of a fair hearing in the context of the revocation of a licence by the Gaming Board (para. 37). There was also an issue of perceived bias before the gaming board which gave rise to a potentially important additional factor in determining whether the scope of judicial review would be adequate. In *Kingsley*, the reviewing High Court was unable to remit the quashed decision to an impartial body. *Kingsley* suggests that if there is only one relevant licensing authority, which is itself tainted by a specific defect, such as having predetermined the licensing application, the availability of judicial review providing the remedy of quashing the decision and remitting it for a fresh decision by the same (tainted) tribunal, cannot comply with Article 6. Nevertheless, *Kinglsley* was relied upon by Lord Hoffmann himself as supporting his conclusions in *Begum* and it is unlikely that it will lead to any substantial departure from that approach.

The requirements of Article 6 (see more generally Chapter 2 at 2.5):

(a)   contrast with the limited approach to bias adopted in *R* v *Reading Borough Council, ex parte Quietlynn Ltd* (1987) 85 LGR 387 (a councillor sitting on a licensing panel for sex establishments when he was well-known for publicly expressing opposition to such establishments), in which Kennedy J held that the more onerous test for judicial bias did not apply to licensing bodies; and

(b)   add considerable weight to the requirements of natural justice (to inform the applicant for a licence of the substance of any objections or representations made against him or her, and to give him or her the opportunity to reply, see *R* v *Huntingdon District Council, ex parte Cowan* [1984] 1 WLR 501).

It is also conceivable that third parties to licensing determinations may demand participatory rights in proceedings by reference to Article 6 ECHR, but they are likely to face difficulty in demonstrating that the impact of the licensing decision amounts to a determination of their civil rights.

In *Balmer-Schafroth* v *Switzerland* (1997) 25 EHRR 598, the Commission upheld the Article 6(1) rights of applicants who lived within five kilometres of a nuclear power station, to participate in the licensing application. The case turned on whether the grant of the licence to the power station constituted a determination of the applicants' rights. The Commission considered that it did, and held that Article 6 applied and had been breached. However, the European Court, while acknowledging the existence of the neighbours' right to protection of their physical integrity, held that the threat to that physical integrity posed by the power station had not been established with a sufficient degree of probability to make the outcome of the licensing procedures directly determinative of the applicants' civil rights (para. 40).

However, where the link between the licensed activity and the claimant is more immediate and causation can be established, third parties may well be able to claim that their civil rights have been determined by the licensing decision. See, by way of analogy, the case of *Lopez Ostra* v *Spain* (1995) 20 EHRR 277, where the European Court held that an individual's right to a home was violated by a clear and significant risk to health caused by a polluting factory. Although Article 6 was not pleaded in that case, *Lopez Ostra* v *Spain* demonstrates that the licensed activities can have a profound impact on the lives of others. In such cases, those affected may well be able to demand a right to participate in the licensing proceedings. A parallel issue has been canvassed in respect of planning decisions with cases such as *R* v *Secretary of State, ex parte Friends Provident* [2002] 1 WLR 1450, at paras 61–69 where it was held that a third party objector's civil rights were affected by the planning decision at issue (permission for a large retail centre which would adversely affect the claimant's commercial interests). By contrast, in *Adlard* (at first instance before Collins J [2002] NPC 10, at paras 19–21), it is made clear that not every case concerning an objector to a planning application will engage the objector's Article 6 rights.

Although concerned with liquor licensing, which is not regulated by local authorities, an analogy may be drawn with *R* v *Newcastle Licensing Justices, ex parte Bushell* [2003] EWHC 1937. In that case Owen J found that third-party objectors to a licensing decision could have their civil rights determined by the transfer of an old on-licence to their area under ss. 12 and 15 of the Licensing Act 1964 (because Article 8 was engaged by the effect on the objector's enjoyment of their homes). These provisions limit the power of licensing justices to refuse such a transfer and it was argued that there was accordingly a breach of Article 6. This was rejected on the basis that the availability of other means by which the claimants and others could control the activitiy in question, by bringing proceedings in nuisance or by applying for a revocation of the licence, meant that any restriction on the right to a fair trial was proportionate.

In a number of licensing contexts, carrying out the relevant activity without a licence, or in breach of the licence (or any conditions imposed), can lead to criminal prosecution. Article 6(1) is of relevance to any criminal charge, and a number of more stringent protections are applied (see Chapter 2). Nevertheless, other Articles may come into play in the licensing enforcement context. Thus, in *Westminster City Council* v *Blenheim Leisure (Restaurants) Ltd* (1999) JP 163, the Divisional Court was considering whether knowledge was required by a licence holder for him to be liable for the offence of providing public entertainment in breach of licence conditions. One of the conditions to the licence (rule 9) required the licensee to maintain good order on the premises. Brooke LJ commented:

> The council would do well, in my judgment, to tighten up the language of Rule 9 if it wishes to be able to use it to prohibit activities like these on licensed premises after the Human Rights Act 1998 comes into force. The extension of the very vague concept of the maintenance of good order to the control of the activities of prostitutes may have passed muster in the days when English common law offences did not receive critical scrutiny from national judicial guardians of a rights-based jurisprudence, but those days will soon be over. English judges will then be applying a Human Rights Convention which has the effect of prescribing that a criminal offence must be clearly defined in law. I do not accept [Counsel's] submission that it is impossible to define the kind of conduct his clients desire to prohibit with greater precision, or that it is satisfactory to leave it to individual magistrates to decide, assisted only by some fairly arcane case law, whether or not activities of the type of which the Council complains in this case amount to a breach of good order so as to render the licensees liable to criminal penalties.
>
> These matters are, however, for the future.

His Lordship's warning is in line with the decision of the European Court of Human Rights in *Hashman and Harrup* v *UK* (1999) 30 EHRR 241, where it found that an order by a magistrates' court binding over a person to keep the peace and not to behave *contra bonos mores* was a breach of Article 10 ECHR. In particular, the concept of being bound over to keep the peace and not to behave *contra bonos mores* was found to be so vague as not to be prescribed by law in Convention terms (see further Chapter Two). The European Court did not go on to consider the further alleged breaches of Articles 5 (right to liberty and security) and 11 (freedom of assembly and association). This case may also provide room to argue that Article 6 has been breached. Colin Manchester, *Entertainment Licensing Law and Practice* (HLT Publications/Old Bailey Press), at para. 1.09, also suggests (somewhat surprisingly) that Article 7 ECHR (no punishment without law) issues may also be raised.

12.4   ARTICLE 1 OF PROTOCOL 1: PROTECTION OF PROPERTY

Article 1 of Protocol 1 states:

> Every natural or legal person is entitled to the peaceful enjoyment of his possessions. No one shall be deprived of his possessions except in the public interest and subject to the conditions provided for by law and by the general principles of international law.
>
> The preceding provisions shall not, however, in any way impair the right of a State to enforce such laws as it deems necessary to control the use of property in accordance with the general interest or to secure the payment of taxes or other contributions or penalties.

The European Court of Human Rights' analysis of Article 1 of Protocol 1 is that it in fact consists of three distinct rules:

(a)   the general principle of peaceful enjoyment of property;
(b)   that the deprivation of property should be governed by the stated conditions; and
(c)   that states are entitled to control the use of property.

It is necessary to consider (b) and (c) before considering whether (a) has been complied with (see *Sporrong and Lönnroth* v *Sweden* (1982) 5 EHRR 35).

The range of property which is potentially protected by Article 1 of Protocol 1 is wide and encompasses most licences. For example, in *Tre Traktörer Atkiebolag* v *Sweden* (1989) 13 EHRR 309, the withdrawal of an alcohol licence from a restaurant was held to amount to a property right which was capable of being so protected.

That said, there are limitations to what is capable of amounting to an interference with property rights within the ambit of Article 1 of Protocol 1. One important limitation is that Article 1 of Protocol 1 only protects property which has already been acquired; it does not give an individual a right to possessions which he or she does not have (see *Marckx* v *Belgium* (1979) 2 EHRR 330). There may be cases where an individual has a legitimate expectation that a licence will be granted and this may constitute as a possession (see *Pine Valley Developments Ltd v Ireland* (1991) 12 EHRR 319. In the Scottish case of *Catscratch Ltd v Glasgow Licensing Board*, 4 June 2001 Lord Johnston accepted that in certain circumstances it may be impossible to distinguish a failure to extend a licence from the removal of a licence (see also *Quark Fishing Ltd v Secretary of State for Foreign and Commonwealth Affairs* [2003] ACD 96. Another limitation is that changes to the conditions under which a licence operates may well not amount to a prima facie interference with Article 1 of Protocol 1 rights — see *Royden v Wirral* [2003] BLGR 290, in which Sir Christopher Bellamy QC, sitting as a Deputy High Court Judge, held that there was no interference with property rights capable of amounting to a breach of Article 1 of Protocol 1 where restrictions on the number of hackney carriage vehicle licences were lifted, to the financial detriment of an existing licence holder, as it could not be said that the claimant had a legitimate expectation that a policy of restricting the number of hackney carriage vehicles licenced in the area would continue indefinitely (see judgment at para. 135).

While the European Court has been willing to cast the net fairly widely in its definition of 'possessions' for the purpose of engaging Article 1 of Protocol 1, it is more difficult to establish that there has been an unjustified interference with or deprivation of that right. The court will focus on whether the interference or control used reflects a fair balance between the needs of the community and the rights of the individual affected, such that there is a reasonable relationship of proportionality between the means of interference with property rights and the aim pursued (*Mellacher v Austria* (1989) 12 EHRR 291, at para. 48; *Chassagnou and others v France* (1999) 7 BHRC 151, at para. 75).

It may be thought, therefore, that the effect of this approach would be to require licensing authorities to give robust and sound justifications for the revoking of licences, in line with the approach to proportionality enunciated in cases such as *R v Secretary of State for the Home Department, ex parte Daly* [2001] 2 AC 532. There is, however, a need for caution. The approach to proportionality, and the need for deference to Parliament and decision-makers, varies considerably between different articles of the Convention and according to the factual context of particular cases. Article 1 of Protocol 1 is one of those articles in which the courts will be least likely to interfere (see *James v UK* (1986) 8 EHRR 123 for the classic exposition of the proportionality test as applied in Article 1 of Protocol 1). It is doubtful that the approach to proportionality under Article 1 of Protocol 1 differs substantially from the old domestic *Wednesbury* approach (in *James* it was said that the court would need to consider whether the measures were 'manifestly without reasonable foundation').

In any event, the intensity of scrutiny is considerably blunted where the court considers that what lies behind the decision is policy considerations of a social, economic or political nature. If the court considers that such considerations underpin the decision under challenge they will emphasize that the fair balance test is not a recipe for review of the merits of the decision (see *R* v *Sameroo* [2001] UKHRR 1622, at paras 26–36; *R* v *Secretary of State for the Home Department, ex parte Farrakhan* [2002] EWCA Civ 606, at para. 67; *Royden* v *Wirral*, [2003] BLGR 290).

12.5 OTHER CONVENTION RIGHTS: EXAMPLES AND ISSUE SPOTTING

12.5.1 Article 14: non-discrimination

Article 14 ECHR prohibits discrimination on the grounds of sex, race, colour, language, religion, political opinion, national or social origin, association with a national minority, property, birth, or other status. It has no free-standing existence (*Belgian Linguistic (No. 1)* (1968) 1 EHRR 252) but applies to unequal treatment in the exercise of other Convention rights. Importantly, it is not necessary for there to have been a violation of the substantive Convention right for there to have been a violation of Article 14. Therefore, Article 14 will be important across the range of licensing. It can be relied upon whenever Article 1 of Protocol 1 is engaged, and the establishment of unequal treatment within the scope of Article 14 ECHR may found a violation of that Article even when (say) the revocation of a licence can be justified for the purposes of Article 1 of Protocol 1.

12.5.2 Article 8

The wide protection given to private life and home life may well be highly significant in a numbering of licensing contexts. For example, the licensing of late night activity (such as under the Late Night Refreshment Homes Act 1982) could interfere with neighbours' rights to enjoy home life (see, by analogy, noise nuisance caused by aircraft (*Rayner* v *UK* (1986) 47 DR 5). In *R* v *Newcastle Licensing Justices, ex parte Bushell* [2003] EWHC 1937, Owen J was satisfied that there could be an interference with the claimant's Article 8 rights because it could lead to an increase in 'unacceptable . . . loutish and drunken behaviour' in and about their homes. The availability of other remedies, however, meant that there was no breach of the claimant's human rights from the fact that there was only a limited review of the transfer of old on-licences by the licensing justices under ss. 12 and 15 of the Licensing Act 1964 (it was not said that Article 8 was itself breached, rather that because it was engaged there was a breach of Article 6).

Conversely, where a licensing body has enforcement powers to take action against unlicensed activity, it is possible that its failure to act could in itself amount to an interference with a person's right to home life (see *Lopez Ostra* v *Spain* (1994) 20 EHRR 277).

Further, the European Court has accepted, in *Niemietz* v *Germany* (1992) 16 EHRR 97, that the boundary between private life and professional life is not absolute. Excessive interference by, say, a market authority, in imposing conditions, could conceivably affect an individual's right to a private life.

12.5.3   Article 10

Decisions of licensing authorities in the regulation of cinemas, theatres, public entertainment, and sex shops, may well raise issues about whether any interference with freedom of expression is justified.

12.6   CONCLUSION

It is possible that in certain cases, the HRA 1998 will led to closer scrutiny of licensing bodies where they are required to justify their decisions under Article 1 of Protocol 1. The issue of whether or not the appeal system complies with Article 6 ECHR may well be of importance in a number of cases and the jurisprudence on this point is still evolving. Depending on the context, the other substantive Articles of the Convention may have some impact in increasing the intensity of judicial review of the decisions of licensing bodies.

Chapter Thirteen

Rating and the Council Tax

Timothy Mould

13.1 TAXATION AND ARTICLE 1 OF PROTOCOL 1

Both the non-domestic rate and the council tax are essentially taxes payable by the occupiers or owners of units of real property. In each case, the tax payable is ordinarily assessed by reference to the value of the unit of property, estimated in accordance with rules prescribed by the relevant Local Government Finance Act. Part III of the Local Government Finance Act 1988 provides for the non-domestic rate; Part I of the Local Government Finance Act 1992 provides for the council tax. In each case, the statutory scheme is to be found not only in the primary legislation, but also in a series of supporting statutory instruments.

Article 1 of Protocol 1 (protection of property) provides:

> Every natural or legal person is entitled to the peaceful enjoyment of his possessions. No one shall be deprived of his possessions except in the public interest and subject to the conditions provided for by law and by the general principles of international law.
>
> The preceding provisions shall not, however, in any way impair the right of a State to enforce such laws as it deems necessary to control the use of property in accordance with the general interest or to secure the payment of taxes or other contributions or penalties.

In *Gasus-Dosier-und Fordertechnik GmbH* v *Netherlands* (1995) 20 EHRR 403, the European Court of Human Rights held (at para. 55) that this Article comprises three distinct rules. The first, which is expressed in the first sentence of the first paragraph and is of a general nature, lays down the principle of peaceful enjoyment of property. The second, in the second sentence of the same paragraph, covers deprivation of possessions and makes it subject to certain conditions. The third, contained in the second paragraph, recognizes that the contracting states are entitled to control the use of property in accordance with the general interest, or to secure the payment of taxes or other contributions or penalties. The three rules are connected. The second and third rules are concerned with particular instances of interference with the right to peaceful enjoyment of property. They should therefore be construed in the light of the general principle enunciated in the first rule.

The European Court went on to consider the effect of the third rule on contracting states' domestic tax legislation. It said (at para. 59):

[The second paragraph of the Article] explicitly reserves the right of Contracting States to pass such laws as they may deem necessary to secure the payment of taxes. The importance which the drafters of the Convention attached to this aspect of the second paragraph of Article 1 may be gauged from the fact that at a stage when the proposed text did not contain such explicit reference to taxes, it was already understood to reserve the State's power to pass whatever fiscal laws they considered desirable, provided always that measures in this field did not amount to arbitrary confiscation.

In passing such laws, therefore, contracting states must be allowed a wide margin of appreciation, and the European Court has stated its willingness to respect the legislature's assessment of matters such as measures to enforce the payment of tax unless they are shown to be 'devoid of reasonable foundation' (at para. 60).

Nevertheless, the European Court in *Gasus-Dosier* reiterated that, in considering whether any particular taxation measure was reasonably founded, there must be a reasonable relationship of proportionality between the means employed and the aim pursued. In other words, the interference with the person's property must achieve a fair balance between the demands of the general interest of the community (i.e. in levying and securing payment of tax revenue judged by the contracting state to be required in order to meet the demands for public expenditure) and the requirement to protect the individual's property rights. In the instant case, the complaint was that domestic tax legislation which enabled the tax authorities to enjoy preferential status over other commercial creditors of the tax debtor, was disproportionate to the statutory objective of securing the payment of tax in the public interest. Having reviewed the circumstances of the case, the European Court held that the requirement of proportionality had been satisfied.

In *Gasus-Dosier*, the European Court was careful to point out that it was unnecessary in the circumstances of that case to determine whether the second paragraph of Article 1 of Protocol 1 extended not only to procedural tax laws (i.e. laws which regulate the formalities of taxation, including the enforcement of tax debts), but also to substantive tax laws (i.e. laws which lay down the circumstances under which tax is due and the amounts payable). Any doubts over that point appear to have been resolved by the European Court's decision in *National and Provincial Building Society and others* v *UK* (1997) 25 EHRR 127. That case concerned domestic legislation of retrospective effect, the purpose of which was to close a 'gap' in the tax liability on interest paid by the applicant building societies, which had arisen due to the avoidance of certain transitional Regulations following a judicial review. The building societies claimed that the retrospective legislation breached Article 1 of Protocol 1. Referring to *Gasus-Dosier*, the European Court said (at para. 80):

> According to the Court's well-established case law, an interference, including one resulting from a measure to secure the payment of taxes, must strike a 'fair balance' between the demands of the general interest of the community and the requirements of the protection of the individual's fundamental rights. The concern to achieve this balance is reflected in the structure of Article 1 as a whole, including the second paragraph: there must therefore be a reasonable relationship of proportionality between the means employed and the aims pursued.
>
> Furthermore, in determining whether this requirement has been met, it is recognised that a Contracting State, not least when framing and implementing policies in the area of taxation, enjoys a wide margin of appreciation and the Court will respect the legislature's assessment in such matters unless it is devoid of reasonable foundation.

The Court went on to find that the actions taken by the United Kingdom in promoting the retrospective legislation to 'close the gap' did not upset the balance to be struck between the individual's right to protection of his property and the public interest in securing the payment of taxes.

These cases, therefore, confirm the wide margin of appreciation which contracting states enjoy in the field of tax legislation and policy. It is reasonable to assume that the domestic courts will adopt the same cautious approach in relation to cases brought under the HRA 1998 in the field of tax, including local taxation under the non-domestic rating and council tax regime. Such an approach would also be consistent with the courts' unwillingness to review decisions in the field of fiscal policy under domestic law (see, e.g., *R v Environment Secretary, ex parte Hammersmith and Fulham London Borough Council* [1991] 1 AC 521). It is reflected in *Edison First Power Ltd v Secretary of State for the Environment, Transport and the Regions* [2003] 4 All ER 209, in which the House of Lords rejected the submission that the special rules for determining the rateable value of centrally listed electricity generators were intrinsically confiscatory, discriminatory, unfair, and irrational, and so contrary to Article 1 of Protocol 1. See also *R v Valuation Office Agency, ex parte Corus UK Ltd* [2002] RA 1, in which the High Court rejected the submission that the valuation officer's decision to make a retrospective alteration to the rating list, resulting in a substantial increase in the ratepayer's liability to non-domestic rates, was in breach of Article 1 of Protocol 1 and Article 14. Those decisions of the European Court which are of relevance to the non-domestic rating and council tax regimes, indicate that the benefit of incorporation in this field is likely to be felt by those individuals who are looking to reinforce procedural safeguards in the course of enforcement proceedings. Apart from Article 1 of Protocol 1, the relevant Convention rights are likely to be

Articles 5 (right to liberty and security), 6 (right to a fair trial), and 14 (prohibition on discrimination).

13.2 LIABILITY TO PAY RATES OR THE COUNCIL TAX

As has already been noted (at 13.1), the European Court of Human Rights recognizes a wide margin of appreciation for contracting states in relation to tax policy and legislation. It is a common feature of systems of taxation that the overall tax burden falls differentially upon individual taxpayers and groups of taxpayers. It is also common for domestic tax systems to exempt certain persons or groups of persons from liability, or alternatively to relieve other persons or groups of persons from liability in part. Such matters are primarily political questions based upon each contracting state's assessment of what is appropriate having regard to the economic and social issues involved. The fate of the community charge or 'poll tax' legislation in the United Kingdom in the late 1980s and early 1990s is illustrative of the political controversy generated by an attempt to replace the traditional rating model, i.e. liability based upon the value of each unit of property (or hereditament) occupied by the taxpayer, with a standard rate tax falling equally on the majority of taxpayers. There is unlikely to be great scope, therefore, for impugning the validity of the basic legal framework of either the non-domestic rate or the council tax by reference to Article 1 of Protocol 1 (*Edison First Power Ltd*; see 13.1).

There may, however, be scope for challenging aspects of the legal framework of liability, exemption and relief in relation to the non-domestic rate or the council tax, even within the limited scope of 'arbitrariness' on the part of the contracting state (*Gasus-Dosier*; see 13.1). In particular, issues may arise under Article 14 ECHR when taken together with Article 1 of Protocol 1 (see *Darby* v *Sweden* (1991) 13 EHRR 774). In that case, the taxpayer, who was not a registered Swedish resident, became liable to pay a special tax under Swedish law, the proceeds of which were intended to finance the Church of Sweden. The applicant taxpayer had no connection with that church. At the same time, registered Swedish residents who, like the applicant, were non-members of the same church, were exempted from paying the church tax. The European Court said (at para. 31):

> Article 14 protects individuals placed in similar situations from discrimination in their enjoyment of their rights under the Convention and its Protocols. However, a difference in the treatment of one of these individuals will only be discriminatory if it 'has no objective and reasonable justification', that is if it does not pursue a 'legitimate aim' and if there is no 'reasonable relationship of proportionality between the means employed and the aim sought to be realised'.

The European Court went on to find a violation of both Article 14 ECHR and Article 1 of Protocol 1, because the difference in treatment of the applicant taxpayer under Swedish law simply on the ground of his being non-resident had no legitimate aim under the Convention (see para. 34).

It is possible that the English courts may entertain similar challenges founded upon Article 14 ECHR and Article 1 of Protocol 1 in relation to liability to the non-domestic rate or council tax. By way of example, para. 16 of Sch. 5 to the Local Government Finance Act 1988, exempts the occupiers of certain categories of property used for the disabled from liability to non-domestic rates. The courts have found it difficult to understand the underlying logic to the dividing line established by the statute between liability to and exemption from rates in relation to such property. In *Evans* v *Suffolk County Council* [1997] RA 120, the President of the Lands Tribunal, ruling that certain short-stay residential accommodation for the disabled was not exempted from liability to non-domestic rates, said:

> I derive no satisfaction from this outcome. Insofar as it seems to have been the intention of Parliament to relieve from the burden of rates those facilities provided by local authorities for the care and welfare of the elderly disabled and handicapped, a common sense approach would treat Mills Meadow as such a facility, owned and operated by the Social Services Department of the council wholly for the purpose of providing for the needs of such people.
>
> However, the tribunal's task is to interpret and to act in accordance with the meaning of the legislation. In *Vandyk* v *Oliver* Lord Wilberforce said of the predecessor of the present provisions (s. 45 of the General Rates Act 1967) at p. 11:
>
> > In *Almond* v *Birmingham Corporation* Lord Reid found himself quite unable to understand the scope of section 45 and the Lands Tribunal, both in the present case and other cases, has forcefully pointed out the very great difficulties for normal minds which this complicated legislation produces. If the scope of section 45 is to be extended far beyond local authorities and charities to many thousands of citizens, many of them ill or handicapped, or if the contrary is the case, Parliament really ought to make its dispositions intelligible. I would hope too that it might make them fair and rational.
>
> I do not think the enactment of Schedule 5 to the 1988 Act and paragraph 16 of that schedule in particular, has materially improved the situation from what it was at the time of Lord Wilberforce's comments. The dispositions of Parliament are still scarcely intelligible, nor does it seem to me that they are any more fair or rational. The division which now exists between domestic property subject to the council tax, and non domestic property subject to rating, has if anything further complicated the situation. I doubt whether Lord Wilberforce or the late Lord Reid would take a more favourable view today.

Ratepayers and council tax payers whose circumstances place them near the boundary between liability and exemption or relief may, therefore, wish to consider carefully whether that boundary is one which appears arbitrary; and, if so, to investigate whether any legitimate aim in taxation policy is discernible for drawing it at that point.

13.3 ENFORCEMENT OF PAYMENT OF RATES AND COUNCIL TAX

In relation to both non-domestic rating and the council tax, a detailed regime for the collection and enforcement of payment of the tax due is to be found in subordinate legislation (see the Non-Domestic Rating (Collection and Enforcement) (Local Lists) Regulations 1989 (SI 1989/1058) and the Council Tax (Administration and Enforcement) Regulations 1992 (SI 1992/613)). In the case of each system of taxation, the Regulations provide that measures taken to enforce non-payment shall be preceded by formal demands for the sums due and a formal finding of liability (a 'liability order') made (on the application of the billing authority) by a magistrates' court. In the case of non-domestic rates, the principal enforcement measure is the levying of distress against the tax debtor's goods. The Regulations provide a detailed procedural regime for the levying of distress, with procedural safeguards by way of an appeal to the magistrates' court in order to secure compliance with that regime by the distraining authority. In the case of the council tax, enforcement may be by way of an attachment of earnings order in the case of a tax debtor in employment. Again, the Regulations provide in detail for the operation of such an order by the billing authority, including the stipulation of limits on the amount which may be deducted by reference to the tax debtor's wage. Distress is also available to enforce payment of the council tax, subject to procedural safeguards which reflect those which apply in relation to the non-domestic rate (above). In the case of an individual, both enforcement regimes provide for commitment of the tax debtor to prison as a last resort in order to secure payment of outstanding amounts of rates or council tax. The billing authority must apply to the magistrates' court. The justices may issue a warrant of commitment only if satisfied that the individual debtor's failure to pay results from his or her wilful refusal or culpable neglect. The House of Lords has confirmed the essentially coercive nature of the remedy (see *Re Smith (a bankrupt)* [1990] 2 AC 215). Where, however, a warrant of commitment has been issued and a suspended term of imprisonment set, and yet the debtor has failed to pay, the justices may properly commit the debtor for punishment in order to maintain the effectiveness of the coercive regime (see *R* v *Cannock Justices, ex parte Ireland* [1996] RA 463, CA).

It is unlikely that the measures available to billing authorities under the relevant Regulations to enforce payment of non-domestic rates and council tax will themselves be found by the courts to be incompatible with the relevant Convention rights. The seizure of property in order to secure payment of taxes is, in principle, compatible with Article 1 of Protocol 1 (and see *Gasus-Dosier* at 13.1). The European Court has considered the regime of commitment to prison for failure to pay (in the context of the community charge or 'poll tax') in *Benham* v *UK* (1995) 22 EHRR 293 and *Perks* v *UK* [2000] RA 487. In both cases, the Court accepted that the regime accorded with Article 5 ECHR, in particular:

1. ... No one shall be deprived of his liberty save in the following cases and in accordance with a procedure prescribed by law:

...

(b) the lawful arrest or detention of a person for non-compliance with the lawful order of a court or in order to secure the fulfilment of any obligation prescribed by law; ...

In both cases, the High Court had quashed decisions by justices to commit to prison. The justices' decisions had been quashed for failing properly to operate the statutory procedure for commitment and for failing properly to consider alternative methods of enforcing payment of the arrears. The claimants argued that their rights under Article 5 ECHR had been breached because the justices had exceeded their jurisdiction and acted arbitrarily. They claimed compensation. The European Court rejected the claims under Article 5: although the justices had erred in domestic law, those errors were within jurisdiction and involved no violation of Article 5(1)(b) (see *Benham*, at paras 40–43 and 46–47; *Perks* at 511–13). In *Perks*, the Court said (at 514):

As regards the allegation that the applicants' detention could not be justified under Article 5 paragraph 1(b) of the Convention, the court notes that a similar argument was implicitly rejected in the *Benham* case. The court accepts that the purpose of the detention orders in the present applications was to secure the fulfilment of the applicants' obligations to pay the community charge owed by them and were, thus, compatible with the objectives of Article 5 paragraph 1(b).

Applicants who are aggrieved by enforcement action taken against them by billing authorities under the Regulations are more likely to focus on the proportionality of the authority's action in the circumstances of the given case. *Gasus-Dosier* illustrates this approach in the context of the seizure of property and the possible violation of Article 1 of Protocol 1. In so doing, there will be opportunities at least to reinforce and possibly to extend the scope or intensity of review of the actions of the billing authority in the given case, whether by the magistrates' courts under the Regulations, or by the higher courts on application by way of case stated or judicial review. There may also be the opportunity to recover compensation in a case where the enforcement action taken is proven to have been so disproportionate as to have violated the taxpayer's Convention rights. Where Article 5 rights are engaged (as in the case of commitment to prison), the HRA 1998 vouchsafes the right to claim damages in respect of the acts of the justices, at least to the extent that such acts may attract compensation under Article 5(5) (see s. 9(3) of the HRA 1998). Entitlement to Article 5(5) compensation depends upon proving a violation of Article 5 (see *Perks* (above), at 515). Note, in this context, that the Court in *Benham* and *Perks* left open the possibility of a violation of Article 5 on the grounds of bad faith or arbitrariness on the part of the justices, albeit that their decision is formally in accordance with the statutory procedures (see *Perks*, at 515).

Domestic law treats court action by billing authorities to enforce the payment of rates and council tax as civil litigation, i.e. matters falling within the civil jurisdiction of magistrates' courts. The European Court has held that proceedings on an application to commit an individual to prison for failure to pay a local tax are criminal in nature for the purposes of Article 6 ECHR (see *Benham* (above), at paras 54–56). Any proceedings for commitment will, therefore, merit careful scrutiny to see whether the requirements of Article 6 have been complied with. In most cases, there is likely to be compliance by virtue of the billing authority and the magistrates' court following the procedures established by the Regulations and case law. In the *Benham* and *Perks* cases, the basis for the finding of a violation of Article 6 was the lack of any right to free legal representation in contravention of Article 6(3)(c). That omission has since been cured by extending the availability of legal advice and assistance to commitment proceedings. Nevertheless, there may be cases where the Article 6 rights provide additional safeguards to the debtor. The principles in domestic law upon which the High Court has reviewed a decision of magistrates to commit a tax debtor to prison are stated in *R v Thanet District Council, ex parte Haddow* [1992] RA 245, at 250:

> So before we can interfere with the justices' decision, it has to be demonstrated that the decision was astonishing or so widely disproportionate that no reasonable bench of justices could arrive at it. In other words, the real question here is that of *Wednesbury* reasonableness.

The question will now arise as to whether the decision of the magistrates is a proportionate response in the circumstances of the case. The issue of proportionality may raise new issues beyond the question of reasonableness (see *R v Secretary of State for the Home Department, ex parte Daly* [2001] 2 WLR 1622, HL, at 1634–1636. This may require the Court to engage in a more intensive review of proceedings before the justices and of the terms of the warrant. For example, under domestic law the justices may lawfully activate a suspended warrant of commitment to prison in the absence of the debtor, provided that they are satisfied that he or she has received proper notice of the relevant hearing date and that it is reasonable to proceed in his absence (see *R v Newcastle Justices, ex parte Devine* [1998] RA 97; *R v Erewash Borough Council, ex parte Smedbury* [1994] RVR 60). It being open to the justices in any case to enforce the debtor's attendance by issuing a warrant for his or her arrest, the issue will now arise whether a decision to proceed in his or her absence is out of proportion to the circumstances and so violates the debtor's right under Articles 5 and 6 of the Convention.

Appendix One

Human Rights Act 1998

CHAPTER 42

ARRANGEMENT OF SECTIONS

HUMAN RIGHTS ACT 1998

1998 CHAPTER 42

An Act to give further effect to rights and freedoms guaranteed under the European Convention on Human Rights; to make provision with respect to holders of certain judicial offices who become judges of the European Court of Human Rights; and for connected purposes. [9th November 1998]

BE IT ENACTED by the Queen's most Excellent Majesty, by and with the advice and consent of the Lords Spiritual and Temporal, and Commons, in this present Parliament assembled, and by the authority of the same, as follows:—

Introduction

1. The Convention Rights

(1) In this Act 'the Convention rights' means the rights and fundamental freedoms set out in—

    (a)   Articles 2 to 12 and 14 of the Convention,

    (b)   Articles 1 to 3 of the First Protocol, and

    (c)   Articles 1 and 2 of the Sixth Protocol,

as read with Articles 16 to 18 of the Convention.

(2) Those Articles are to have effect for the purposes of this Act subject to any designated derogation or reservation (as to which see sections 14 and 15),

(3) The Articles are set out in Schedule 1.

(4) The [Lord Chancellor] may by order make such amendments to this Act as he considers appropriate to reflect the effect, in relation to the United Kingdom, of a protocol.

(5) In subsection (4) 'protocol' means a protocol to the Convention—

    (a)   which the United Kingdom has ratified; or

    (b)   which the United Kingdom has signed with a view to ratification.

(6) No amendment may be made by an order under subsection (4) so as to come into force before the protocol concerned is in force in relation to the United Kingdom.

2. Interpretation of Convention rights

(1) A court or tribunal determining a question which has arisen in connection with a Convention right must take into account any—

    (a)   judgment, decision, declaration or advisory opinion of the European Court of Human Rights,

    (b)   opinion of the Commission given in a report adopted under Article 31 of the Convention,

(c)   decision of the Commission in connection with Article 26 or 27(2) of the Convention, or

(d)   decision of the Committee of Ministers taken under Article 46 of the Convention,

whenever made or given, so far as, in the opinion of the court or tribunal, it is relevant to the proceedings in which that question has arisen.

(2)   Evidence of any judgment, decision, declaration or opinion of which account may have to be taken under this section is to be given in proceedings before any court or tribunal in such manner as may be provided by rules.

(3)   In this section 'rules' means rules of court or, in the case of proceedings before a tribunal, rules made for the purposes of this section—

(a)   by the Lord Chancellor or the Secretary of State, in relation to any proceedings outside Scotland:

(b)   by the Secretary of State, in relation to proceedings in Scotland; or

(c)   by a Northern Ireland department, in relation to proceedings before a tribunal in Northern Ireland—

(i)   which deals with transferred matters; and

(ii)   for which no rules made under paragraph (a) are in force.

Legislation

3.   Interpretation of legislation

(1)   So far as it is possible to do so, primary legislation and subordinate legislation must be read and given effect in a way which is compatible with the Convention rights.

(2)   This section—

(a)   applies to primary legislation and subordinate legislation whenever enacted;

(b)   does not affect the validity, continuing operation or enforcement of any incompatible primary legislation; and

(c)   does not affect the validity, continuing operation or enforcement of any incompatible subordinate legislation if (disregarding any possibility of revocation) primary legislation prevents removal of the incompatibility.

4.   Declaration of incompatibility

(1)   Subsection (2) applies in any proceedings in which a court determines whether a provision of primary legislation is compatible with a Convention right.

(2)   If the court is satisfied that the provision is incompatible with a Convention right, it may make a declaration of that incompatibility.

(3)   Subsection (4) applies in any proceedings in which a court determines whether a provision of subordinate legislation, made in the exercise of a power conferred by primary legislation, is compatible with a Convention right.

(4) If the court is satisfied—

(a) that the provision is incompatible with a Convention right, and

(b) that (disregarding any possibility of revocation) the primary legislation concerned prevents removal of the incompatibility,

it may make a declaration of that incompatibility.

(5) In this section 'court' means—

(a) the House of Lords;

(b) the Judicial Committee of the Privy Council;

(c) the Courts-Martial Appeal Court;

(d) in Scotland, the High Court of Justiciary sitting otherwise than as a trial court or the Court of Session;

(e) in England and Wales or Northern Ireland, the High Court or the Court of Appeal.

(6) A declaration under this section ('a declaration of incompatibility')—

(a) does not affect the validity, continuing operation or enforcement of the provision in respect of which it is given; and

(b) is not binding on the parties to the proceedings in which it is made.

5. Right of Crown to intervene

(1) Where a court is considering whether to make a declaration of incompatibility, the Crown is entitled to notice in accordance with rules of court.

(2) In any case to which subsection (1) applies—

(a) a Minister of the Crown (or a person nominated by him),

(b) a member of the Scottish Executive,

(c) a Northern Ireland Minister,

(d) a Northern Ireland department,

is entitled, on giving notice in accordance with rules of court, to be joined as a party to the proceedings.

(3) Notice under subsection (2) may be given at any time during the proceedings.

(4) A person who has been made a party to criminal proceedings (other than in Scotland) as the result of a notice under subsection (2) may, with leave, appeal to the House of Lords against any declaration of incompatibility made in the proceedings.

(5) In subsection (4)—

'criminal proceedings' includes all proceedings before the Courts-Martial Appeal Court; and

'leave' means leave granted by the court making the declaration of incompatibility or by the House of Lords.

Public authorities

6. Acts of public authorities

(1)   It is unlawful for a public authority to act in a way which is incompatible with a Convention right.

(2)   Subsection (1) does not apply to an act if—

(a)   as the result of one or more provisions of primary legislation, the authority could not have acted differently; or

(b)   in the case of one or more provisions of, or made under, primary legislation which cannot be read or given effect in a way which is compatible with the Convention rights, the authority was acting so as to give effect to or enforce those provisions.

(3)   In this section 'public authority' includes—

(a)   a court or tribunal, and

(b)   any person certain of whose functions are functions of a public nature, but does not include either House of Parliament or a person exercising functions in connection with proceedings in Parliament.

(4)   In subsection (3) 'Parliament' does not include the House of Lords in its judicial capacity.

(5)   In relation to a particular act, a person is not a public authority by virtue only of subsection (3)(b) if the nature of the act is private.

(6)   'An act' includes a failure to act but does not include a failure to—

(a)   introduce in, or lay before, Parliament a proposal for legislation; or

(b)   make any primary legislation or remedial order.

7. Proceedings

(1)   A person who claims that a public authority has acted (or proposes to act) in a way which is made unlawful by section 6(1) may—

(a)   bring proceedings against the authority under this Act in the appropriate court or tribunal, or

(b)   rely on the Convention right or rights concerned in any legal proceedings.

but only if he is (or would be) a victim of the unlawful act.

(2)   In subsection (1)(a) 'appropriate court or tribunal' means such court or tribunal as may be determined in accordance with rules; and proceedings against an authority include a counterclaim or similar proceeding.

(3)   If the proceedings are brought on an application for judicial review, the applicant is to be taken to have a sufficient interest in relation to the unlawful act only if he is, or would be, a victim of that act.

(4)   If the proceedings are made by way of a petition for judicial review in Scotland, the applicant shall be taken to have title and interest to sue in relation to the unlawful act only if he is, or would be, a victim of that act.

(5) Proceedings under subsection (1)(a) must be brought before the end of—

(a) the period of one year beginning with the date on which the act complained of took place; or

(b) such longer period as the court or tribunal considers equitable having regard to all the circumstances,

but that is subject to any rule imposing a stricter time limit in relation to the procedure in question.

(6) In subsection (1)(b) 'legal proceedings' includes—

(a) proceedings brought by or at the instigation of a public authority; and

(b) an appeal against the decision of a court or tribunal.

(7) For the purposes of this section, a person is a victim of an unlawful act only if he would be a victim for the purposes of Article 34 of the Convention if proceedings were brought in the European Court of Human Rights in respect of that act.

(8) Nothing in this Act creates a criminal offence.

(9) In this section 'rules' means—

(a) in relation to proceedings before a court or tribunal outside Scotland, rules made by the Lord Chancellor or the Secretary of State for the purposes of this section or rules of court,

(b) in relation to proceedings before a court or tribunal in Scotland, rules made by the Secretary of State for those purposes,

(c) in relation to proceedings before a tribunal in Northern Ireland—

(i) which deals with transferred matters; and

(ii) for which no rules made under paragraph (a) are in force,

rules made by a Northern Ireland department for those purposes.

and includes provision made by order under section 1 of the Courts and Legal Services Act 1990.

(10) In making rules, regard must be had to section 9.

(11) The Minister who has power to make rules in relation to a particular tribunal may, to the extent he considers it necessary to ensure that the tribunal can provide an appropriate remedy in relation to an act (or proposed act) of a public authority which is (or would be) unlawful as a result of section 6(1), by order add to—

(a) the relief or remedies which the tribunal may grant; or

(b) the grounds on which it may grant any of them.

(12) An order made under subsection (11) may contain such incidental, supplemental, consequential or transitional provision as the Minister making it considers appropriate.

(13) 'The Minister' includes the Northern Ireland department concerned.

8. Judicial remedies

(1) In relation to any act (or proposed act) of a public authority which the court finds is (or would be) unlawful, it may grant such relief or remedy, or make such order, within its powers as it considers just and appropriate.

(2)   But damages may be awarded only by a court which has power to award damages, or to order the payment of compensation, in civil proceedings.

(3)   No award of damages is to be made unless, taking account of all the circumstances of the case, including—

(a)   any other relief or remedy granted, or order made, in relation to the act in question (by that or any other court), and

(b)   the consequences of any decision (of that or any other court) in respect of that act, the court is satisfied that the award is necessary to afford just satisfaction to the person in whose favour it is made.

(4)   In determining—

(a)   whether to award damages, or

(b)   the amount of an award, the court must take into account the principles applied by the European Court of Human Rights in relation to the award of compensation under Article 41 of the Convention.

(5)   A public authority against which damages are awarded is to be treated—

(a)   in Scotland, for the purposes of section 3 of the Law Reform (Miscellaneous Provisions) (Scotland) Act 1940 as if the award were made in an action of damages in which the authority has been found liable in respect of loss or damage to the person to whom the award is made;

(b)   for the purposes of the Civil Liability (Contribution) Act 1978 as liable in respect of damage suffered by the person to whom the award is made.

(6)   In this section—

'court' includes a tribunal;

'damages' means damages for an unlawful act of a public authority; and

'unlawful' means unlawful under section 6(1).

9.   Judicial acts

(1)   Proceedings under section 7(1)(a) in respect of a judicial act may be brought only—

(a)   by exercising a right of appeal;

(b)   on an application (in Scotland a petition) for judicial review; or

(c)   in such other forum as may be prescribed by rules.

(2)   That does not affect any rule of law which prevents a court from being the subject of judicial review.

(3)   In proceedings under this Act in respect of a judicial act done in good faith, damages may not be awarded otherwise than to compensate a person to the extent required by Article 5(5) of the Convention.

(4)   An award of damages permitted by subsection (3) is to be made against the Crown; but no award may be made unless the appropriate person, if not a party to the proceedings, is joined.

(5)   In this section—

'appropriate person' means the Minister responsible for the court concerned, or a person or government department nominated by him;

'court' includes a tribunal;

'judge' includes a member of a tribunal, a justice of the peace and a clerk or other officer entitled to exercise the jurisdiction of a court;

'judicial act' means a judicial act of a court and includes an act done on the instructions, or on behalf, of a judge; and

'rules' has the same meaning as in section 7(9).

Remedial action

10. Power to take remedial action

(1) This section applies if—

(a) a provision of legislation has been declared under section 4 to be incompatible with a Convention right and, if an appeal lies—

(i) all persons who may appeal have stated in writing that they do not intend to do so;

(ii) the time for bringing an appeal has expired and no appeal has been brought within that time; or

(iii) an appeal brought within that time has been determined or abandoned; or

(b) it appears to a Minister of the Crown or Her Majesty in Council that, having regard to a finding of the European Court of Human Rights made after the coming into force of this section in proceedings against the United Kingdom, a provision of legislation is incompatible with an obligation of the United Kingdom arising from the Convention.

(2) If a Minister of the Crown considers that there are compelling reasons for proceeding under this section, he may by order make such amendments to the legislation as he considers necessary to remove the incompatibility.

(3) If, in the case of subordinate legislation, a Minister of the Crown considers—

(a) that it is necessary to amend the primary legislation under which the subordinate legislation in question was made, in order to enable the incompatibility to be removed, and

(b) that there are compelling reasons for proceeding under this section, he may by order make such amendments to the primary legislation as he considers necessary.

(4) This section also applies where the provision in question is in subordinate legislation and has been quashed, or declared invalid, by reason of incompatibility with a Convention right and the Minister proposes to proceed under paragraph 2(b) of Schedule 2.

(5) If the legislation is an Order in Council, the power conferred by sub-section (2) or (3) is exercisable by Her Majesty in Council.

(6)   In this section 'legislation' does not include a Measure of the Church Assembly or of the General Synod of the Church of England.

(7)   Schedule 2 makes further provision about remedial orders.

Other rights and proceedings

11.   Safeguard for existing human rights

A person's reliance on a Convention right does not restrict—

(a)   any other right or freedom conferred on him by or under any law having effect in any part of the United Kingdom; or

(b)   his right to make any claim or bring any proceedings which he could make or bring apart from sections 7 to 9.

12.   Freedom of expression

(1)   This section applies if a court is considering whether to grant any relief which, if granted, might affect the exercise of the Convention right to freedom of expression.

(2)   If the person against whom the application for relief is made ('the respondent') is neither present nor represented, no such relief is to be granted unless the court is satisfied—

(a)   that the applicant has taken all practicable steps to notify the respondent; or

(b)   that there are compelling reasons why the respondent should not be notified.

(3)   No such relief is to be granted so as to restrain publication before trial unless the court is satisfied that the applicant is likely to establish that publication should not be allowed.

(4)   The court must have particular regard to the importance of the Convention right to freedom of expression and, where the proceedings relate to material which the respondent claims, or which appears to the court, to be journalistic, literary or artistic material (or to conduct connected with such material), to—

(a)   the extent to which—

(i)   the material has, or is about to, become available to the public; or

(ii)   it is, or would be, in the public interest for the material to be published;

(b)   any relevant privacy code.

(5)   In this section—

'court' includes a tribunal; and

'relief' includes any remedy or order (other than in criminal proceedings)

13.   Freedom of thought, conscience and religion

(1)   If a court's determination of any question arising under this Act might affect the exercise by a religious organisation (itself or its members collectively)

of the Convention right to freedom of thought, conscience and religion, it must have particular regard to the importance of that right.

(2)   In this section 'court' includes a tribunal.

Derogations and reservations

14.   Derogations

(1)   In this Act 'designated derogation' means any derogation by the United Kingdom from an Article of the Convention, or of any protocol to the Convention, which is designated for the purposes of this Act in an order made by the [Lord Chancellor].

(2)   . . .

(3)   If a designated derogation is amended or replaced it ceases to be a designated derogation.

(4)   But subsection (3) does not prevent the [Lord Chancellor] from exercising his power under subsection (1) to make a fresh designation order in respect of the Article concerned.

(5)   The [Lord Chancellor] must by order make such amendments to Schedule 3 as he considers appropriate to reflect—

    (a)   any designation order; or

    (b)   the effect of subsection (3).

(6)   A designation order may be made in anticipation of the making by the United Kingdom of a proposed derogation.

15.   Reservations

(1)   In this Act 'designated reservation' means—

    (a)   the United Kingdom's reservation to Article 2 of the First Protocol to the Convention; and

    (b)   any other reservation by the United Kingdom to an Article of the Convention, or of any protocol to the Convention, which is designated for the purposes of this Act in an order made by the [Lord Chancellor].

(2)   The text of the reservation referred to in subsection (1)(a) is set out in Part II of Schedule 3.

(3)   If a designated reservation is withdrawn wholly or in part it ceases to be a designated reservation.

(4)   But subsection (3) does not prevent the [Lord Chancellor] from exercising his power under subsection (1)(b) to make a fresh designation order in respect of the Article concerned.

(5)   The [Lord Chancellor] must by order make such amendments to this Act as he considers appropriate to reflect—

    (a)   any designation order; or

    (b)   the effect of subsection (3).

16. Period for which designated derogations have effect

(1)   If it has not already been withdrawn by the United Kingdom, a designated derogation ceases to have effect for the purposes of this Act at the end of the period of five years beginning with the date on which the order designating it was made.

(2)   At any time before the period—

(a)   fixed by subsection (1), or

(b)   extended by an order under this subsection, comes to an end, the [Lord Chancellor] may by order extend it by a further period of five years.

(3)   An order under section 14(1) ceases to have effect at the end of the period for consideration, unless a resolution has been passed by each House approving the order.

(4)   Subsection (3) does not affect—

(a)   anything done in reliance on the order; or

(b)   the power to make a fresh order under section 14(1).

(5)   In subsection (3) 'period for consideration' means the period of forty days beginning with the day on which the order was made.

(6)   In calculating the period for consideration, no account is to be taken of any time during which—

(a)   Parliament is dissolved or prorogued; or

(b)   both Houses are adjourned for more than four days.

(7)   If a designated derogation is withdrawn by the United Kingdom, the [Lord Chancellor] must by order make such amendments to this Act as he considers are required to reflect that withdrawal.

17. Periodic review of designated reservations

(1)   The appropriate Minister must review the designated reservation referred to in section 15(1)(a)—

(a)   before the end of the period of five years beginning with the date on which section 1(2) came into force; and

(b)   if that designation is still in force, before the end of the period of five years beginning with the date on which the last report relating to it was laid under subsection (3).

(2)   The appropriate Minister must review each of the other designated reservations (if any)—

(a)   before the end of the period of five years beginning with the date on which the order designating the reservation first came into force; and

(b)   if the designation is still in force, before the end of the period of five years beginning with the date on which the last report relating to it was laid under subsection (3).

(3)   The Minister conducting a review under this section must prepare a report on the result of the review and lay a copy of it before each House of Parliament.

Judges of the European Court of Human Rights

18. Appointment to European Court of Human Rights

(1) In this section 'judicial office' means the office of—

(a) Lord Justice of Appeal, Justice of the High Court or Circuit judge, in England and Wales;

(b) judge of the Court of Session or sheriff, in Scotland;

(c) Lord Justice of Appeal, judge of the High Court or county court judge, in Northern Ireland.

(2) The holder of a judicial office may become a judge of the European Court of Human Rights ('the Court') without being required to relinquish his office.

(3) But he is not required to perform the duties of his judicial office while he is a judge of the Court.

(4) In respect of any period during which he is a judge of the Court—

(a) a Lord Justice of Appeal or Justice of the High Court is not to count as a judge of the relevant court for the purposes of section 2(1) or 4(1) of the Supreme Court Act 1981 (maximum number of judges) nor as a judge of the Supreme Court for the purposes of section 12(1) to (6) of that Act (salaries etc.);

(b) a judge of the Court of Session is not to count as a judge of that court for the purposes of section 1(1) of the Court of Session Act 1988 (maximum number of judges) or of section 9(1)(c) of the Administration of Justice Act 1973 ('the 1973 Act') (salaries etc.);

(c) a Lord Justice of Appeal or judge of the High Court in Northern Ireland is not to count as a judge of the relevant court for the purposes of section 2(1) or 3(1) of the Judicature (Northern Ireland) Act 1978 (maximum number of judges) nor as a judge of the Supreme Court of Northern Ireland for the purposes of section 9(1)(d) of the 1973 Act (salaries etc.);

(d) a Circuit judge is not to count as such for the purposes of section 18 of the Courts Act 1971 (salaries etc.);

(e) a sheriff is not to count as such for the purposes of section 14 of the Sheriff Courts (Scotland) Act 1907 (salaries etc.);

(f) a county court judge of Northern Ireland is not to count as such for the purposes of section 106 of the County Courts Act (Northern Ireland) 1959 (salaries etc.).

(5) If a sheriff principal is appointed a judge of the Court, section 11(1) of the Sheriff Courts (Scotland) Act 1971 (temporary appointment of sheriff principal) applies, while he holds that appointment, as if his office is vacant.

(6) Schedule 4 makes provision about judicial pensions in relation to the holder of a judicial office who serves as a judge of the Court.

(7) The Lord Chancellor or the Secretary of State may by order make such transitional provision (including, in particular, provision for a temporary increase

in the maximum number of judges) as he considers appropriate in relation to any holder of a judicial office who has completed his service as a judge of the Court.

Parliamentary procedure

19. Statements of compatibility

(1) A Minister of the Crown in charge of a Bill in either House of Parliament must, before Second Reading of the Bill—

(a) make a statement to the effect that in his view the provisions of the Bill are compatible with the Convention rights ('a statement of compatibility'); or

(b) make a statement to the effect that although he is unable to make a statement of compatibility the government nevertheless wishes the House to proceed with the Bill.

(2) The statement must be in writing and be published in such manner as the Minister making it considers appropriate.

Supplemental

20. Orders etc. under this Act

(1) Any power of a Minister of the Crown to make an order under this Act is exercisable by statutory instrument.

(2) The power of the Lord Chancellor or the Secretary of State to make rules (other than rules of court) under section 2(3) or 7(9) is exercisable by statutory instrument.

(3) Any statutory instrument made under section 14, 15 or 16(7) must be laid before Parliament.

(4) No order may be made by the Lord Chancellor or the Secretary of State under section 1(4), 7(11) or 16(2) unless a draft of the order has been laid before, and approved by, each House of Parliament.

(5) Any statutory instrument made under section 18(7) or Schedule 4, or to which subsection (2) applies, shall be subject to annulment in pursuance of a resolution of either House of Parliament.

(6) The power of a Northern Ireland department to make—

(a) rules under section 2(3)(c) or 7(9)(c), or

(b) an order under section 7(11), is exercisable by statutory rule for the purposes of the Statutory Rules (Northern Ireland) Order 1979.

(7) Any rules made under section 2(3)(c) or 7(9)(c) shall be subject to negative resolution; and section 41(6) of the Interpretation Act (Northern Ireland) 1954 (meaning of 'subject to negative resolution') shall apply as if the power to make the rules were conferred by an Act of the Northern Ireland Assembly.

(8) No order may be made by a Northern Ireland department under section

7(11) unless a draft of the order has been laid before, and approved by, the Northern Ireland Assembly.

21. Interpretation etc.

(1) In this Act—

'amend' includes repeal and apply (with or without modifications);

'the appropriate Minister' means the Minister of the Crown having charge of the appropriate authorised government department (within the meaning of the Crown Proceedings Act 1947);

'the Commission' means the European Commission of Human Rights;

'the Convention' means the Convention for the Protection of Human Rights and Fundamental Freedoms, agreed by the Council of Europe at Rome on 4th November 1950 as it has effect for the time being in relation to the United Kingdom;

'declaration of incompatibility' means a declaration under section 4;

'Minister of the Crown' has the same meaning as in the Ministers of the Crown Act 1975;

'Northern Ireland Minister' includes the First Minister and the deputy First Minister in Northern Ireland;

'primary legislation' means any—

(a) public general Act;

(b) local and personal Act;

(c) private Act;

(d) Measure of the Church Assembly;

(e) Measure of the General Synod of the Church of England;

(f) Order in Council—

(i) made in exercise of Her Majesty's Royal Prerogative;

(ii) made under section 38(1)(a) of the Northern Ireland Constitution Act 1973 or the corresponding provision of the Northern Ireland Act 1998; or

(iii) amending an Act of a kind mentioned in paragraph (a), (b) or (c);

and includes an order or other instrument made under primary legislation (otherwise than by the National Assembly for Wales, a member of the Scottish Executive, a Northern Ireland Minister or a Northern Ireland department) to the extent to which it operates to bring one or more provisions of that legislation into force or amends any primary legislation;

'the First Protocol' means the protocol to the Convention agreed at Paris on 20th March 1952;

'the Sixth Protocol' means the protocol to the Convention agreed at Strasbourg on 28th April 1983;

'the Eleventh Protocol' means the protocol to the Convention (restructuring the control machinery established by the Convention) agreed at Strasbourg on 11th May 1994;

'remedial order' means an order under section 10;

'subordinate legislation' means any—

    (a)   Order in Council other than one—

       (i)   made in exercise of Her Majesty's Royal Prerogative;

       (ii)   made under section 38(1)(a) of the Northern Ireland Constitution Act 1973 or the corresponding provision of the Northern Ireland Act 1998; or

       (iii)   amending an Act of a kind mentioned in the definition of primary legislation;

    (b)   Act of the Scottish Parliament;

    (c)   Act of the Parliament of Northern Ireland;

    (d)   Measure of the Assembly established under section 1 of the Northern Ireland Assembly Act 1973;

    (e)   Act of the Northern Ireland Assembly;

    (f)   order, rules, regulations, scheme, warrant, byelaw or other instrument made under primary legislation (except to the extent to which it operates to bring one or more provisions of that legislation into force or amends any primary legislation);

    (g)   order, rules, regulations, scheme, warrant, byelaw or other instrument made under legislation mentioned in paragraph (b), (c), (d) or (e) or made under an Order in Council applying only to Northern Ireland;

    (h)   order, rules, regulations, scheme, warrant, byelaw or other instrument made by a member of the Scottish Executive, a Northern Ireland Minister or a Northern Ireland department in exercise of prerogative or other executive functions of Her Majesty which are exercisable by such a person on behalf of Her Majesty;

'transferred matters' has the same meaning as in the Northern Ireland Act 1998; and

'tribunal' means any tribunal in which legal proceedings may be brought.

(2)   The references in paragraphs (b) and (c) of section 2(1) to Articles are to Articles of the Convention as they had effect immediately before the coming into force of the Eleventh Protocol.

(3)   The reference in paragraph (d) of section 2(1) to Article 46 includes a reference to Articles 32 and 54 of the Convention as they had effect immediately before the coming into force of the Eleventh Protocol.

(4)   The references in section 2(1) to a report or decision of the Commission or a decision of the Committee of Ministers include references to a report or decision made as provided by paragraphs 3, 4 and 6 of Article 5 of the Eleventh Protocol (transitional provisions).

(5)   Any liability under the Army Act 1955, the Air Force Act 1955 or the Naval Discipline Act 1957 to suffer death for an offence is replaced by a liability to imprisonment for life or any less punishment authorised by those Acts; and those Acts shall accordingly have effect with the necessary modifications.

22. Short title, commencement, application and extent

(1)   This Act may be cited as the Human Rights Act 1998.

(2)   Sections 18, 20 and 21(5) and this section come into force on the passing of this Act.

(3)   The other provisions of this Act come into force on such day as the Secretary of State may by order appoint; and different days may be appointed for different purposes.

(4)   Paragraph (b) of subsection (1) of section 7 applies to proceedings brought by or at the instigation of a public authority whenever the act in question took place; but otherwise that subsection does not apply to an act taking place before the coming into force of that section.

(5)   This Act binds the Crown.

(6)   This Act extends to Northern Ireland.

(7)   Section 21(5), so far as it relates to any provision contained in the Army Act 1955, the Air Force Act 1955 or the Naval Discipline Act 1957, extends to any place to which that provision extends.

SCHEDULES

Section 1(3)

SCHEDULE 1
THE ARTICLES

PART I
THE CONVENTION

RIGHTS AND FREEDOMS

Article 2
Right to life

1.   Everyone's right to life shall be protected by law. No one shall be deprived of his life intentionally save in the execution of a sentence of a court following his conviction of a crime for which this penalty is provided by law.

2.   Deprivation of life shall not be regarded as inflicted in contravention of this Article when it results from the use of force which is no more than absolutely necessary:

(a)   in defence of any person from unlawful violence;

(b)   in order to effect a lawful arrest or to prevent the escape of a person lawfully detained;

(c)   in action lawfully taken for the purpose of quelling a riot or insurrection.

Article 3
Prohibition of torture

No one shall be subjected to torture or to inhuman or degrading treatment or punishment.

Article 4
Prohibition of slavery and forced labour

1.   No one shall be held in slavery or servitude.

2.   No one shall be required to perform forced or compulsory labour.

3.   For the purpose of this Article the term 'forced or compulsory labour' shall not include:

(a)   any work required to be done in the ordinary course of detention imposed according to the provisions of Article 5 of this Convention or during conditional release from such detention;

(b)   any service of a military character or, in case of conscientious objectors in countries where they are recognised, service exacted instead of compulsory military service;

(c)   any service exacted in case of an emergency or calamity threatening the life or well-being of the community;

(d)   any work or service which forms part of normal civic obligations.

Article 5
Right to liberty and security

1.   Everyone has the right to liberty and security of person. No one shall be deprived of his liberty save in the following cases and in accordance with a procedure prescribed by law:

(a)   the lawful detention of a person after conviction by a competent court;

(b)   the lawful arrest or detention of a person for non-compliance with the lawful order of a court or in order to secure the fulfilment of any obligation prescribed by law;

(c)   the lawful arrest or detention of a person effected for the purpose of bringing him before the competent legal authority on reasonable suspicion of having committed an offence or when it is reasonably considered necessary to prevent his committing an offence or fleeing after having done so;

(d)   the detention of a minor by lawful order for the purpose of educational supervision or his lawful detention for the purpose of bringing him before the competent legal authority;

(e)   the lawful detention of persons for the prevention of the spreading of infectious diseases, of persons of unsound mind, alcoholics or drug addicts or vagrants;

(f)   the lawful arrest or detention of a person to prevent his effecting an unauthorised entry into the country or of a person against whom action is being taken with a view to deportation or extradition.

2.   Everyone who is arrested shall be informed promptly, in a language which he understands, of the reasons for his arrest and of any charge against him.

3.   Everyone arrested or detained in accordance with the provisions of paragraph 1(c) of this Article shall be brought promptly before a judge or other officer authorised by law to exercise judicial power and shall be entitled to trial within a reasonable time or to release pending trial. Release may be conditioned by guarantees to appear for trial.

4.   Everyone who is deprived of his liberty by arrest or detention shall be entitled to take proceedings by which the lawfulness of his detention shall be decided speedily by a court and his release ordered if the detention is not lawful.

5.   Everyone who has been the victim of arrest or detention in contravention of the provisions of this Article shall have an enforceable right to compensation.

Article 6
Right to a fair trial

1.   In the determination of his civil rights and obligations or of any criminal charge against him, everyone is entitled to a fair and public hearing within a reasonable time by an independent and impartial tribunal established by law. Judgment shall be pronounced publicly but the press and public may be excluded from all or part of the trial in the interest of morals, public order or national security in a democratic society, where the interests of juveniles or the protection of the private life of the parties so require, or to the extent strictly necessary in the opinion of the court in special circumstances where publicity would prejudice the interests of justice.

2.   Everyone charged with a criminal offence shall be presumed innocent until proved guilty according to law.

3.   Everyone charged with a criminal offence has the following minimum rights:

(a)   to be informed promptly, in a language which he understands and in detail, of the nature and cause of the accusation against him;

(b)   to have adequate time and facilities for the preparation of his defence;

(c)   to defend himself in person or through legal assistance of his own choosing or, if he has not sufficient means to pay for legal assistance, to be given it free when the interests of justice so require;

(d)   to examine or have examined witnesses against him and to obtain the attendance and examination of witnesses on his behalf under the same conditions as witnesses against him;

(e)   to have the free assistance of an interpreter if he cannot understand or speak the language used in court.

Article 7
No punishment without law

1.   No one shall be held guilty of any criminal offence on account of any act or omission which did not constitute a criminal offence under national or

international law at the time when it was committed. Nor shall a heavier penalty be imposed than the one that was applicable at the time the criminal offence was committed.

2. This Article shall not prejudice the trial and punishment of any person for any act or omission which, at the time when it was committed, was criminal according to the general principles of law recognised by civilised nations.

Article 8
Right to respect for private and family life

1. Everyone has the right to respect for his private and family life, his home and his correspondence.

2. There shall be no interference by a public authority with the exercise of this right except such as is in accordance with the law and is necessary in a democratic society in the interests of national security, public safety or the economic well-being of the country, for the prevention of disorder or crime, for the protection of health or morals, or for the protection of the rights and freedoms of others.

Article 9
Freedom of thought, conscience and religion

1. Everyone has the right to freedom of thought, conscience and religion; this right includes freedom to change his religion or belief and freedom, either alone or in community with others and in public or private, to manifest his religion or belief, in worship, teaching, practice and observance.

2. Freedom to manifest one's religion or beliefs shall be subject only to such limitations as are prescribed by law and are necessary in a democratic society in the interests of public safety, for the protection of public order, health or morals, or for the protection of the rights and freedoms of others.

Article 10
Freedom of expression

1. Everyone has the right to freedom of expression. This right shall include freedom to hold opinions and to receive and impart information and ideas without interference by public authority and regardless of frontiers. This Article shall not prevent States from requiring the licensing of broadcasting, television or cinema enterprises.

2. The exercise of these freedoms, since it carries with it duties and responsibilities, may be subject to such formalities, conditions, restrictions or penalties as are prescribed by law and are necessary in a democratic society, in the interests of national security, territorial integrity or public safety, for the prevention of disorder or crime, for the protection of health or morals, for the protection of the

reputation or rights of others, for preventing the disclosure of information received in confidence, or for maintaining the authority and impartiality of the judiciary.

Article 11
Freedom of assembly and association

1.   Everyone has the right to freedom of peaceful assembly and to freedom of association with others, including the right to form and to join trade unions for the protection of his interests.

2.   No restrictions shall be placed on the exercise of these rights other than such as are prescribed by law and are necessary in a democratic society in the interests of national security or public safety, for the prevention of disorder or crime, for the protection of health or morals or for the protection of the rights and freedoms of others. This Article shall not prevent the imposition of lawful restrictions on the exercise of these rights by members of the armed forces, of the police or of the administration of the State.

Article 12
Right to marry

Men and women of marriageable age have the right to marry and to found a family, according to the national laws governing the exercise of this right.

Article 14
Prohibition of discrimination

The enjoyment of the rights and freedoms set forth in this Convention shall be secured without discrimination on any ground such as sex, race, colour, language, religion, political or other opinion, national or social origin, association with a national minority, property, birth or other status.

Article 16
Restrictions on political activity of aliens

Nothing in Articles 10, 11 and 14 shall be regarded as preventing the High Contracting Parties from imposing restrictions on the political activity of aliens.

Article 17
Prohibition of abuse of rights

Nothing in this Convention may be interpreted as implying for any State, group or person any right to engage in any activity or perform any act aimed at the destruction of any of the rights and freedoms set forth herein or at their limitation to a greater extent than is provided for in the Convention.

Article 18
Limitation on use of restrictions on rights

The restrictions permitted under this Convention to the said rights and freedoms shall not be applied for any purpose other than those for which they have been prescribed.

PART II
THE FIRST PROTOCOL

Article 1
Protection of property

Every natural or legal person is entitled to the peaceful enjoyment of his possessions. No one shall be deprived of his possessions except in the public interest and subject to the conditions provided for by law and by the general principles of international law.

The preceding provisions shall not, however, in any way impair the right of a State to enforce such laws as it deems necessary to control the use of property in accordance with the general interest or to secure the payment of taxes or other contributions or penalties.

Article 2
Right to education

No person shall be denied the right to education. In the exercise of any functions which it assumes in relation to education and to teaching, the State shall respect the right of parents to ensure such education and teaching in conformity with their own religious and philosophical convictions.

Article 3
Right to free elections

The High Contracting Parties undertake to hold free elections at reasonable intervals by secret ballot, under conditions which will ensure the free expression of the opinion of the people in the choice of the legislature.

PART III
THE SIXTH PROTOCOL

Article 1
Abolition of the death penalty

The death penalty shall be abolished. No one shall be condemned to such penalty or executed.

Article 2
Death penalty in time of war

A State may make provision in its law for the death penalty in respect of acts committed in time of war or of imminent threat of war; such penalty shall be applied only in the instances laid down in the law and in accordance with its provisions. The State shall communicate to the Secretary General of the Council of Europe the relevant provisions of that law.

SCHEDULE 2
REMEDIAL ORDERS

Orders

1.—(1) A remedial order may—

(a)   contain such incidental, supplemental, consequential or transitional provision as the person making it considers appropriate;

(b)   be made so as to have effect from a date earlier than that on which it is made;

(c)   make provision for the delegation of specific functions;

(d)   make different provision for different cases.

(2)   The power conferred by sub-paragraph (1)(a) includes—

(a)   power to amend primary legislation (including primary legislation other than that which contains the incompatible provision); and

(b)   power to amend or revoke subordinate legislation (including subordinate legislation other than that which contains the incompatible provision).

(3)   A remedial order may be made so as to have the same extent as the legislation which it affects.

(4)   No person is to be guilty of an offence solely as a result of the retrospective effect of a remedial order.

Procedure

2.   No remedial order may be made unless—

(a)   a draft of the order has been approved by a resolution of each House of Parliament made after the end of the period of 60 days beginning with the day on which the draft was laid; or

(b)   it is declared in the order that it appears to the person making it that, because of the urgency of the matter, it is necessary to make the order without a draft being so approved.

Orders laid in draft

3.—(1)   No draft may be laid under paragraph 2(a) unless—

(a)   the person proposing to make the order has laid before Parliament a document which contains a draft of the proposed order and the required information; and

(b)   the period of 60 days, beginning with the day on which the document required by this sub-paragraph was laid, has ended.

(2)   If representations have been made during that period, the draft laid under paragraph 2(a) must be accompanied by a statement containing—

(a)   a summary of the representations; and

(b)   if, as a result of the representations, the proposed order has been changed, details of the changes.

Urgent cases

4.—(1)   If a remedial order ('the original order') is made without being approved in draft, the person making it must lay it before Parliament, accompanied by the required information, after it is made.

(2)   If representations have been made during the period of 60 days beginning with the day on which the original order was made, the person making it must (after the end of that period) lay before Parliament a statement containing—

(a)   a summary of the representations; and

(b)   if, as a result of the representations, he considers it appropriate to make changes to the original order, details of the changes.

(3)   If sub-paragraph (2)(b) applies, the person making the statement must—

(a)   make a further remedial order replacing the original order; and

(b)   lay the replacement order before Parliament.

(4)   If, at the end of the period of 120 days beginning with the day on which the original order was made, a resolution has not been passed by each House approving the original or replacement order, the order ceases to have effect (but without that affecting anything previously done under either order or the power to make a fresh remedial order).

Definitions

5.   In this Schedule—

'representations' means representations about a remedial order (or proposed remedial order) made to the person making (or proposing to make) it and includes any relevant Parliamentary report or resolution; and 'required information' means—

(a)   an explanation of the incompatibility which the order (or proposed order) seeks to remove, including particulars of the relevant declaration, finding or order; and

(b)   a statement of the reasons for proceeding under section 10 and for making an order in those terms.

Calculating periods

6.   In calculating any period for the purposes of this Schedule, no account is to be taken of any time during which—

(a)   Parliament is dissolved or prorogued; or

(b)   both Houses are adjourned for more than four days.

[7.—(1)   This paragraph applies in relation to—

(a)   any remedial order made, and any draft of such an order proposed to be made,—

(i)   by the Scottish Ministers; or

(ii)   within devolved competence (within the meaning of the Scotland Act 1998) by Her Majesty in Council; and

(b)   any document or statement to be laid in connection with such an order (or proposed order).

(2)   This Schedule has effect in relation to any such order (or proposed order), document or statement subject to the following modifications.

(3)   Any reference to Parliament, each House of Parliament or both Houses of Parliament shall be construed as a reference to the Scottish Parliament.

(4)   Paragraph 6 does not apply and instead, in calculating any period for the purposes of this Schedule, no account is to be taken of any time during which the Scottish Parliament is dissolved or is in recess for more than four days.]

SCHEDULE 3
[DEROGATION AND RESERVATION]

[PART I
DEROGATION

United Kingdom's derogation from Article 5(1)

The United Kingdom Permanent Representative to the Council of Europe presents his compliments to the Secretary General of the Council, and has the honour to convey the following information in order to ensure compliance with the obligations of Her Majesty's Government in the United Kingdom under Article 15(3) of the Convention for the Protection of Human Rights and Fundamental Freedoms signed at Rome on 4 November 1950.

Public emergency in the United Kingdom

The terrorist attacks in New York, Washington, D.C. and Pennsylvania on 11th September 2001 resulted in several thousand deaths, including many British victims and others from 70 different countries. In its resolutions 1368 (2001) and 1373 (2001), the United Nations Security Council recognised the attacks as a threat to international peace and security.

The threat from international terrorism is a continuing one. In its resolution 1373 (2001), the Security Council, acting under Chapter VII of the United Nations Charter, required all States to take measures to prevent the commission of terrorist attacks, including by denying safe haven to those who finance, plan, support or commit terrorist attacks.

There exists a terrorist threat to the United Kingdom from persons suspected of involvement in international terrorism. In particular, there are foreign nationals present in the United Kingdom who are suspected of being concerned in the commission, preparation or instigation of acts of international terrorism, of being members of organisations or groups which are so concerned or of having links with members of such organisations or groups, and who are a threat to the national security of the United Kingdom.

As a result, a public emergency, within the meaning of Article 15(1) of the Convention, exists in the United Kingdom.

The Anti-terrorism, Crime and Security Act 2001

As a result of the public emergency, provision is made in the Anti-terrorism, Crime and Security Act 2001, inter alia, for an extended power to arrest and detain a foreign national which will apply where it is intended to remove or deport the person from the United Kingdom but where removal or deportation is not for the time being possible, with the consequence that the detention would be unlawful under existing domestic law powers. The extended power to arrest and detain will apply where the Secretary of State issues a certificate indicating his belief that the person's presence in the United Kingdom is a risk to national security and that he suspects the person of being an international terrorist. That certificate will be subject to an appeal to the Special Immigration Appeals Commission ('SIAC'), established under the Special Immigration Appeals Commission Act 1997, which will have power to cancel it if it considers that the certificate should not have been issued. There will be an appeal on a point of law from a ruling by SIAC. In addition, the certificate will be reviewed by SIAC at regular intervals SIAC will also be able to grant bail, where appropriate, subject to conditions. It will be open to a detainee to end his detention at any time by agreeing to leave the United Kingdom.

The extended power of arrest and detention in the Anti-terrorism, Crime and Security Act 2001 is a measure which is strictly required by the exigencies of the situation. It is a temporary provision which comes into force for an initial period of 15 months and then expires unless renewed by Parliament. Thereafter, it is subject to annual renewal by Parliament. If, at any time, in the Government's assessment, the public emergency no longer exists or the extended power is no longer strictly required by the exigencies of the situation, then the Secretary of State will, by Order, repeal the provision.

Domestic law powers of detention (other than under the Anti-terrorism, Crime and Security Act 2001)

The Government has powers under the Immigration Act 1971 ('the 1971 Act') to remove or deport persons on the ground that their presence in the United Kingdom is not conducive to the public good on national security grounds. Persons can also be arrested and detained under Schedules 2 and 3 to the 1971 Act pending their removal or deportation. The courts in the United Kingdom have ruled that this power of detention can only be exercised during the period necessary, in all the circumstances of the particular case, to effect removal and that, if it becomes clear that removal is not going to be possible within a reasonable time, detention will be unlawful (*R* v *Governor of Durham Prison, ex parte Singh* [1984] 1 All ER 983).

Article 5(1)(f) of the Convention

It is well established that Article 5(1)(f) permits the detention of a person with a view to deportation only in circumstance where 'action is being taken with a view to deportation' (*Chahal* v *United Kingdom* (1996) 23 EHRR 413 at paragraph 112). In that case the European Court of Human Rights indicated that detention will cease to be permissible under Article 5(1)(f) if deportation proceedings are not prosecuted with due diligence and that it was necessary in such cases to determine whether the duration of the deportation proceedings was excessive (paragraph 113).

In some cases, where the intention remains to remove or deport a person on national security grounds, continued detention may not be consistent with Article 5(1)(f) as interpreted by the Court in the *Chahal* case. This may be the case, for example, if the person has established that removal to their own country might result in treatment contrary to Article 3 of the Convention. In such circumstances, irrespective of the gravity of the threat to national security posed by the person concerned, it is well established that Article 3 prevents removal or deportation to a place where there is a real risk that the person will suffer treatment contrary to that article. If no alternative destination is immediately available then removal or deportation may not, for the time being, be possible even though the ultimate intention remains to remove or deport the person once satisfactory arrangements can be made. In addition, it may not be possible to prosecute the person for a criminal offence given the strict rules on the admissibility of evidence in the criminal justice system of the United Kingdom and the high standard of proof required.

Derogation under Article 15 of the Convention

The Government has considered whether the exercise of the extended power to detain contained in the Anti-terrorism. Crime and Security Act 2001 may be inconsistent with the obligations under Article 5(1) of the Convention. As indicated above, there may be cases where, notwithstanding a continuing intention to remove or deport a person who is being detained, it is not possible to say that 'action is being taken with a view to deportation' within the meaning of Article 5(1)(f) as interpreted by the Court in the *Chahal* case. To the extent, therefore, that the exercise of the extended power may be inconsistent with the United Kingdom's obligations under Article 5(1), the Government has decided to avail itself of the right of derogation conferred by Article 15(1) of the Convention and will continue to do so until further notice.

Strasbourg, 18 December 2001]

[PART II
RESERVATION]

At the time of signing the present (First) Protocol, I declare that, in view of certain provisions of the Education Acts in the United Kingdom, the principle affirmed in the second sentence of Article 2 is accepted by the United Kingdom only so far as it is compatible with the provision of efficient instruction and training, and the avoidance of unreasonable public expenditure.

Dated 20 March 1952. Made by the United Kingdom Permanent Representative to the Council of Europe.

SCHEDULE 4
JUDICIAL PENSIONS

Duty to make orders about pensions

1.—(1)   The appropriate Minister must by order make provision with respect to pensions payable to or in respect of any holder of a judicial office who serves as an ECHR judge.

(2)   A pensions order must include such provision as the Minister making it considers is necessary to secure that—

(a)   an ECHR judge who was, immediately before his appointment as an ECHR judge, a member of a judicial pension scheme is entitled to remain as a member of that scheme;

(b)   the terms on which he remains a member of the scheme are those which would have been applicable had he not been appointed as an ECHR judge; and

(c)   entitlement to benefits payable in accordance with the scheme continues to be determined as if, while serving as an ECHR judge, his salary was that which would (but for section 18(4)) have been payable to him in respect of his continuing service as the holder of his judicial office.

Contributions

2.   A pensions order may, in particular, make provision—

(a)   for any contributions which are payable by a person who remains a member of a scheme as a result of the order, and which would otherwise be payable by deduction from his salary, to be made otherwise than by deduction from his salary as an ECHR judge; and

(b)   for such contributions to be collected in such manner as may be determined by the administrators of the scheme.

Amendments of other enactments

3.   A pensions order may amend any provision of, or made under, a pensions Act in such manner and to such extent as the Minister making the order considers necessary or expedient to ensure the proper administration of any scheme to which it relates.

Definitions

4.   In this Schedule—

'appropriate Minister' means—

(a)   in relation to any judicial office whose jurisdiction is exercisable exclusively in relation to Scotland, the Secretary of State; and

(b)   otherwise, the Lord Chancellor;

'ECHR judge' means the holder of a judicial office who is serving as a judge of the Court;

'judicial pension scheme' means a scheme established by and in accordance with a pensions Act;

'pensions Act means—

(a)   the County Courts Act (Northern Ireland) 1959;

(b)   the Sheriffs' Pensions (Scotland) Act 1961;

(c)   the Judicial Pensions Act 1981; or

(d)   the Judicial Pensions and Retirement Act 1993; and

'pensions order' means an order made under paragraph 1.

Appendix Two

European Convention on Human Rights

CONVENTION FOR THE PROTECTION OF HUMAN RIGHTS AND
FUNDAMENTAL FREEDOMS AS AMENDED BY PROTOCOL NO. 11
(Date of entry into force 1 November 1998)

The governments signatory hereto, being members of the Council of Europe,

Considering the Universal Declaration of Human Rights proclaimed by the General Assembly of the United Nations on 10th December 1948.

Considering that this Declaration aims at securing the universal and effective recognition and observance of the Rights therein declared;

Considering that the aim of the Council of Europe is the achievement of greater unity between its members and that one of the methods by which that aim is to be pursued is the maintenance and further realisation of human rights and fundamental freedoms;

Reaffirming their profound belief in those fundamental freedoms which are the foundation of justice and peace in the world and are best maintained on the one hand by an effective political democracy and on the other by a common understanding and observance of the human rights upon which they depend:

Being resolved, as the governments of European countries which are like-minded and have a common heritage of political traditions, ideals, freedom and the rule of law, to take the first steps for the collective enforcement of certain of the rights stated in the Universal Declaration,

Have agreed as follows:

Article 1
Obligation to respect human rights

The High Contracting Parties shall secure to everyone within their jurisdiction the rights and freedoms defined in Section I of this Convention.

Section I—Rights and freedoms

Article 2
Right to life

1.   Everyone's right to life shall be protected by law. No one shall be deprived of his life intentionally save in the execution of a sentence of a court following his conviction of a crime for which this penalty is provided by law.

2.   Deprivation of life shall not be regarded as inflicted in contravention of this article when it results from the use of force which is no more than absolutely necessary;

(a)   in defence of any person from unlawful violence;

(b)   in order to effect a lawful arrest or to prevent the escape of a person lawfully detained;

(c)   in action lawfully taken for the purpose of quelling a riot or insurrection.

Article 3
Prohibition of torture

No one shall be subjected to torture or to inhuman or degrading treatment or punishment.

Article 4
Prohibition of slavery and forced labour

1.   No one shall be held in slavery or servitude.

2.   No one shall be required to perform forced or compulsory labour.

3.   For the purpose of this article the term 'forced or compulsory labour' shall not include:

(a)   any work required to be done in the ordinary course of detention imposed according to the provisions of Article 5 of this Convention or during conditional release from such detention;

(b)   any service of a military character or, in case of conscientious objectors in countries where they are recognised, service exacted instead of compulsory military service;

(c)   any service exacted in case of an emergency or calamity threatening the life or well-being of the community;

(d)   any work or service which forms part of normal civic obligations.

Article 5
Right to liberty and security

1.   Everyone has the right to liberty and security of person. No one shall be deprived of his liberty save in the following cases and in accordance with a procedure prescribed by law:

(a)   the lawful detention of a person after conviction by a competent court;

(b)   the lawful arrest or detention of a person for non-compliance with the lawful order of a court or in order to secure the fulfilment of any obligation prescribed by law;

(c)   the lawful arrest or detention of a person effected for the purpose of bringing him before the competent legal authority on reasonable suspicion of having committed an offence or when it is reasonably considered necessary to prevent his committing an offence or fleeing after having done so;

(d)   the detention of a minor by lawful order for the purpose of educational supervision or his lawful detention for the purpose of bringing him before the competent legal authority;

(e)   the lawful detention of persons for the prevention of the spreading of infectious diseases, of persons of unsound mind, alcoholics or drug addicts or vagrants;

(f)   the lawful arrest or detention of a person to prevent his effecting an unauthorised entry into the country or of a person against whom action is being taken with a view to deportation or extradition.

2.   Everyone who is arrested shall be informed promptly, in a language which he understands, of the reasons for his arrest and of any charge against him

3.   Everyone arrested or detained in accordance with the provisions of paragraph 1.c of this article shall be brought promptly before a judge or other officer authorised by law to exercise judicial power and shall be entitled to trial within a reasonable time or to release pending trial. Release may be conditioned by guarantees to appear for trial.

4.   Everyone who is deprived of his liberty by arrest or detention shall be entitled to take proceedings by which the lawfulness of his detention shall be decided speedily by a court and his release ordered if the detention is not lawful.

5.   Everyone who has been the victim of arrest or detention in contravention of the provisions of this article shall have an enforceable right to compensation.

Article 6
Right to a fair trial

1.   In the determination of his civil rights and obligations or of any criminal charge against him, everyone is entitled to a fair and public hearing within a reasonable time by an independent and impartial tribunal established by law. Judgment shall be pronounced publicly but the press and public may be excluded from all or part of the trial in the interests of morals, public order or national security in a democratic society, where the interests of juveniles or the protection of the private life of the parties so require, or to the extent strictly necessary in the opinion of the court in special circumstances where publicity would prejudice the interests of justice.

2. Everyone charged with a criminal offence shall be presumed innocent until proved guilty according to law.

3. Everyone charged with a criminal offence has the following minimum rights:

(a) to be informed promptly, in a language which he understands and in detail, of the nature and cause of the accusation against him;

(b) to have adequate time and facilities for the preparation of his defence;

(c) to defend himself in person or through legal assistance of his own choosing or, if he has not sufficient means to pay for legal assistance, to be given it free when the interests of justice so require;

(d) to examine or have examined witnesses against him and to obtain the attendance and examination of witnesses on his behalf under the same conditions as witnesses against him;

(e) to have the free assistance of an interpreter if he cannot understand or speak the language used in court.

Article 7
No punishment without law

1. No one shall be held guilty of any criminal offence on account of any act or omission which did not constitute a criminal offence under national or international law at the time when it was committed. Nor shall a heavier penalty he imposed than the one that was applicable at the time the criminal offence was committed.

2. This article shall not prejudice the trial and punishment of any person for any act or omission which, at the time when it was committed, was criminal according to the general principles of law recognised by civilised nations.

Article 8
Right to respect for private and family life

1. Everyone has the right to respect for his private and family life, his home and his correspondence.

2. There shall be no interference by a public authority with the exercise of this right except such as is in accordance with the law and is necessary in a democratic society in the interests of national security, public safety or the economic well-being of the country, for the prevention of disorder or crime, for the protection of health or morals, or for the protection of the rights and freedoms of others.

Article 9
Freedom of thought, conscience and religion

1. Everyone has the right to freedom of thought, conscience and religion; this right includes freedom to change his religion or belief and freedom, either alone

or in community with others and in public or private, to manifest his religion or belief, in worship, teaching, practice and observance.

2.   Freedom to manifest one's religion or beliefs shall be subject only to such limitations as are prescribed by law and are necessary in a democratic society in the interests of public safety, for the protection of public order, health or morals, or for the protection of the rights and freedoms of others.

Article 10
Freedom of expression

1.   Everyone has the right to freedom of expression. This right shall include freedom to hold opinions and to receive and impart information and ideas without interference by public authority and regardless of frontiers. This article shall not prevent States from requiring the licensing of broadcasting, television or cinema enterprises.

2.   The exercise of these freedoms, since it carries with it duties and responsibilities, may be subject to such formalities, conditions, restrictions or penalties as are prescribed by law and are necessary in a democratic society, in the interests of national security, territorial integrity or public safety, for the prevention of disorder or crime, for the protection of health or morals, for the protection of the reputation or rights of others, for preventing the disclosure of information received in confidence, or for maintaining the authority and impartiality of the judiciary.

Article 11
Freedom of assembly and association

1.   Everyone has the right to freedom of peaceful assembly and to freedom of association with others, including the right to form and to join trade unions for the protection of his interests.

2.   No restrictions shall be placed on the exercise of these rights other than such as are prescribed by law and are necessary in a democratic society in the interests of national security or public safety, for the prevention of disorder or crime, for the protection of health or morals or for the protection of the rights and freedoms of others. This article shall not prevent the imposition of lawful restrictions on the exercise of these rights by members of the armed forces, of the police or of the administration of the State.

Article 12
Right to marry

Men and women of marriageable age have the right to marry and to found a family, according to the national laws governing the exercise of this right.

Article 13
Right to an effective remedy

Everyone whose rights and freedoms as set forth in this Convention are violated shall have an effective remedy before a national authority notwithstanding that the violation has been committed by persons acting in an official capacity.

Article 14
Prohibition of discrimination

The enjoyment of the rights and freedoms set forth in this Convention shall be secured without discrimination on any ground such as sex, race, colour, language, religion, political or other opinion, national or social origin, association with a national minority, property, birth or other status.

Article 15
Derogation in time of emergency

1.   In time of war or other public emergency threatening the life of the nation any High Contracting Party may take measures derogating from its obligations under this Convention to the extent strictly required by the exigencies of the situation, provided that such measures are not inconsistent with its other obligations under international law.

2.   No derogation from Article 2, except in respect of deaths resulting from lawful acts of war, or from Articles 3, 4 (paragraph 1) and 7 shall be made under this provision.

3.   Any High Contracting Party availing itself of this right of derogation shall keep the Secretary General of the Council of Europe fully informed of the measures which it has taken and the reasons therefor. It shall also inform the Secretary General of the Council of Europe when such measures have ceased to operate and the provisions of the Convention are again being fully executed.

Article 16
Restrictions on political activity of aliens

Nothing in Articles 10, 11 and 14 shall be regarded as preventing the High Contracting Parties from imposing restrictions on the political activity of aliens.

Article 17
Prohibition of abuse of rights

Nothing in this Convention may be interpreted as implying for any State, group or person any right to engage in any activity or perform any act aimed at the destruction of any of the rights and freedoms set forth herein or at their limitation to a greater extent than is provided for in the Convention.

Article 18
Limitation on use of restrictions on rights

The restrictions permitted under this Convention to the said rights and freedoms shall not be applied for any purpose other than those for which they have been prescribed.

Section II—European Court of Human Rights

Article 19
Establishment of the Court

To ensure the observance of the engagements undertaken by the High Contracting Parties in the Convention and the Protocols thereto, there shall be set up a European Court of Human Rights, hereinafter referred to as 'the Court'. It shall function on a permanent basis.

Article 20
Number of judges

The Court shall consist of a number of judges equal to that of the High Contracting Parties.

Article 21
Criteria for office

1. The judges shall be of high moral character and must either possess the qualifications required for appointment to high judicial office or be jurisconsults of recognised competence.
2. The judges shall sit on the Court in their individual capacity.
3. During their term of office the judges shall not engage in any activity which is incompatible with their independence, impartiality or with the demands of a full-time office; all questions arising from the application of this paragraph shall be decided by the Court.

Article 22
Election of judges

1. The judges shall be elected by the Parliamentary Assembly with respect to each High Contracting Party by a majority of votes cast from a list of three candidates nominated by the High Contracting Party.
2. The same procedure shall be followed to complete the Court in the event of the accession of new High Contracting Parties and in filling casual vacancies.

Article 23
Terms of office

1.   The judges shall be elected for a period of six years. They may be re-elected. However, the terms of office of one-half of the judges elected at the first election shall expire at the end of three years.

2.   The judges whose terms of office are to expire at the end of the initial period of three years shall be chosen by lot by the Secretary General of the Council of Europe immediately after their election.

3.   In order to ensure that, as far as possible, the terms of office of one-half of the judges are renewed every three years, the Parliamentary Assembly may decide, before proceeding to any subsequent election, that the term or terms of office of one or more judges to be elected shall be for a period other than six years but not more than nine and not less than three years.

4.   In cases where more than one term of office is involved and where the Parliamentary Assembly applies the preceding paragraph, the allocation of the terms of office shall be effected by a drawing of lots by the Secretary General of the Council of Europe immediately after the election.

5.   A judge elected to replace a judge whose term of office has not expired shall hold office for the remainder of his predecessor's term.

6.   The terms of office of judges shall expire when they reach the age of 70.

7.   The judges shall hold office until replaced. They shall, however, continue to deal with such cases as they already have under consideration.

Article 24
Dismissal

No judge may be dismissed from his office unless the other judges decide by a majority of two-thirds that he has ceased to fulfil the required conditions.

Article 25
Registry and legal secretaries

The Court shall have a registry, the functions and organisation of which shall be laid down in the rules of the Court. The Court shall be assisted by legal secretaries.

Article 26
Plenary Court

The plenary Court shall

(a)   elect its President and one or two Vice-Presidents for a period of three years; they may be re-elected;

(b)   set up Chambers, constituted for a fixed period of time;

(c) elect the Presidents of the Chambers of the Court; they may be re-elected;

(d) adopt the rules of the Court, and

(e) elect the Registrar and one or more Deputy Registrars.

Article 27
Committees, Chambers and Grand Chamber

1. To consider cases brought before it, the Court shall sit in committees of three judges, in Chambers of seven judges and in a Grand Chamber of seventeen judges. The Court's Chambers shall set up committees for a fixed period of time.

2. There shall sit as an *ex officio* member of the Chamber and the Grand Chamber the judge elected in respect of the State Party concerned or, if there is none or if he is unable to sit, a person of its choice who shall sit in the capacity of judge.

3. The Grand Chamber shall also include the President of the Court, the Vice-Presidents, the Presidents of the Chambers and other judges chosen in accordance with the rules of the Court. When a case is referred to the Grand Chamber under Article 43, no judge from the Chamber which rendered the judgment shall sit in the Grand Chamber, with the exception of the President of the Chamber and the judge who sat in respect of the State Party concerned.

Article 28
Declarations of inadmissibility by committees

A committee may, by a unanimous vote, declare inadmissible or strike out of its list of cases an application submitted under Article 34 where such a decision can be taken without further examination. The decision shall be final.

Article 29
Decisions by Chambers on admissibility and merits

1. If no decision is taken under Article 28, a Chamber shall decide on the admissibility and merits of individual applications submitted under Article 34.

2. A Chamber shall decide on the admissibility and merits of inter-State applications submitted under Article 33.

3. The decision on admissibility shall be taken separately unless the Court, in exceptional cases, decides otherwise.

Article 30
Relinquishment of jurisdiction to the Grand Chamber

Where a case pending before a Chamber raises a serious question affecting the interpretation of the Convention or the protocols thereto, or where the resolution of a question before the Chamber might have a result inconsistent with a judgment previously delivered by the Court, the Chamber may, at any time before it has rendered its judgment, relinquish jurisdiction in favour of the Grand Chamber, unless one of the parties to the case objects.

Article 31
Powers of the Grand Chamber

The Grand Chamber shall

(a)   determine applications submitted either under Article 33 or Article 34 when a Chamber has relinquished jurisdiction under Article 30 or when the case has been referred to it under Article 43; and

(b)   consider requests for advisory opinions submitted under Article 47.

Article 32
Jurisdiction of the Court

1.   The jurisdiction of the Court shall extend to all matters concerning the interpretation and application of the Convention and the protocols thereto which are referred to it as provided in Article 33, 34 and 47.

2.   In the event of dispute as to whether the Court has jurisdiction, the Court shall decide.

Article 33
Inter-State cases

Any High Contracting Party may refer to the Court any alleged breach of the provisions of the Convention and the protocols thereto by another High Contracting Party

Article 34
Individual applications

The Court may receive applications from any person, non-governmental organisation or group of individuals claiming to be the victim of a violation by one of the High Contracting Parties of the rights set forth in the Convention or the protocols thereto. The High Contracting Parties undertake not to hinder in any way the effective exercise of this right.

Article 35
Admissibility criteria

1.   The Court may only deal with the matter after all domestic remedies have been exhausted, according to the generally recognised rules of international law, and within a period of six months from the date on which the final decision was taken.

2.   The Court shall not deal with any application submitted under Article 34 that

(a)   is anonymous; or

(b)   is substantially the same as a matter that has already been examined by the Court or has already been submitted to another procedure of international investigation or settlement and contains no relevant new information.

3.   The Court shall declare inadmissible any individual application submitted under Article 34 which it considers incompatible with the provisions of the Convention or the protocols thereto, manifestly ill-founded, or an abuse of the right of application.

4.   The Court shall reject any application which it considers inadmissible under this Article. It may do so at any stage of the proceedings.

Article 36
Third party intervention

1.   In all cases before a Chamber of the Grand Chamber, a High Contracting Party one of whose nationals is an applicant shall have the right to submit written comments and to take part in hearings.

2.   The President of the Court may, in the interest of the proper administration of justice, invite any High Contracting Party which is not a party to the proceedings or any person concerned who is not the applicant to submit written comments or take part in hearings.

Article 37
Striking out applications

1.   The Court may at any stage of the proceedings decide to strike an application out of its list of cases where the circumstances lead to the conclusion that

(a)   the applicant does not intend to pursue his application; or

(b)   the matter has been resolved; or

(c)   for any other reason established by the Court, it is no longer justified to continue the examination of the application.

However, the Court shall continue the examination of the application if respect for human rights as defined in the Convention and the protocols thereto so requires.

2.   The Court may decide to restore an application to its list of cases if it considers that the circumstances justify such a course.

Article 38
Examination of the case and friendly settlement proceedings

1.   If the Court declares the application admissible, it shall

(a)   pursue the examination of the case, together with the representatives of the parties, and if need be, undertake an investigation, for the effective conduct of which the States concerned shall furnish all necessary facilities;

(b)   place itself at the disposal of the parties concerned with a view to securing a friendly settlement of the matter on the basis of respect for human rights as defined in the Convention and the protocols thereto.

2.   Proceedings conducted under paragraph 1.b shall be confidential.

Article 39
Finding of a friendly settlement

If a friendly settlement is effected, the Court shall strike the case out of its list by means of a decision which shall be confined to a brief statement of the facts and of the solution reached.

Article 40
Public hearings and access to documents

1.   Hearings shall be in public unless the Court in exceptional circumstances decides otherwise.

2.   Documents deposited with the Registrar shall be accessible to the public unless the President of the Court decides otherwise.

Article 41
Just satisfaction

If the Court finds that there has been a violation of the Convention or the protocols thereto, and if the internal law of the High Contracting Party concerned allows only partial reparation to be made, the Court shall, if necessary afford just satisfaction to the injured party.

Article 42
Judgments of Chambers

Judgments of Chambers shall become final in accordance with the provisions of Article 44, paragraph 2.

Article 43
Referral to the Grand Chamber

1.   Within a period of three months from the date of the judgment of the Chamber, any party to the case may, in exceptional cases, request that the case be referred to the Grand Chamber.

2.   A panel of five judges of the Grand Chamber shall accept the request if the case raises a serious question affecting the interpretation or application of the Convention or the protocols thereto, or a serious issue of general importance.

3.   If the panel accepts the request, the Grand Chamber shall decide the case by means of a judgment.

Article 44
Final judgments

1.   The judgment of the Grand Chamber shall be final.

2.   The judgment of a Chamber shall become final

(a)   when the parties declare that they will not request that the case be referred to the Grand Chamber; or

(b)   three months after the date of the judgment, if reference of the case to the Grand Chamber has not been requested; or

(c)   when the panel of the Grand Chamber rejects the request to refer under Article 43.

3.   The final judgment shall be published.

Article 45
Reasons for judgments and decisions

1.   Reasons shall be given for judgments as well as for decisions declaring applications admissible or inadmissible.

2.   If a judgment does not represent, in whole or in part, the unanimous opinion of the judges, any judge shall be entitled to deliver a separate opinion.

Article 46
Binding force and execution of judgments

1.   The High Contracting Parties undertake to abide by the final judgment of the Court in any case to which they are parties.

2.   The final judgment of the Court shall be transmitted to the Committee of Ministers, which shall supervise its execution.

Article 47
Advisory opinions

1.   The Court may, at the request of the Committee of Ministers, give advisory opinions on legal questions concerning the interpretation of the Convention and the protocols thereto.

2.   Such opinions shall not deal with any question relating to the content or scope of the rights or freedoms defined in Section I of the Convention and the protocols thereto, or with any other question which the Court or the Committee of Ministers might have to consider in consequence of any such proceedings as could be instituted in accordance with the Convention.

3.   Decisions of the Committee of Ministers to request an advisory opinion of the Court shall require a majority vote of the representatives entitled to sit on the Committee.

Article 48
Advisory jurisdiction of the Court

The Court shall decide whether a request for an advisory opinion submitted by the Committee of Ministers is within its competence as defined in Article 47.

Article 49
Reasons for advisory opinions

1. Reasons shall be given for advisory opinions of the Court.
2. If the advisory opinion does not represent, in whole or in part, the unanimous opinion of the judges, any judge shall be entitled to deliver a separate opinion.
3. Advisory opinions of the Court shall be communicated to the Committee of Ministers.

Article 50
Expenditure on the Court

The expenditure on the Court shall be borne by the Council of Europe.

Article 51
Privileges and immunities of judges

The judges shall be entitled, during the exercise of their functions, to the privileges and immunities provided for in Article 40 of the Statute of the Council of Europe and in the agreements made thereunder.

Section III—Miscellaneous provisions

Article 52
Inquiries by the Secretary General

On receipt of a request from the Secretary General of the Council of Europe any High Contracting Party shall furnish an explanation of the manner in which its internal law ensures the effective implementation of any of the provisions of the Convention.

Article 53
Safeguard for existing human rights

Nothing in this Convention shall be construed as limiting or derogating from any of the human rights and fundamental freedoms which may be ensured under the laws of any High Contracting Party or under any other agreement to which it is a Party.

Article 54
Powers of the Committee of Ministers

Nothing in this Convention shall prejudice the powers conferred on the Committee of Ministers by the Statute of the Council of Europe.

Article 55
Exclusion of other means of dispute settlement

The High Contracting Parties agree that, except by special agreement, they will not avail themselves of treaties, conventions or declarations in force between them for the purpose of submitting, by way of petition, a dispute arising out of the interpretation or application of this Convention to a means of settlement other than those provided for in this Convention.

Article 56
Territorial application

1.   Any State may at the time of its ratification or at any time thereafter declare by notification addressed to the Secretary General of the Council of Europe that the present Convention shall, subject to paragraph 4 of this Article, extend to all or any of the territories for whose international relations it is responsible.

2.   The Convention shall extend to the territory or territories named in the notification as from the thirtieth day after the receipt of this notification by the Secretary General of the Council of Europe.

3.   The provisions of this Convention shall be applied in such territories with due regard, however, to local requirements.

4.   Any State which has made a declaration in accordance with paragraph 1 of this article may at any time thereafter declare on behalf of one or more of the territories to which the declaration relates that it accepts the competence of the Court to receive applications from individuals, non-governmental organisations or groups of individuals as provided by Article 34 of the Convention.

Article 57
Reservations

1.   Any State may, when signing this Convention or when depositing its instrument of ratification, make a reservation in respect of any particular provision of the Convention to the extent that any law then in force in its territory is not in conformity with the provision. Reservations of a general character shall not be permitted under this article.

2.   Any reservation made under this article shall contain a brief statement of the law concerned.

Article 58
Denunciation

1.   A High Contracting Party may denounce the present Convention only after the expiry of five years from the date on which it became a party to it and after six months' notice contained in a notification addressed to the Secretary General of the Council of Europe, who shall inform the other High Contracting Parties.

2.   Such a denunciation shall not have the effect of releasing the High Contracting Party concerned from its obligations under this Convention in respect of any act which, being capable of constituting a violation of such obligations, may have been performed by it before the date at which the denunciation became effective.

3.   Any High Contracting Party which shall cease to be a member of the Council of Europe shall cease to be a Party to this Convention under the same conditions.

4.   The Convention may be denounced in accordance with the provisions of the preceding paragraphs in respect of any territory to which it has been declared to extend under the terms of Article 56.

Article 59
Signature and ratification

1.   This Convention shall be open to the signature of the members of the Council of Europe. It shall be ratified. Ratifications shall be deposited with the Secretary General of the Council of Europe.

2.   The present Convention shall come into force after the deposit of ten instruments of ratification.

3.   As regards any signatory ratifying subsequently, the Convention shall come into force at the date of the deposit of its instrument of ratification.

4.   The Secretary General of the Council of Europe shall notify all the members of the Council of Europe of the entry into force of the Convention, the names of the High Contracting Parties who have ratified it, and the deposit of all instruments of ratification which may be effected subsequently.

Done at Rome this 4th day of November 1950, in English and French, both texts being equally authentic, in a single copy which shall remain deposited in the archives of the Council of Europe.

The Secretary General shall transmit certified copies to each of the signatories.

PROTOCOL [NO. 1] TO THE CONVENTION FOR THE PROTECTION OF HUMAN RIGHTS AND FUNDAMENTAL FREEDOMS, AS AMENDED BY PROTOCOL NO. 11

The governments signatory hereto, being members of the Council of Europe,

Being resolved to take steps to ensure the collective enforcement of certain rights and freedoms other than those already included in Section 1 of the Convention for the Protection of Human Rights and Fundamental Freedoms signed at Rome on 4 November 1950 (hereinafter referred to as 'the Convention'),

Have agreed as follows:

Article 1
Protection of property

Every natural or legal person is entitled to the peaceful enjoyment of his possessions. No one shall be deprived of his possessions except in the public interest and subject to the conditions provided for by law and by the general principles of international law.

The preceding provisions shall not, however, in any way impair the right of a State to enforce such laws as it deems necessary to control the use of property in accordance with the general interest or to secure the payment of taxes or other contributions or penalties.

Article 2
Right to education

No person shall be denied the right to education. In the exercise of any functions which it assumes in relation to education and to teaching, the State shall respect the right of parents to ensure such education and teaching in conformity with their own religious and philosophical convictions.

Article 3
Right to free elections

The High Contracting Parties undertake to hold free elections at reasonable intervals by secret ballot, under conditions which will ensure the free expression of the opinion of the people in the choice of the legislature.

Article 4
Territorial application

Any High Contracting Party may at the time of signature or ratification or at any time thereafter communicate to the Secretary General of the Council of Europe a declaration stating the extent to which it undertakes that the provisions of the present Protocol shall apply to such of the territories for the international relations of which it is responsible as are named therein.

Any High Contracting Party which has communicated a declaration in virtue of the preceding paragraph may from time to time communicate a further declaration modifying the terms of any former declaration or terminating the application of the provisions of this Protocol in respect of any territory.

A declaration made in accordance with this article shall be deemed to have been made in accordance with paragraph 1 of Article 56 of the Convention.

Article 5
Relationship to the Convention

As between the High Contracting Parties the provisions of Articles 1, 2, 3 and 4 of this Protocol shall be regarded as additional articles to the Convention and all the provisions of the Convention shall apply accordingly.

Article 6
Signature and ratification

This Protocol shall be open for signature by the members of the Council of Europe, who are the signatories of the Convention; it shall be ratified at the same time as or after the ratification of the Convention. It shall enter into force after the deposit of ten instruments of ratification. As regards any signatory ratifying subsequently, the Protocol shall enter into force at the date of the deposit of its instrument of ratification.

The instruments of ratification shall be deposited with the Secretary General of the Council of Europe, who will notify all members of the names of those who have ratified.

Done at Paris on the 20th day of March 1952, in English and French, both texts being equally authentic, in a single copy which shall remain deposited in the archives of the Council of Europe. The Secretary General shall transmit certified copies to each of the signatory governments.

PROTOCOL NO. 4 TO THE CONVENTION FOR THE PROTECTION OF HUMAN RIGHTS AND FUNDAMENTAL FREEDOMS, SECURING CERTAIN RIGHTS AND FREEDOMS OTHER THAN THOSE ALREADY INCLUDED IN THE CONVENTION AND IN THE FIRST PROTOCOL THERETO, AS AMENDED BY PROTOCOL NO. 11

The governments signatory hereto, being members of the Council of Europe,

Being resolved to take steps to ensure the collective enforcement of certain rights and freedoms other than those already included in Section 1 of the Convention for the Protection of Human Rights and Fundamental Freedoms signed at Rome on 4th November 1950 (hereinafter referred to as the 'Convention') and in Articles 1 to 3 of the First Protocol to the Convention, signed at Paris on 20th March 1952,

Have agreed as follows:

Article 1
Prohibition of imprisonment for debt

No one shall be deprived of his liberty merely on the ground of inability to fulfil a contractual obligation.

Article 2
Freedom of movement

1.   Everyone lawfully within the territory of a State shall, within that territory, have the right to liberty of movement and freedom to choose his residence.

2.   Everyone shall be free to leave any country, including his own.

3.   No restrictions shall be placed on the exercise of these rights other than such as are in accordance with law and are necessary in a demoncratic society in the interests of national security or public safety, for the maintenance of *ordre public*, for the prevention of crime, for the protection of health or morals, or for the protection of the rights and freedoms of others.

4.   The rights set forth in paragraph I may also be subject, in particular areas, to restrictions imposed in accordance with law and justified by the public interest in a democratic society.

Article 3
Prohibition of expulsion of nationals

1.   No one shall be expelled, by means either of an individual or of a collective measure, from the territory of the State of which he is a national.

2.   No one shall be deprived of the right to enter the territory of the state of which he is a national.

Article 4
Prohibition of collective expulsion of aliens

Collective expulsion of aliens is prohibited.

Article 5
Territorial application

1.   Any High Contracting Party may, at the time of signature or ratification of this Protocol, or at any time thereafter, communicate to the Secretary General of the Council of Europe a declaration stating the extent to which it undertakes that the provisions of this Protocol shall apply to such of the territories for the international relations of which it is responsible as are named therein.

2.   Any High Contracting Party which has communicated a declaration in virtue of the preceding paragraph may, from time to time, communicate a further

declaration modifying the terms of any former declaration or terminating the application of the provisions of this Protocol in respect of any territory.

3. A declaration made in accordance with this article shall be deemed to have been made in accordance with paragraph 1 of Article 56 of the Convention.

4. The territory of any State to which this Protocol applies by virtue of ratification or acceptance by that State, and each territory to which this Protocol is applied by virtue of a declaration by that State under this article, shall be treated as separate territories for the purpose of the references in Articles 2 and 3 to the territory of a State.

5. Any State which has made a declaration in accordance with paragraph 1 or 2 of this Article may at any time thereafter declare on behalf of one or more of the territories to which the declaration relates that it accepts the competence of the Court to receive applications from individuals, non-governmental organisations or groups of individuals as provided in Article 34 of the Convention in respect of all or any of Articles 1 to 4 of this Protocol.

Article 6
Relationship to the Convention

As between the High Contracting Parties the provisions of Articles 1 to 5 of this Protocol shall be regarded as additional Articles to the Convention, and all the provisions of the Convention shall apply accordingly.

Article 7
Signature and ratification

1. This Protocol shall be open for signature by the members of the Council of Europe who are the signatories of the Convention; it shall be ratified at the same time as or after the ratification of the Convention. It shall enter into force after the deposit of five instruments of ratification. As regards any signatory ratifying subsequently, the Protocol shall enter into force at the date of the deposit of its instrument of ratification.

2. The instruments of ratification shall be deposited with the Secretary General of the Council of Europe, who will notify all members of the names of those who have ratified.

In witness whereof the undersigned, being duly authorised thereto, have signed this Protocol.

Done at Strasbourg, this 16th day of September 1963, in English and in French both texts being equally authoritative, in a single copy which shall remain deposited in the archives of the Council of Europe. The Secretary General shall transmit certified copies to each of the signatory states.

PROTOCOL NO. 6 TO THE CONVENTION FOR THE PROTECTION OF HUMAN RIGHTS AND FUNDAMENTAL FREEDOMS CONCERNING THE ABOLITION OF THE DEATH PENALTY, AS AMENDED BY PROTOCOL NO. 11

The member States of the Council of Europe, signatory to this Protocol to the Convention for the Protection of Human Rights and Fundamental Freedoms signed at Rome on 4 November 1950 (hereinafter referred to as 'the Convention'),

Considering that the evolution that has occurred in several member States of the Council of Europe expresses a general tendency in favour of abolition of the death penalty;

Have agreed as follows:

Article 1
Abolition of the death penalty

The death penalty shall be abolished. No-one shall be condemned to such penalty or executed.

Article 2
Death penalty in time of war

A State may make provision in its law for the death penalty in respect of acts committed in time of war or of imminent threat of war; such penalty shall be applied only in the instances laid down in the law and in accordance with its provisions. The State shall communicate to the Secretary General of the Council of Europe the relevant provisions of that law.

Article 3
Prohibition of derogations

No derogation from the provisions of this Protocol shall be made under Article 15 of the Convention.

Article 4
Prohibition of reservations

No reservation may be made under Article 57 of the Convention in respect of the provisions of this Protocol.

Article 5
Territorial application

1.   Any State may at the time of signature or when depositing its instrument of ratification, acceptance or approval, specify the territory or territories to which this Protocol shall apply.

2.   Any State may at any later date, by a declaration addressed to the Secretary General of the Council of Europe, extend the application of this Protocol to any other territory specified in the declaration. In respect of such territory the Protocol shall enter into force on the first day of the month following the date of receipt of such declaration by the Secretary General.

3.   Any declaration made under the two preceding paragraphs may, in respect of any territory specified in such declaration, be withdrawn by a notification addressed to the Secretary General. The withdrawal shall become effective on the first day of the month following the date of receipt of such notification by the Secretary General.

Article 6
Relationship to the Convention

As between the States Parties the provisions of Articles 1 to 5 of this Protocol shall be regarded as additional articles to the Convention and all the provisions of the Convention shall apply accordingly.

Article 7
Signature and ratification

The Protocol shall be open for signature by the member States of the Council of Europe, signatories to the Convention. It shall be subject to ratification, acceptance or approval. A member State of the Council of Europe may not ratify, accept or approve this Protocol unless it has, simultaneously or previously, ratified the Convention. Instruments of ratification, acceptance or approval shall be deposited with the Secretary General of the Council of Europe.

Article 8
Entry into force

1.   This Protocol shall enter into force on the first day of the month following the date on which five member States of the Council of Europe have expressed their consent to be bound by the Protocol in accordance with the provisions of Article 7.

2.   In respect of any member State which subsequently expresses its consent to be bound by it, the Protocol shall enter into force on the first day of the month following the date of the deposit of the instrument of ratification, acceptance or approval.

Article 9
Depositary functions

The Secretary General of the Council of Europe shall notify the member States of the Council of:

(a) any signature;

(b) the deposit of any instrument of ratification, acceptance or approval;

(c) any date of entry into force of this Protocol in accordance with Articles 5 and 8;

(d) any other act, notification or communication relating to this Protocol.

In witness whereof the undersigned, being duly authorised thereto, have signed this Protocol.

Done at Strasbourg, this 28th day of April 1983, in English and in French, both texts being equally authentic, in a single copy which shall he deposited in the archives of the Council of Europe. The Secretary General of the Council of Europe shall transmit certified copies to each member State of the Council of Europe.

PROTOCOL NO. 7 TO THE CONVENTION FOR THE PROTECTION OF HUMAN RIGHTS AND FUNDAMENTAL FREEDOMS, AS AMENDED BY PROTOCOL NO. 11

The member States of the Council of Europe signatory hereto.

Being resolved to take further steps to ensure the collective enforcement of certain rights and freedoms by means of the Convention for the Protection of Human Rights and Fundamental Freedoms signed at Rome on 4 November 1950 (hereinafter referred to as 'the Convention').

Have agreed as follows

Article 1
Procedural safeguards relating to expulsion of aliens

1. An alien lawfully resident in the territory of a State shall not be expelled therefrom except in pursuance of a decision reached in accordance with law and shall be allowed:

(a) to submit reasons against his expulsion,

(b) to have his case reviewed, and

(c) to be represented for these purposes before the competent authority or a person or persons designated by that authority.

2. An alien may be expelled before the exercise of his rights under paragraph 1.a, b and c of this Article, when such expulsion is necessary in the interests of public order or is grounded on reasons of national security.

Article 2
Right of appeal in criminal matters

1. Everyone convicted of a criminal offence by a tribunal shall have the right to have his conviction or sentence reviewed by a higher tribunal. The exercise of

this right, including the grounds on which it may be exercised, shall be governed by law.

2. This right may be subject to exceptions in regard to offences of a minor character, as prescribed by law, or in cases in which the person concerned was tried in the first instance by the highest tribunal or was convicted following an appeal against acquittal.

Article 3
Compensation for wrongful conviction

When a person has by a final decision been convicted of a criminal offence and when subsequently his conviction has been reversed, or he has been pardoned, on the ground that a new or newly discovered fact shows conclusively that there has been a miscarriage of justice, the person who has suffered punishment as a result of such conviction shall be compensated according to the law or the practice of the State concerned, unless it is proved that the non-disclosure of the unknown fact in time is wholly or partly attributable to him.

Article 4
Right not to be tried or punished twice

1. No one shall be liable to be tried or punished again in criminal proceedings under the jurisdiction of the same State for an offence for which he has already been finally acquitted or convicted in accordance with the law and penal procedure of that State.

2. The provisions of the preceding paragraph shall not prevent the reopening of the case in accordance with the law and penal procedure of the State concerned, if there is evidence of new or newly discovered facts, or if there has been a fundamental defect in the previous proceedings, which could affect the outcome of the case.

3. No derogation from this Article shall be made under Article 15 of the Convention.

Article 5
Equality between spouses

Spouses shall enjoy equality of rights and responsibilities of a private law character between them, and in their relations with their children, as to marriage, during marriage and in the event of its dissolution. This Article shall not prevent States from taking such measures as are necessary in the interests of the children.

Article 6
Territorial application

1. Any State may at the time of signature or when depositing its instrument of ratification, acceptance or approval, specify the territory or territories to which the

Protocol shall apply and state the extent to which it undertakes that the provisions of this Protocol shall apply to such territory or territories.

2.　Any State may at any later date, by a declaration addressed to the Secretary General of the Council of Europe, extend the application of this Protocol to any other territory specified in the declaration. In respect of such territory the Protocol shall enter into force on the first day of the month following the expiration of a period of two months after the date of receipt by the Secretary General of such declaration.

3.　Any declaration made under the two preceding paragraphs may, in respect of any territory specified in such declaration, be withdrawn or modified by a notification addressed to the Secretary General. The withdrawal or modification shall become effective on the first day of the month following the expiration of a period of two months after the date of receipt of such notification by the Secretary General.

4.　A declaration made in accordance with this Article shall be deemed to have been made in accordance with paragraph 1 of Article 56 of the Convention.

5.　The territory of any State to which this Protocol applies by virtue of ratification, acceptance or approval by that State, and each territory to which this Protocol is applied by virtue of a declaration by that State under this Article, may be treated as separate territories for the purpose of the reference in Article 1 to the territory of a State.

6.　Any State which has made a declaration in accordance with paragraph 1 or 2 of this Article may at any time thereafter declare on behalf of one or more of the territories to which the declaration relates that it accepts the competence of the Court to receive applications from individuals, non-governmental organisations or groups of individuals as provided in Article 34 of the Convention in respect of Articles 1 to 5 of this Protocol.

Article 7
Relationship to the Convention

As between the States Parties, the provisions of Article 1 to 6 of this Protocol shall be regarded as additional Articles to the Convention, and all the provisions of the Convention shall apply accordingly.

Article 8
Signature and ratification

This Protocol shall be open for signature by member States of the Council of Europe which have signed the Convention. It is subject to ratification, acceptance or approval. A member State of the Council of Europe may not ratify, accept or approve this Protocol without previously or simultaneously ratifying the Convention. Instruments of ratification, acceptance or approval shall be deposited with the Secretary General of the Council of Europe.

Article 9
Entry into force

1. This Protocol shall enter into force on the first day of the month following the expiration of a period of two months after the date on which seven member States of the Council of Europe have expressed their consent to be bound by the Protocol in accordance with the provisions of Article 8.

2. In respect of any member State which subsequently expresses its consent to be bound by it, the Protocol shall enter into force on the first day of the month following the expiration of a period of two months after the date of the deposit of the instrument of ratification, acceptance or approval.

Article 10
Depositary functions

The Secretary General of the Council of Europe shall notify all the member States of the Council of Europe of:

(a)   any signature;

(b)   the deposit of any instrument of ratification, acceptance or approval.

(c)   any date of entry into force of this Protocol in accordance with Articles 6 and 9;

(d)   any other act, notification or declaration relating to this Protocol.

In witness whereof the undersigned, being duly authorised thereto, have signed this Protocol.

Done at Strasbourg, this 22nd day of November 1984, in English and French, both texts being equally authentic, in a single copy which shall be deposited in the archives of the Council of Europe. The Secretary General of the Council of Europe shall transmit certified copies to each member State of the Council of Europe.

PROTOCOL NO. 12 TO THE CONVENTION FOR THE PROTECTION OF HUMAN RIGHTS AND FUNDAMENTAL FREEDOMS

The member states of the Council of Europe signatory hereto.

Having regard to the fundamental principle according to which all persons are equal before the law and are entitled to the equal protection of the law;

Being resolved to take further steps to promote the equality of all persons through the collective enforcement of a general prohibition of discrimination by means of the Convention for the Protection of Human Rights and Fundamental Freedoms signed at Rome on 4 November 1950 (hereinafter referred to as 'the Convention');

Reaffirming that the principle of non-discrimination does not prevent States Parties from taking measures in order to promote full and effective equality,

provided that there is an objective and reasonable justification for those measures.
Have agreed as follows:

Article 1
General prohibition of discrimination

1.   The enjoyment of any right set forth by law shall be secured without discrimination on any ground such as sex, race, colour, language, religion, political or other opinion, national or social origin, association with a national minority, property, birth or other status.

2.   No one shall be discriminated against by any public authority on any ground such as those mentioned in paragraph 1.

Article 2
Territorial application

1.   Any state may, at the time of signature or when depositing its instrument of ratification acceptance or approval, specify the territory or territories to which this Protocol shall apply.

2.   Any state may at any later date, by a declaration addressed to the Secretary General of the Council of Europe, extend the application of this Protocol to any other territory specified in the declaration, in respect of such territory the Protocol shall enter into force on the first day of the month following the expiration of a period of three months after the date of receipt by the Secretary General of such declaration.

3.   Any declaration made under the two preceding paragraphs may, in respect of any territory specified in such declaration, be withdrawn or modified by a notification addressed to the Secretary General. The withdrawal or modification shall become effective on the first day of the month following the expiration of a period of three months after the date of receipt of such notification by the Secretary General.

4.   A declaration made in accordance with this article shall be deemed to have been made in accordance with paragraph 1 of Article 56 of the Convention.

5.   Any state which has made a declaration in accordance with paragraph 1 or 2 of this article may at any time thereafter declare on behalf of one or more of the territories to which the declaration relates that it accepts the competence of the Court to receive applications from individuals, non-governmental organisations or groups of individuals as provided by Article 34 of the Convention in respect of Article 1 of this Protocol.

Article 3
Relationship to the Convention

As between the States Parties, the provisions of Articles 1 and 2 of this Protocol shall be regarded as additional articles to the Convention, and all the provisions of the Convention shall apply accordingly.

Article 4
Signature and ratification

This Protocol shall be open for signature by member states of the Council of Europe which have signed the Convention. It is subject to ratification, acceptance or approval. A member state of the Council of Europe may not ratify, accept or approve this Protocol without previously or simultaneously ratifying the Convention. Instruments of ratification, acceptance or approval shall be deposited with the Secretary General of the Council of Europe.

Article 5
Entry into force

1.   This Protocol shall enter into force on the first day of the month following the expiration of a period of three months after the date on which ten member states of the Council of Europe have expressed their consent to be bound by the Protocol in accordance with the provisions of Article 4.

2.   In respect of any member state which subsequently expresses its consent to be bound by it, the Protocol shall enter into force on the first day of the month following the expiration of a period of three months after the date of the deposit of the instrument of ratification, acceptance or approval.

Article 6
Depositary functions

The Secretary General of the Council of Europe shall notify all the member states of the Council of Europe of:

(a)   any signature;

(b)   the deposit of any instrument of ratification, acceptance or approval;

(c)   any date of entry into force of this Protocol in accordance with Article 2 and 5;

(d)   any other act, notification or communication relating to this Protocol.

In witness whereof the undersigned, being duly authorised thereto, have signed this Protocol.

Done at . . . . this . . . . day of . . . . . 2000, in English and French, both texts being equally authentic, in a single copy which shall be deposited in the archives of the Council of Europe. The Secretary General of the Council of Europe shall transmit certified copies to each member state of the Council of Europe.

Index

LIBRARY, UNIVERSITY COLLEGE CHESTER